A HISTORY OF SOVIET RUSSIA

A HISTORY OF SOVIET RUSSIA

by E. H. Carr

in fourteen volumes

*with R. W. Davies

A HISTORY OF SOVIET RUSSIA 4

THE
INTERREGNUM
1923-1924

BY
E. H. CARR
Fellow of Trinity College, Cambridge

First published 1954
Reprinted 1960, 1965, 1978

Published by
THE MACMILLAN PRESS LTD
London and Basingstoke
Associated companies in Delhi
Dublin Hong Kong Johannesburg Lagos
Melbourne New York Singapore Tokyo

Printed in Hong Kong by
CHINA TRANSLATION AND PRINTING SERVICES

British Library Cataloguing in Publication Data

Carr, Edward Hallett
    The interregnum, 1923–1924 — (Carr, Edward
    Hallett. History of Soviet Russia; 4)
    1. Russia — Social conditions — 1917–
    I. Title
    309.1′47′0841   HN523

    ISBN 0–333–09723–8
    ISBN 0–333–24216–5   Boxed set

PREFACE

IN the preface to the first volume of *The Bolshevik Revolution, 1917–1923*, published in 1950, I expressed the intention of proceeding, on the completion of this work, to " the second instalment of the whole project " under the title *The Struggle for Power, 1923–1928*. Further consideration and fuller examination of the material have led me to modify this plan in several respects. In the first place, the last months of Lenin's last illness and the first weeks after his death, the interval from March 1923 to May 1924, appeared to constitute a sort of intermediate period — a truce or interregnum in party and Soviet affairs — when controversial decisions were, so far as possible, avoided or held in suspense: in the new plan this period occupies a separate volume, now published under the title *The Interregnum, 1923–1924*. Next, it was found that the period from 1924 to 1928, while constituting in many respects a unity, could more conveniently be divided into two sections. Finally, the title originally suggested for this period seemed too trivial, and inadequate to the fundamental issues involved in the struggle. According to my present plan, the third instalment of my project will bear the title *Socialism in One Country, 1924–1926*, will cover the period approximately from the summer of 1924 to the first months of 1926, and will occupy two volumes. The proclamation of " socialism in one country " will provide the occasion for some reflexions, which I feel to be appropriate at this stage, on the relation between the Bolshevik revolution and the material, political and cultural legacy of the Russian past.

I have once more to acknowledge a continuing debt of gratitude to many of those who helped me in the earlier stages of my task. The most important sources of my material have again been the British Museum and the libraries of the London School of Economics and of the Royal Institute of International Affairs. I have also been able to use the libraries of the School of Slavonic Studies of the University of London and of the Institute of Agrarian Affairs of Oxford University, the Bibliothèque de Documentation Internationale Contemporaine of the University of Paris, and the libraries of the International Labour Office at Geneva and of the Internationaal Instituut voor Sociale Geschiedenis at Amsterdam. It was in the last-named institute that I found the typewritten copy of the hitherto unpublished " platform of the 46 " from which I made the translation printed in the present

v

volume. I wish to express my very warm thanks to the librarians of all these institutions and their staffs for their invaluable assistance and for the untiring patience with which they have received and satisfied my exacting demands on them.

The present volume has suffered, in comparison with its predecessors, from the fact that I have had no opportunity of visiting the United States while I have been engaged on it. But I have been deeply indebted to Mrs. Olga Gankin of the Hoover Library and Institute at Stanford for her unfailing kindness in answering my most pertinacious enquiries and in supplying information from the rich and still partly unexplored resources of the library. Few scholars appear so far to have worked on the Trotsky archives in the Houghton Library of Harvard University ; nor, so far as I know, has any systematic account yet been published of what they contain. This is a most serious gap in our knowledge of Soviet history.

My special thanks are due to Mr. Isaac Deutscher, the biographer of Stalin and Trotsky, both for reading and criticizing a substantial part of my manuscript and for putting at my disposal notes made by him from the Trotsky archives during a visit in 1951; to Herr Heinrich Brandler for giving me his personal recollections of the events of 1923; to Mr. Maurice Dobb and Mr. H. C. Stevens for lending me books and pamphlets which I should otherwise have missed; to Mrs. Degras for once more volunteering to read the proofs, and to Dr. Ilya Neustadt for compiling the index — two particularly onerous tasks, the discharge of which places both the author and his readers very much in their debt.

E. H. CARR

January 5, 1954

CONTENTS

PART I

THE SCISSORS CRISIS

PART II

THE CAPITALIST WORLD

PART III

THE TRIUMVIRATE IN POWER

PART I

THE SCISSORS CRISIS

CHAPTER I

MARKING TIME

IN the winter of 1922–1923, after two years of NEP, a note-worthy revival was discernible in the Soviet economy — a revival due partly to the natural process of recovery from the long ordeal of war and civil war, partly to the excellent harvest of 1922, and partly to the new policies which had been inaugurated in March 1921. Production had risen steeply both in agriculture and in rural and artisan industry, and less steeply in factory industries producing consumer goods (and as yet hardly at all in the heavy industries producing capital goods); while the peasant was the principal beneficiary of NEP, the industrial worker had been freed from labour conscription, and his miserable standard of living had to some extent risen; both internal and foreign trade were being developed; the foundation of a fiscal system and a working state budget had been laid, and the first steps taken towards the creation of a stable currency. On the other hand, none of these aims was distinctively socialist. The structure of the economy was capitalist or pre-capitalist except for the nationalized industries; and these had been obliged to adapt themselves to a quasi-capitalist environment through the obligation laid on them to conduct their business on commercial principles. The successes of NEP had been achieved by resort to capitalist methods and brought with them two incidental consequences which Marxists had always regarded as characteristic evils of capitalism — large-scale unemployment and violent price fluctuations. The problem which had dogged the victorious revolution since 1917, and was inherent in the attempt to effect the transition to socialism in a predominantly peasant community, was its dependence on the support of the peasantry. In 1921 a temporary solution seemed to have been found in the adoption of NEP; the alliance with the peasantry had been so securely welded that it would hold until the spread of the proletarian revolution to Europe brought relief to the struggling Russian proletariat. But, at the moment of Lenin's final withdrawal from the scene, this assumption was for the first time severely challenged. A revival of economic tension, primarily due to wild fluctuations in market prices, opened a new rift between industry and agriculture, between proletariat and peasantry, and called in question the tenability of the NEP compromise.

Attention has already been drawn to certain inconsistencies in the attitude to NEP revealed in the pronouncements of the party and of Lenin himself, turning on the equivocal position of the peasant as the necessary ally of the proletariat but the ultimate obstacle to be overcome on the road to socialism.[1] Lenin had been fully conscious at an early stage of NEP of the anomalies inherent in it :

> There are more contradictions in our economic reality than there were before the new economic policy : partial, small improvements in the economic position among some strata of the population, among a few ; complete inability to make economic resources square with indispensable needs among the rest, among the many. These contradictions have grown greater. And it is understandable that, so long as we are going through a sharp turn, it is impossible to escape from these contradictions all at once.[2]

When, at the eleventh party congress in the spring of 1922, under pressure from those who dwelt on the disastrous consequences of NEP for industry, Lenin announced the ending of the " retreat ",[3] it was a natural deduction that there would be no more concessions to the peasant. Yet at the same congress he dwelt with the utmost emphasis on the need to " restore the link ", to come to the help of " the ruined, impoverished, miserably hungry " small peasant — " or he will send us to all the devils ".[4] In his speech at the fourth congress of Comintern in November 1922 — his last public speech but one — Lenin spoke both of the satisfaction that had been given to the peasant and of the need for state subsidies for heavy industry (" unless we find them, we are lost ").[5] A week

[1] See *The Bolshevik Revolution, 1917–1923*, Vol. 2, pp. 274-279.
[2] Lenin, *Sochineniya*, xxvii, 71.
[3] See *The Bolshevik Revolution, 1917–1923*, Vol. 2, p. 277.
[4] Lenin, *Sochineniya*, xxvii, 231.
[5] See *The Bolshevik Revolution, 1917–1923*, Vol. 2, pp. 295, 316-317.

later, in his last speech of all, he referred to the " retreat " as still in progress, and added frankly :

> Where and how we must now re-form ourselves, adapt ourselves, re-organize ourselves so that after the retreat we may begin a stubborn move forward, we still do not know.[1]

In one of his last articles, written in January 1923, he described the Soviet order as " founded on the collaboration of two classes, the workers and the peasants ", and laid down what he regarded as the major task of the party :

> If serious class antagonisms arise between these two classes, then a split will be unavoidable ; but in our social order there are no fixed and inevitable grounds for such a split, and the chief task of our central committee and central control commission, and of our party as a whole, is to watch attentively those circumstances out of which a split might arise and anticipate them, since in the last resort the fate of our republic will depend on whether the peasant mass goes with the working class and remains faithful to its alliance with that class, or whether it allows the " nepmen ", i.e. the new bourgeoisie, to divide it from the workers, to split it away from them.[2]

Thus, while Lenin had appeared in 1922 to voice the demand for a resumption of the march towards socialism, his last injunction was to keep the link with the peasantry in being at all costs. So long as the compromise held, all was well. But, in any crisis which made the existing compromise unworkable without further concessions to one side or the other, any course of action could be supported by appropriate quotations from the fountain-head.

The first signs of crisis began to appear when, in the winter of 1922–1923, the terms of trade between agricultural and industrial goods, hitherto favourable to the former, began to move slowly but steadily in favour of industry. NEP had given the peasant the opportunity to recoup himself, after the privations and terrors of war communism, by extracting from the town-dwellers a high price for his products ; the land law of May 1922, confirmed by the new agrarian code at the end of the year, gave

---

[1] Lenin, *Sochineniya*, xxvii, 362.
[2] *Ibid.* xxvii, 405 ; Lenin's " testament " also emphasized agreement between workers and peasants as the fundamental basis on which the party rested (see p. 258 below).

him security of tenure ;[1] and the steps taken to restore orthodox finance and stabilize the currency promised protection to the peasant against a currency inflation the cost of which had fallen heavily on him. After the wonderful harvest of 1922, the peasant was more prosperous than at any time since the revolution, and was, as Lenin noted, well satisfied with his lot.[2] It was true that the process of equalization of holdings and resources between different categories of peasants which was set in motion after the October revolution and intensified by the requisitions of war communism had now been reversed. The inherent tendency of NEP to encourage ·differentiation between different strata of the peasantry continued unchecked. At one end of the scale more poor peasants were sinking below the level of self-sufficiency and had to hire out their land or their labour in order to live ; at the other end the *kulaks* were producing larger surpluses for disposal on the market. The extension within the peasantry of the practices of leasing land and hiring labour, which had been held in check in the first years of the revolution, was the symptom of this differentiation.[3] According to statistics compiled by Vserabotzemles, the agricultural workers' trade union, at the end of 1923, 400,000 peasants (or 2 per cent of the total number) employed

---

[1] See *The Bolshevik Revolution, 1917–1923*, Vol. 2, pp. 289, 296-297.

[2] See *ibid.* Vol. 2, p. 295.

[3] S. G. Strumilin, *Na Khozyaistvennom Fronte* (1925), pp. 230-261, contains a careful statistical study of these processes originally published in April 1923. A detailed analysis, which appeared in the trade union newspaper, *Trud*, of the peasantry in one province of the Ukraine (Odessa) showed that out of 577,000 households 11,000 had no cultivated land at all, another 162,000 had no animal, and could not grow enough to be self-supporting. A further 137,000 had one animal ; their situation was precarious. Peasants who were not self-supporting could not find employment in the towns (industrial unemployment was worse in the Ukraine than elsewhere — see p. 50 below), or in the collective farms, which were not in a flourishing condition, or in the Sovkhozy (see *The Bolshevik Revolution, 1917–1923*, Vol. 2, pp. 155-156, 289-290), which were more or less derelict, employing only 3000 workers in the whole province, and leasing most of their land. There was therefore no option but to become *batraks*, i.e. hired workers on the land of more prosperous peasants. In brief, " a sharp division exists between ' strong ' and ' weak ' households " and " the ' weak ' households perish, filling the ranks of the *batraks* " (*Trud*, September 26, 1923). A year later, at the thirteenth party congress, Kamenev, apparently quoting from a monograph issued by the central statistical administration, classified the peasant population as follows : 63 per cent poor peasants, forming 74 per cent of the total number of households, cultivating 40 per cent of the area under crops, and owning 50 per cent of the animals ; 23 per cent middle peasants, forming 18 per cent of the households, cultivating 25 per cent of the area under

600,000 hired workers.[1]   Both figures certainly represent a serious
understatement.   But the proportion of employed to employers
shows that the process had not yet gone very far.   For the moment,
the picture of a prosperous and contented peasantry which had
left behind for ever the horrors of requisitioning and war communism represented a fair approximation to the truth; and the
arguments for letting well alone seemed still impregnable.
Towards the end of 1922, after the excellent harvest of that
year, a small quantity of grain had been exported from Soviet
Russia for the first time since the revolution; and a lively demand
was now heard for action to stem the progressive fall in grain
prices by promoting exports of grain.   Narkomfin, the champion
at this time of peasant interests and now also concerned to
build up the foreign currency reserves of Gosbank, came out
strongly in favour of grain exports; and, on its instigation,
the tenth All-Russian Congress of Soviets in December 1922
came out with a recommendation to expand exports of grain and
raw materials.[2]   The distribution of seed to the peasants on an
unprecedented scale was announced in a decree of January 17,
1923, which described an increase of the areas under crops as
"the foundation of the welfare not only of the peasant, but of
the whole state"; and another decree promised land "in border
regions where land is abundant" to agricultural immigrants.[3]

Industry presented a more difficult problem than agriculture,
if only for the basic reason that, while agriculture, in the favourable
harvest of 1922, had attained some three-quarters of average pre-
war production over the same area, industry had at the same period

crops, and owning 25 per cent of the animals; and 14 per cent rich peasants
forming 8 per cent of the households, cultivating 34 per cent of the area under
crops and owning 25 per cent of the animals (*Trinadtsatyi S"ezd Rossiiskoi
Kommunisticheskoi Partii (Bol'shevikov)* (1924), pp. 408-409). Examples of the
way in which legal limitations on the right to hire labour were evaded by such
devices as fictitious marriages or adoption, or the rendering of labour in return
for advances of grain or seed, are given in L. Kritsman, *Klassovoe Rassloenie v
Sovetskoi Derevne* (1926), pp 163-164.

[1] *XI Vserossiiskii S"ezd Sovetov* (1924), p. 47; the statistics also showed
100,000 workers on Soviet farms, 100,000 in forestry and 100,000 on specialized
farms of agricultural production (fruit, vegetables, etc.). For an account of
Vserabotzemles see *Trud*, December 2, 1923, it was founded in 1920 for
workers on Soviet farms or in artels and communes (these being later excluded),
but it never became an effective organization.

[2] *S"ezdy Sovetov v Dokumentakh*, i (1959), 227.

[3] *Sobranie Uzakonenii, 1923*, No. 4, art. 73; No. 10, art. 128.

reached little more than a quarter of its pre-war output.[1] What
had happened to agriculture under NEP, whether welcome or
not, was exactly what had been foreseen. What had happened to
industry was far more complex and baffling. Industry fell into
three categories. The first consisted of rural industry and small
artisan industry conducted mainly in the countryside. This had
shared in the impetus given by NEP to agriculture, and had
recovered since 1921 at a far more rapid rate than factory industry,
and to some extent at its expense.[2] But such a development merely
tended to make the rural community more self-supporting, to
strengthen the *kulak* element in the countryside, and to destroy
the " link " between peasantry and proletariat, between country
and town, which NEP purported to establish. The second
category consisted of factory industry producing consumer goods
for the market : this had recovered in the summer of 1922, through
the formation of quasi-monopolistic syndicates, from the *razbazarovanie* crisis of the previous winter,[3] but was now on the
verge of a new crisis due to the inflation of prices inherent in this
process. The third category consisted of heavy industry producing
capital goods or supplies and services essential to the economy as a
whole, and not working primarily for a consumer market : the
metallurgical industry and the heavy engineering and chemical
industries, together with mining and transport, were the principal
items in this category. An important distinction between the
two categories of large-scale industry was in the method of their
financing. Since the revival of the banking system at the end of
1921,[4] the consumer industries had been financed by Gosbank
and Prombank on commercial principles and in virtue of their
profit-earning capacity. Heavy industry and transport, operating
at a loss and unable to obtain bank credits, continued to be
financed by direct subventions from the state, out of which they
paid their wages bills or purchased raw materials and equipment.[5]

---

[1] *Dvenadtsatyi S"ezd Rossiiskoi Kommunisticheskoi Partii* (*Bol'shevikov*)
(1923), p. 25 ; for the figures of industrial production see Y. S. Rozenfeld,
Promyshlennaya Politika SSSR (1926), p. 515.

[2] See *The Bolshevik Revolution, 1917–1923*, Vol. 2, pp. 297-299, 310.

[3] See *ibid*. Vol. 2, pp. 312-315.

[4] See *ibid*. Vol. 2, pp. 356-357.

[5] In the financial year 1922–1923 state subventions to heavy industry still
exceeded bank credits to the rest of industry : in subsequent years this relation
was reversed (Y. S. Rozenfeid, *Promyshlennaya Politika SSSR* (1926), p. 412 .

Without such subventions production and services essential to the economy as a whole would have come to a standstill.

While, therefore, both categories of large-scale industry were involved in the crisis of 1923, very different considerations affected them. Since the autumn of 1921 the consumer industries had been constantly adjured to apply the principles of *khozraschet* and warned that their efficiency would be measured by their capacity to earn profits. Thanks to generous credit facilities, and to the monopoly position established by the syndicates, they had driven up prices and earned substantial profits By the summer of 1923 they had increased their production, built up their stocks and restored their working capital. Nor was it easy to blame them. The formal decree defining and confirming the status of the industrial trusts, which was issued only just before the twelfth party congress, described them as enterprises operating " with the object of earning a profit ".[1] As late as July 1923 Vesenkha issued an order which repeated and elaborated the prescriptions of the decree and referred to profit-making as " the guiding principle of the activity of the trusts ".[2] It was, however, this policy which led, or largely contributed, to the scissors crisis.

Heavy industry was in a far graver plight. In 1922 it had recovered scarcely at all from the low level of the two preceding years.[3] It suffered in a higher degree than the consumer industries from those basic weaknesses which were the direct result of war, revolution and civil war : an obsolete and worn-out plant, shortage of raw materials, dispersal of its always limited resources in skilled labour, and swollen overhead costs.[4] No serious reorganization

---

[1] See *The Bolshevik Revolution, 1917–1923*, Vol. 2, p. 309.

[2] *Sbornik Dekretov, Postanovlenii, Rasporyazhenii i Prikazov po Narodnomu Khozyaistvu*, No. 7 (16), July 1923, pp. 37–38 ; it was read by Rykov at the thirteenth party conference in January 1924 (*Trinadtsataya Konferentsiyu Ros siiskoi Kommunisticheskoi Partii (Bol'shevikov)* (1924), pp. 9–10) as an example of the erroneous policy prevailing in 1923. Its author was Pyatakov.

[3] See *The Bolshevik Revolution, 1917–1923*, Vol. 2, pp. 311, 315–316.

[4] At the Sormovo engineering works the number of workers directly engaged on production fell between 1913 and 1922 from 6497 to 3708 ; subsidiary workers increased in the same period from 4187 to 6121 and employees from 1230 to 2188 ; the proportion of subsidiary workers and employees to workers engaged on production rose from 83 per cent in 1913 to 224 per cent in 1922 (*Trud*, February 3, 1923). In all major industries, except the chemical industry (where the increase was smaller), the proportion of employees to workers was estimated to have doubled since 1913 (*ibid.* October 25, 1923).

B

to take account of changed conditions had been possible so long
as the civil war lasted; and NEP in its initial stages had been
unfavourable to measures of centralization. At the outset, therefore, and even after the formation of the trusts, the picture presented by heavy industry was of a large number of factories each
working at a small fraction of its capacity.[1] None of the devices
which enabled the consumer industries, once the first shock was
over, to adapt themselves to commercial conditions, and to meet
some, at least, of the problems of reorganization and rationalization on a rising market, was open to heavy industry producing
capital goods. The need for rationalization was here more urgent
than anywhere: the first step towards the salving of heavy
industry was to concentrate the contracted volume of production
in the least obsolete and least inefficient factories. But this
involved the wholesale dismissal of skilled workers who formed
the core of the class-conscious proletariat and the main bulwark
of Bolshevism in the working-class. The party leaders long
shrank from the application of the ruthless, but necessary, surgical
knife.[2] In February 1923 Vesenkha set up a commission for the
concentration of industry.[3] But effective measures of concentration also required, on a short view, additional capital expenditure
and increased demands on the state budget. From these complex

[1] Figures for the first quarter of 1923 are given in Y. S. Rozenfeld, *Promyshlennaya Politika SSSR* (1926), pp. 222-223. Conditions were best in Moscow
where the factories of the engineering trust were working at 38 per cent of
capacity; the corresponding figure for the Petrograd engineering trust was 11
per cent, and the Putilov works in Petrograd were working at only 4·3 per cent
of capacity. Conditions were better in the consumer industries, though according to the figure given to the twelfth party congress, industry as a whole was only
working at 30 per cent of capacity (*Dvenadtsatyi S"ezd Rossiiskoi Kommunisticheskoi Partii (Bol'shevikov)* (1923), p. 339).

[2] In January 1923 the decision was taken in the interests of rationalization
to close down the Putilov engineering works in Petrograd, one of the great
Bolshevik strongholds in 1917; Zinoviev appealed to the Politburo and secured
a reversal of the decision at the last moment (L. Trotsky, *The Real Situation in
Russia* (n.d. [1928], pp. 276-277). Six months later the organ of STO argued
that, in spite of the urgent need to reduce high costs, the rationalization of the
Petrograd engineering industry "must not increase unemployment" (*Ekonomicheskaya Zhizn'*, June 17, 1923). Shortly afterwards, the Petrograd engineering
trust was reported to be working at a loss, of which 90 per cent was attributable to the Putilov factory (*Trud*, August 23, 1923); Rykov in a speech of
December 29, 1923, confirmed that both it and the Bryansk engineering works
had been kept open "for political reasons" (*Pravda*, January 3, 1924).

[3] Y. S. Rozenfeld, *Promyshlennaya Politika SSSR* (1926), pp. 224-225.

embarrassments there was no escape. The capital industries could achieve no recovery in the backward Russian economy, where accumulation of capital through voluntary savings could not be expected, without state intervention and state credits, and without a radical process of reorganization which in its immediate results was bound to bear heavily on the industrial workers. On any view the balance-sheet of NEP in respect of industry was highly disquieting. It had stimulated those primitive and backward local industries which tend to be superseded in any advanced economy; it had failed altogether to help the heavy industries, the essential key to industrial progress; and it had enabled the large consumer industries to survive only by measures of self-help which bore hardly on the peasant and were bound in the long run to destroy the balance between town and country which it was the main purpose of NEP to promote.

The state of trade and distribution was no less disquieting than that of industry. It was disquieting from two points of view. In the first place, NEP brought into the open the mass of private traders who had eked out an illegal existence in the penumbra of war communism, and encouraged the appearance of many more, so that the great bulk of retail trade was now conducted by private traders, greater and lesser nepmen, whose energy and resourcefulness, in conditions of free competition, drove the state trading institutions and the cooperatives from a large part of the field. Figures compiled early in 1924 showed that 83·4 per cent of retail trade was in private hands, leaving 10 per cent to the cooperatives and only 6·6 per cent to the state organs and institutions.[1] Soviet trusts themselves often used nepmen as agents in transactions with one another, and were known to offer larger discounts to private traders than to state institutions; Gosbank was sometimes accused of favouring private traders in the allocation of credits.[2] A complaint was even heard that trusts and other Soviet economic institutions protected their nepmen-agents against the

---

[1] *Trinadtsatyi S"ezd Rossiiskoi Kommunisticheskoi Partii (Bol'shevikov)* (1924), p. 404. On the other hand, the government held the commanding position in wholesale trade : of the total volume of trade, Zinoviev said that 36 per cent was in government hands, leaving 64 per cent for private capital (*ibid.* p. 93).

[2] Z. V. Atlas, *Ocherki po Istorii Denezhnogo Obrashcheniya v SSSR (1917–1925)* (1940), p. 185.

tax-gatherers of Narkomfin by refusing, on the score of " commercial secrecy ", to divulge payments made to them.[1] Such phenomena, however anomalous at first sight, were only to be expected. Once *khozraschet* and unfettered competition were the order of the day, the trained and experienced merchant enjoyed every advantage over the newly created and bureaucratically inspired state trading institutions and even over the cooperatives, especially since the efficiency and independence of the latter had been sapped in the long struggle with the state authorities. It was admitted that prices of commodities in the private market were generally lower than in the state shops ; and Lezhava, the president of the commission for internal trade (Komvnutorg), applied to the private trader a well-known Russian proverb : " Let him be a cur for all I care, if he brings the goods ".[2]

The second ground for disquiet was the high cost, and low efficiency, of the distributive machine as a whole, whether in public or in private hands. Inefficiency in distribution sprang from the same causes as low productivity in industry : to make good the destruction and disintegration wrought by the successive ravages of war, revolution and civil war was, both in human and in material terms, an uphill task. Indices of wholesale and retail prices constructed on the basis of corresponding prices for 1913 showed that the margin between wholesale and retail prices had widened by some 20 per cent since that time, and was widening still further throughout 1923.[3] While Narkomfin continued to blame the trusts and syndicates for the high prices of industrial goods, the middleman was the more popular scapegoat. The press of 1923 was full of apparently well-grounded complaints about the number of hands through which goods passed on their way from the factory to the consumer and the profits and commissions exacted at each stage. Since a revival of trade was an essential condition of NEP, it was not inappropriate that the first

[1] *Vtoroi S"ezd Sovetov Soyuza Sovetskikh Sotsialisticheskikh Respublik* (1924), p. 158.

[2] *Trud*, October 5, 1923 ; *Ekonomicheskaya Zhizn'*, October 15, 1923. For Komvnutorg see *The Bolshevik Revolution, 1917–1923*, Vol. 2, p. 344.

[3] See the table in L. N. Yurovsky, *Na Putyakh k Denezhnoi Reforme* (2nd ed., 1924), p. 75 (quoted on p. 33 below) ; a different calculation (*ibid.* p. 85) shows an even wider margin. The English translation of this work under the title *Currency Problems and Policy of the Soviet Union* (1924) is somewhat abbreviated, but contains a supplementary chapter.

serious crisis of the new economic policy should take the form of a
crisis of prices.

The criticism of current economic policy which, though still
largely inarticulate and unformulated, began to be heard more
and more insistently in the winter of 1922–1923 turned first and
foremost on the need to come to the aid of the heavy industrial
sector of the economy. The organ of STO, *Ekonomicheskaya
Zhizn'*, devoted a leading article on January 25, 1923, to a demand
for economies in the budget (in what sector of it was discreetly
left unstated) in order to release funds to help heavy industry.
A spokesman of industry protested in *Trud* on March 10, 1923,
against talk of further state intervention in favour of the peasant
at the expense of industry : industry " requires from the state
not a diminution of protection, but on the contrary an increase
of it ". But such pleas, once they went beyond vague generalities,
quickly led to conclusions incompatible with the official party line,
since they could be satisfied only by increasing the budget deficit
and by swelling still further the volume of paper currency, or
by increasing the burden of taxation on the peasant. The year
1923 became a time of constant and bitter struggle between
Narkomfin, its course now firmly set for financial reform and a
balanced budget, and therefore determined at all costs to cut down
state subsidies to industry, and those who believed that the
restoration of heavy industry, through a simultaneous process of
concentration and expansion, both involving capital outlays, was
in the long run the only path to economic recovery and the
advance towards socialism. Since the restoration of heavy
industry was necessarily dependent on the development of
planning, the second view tended to find its most vocal advocates
in Gosplan, on which the hopes of Trotsky had also long centred.[1]
To the demands of Narkomfin for economies the spokesmen of
Gosplan retorted that only those economies were laudable which
did not result in " stagnation in our economy and serious difficulties in restoring it owing to the further deterioration of transport and heavy industry ", and that a sound policy of advances
to industry was being sacrificed to fiscal considerations.[2] On the
other hand, the campaign to increase grain exports, which was

[1] See *The Bolshevik Revolution, 1917–1923*, Vol. 2, pp. 379-381.
[2] *Ekonomicheskaya Zhizn'*, April 24, 1923 (article by V. Smirnov), May 19, 1923.

strongly supported by Narkomfin for the double purpose of aiding
the peasant and of building up reserves of gold and foreign currency, encountered opposition in Gosplan, where the majority
of the presidium held its ground and remained firmly wedded
to the policy of cheap food and the planned development of
industry. Strumilin cogently stated the arguments against grain
exports. He conjured up the ·danger of restoring Russia to her
former status as " an agricultural colony of the bourgeois west "
with the consequences of the destruction of Russian industry and
the renewed dependence of Russia on the capitalist world. It
was pointed out that only the well-to-do peasants who had grain
to sell — not more than 15-20 per cent of the whole — would
benefit by a rise in prices ; the great mass of the peasantry was
either barely self-supporting or a purchaser of grain. In any case
it was an " elementary truth " that the healthy development of
agriculture was dependent on the expansion of industry.[1] But
these theoretically powerful arguments of a long-term character
carried little weight with political leaders faced with the urgent
need to provide the peasant with strong enough incentives to
produce the wherewithal to feed urban populations and prevent
the price-level turning further against him ; increased facilities
for the export of grain seemed, under the conditions of NEP, the
convenient and most effective means of attaining this vital object.

Responsible party critics of economic policy in the first months
of 1923 fell into two groups. The first group was concerned
with the adverse effects of NEP on heavy industry, and sought
first and foremost to mitigate these effects through an extension
of state subsidies — if necessary, by curtailing the benefits which
NEP had conferred on the peasant or increasing the burdens on
him. Preobrazhensky, always keen to expose the shortcomings
and anomalies of NEP,[2] who had criticized Lenin as early as
December 1921 for describing war communism as a mistake, and
argued that this mistaken terminology might lead later to mistakes
about the goal of the revolution,[3] was the outstanding theorist
of the group, Pyatakov, the vice-president of Vesenkha, its ablest

[1] S. G. Strumilin, *Na Khozyaistvennom Fronte* (1925), pp. 215-217 ; the
article setting forth these arguments was originally published in April 1923.

[2] See *The Bolshevik Revolution, 1917-1923*, Vol. 2, pp. 291-293, 379.

[3] *Vserossiiskaya Konferentsiya RKP (Bol'shevikov)*, No. 2 (December 20,
1921), p. 22.

representative in the economic administration. Trotsky stood
near to the position of this group, but did not share it to the full.
He had whole-heartedly accepted NEP ; he had indeed been the
first to propose it.[1] But he insisted on the purpose of NEP as
" the utilization by the workers' state of the methods, procedures
and institutions of capitalist society in order to build, or to prepare
the way to build, a socialist economy " ; [2] and he was predisposed
to welcome any measure which signified the ending of the
" retreat ". This attitude was linked with his insistence on the
need for planning, since planning was the condition of a revival
of heavy industry and therefore of a renewed advance towards
socialism.[3] It was no accident that Trotsky should have become
in the winter of 1922–1923 the spokesman of industry in the
Politburo, where he more than once pressed the demand for a
more generous credit policy.[4] There was thus ample material
available to those who began in 1923 to charge Trotsky with
" underestimating " the peasantry, though the charge was not
altogether justified in the form in which it was made, and later
assumed dimensions wholly disproportionate to the grain of truth
contained in it. A second group of which Krasin was the most
important party representative, but which probably enjoyed wide
support among officials and managers in industry,[5] regarded the
extraction of further surpluses from the peasant as impracticable
or undesirable, and pursued the hope of foreign credits. This

[1] See The Bolshevik Revolution, 1917–1923, Vol. 2, p. 280.

[2] Dvenadtsatyi S"ezd Rossiiskoi Kommunisticheskoi Partii (Bol'shevikov)
(1923), p. 282.

[3] Trotsky said at the twelfth party congress : " If we had not worked at an
economic plan, checking it, verifying it, modifying it in course of execution, our
transport, our heavy industry would have gone to the scrap-heap. Of course
heavy industry would have been resuscitated through the market in 10 or 20
years, but by that time in the form of private capitalist industry " (ibid. p. 307).

[4] Trotsky's note to the Politburo, on this point, of February 13, 1923, is in
the Trotsky archives, T 778 ; support for industry was also implicit in Trotsky's
insistence at this time on more comprehensive planning and greater power for
Gosplan (see The Bolshevik Revolution, 1917–1923, Vol. 2, pp. 379-380).

[5] It was compromising to Krasin in party circles that his views corresponded
so closely with those of a group of former bourgeois professors and economists,
who were still teaching in Soviet universities ; during 1922 this group issued
several numbers of a journal entitled Ekonomist, which was still tolerated as a
learned publication, and the main theme of which was the impossibility of
restoring the Soviet economy without foreign aid based on a return to capitalist
principles. Krasin's views seem at this time to have been regarded in the party
as useful for export, but were not otherwise taken very seriously.

group not only accepted NEP to the full, but wished to carry it to what seemed the logical conclusion of a more conciliatory attitude towards the capitalist Powers. The weakness of this proposal was that the experiences of the Genoa and Hague conferences had demonstrated the stringency of the terms on which foreign credits could be obtained, and that Lenin, by rejecting the Urquhart agreement against Krasin's advice,[1] appeared to have turned away from this policy.

Such was the situation when, in the weeks following Lenin's second severe stroke of March 9, 1923, preparations were hastily made for the twelfth party congress.[2] During the preliminary discussions in the Politburo, Trotsky referred to his " differences on the economic questions " with the majority, but found the other members unwilling to discuss them or even to admit their existence.[3] The time was not ripe ; the issues themselves were not yet fully clear ; and, so long as Lenin himself might yet recover sufficiently to take a hand in party disputes, nobody wanted to bring them to a head. In accordance with precedent draft resolutions on major questions for submission to the congress were prepared in the Politburo and carried its collective authority. It was arranged that the principal report on the policy of the central committee during the past year should be made by Zinoviev, that Trotsky should submit a special resolution on industry and Kamenev one on taxation of the peasant. The agreed texts carried certain differences of nuance, but any open clash of opinion was avoided. Basic economic issues were ventilated at the congress by other members of the party and to some extent even by the leaders. But the prior agreement in the Politburo to refrain from radical and controversial decisions limited the scope of the debate.

Notwithstanding this restraint, no pains were spared by the

[1] See *The Bolshevik Revolution, 1917–1923*, Vol. 3, p. 432.
[2] For these preparations see pp. 272-273 below.
[3] L. Trotsky, *Moya Zhizn'* (Berlin, 1930), ii, 227-228 ; in L. Trotsky, *Stalin* (1946), p. 366, they have become " serious differences ". Rykov a year later referred to the argument as " a little discussion which did not go beyond the limit of the central committee " (*Trinadtsataya Konferentsiya Rossiiskoi Kommunisticheskoi Partii (Bol'shevikov)* (1924), p. 6). For an account of relations between the party leaders on the eve of the twelfth congress see pp. 270-272 below.

party leadership to make the defence of the peasant, and of the
" link " between proletariat and peasantry established by NEP,
the keynote of the congress. On the eve of the congress the
official economic organ proclaimed that the export of grain and
the need to temper the burden of taxation on the peasant were the
two most important issues confronting it.[1] By a symbolical
gesture 30 non-party peasants were given seats in the congress
hall.[2] Zinoviev, as the chief spokesman of the party, made himself
their champion. He warmly rebutted the charge of a " peasant
deviation "; if the policy of the party central committee was a
deviation, Lenin himself, the progenitor of NEP, was the author
of it. The peasant was the key to everything. Taxation must not
fall too heavily on him; export of grain must be encouraged in
order to raise grain prices; the national question must be considered from the angle of the peasantry of the border regions;
the cost of the administrative apparatus must be reduced; even
anti-religious propaganda must be so conducted as " not to
irritate the peasant ".[3] In one passage he seemed to recognize
the vulnerability of NEP by making a half-jesting distinction
between " the new economic policy " and the word " NEP ",
which brought to the mind a picture of " the nepman and his
unpleasant features ". But the gist of the speech was a cautious
verdict in favour of the *status quo*.

> The only important thing, comrades, is that we should
> continue to look at NEP correctly, that we should clearly

[1] *Ekonomicheskaya Zhizn'*, April 16, 1923.
[2] *Dvenadtsatyi S"ezd Rossiiskoi Kommunisticheskoi Partii (Bol'shevikov)*
(1923), p. 416.
[3] Two resolutions of the congress referred to the importance of not insulting
the religious feelings of believers (*VKP(B) v Rezolyutsiyakh* (1941), i, 514, 521).
An article in *Pravda*, May 8, 1923, referred to the deep roots of religion among
the peasant population and the need for " great caution, great skill " in eradicat-
ing them : " otherwise we shall achieve nothing but *the creation of new legends* ".
A circular from the trade union central council requested trade unions " to
behave with complete tolerance and tact to the religious convictions of their
members and not repel them from the unions by insulting their religious feeling
with thoughtless and tactless attacks " (*Trud*, June 9, 1923). The change of
policy in anti-religious propaganda may be connected with an incident mentioned
by Trotsky which must have occurred late in 1922 ; according to L. Trotsky,
Moya Zhizn' (Berlin, 1930), ii, 213, Stalin appointed Yaroslavsky as Trotsky's
deputy in the department of anti-religious propaganda as a step to get it away
from Trotsky's control, and Lenin, after his return to work, expressed dis-
approval of this appointment.

recognize that it is a question of the link with the peasant, not
with the nepman, and that we should understand that we must
resist all those who see in this a so-called " peasant deviation ".[1]

The first resolution recognized that " agriculture will long remain
the foundation of the economy of the Soviet land ", and advocated
export of grain in order to raise grain prices and provide " a
stimulus for the peasant to increase the area under the plough ".
The importance of " the link between the working class and the
peasantry " was once more stressed. Industry must put its own
house in order : " the specific weight of state industry in the whole
economy of the country can be increased only by degrees and only
through the organization of industry to raise its profitability, etc." [2]

At a later stage of the proceedings Kamenev reinforced the
same doctrine in introducing a separate resolution on the taxation
of the peasant. In a speech copiously interlarded with quotations
from Lenin, he explained that the question of " mutual relations
between the proletariat and the peasantry in the Soviet land " was
" the fundamental question of the dictatorship of the proletariat
in the present period ". The land decree of October 26/November
8, 1917, had been the first " treaty " between them ; the introduction of the tax in kind under NEP was the second. Lenin's last
published article, and a report by Frunze from the province of
Ivanovo-Vosnesensk on " the serious discontent of the peasantry
with the policy of the Soviet power ", were quoted in support of
the proposition that the burden on the peasant must be alleviated.
The concrete proposals were to convert the tax in kind into
monetary terms, to unify it, and to raise grain prices by stimulating
exports of grain. This Kamenev described as " the last battle
between capitalism and communism " — to be fought not on the
battlefields of the civil war, but " in the sphere of the peasant
economy ".[3] A briefer and more detailed speech from Sokolnikov
gave some figures. Taxes on the peasant in the current year were
estimated to bring in 390 million gold rubles ; for the next year,
1923–1924, it was proposed to raise the total to 400 millions ; but,
since a 16-18 per cent increase in the area under crops was

[1] *Dvenadtsatyi S"ezd Rossiiskoi Kommunisticheskoi Partii (Bol'shevikov)*
(1923), pp. 23-26, 32-39.
[2] *VKP(B) v Rezolyutsiyakh* (1941), i, 472-473.
[3] *Dvenadtsatyi S"ezd Rossiiskoi Kommunisticheskoi Partii (Bol'shevikov)*
(1923), pp. 388-412.

expected, this would mean a substantial reduction in the demand
on the individual peasant.[1] The resolution recorded the decision
to relieve the burden of taxation on the peasant by offering him
the alternative of payment in cash or in kind, by unifying all
existing taxes into a " single agricultural tax ", and by taking
account of local and individual conditions in fixing the assessment.
Officials were particularly enjoined to explain the necessity and
purpose of the tax to the peasant in sympathetic terms.[2]

Between these impressive pronouncements by Zinoviev and
Kamenev on behalf of the peasant, which fell respectively at the
beginning and almost at the end of the congress, came the complaints of the critics, who spoke in the debate on Zinoviev's
report, and Trotsky's report on industry. Larin, in a speech full
of personal recrimination which clearly put the congress against
him, proposed a 20 per cent increase in taxes on the peasant in
order to secure a correct distribution of resources between
agriculture and industry : this represented the case of industry
in its naked and extreme form. Krasin pleaded the cause of
industry from a different standpoint. In a recent article in
Pravda, which had attracted attention and resentment, he had
protested against too much state interference with industry and
demanded " a maximum of production and a minimum of
control ".[3] In his speech at the congress he showed himself
sceptical of the possibility either of helping the peasant or of
developing industry out of native resources, and continued to pin
his faith on foreign loans and concessions : the weakness of his
case was that, while nobody contested the desirability of this
expedient, few believed it practicable on any terms which the
régime could conceivably accept.[4] Preobrazhensky, whose views

[1] Ibid p. 420.
[2] VKP(B) v Rezolyutsiyakh (1941), i, 488-491.
[3] Pravda, March 24, 1923 ; Martynov, a new convert from Menshevism,
replied (ibid. April 4, 1923) that this plea had been heard " in recent years "
from " managers of all colours and tendencies ", and that Krasin's fundamental
error was a desire to replace political action by economic management before
class contradictions had been eradicated. In a further article Krasin sarcastically
enquired whether the " link " with the peasantry could be achieved through
" the continued ruin of our heavy industry " (ibid. April 15, 1923).
[4] Dvenadtsatyi S"ezd Rossiiskoi Kommunisticheskoi Partii (Bol'shevikov)
(1923), pp. 101-104, 116-119 ; Krasin reiterated his plea in a second speech
(ibid. pp. 351-355). In an interview in Trud, April 17, 1923, he strongly
defended grain exports.

of the relative weight of industry and agriculture in Bolshevik policy were at the opposite pole to those propounded by Zinoviev, confined himself to deploring the lack of any decision of principle about the future of NEP, and then turned aside to attack Krasin's policy of surrender to foreign capitalism as the greater danger.[1] The opposition to the economic policy laid down by the Politburo and announced by Zinoviev had largely fizzled out before Trotsky rose to deliver his report on industry.

Trotsky began by explaining that his report was designed not to record the progress of industry during the past year, but to have " a directive character ". It proved, however, to be analytical rather than " directive ". Trotsky was plainly inhibited by his unwillingness to challenge the majority of the Politburo and by his acceptance of a compromise which was not so much a compromise as an agreement not to bring differences into the open. The conclusions which would have resulted from his analysis were diametrically opposed to those of Zinoviev; but these conclusions he failed to draw — at any rate in any form which would have made the opposition clear. The speech was none the less a full and far-reaching analysis of Trotsky's views at this time. The essential purposes of NEP as he defined it were two : to increase the productive forces of the country, and to organize these forces in such a way as to propel the state along the socialist path.[2] The exchange of products between agriculture and industry which NEP was designed to promote meant, however, on the industrial side, the production of consumer goods. It had brought with it a rapid increase of production in rural industries and in factory industries (notably the textile industry) catering for the domestic consumer. Heavy and medium industries had registered scarcely any advance ; nor was there any inducement for the investment of private capital in them. It was the task of the succeeding period to extend the revival brought about by NEP in light industry to heavy industry, and to " drain off into the mill of socialism as large a part as possible of what we provisionally call the surplus value created by the whole labouring population of our Union ".[3]

Having reached this crucial point, Trotsky left it for a digression

[1] *Dvenadtsatyi S"ezd Rossiiskoi Kommunisticheskoi Partii (Bol'shevikov)* (1923), p. 130.
[2] *Ibid.* pp. 282-283.   [3] *Ibid.* pp. 285-291.

which made his speech famous when the rest of it was conveniently forgotten. He exhibited a diagram showing the relations between prices of agricultural products and prices of industrial products since the previous summer. The two lines converged and intersected in September 1922 (this being the point of parity as measured by 1913 prices), and from that point gradually diverged more and more widely, giving the diagram the aspect of an open pair of scissors.[1] The scissors represented the rapid movement of prices since the autumn of 1922 in favour of industry, counteracting and revoking the movement of prices in favour of agriculture which had set in after the introduction of NEP.[2] According to Trotsky's diagram, industrial prices in March 1923 stood at above 140 per cent of the 1913 level, while agricultural prices had sunk below 80 per cent;[3] and the disparity continued to increase by leaps and bounds. The nature of the crisis was masked for a time by the still progressive currency inflation, since the phenomenal rise in all prices in terms of current rubles was more conspicuous than the smaller but more significant divergence between the rate of increase in the prices of different commodities. Trotsky's speech and diagram brought home to many delegates for the first time the nature of the crisis. The demonstration enabled him to take as the starting-point for his practical conclusions the one point in the economic situation where the most ardent supporters of the peasant were most sensitive to the need for state intervention. The rise in industrial prices struck at the roots of current economic policies by threatening to deprive the peasant of the adequate return for his products which NEP had sought to give him, and by demonstrating the fallacy of the supposition that safety could be found in giving free rein to the processes of the market. These radical deductions were not yet

[1] The diagram, based on figures obtained by Trotsky from Komvnutorg, is reproduced in *Dvenadtsatyi S"ezd Rossiiskoi Kommunisticheskoi Partii (Bol'shevikov)* (1923), p. 393. A similar diagram in M. H. Dobb, *Russian Economic Development since the Revolution* (2nd ed. 1929), p. 222, based on the calculations of Strumilin, the economist of Gosplan, introduces some refinements (and incidentally puts the point of intersection in August instead of September 1922), thus marring the simple outline of the " scissors "; but the broad conclusion is the same.

[2] See *The Bolshevik Revolution, 1917–1923*, Vol. 2, pp. 311-315.

[3] Strumilin's more carefully weighted figures made the disparity still greater, giving percentages of 169 and 60 respectively for February 1923 (S. G. Strumilin, *Na Khozyaistvennom Fronte* (1925), p. 212).

drawn — even by Trotsky himself. But it was not wholly inappropriate that the term " scissors crisis " came to be applied to
the whole economic crisis of 1923, though violent price fluctuations
were only a part of its symptoms.

Trotsky now proceeded to his conclusions, which had been
agreed in advance in the Politburo and were embodied in the draft
resolution. The first, which was now virtually uncontested, was
to promote the export of grain. The second, which was everywhere accepted in principle, though its application was difficult
and controversial, was to increase the efficiency of industry by
measures of concentration and by cutting down overhead costs —
a process which was connected with the development of stricter
and more accurate accountancy. The problem of unemployment
was treated as secondary. Trotsky admitted that " the necessity
of dismissing men and women workers " was a " hard, very hard,
nut ", but thought it a lesser evil than the " concealed unemployment " of inefficient production. The question of wages raised
" no difficulties of principle ", and was dismissed in a single
paragraph with a reference to a commission which had recently
sat under the presidency of Rykov and had removed incipient
" misunderstandings between the industrialists and the trade
unionists ".[1] The only specific recommendation in this field was
to equalize wages between heavy and light industry, so that the
greater prosperity of the latter might benefit the working class
as a whole. More delicate was the acutely controversial question
of the financing of industry. The programme for industry was
set by Vesenkha under the authority of STO. The " financial
pump " should therefore be in the hands of Vesenkha, and
credits should be granted by the Prombank, which was really a
special branch of the State Bank. This would ensure that credits
would be given to enterprises not from the standpoint of capacity
to earn immediate profits, but from the standpoint of prospects
over a number of years.[2]

[1] See pp. 74-75 below.
[2] *Dvenadtsatyi S"ezd Rossiiskoi Kommunisticheskoi Partii (Bol'shevikov)*
(1923), pp. 294-304. For Prombank see *The Bolshevik Revolution, 1917-1923,*
Vol. 2, p. 357. Its first director, Krasnoshchekov, was arrested for financial
malpractices in September 1923 ; an account of his misdemeanours will be
found in *Pravda*, February 12, 1924. Shortly before his arrest, Krasnoshchekov
proposed that Gosbank should be deprived of its credit functions, and the
financing of industry entrusted exclusively to Prombank (*Ekonomicheskaya*

Finally, Trotsky wound up his speech with a long exposition
of the principles of planning, which he himself perhaps regarded
as the essential part of his conclusions, but which others certainly
treated as a theoretical and utopian epilogue. He began by attempting to show how a planned economy grew inevitably out of current
needs and practice. The foundations of planning were already
laid by three factors which could not be brought under the
laws of the market — the Red Army (" the army is a planned
economy "), transport and heavy industry (" which with us works
either for transport, or for the army, or for other branches of
state industry "). In this field planning amounted to no more
than necessary foresight and coordination of requirements. Recalling the adoption by the ninth party congress in the far-off
days of war communism of the idea of " a single economic plan ",[1]
he defined the three stages of the development of planning : first,
" means of production to produce means of production ", then
" means of production to produce objects of consumption " and
finally " objects of consumption ". The function of planning was
ultimately to overcome NEP :

> Our new economic policy was established seriously and for
> a long time, but not for ever. We introduced the " new "
> policy in order on its own foundation and to a large extent by
> using its own methods to overcome it. . . . Ultimately we shall
> extend this planning principle to the whole market, and in so
> doing swallow and eliminate it. In other words our successes
> on the basis of the new economic policy automatically bring us
> nearer to its liquidation, to its replacement by the *newest*
> economic policy, which will be a socialist policy.

But how was progress towards planning to be made ? Trotsky
cited a remark from a report to the congress on the state industry

Zhizn', September 7, 1923). Its first report, issued in the summer of 1923,
showed that between November 1922 and May 1923 it had been primarily
concerned to keep its capital intact, that its charges for advances had been
exorbitant, and that what advances it had made had been almost exclusively to
light industry (*ibid.* August 23, 1923 (Supplement)). On the occasion of a
conference of managers and local representatives of Prombank in Moscow in
June 1923, a scheme was actually mooted to make Prombank a centre for the
financing of heavy industry (*ibid.* June 22, 1923) ; but this can have had little
hope of success, since Prombank was wholly dependent on Gosbank, which was
closely leagued with Narkomfin.
    [1] See *The Bolshevik Revolution, 1917–1923*, Vol. 2, p. 370.

of the Moscow region : " The working class, being in power, has
the possibility, when class interests require it, of giving industry a
credit at the expense of the worker's wage ". " In other words,"
paraphrased Trotsky, " there may be moments when the state
does not pay a full wage or pays only a half, and you, the worker,
give a credit to your state at the expense of your wages." Unless
the worker was prepared to earn surplus value for the workers'
state, there was no way forward to socialism. Having thus firmly
dissociated himself from the attack on the party leadership in
the name of the workers, Trotsky concluded with a postscript
on the inevitable hardships of a period of " primitive socialist
accumulation ".[1]

The speech had ranged far and wide, and the debate that
followed it was desultory. None of the other principal leaders
took part in it. None of the delegates who spoke did anything
to sharpen the issue except Chubar, a worker and an old Bolshevik,
who sourly observed that, while the workers and peasants might
" give a credit to their state " by forgoing a part of their rewards,
many of the specialists employed under NEP merely wanted to
" grab something which will help them to get more firmly on to
their feet as property-owners ", and Lyadov, another old Bolshevik, who uncompromisingly pleaded the cause of heavy
industry and wanted to " deliver " it from "the power of
NEP ".[2] The resolution, after some minor amendments in the
drafting committee, was unanimously adopted by the congress.
It began by asserting that " only the development of industry
can create an unshakable foundation for the dictatorship of
the proletariat ", but immediately added the safeguarding qualification :

> Agriculture, in spite of the fact that it is still at a low
> technical level, has a primary significance for the whole economy
> of Soviet Russia.[3]

[1] *Dvenadtsatyi S"ezd Rossiiskoi Kommunisticheskoi Partii (Bol'shevikov)*
(1923), pp. 306-322 ; the passage on planning has already been quoted in *The
Bolshevik Revolution, 1917-1923*, Vol. 2, p. 382.
    [2] *Dvenadtsatyi S"ezd Rossiiskoi Kommunisticheskoi Partii (Bol'shevikov)*
(1923), pp. 343, 359.
    [3] This clause was added when the draft resolution as approved by the
Politburo was submitted to the party central committee on the eve of the congress ; Trotsky opposed it on the ground that it was irrelevant to a resolution

The duration of this state of affairs depended largely on " the course of events outside Russia, i.e. first and foremost the course of the revolutions in west and east ". But as regards the measures to be adopted at home, which were cautiously said to have " a gradual character ", the resolution remained chiefly on the safe ground of general principles. On the one hand, the revival of state industry depended on agricultural development, since " the necessary working capital can be created only from agriculture in the form of an excess of agricultural products over what is consumed in the countryside ". On the other hand, " the creation of surplus value in state industry is a matter of life and death for the Soviet power, i.e. for the proletariat " ; and the development of industry is " a condition of the development of our agriculture in a socialist, and not a capitalist, direction ". A significant paragraph touched on a basic problem of NEP without indicating the solution :

> Mutual relations between light and heavy industry cannot be settled simply by the method of the market, since this would in fact bring a threat of the ruin of heavy industry in the years immediately to come, with the prospect of its subsequent restoration through the spontaneous operation of the market, but then on the basis of private property.

The conclusions of Trotsky's speech on the export of grain, on the rationalizing and financing of industry and on the principles of planning were duly recorded — sometimes in slightly vaguer terms than those which the speaker had used. Little encouragement was given to those who preached the panacea of credits for industry. " Complaints of the *insufficiency of working capital* " were a proof that the state had taken under its management more industrial enterprises than could be profitably maintained in the existing state of the economy ; the only solution lay in " a radical *concentration of production* in the technically best equipped and geographically best situated enterprises ". An emphatic blessing was given to the principle of one-man management.[1] Attention

on industry, but was outvoted (*Trinadtsataya Konferentsiya Rossiiskoi Kommunisticheskoi Partii (Bol'shevikov)* (1924), pp. 6-7). According to L. Trotsky, *Moya Zhizn'* (Berlin, 1930), ii, 229, the proposal came from Kamenev and was the first move in the campaign to discredit Trotsky on the score of his alleged neglect of the peasantry.

[1] For this section of the resolution see p. 46 below.

C

was drawn to the inadequacy of the machinery of trade and distribution, to the need to increase its efficiency and reduce its cost.
But nothing more radical was recommended than study by the
departments concerned. The resolution as a whole retained the
character of a declaration of principles rather than of a decision
on policy.[1]

The twelfth party congress represented an almost unqualified
victory for the supporters of the economic *status quo*. Trotsky
had analysed the difficulties of heavy industry, but stopped short
of radical solutions which would have been a direct challenge to
the majority of the Politburo. He had impressed the delegates
with the problem of the " scissors ", but had not sought to depict
it as a major crisis or as a symptom of deep-seated disease. The
cloud on the horizon was not yet large or menacing enough to
shake the leaders out of their complacency. No call for urgent
action had come from the congress. When it was over, effect
was given to its principal concrete recommendations through the
governmental machine. The organization of the export of
agricultural products was entrusted to a limited liability company
set up for the purpose under the name Eksportkhleb, and working
under the control of Vneshtorg;[2] and 44 million puds of grain
were exported in the year ending September 30, 1923, of which
28 millions went to Germany.[3] A long decree of May 20, 1923,
provided for the institution of a " single agricultural tax " which
was to replace not only the taxes imposed under NEP, but also
the " general citizens' tax " introduced in February 1922,[4] what
was left of the compulsory labour service, and all local taxation
other than that levied by rural districts and villages. The tax was
to be computed, as before, in units of rye, but payment could be

---

[1] *VKP(B) v Rezolyutsiyakh* (1941), i, 476-488.

[2] *Sobranie Uzakonenii, 1923*, No. 37, art. 394 ; Eksportkhleb acquired four
months later a monopoly both for grain and for dairy products (*ibid*. No. 95,
art. 954).

[3] *Ekonomicheskaya Zhizn'*, October 1-2, 1923 ; average annual exports of
grain between 1900 and 1914 amounted to more than 500 million pounds. An
agreement signed by the Soviet trade delegate in Berlin with a German financial
group for the purchase of grain was ratified by Sovnarkom on July 17, 1923
(*Sbornik Dekretov, Postanovlenii, Rasporyazhenii i Prikazov po Narodnomu
Khozyaistvu*, No. 7 (10), July 1923, p. 49) ; other purchasers of grain were
Finland, Scandinavia and Great Britain (*Dvenadtsatyi S"ezd Rossiiskoi Kommunisticheskoi Partii (Bol'shevikov)* (1923), pp. 20-21).

[4] For this tax see *The Bolshevik Revolution, 1917-1923*, Vol. 2, p. 354.

made either in kind or in currency.[1] As regards industry, no
specific legislation was required to carry out the vague directives
of the congress; and nothing seems to have been done.[2] Advantage
was taken of the reorganization of commissariats on the creation
of the USSR in the summer of 1923 to bring back Rykov to the
presidency of Vesenkha in place of the weak and ineffective
Bogdanov;[3] but Pyatakov, an able administrator and always
ready to press the claims of heavy industry, remained the dominant
personality in that institution.

In the first months of 1923 the Soviet economy under the
influence of NEP had begun to exhibit many of the familiar
features of the capitalist pattern. Each element in it was struggling
to act independently in the pursuit of its own interest, on the
assumption that the maximum prosperity of the whole economy
would result from this process; and the main unifying control
was exercised by the financial authorities through the medium of
monetary and credit policy. It was no accident that the only
field in which an active and forward-looking policy was being
pursued at this time was that of finance. The financial aspect of
NEP, which was the most remote from the original conception,
had become by 1923 its most constructive and least controversial
part. Once the dream of a withering away of money had faded
with the advent of NEP, nobody seriously contested the view
that the function of money could not be performed by a depreciating and almost worthless currency. Here some positive action
was plainly required. After a brief struggle between the "goods
ruble" and the "gold ruble", during which some supporters of

---

[1] *Sobranie Uzakonenii, 1923*, No. 42, art. 451; later in the year the proportion of the tax that might be paid in kind was limited to 50 per cent or less,
according to the province concerned (*ibid.* No. 90, arts. 886, 887).

[2] Trotsky complained nine months later that " at the twelfth congress questions of the planned direction of the economy were discussed only formally "
and that " the ways and means indicated in the resolution of the twelfth congress were until recently scarcely applied at all " (L. Trotsky, *Novyi Kurs*
(1924), p. 4).

[3] Bogdanov was strongly attacked by Trotsky at the congress for his
" fatalism " and tendency towards " a Buddhist philosophy " (*Dvenadtsatyi
S"ezd Rossiiskoi Kommunisticheskoi Partii (Bol'shevikov)* (1923), pp. 370-
372).

the former advocated the stabilization of the currency on the basis of a price-index and not of gold,[1] the die had been cast for a currency based on gold. This decision had been registered in the resolutions of the party conference of December 1921 and of the eleventh party congress in March 1922.[2] The creation in November 1922 of the chervonets, with its equivalent of ten gold rubles and its backing in gold and foreign currency, had been accepted as a vital step forward, and the importance of financial reform to establish a stable currency became an unassailable item of party doctrine. The new mood was well expressed in a long circular issued by STO to regional and provincial economic authorities on the eve of the twelfth party congress. When Lenin had dwelt on the importance under NEP of retaining control of the " commanding heights " the reference had been to the nationalized industries — the core of the future socialist economy and the bulwark behind which the assaults of capitalism could be successfully defied. The STO circular took this familiar phrase and gave it a broader interpretation :

> Trading and financial institutions and agencies acquire [under NEP] first-rate practical importance (cooperatives, state shops, the State Bank etc.). If we do not seize the commanding heights here, we shall not be able to keep the rudder of economic life in our hands.[3]

The essential rôle which Lenin had assigned under NEP to " the commanding heights " of heavy industry was extended to the " commanding heights " of finance and commerce. The extension can hardly have been other than deliberate, and was in any case significant.

The issue of the chervonets at the end of 1922 had been the first step towards currency stabilization, or rather towards the creation of conditions in which the currency could be stabilized. But to attain this result it would be necessary to concentrate

---

[1] The principal advocate of this project was Strumilin, the leading economist of Gosplan, who claimed that the pre-war Austrian currency had been maintained on this basis (S. G. Strumilin, *Na Khozyaistvennom Fronte* (1925), pp. 103-110). Such schemes were also advocated by some western economists, notably by the American Irving Fisher, who was frequently quoted in Soviet literature of the period.

[2] See *The Bolshevik Revolution, 1917–1923*, Vol. 2, pp. 352-354.

[3] *Sobranie Uzakonenii, 1923*, No. 22, art. 258, pp. 404-405.

in the hands of Narkomfin and its agencies stronger powers than they at present possessed. The establishment of a stable currency could not be achieved without wider measures of state intervention than had been contemplated in the first period of NEP, and demanded a reversal of some of the measures then taken. In the process of relaxing controls which had been hailed as the essence of NEP, the occasion had been taken during 1922 to legalize transactions in gold, precious metals and foreign currency, hitherto rigorously prohibited, though often practised illegally ; [1] to permit state institutions and cooperatives to make and receive payments in old Russian gold currency ; [2] and to establish Exchanges, which were open to state institutions, cooperatives and private traders paying income tax in a high category, and on which dealings were regularly conducted in chervonets notes, foreign currencies or foreign bills of exchange, Soviet state bonds, shares or documents of companies registered in Soviet territory, and precious metals. [3]   The result of these measures was the revival of a money market, a bullion market and a stock exchange. It now became necessary, in order to create a monopoly for the chervonets as a legal medium, to restrict some of the freedom thus accorded. The first step was the creation by decree of February 6, 1923, of what was called a " special valuta commission ", consisting of representatives of Vneshtorg, Vesenkha, Gosbank, Komvnutorg and Tsentrosoyuz under the presidency of the representative of Narkomfin, with authority to grant licences entitling institutions or persons to deal on the Exchanges, as well as *ad hoc* licences, for institutions not so entitled, to acquire foreign currency. The purpose of these arrangements was to limit the use of foreign currency to foreign trade transactions and to prevent it from becoming a medium of internal circulation. [4] Then, on February 16, 1923, a general decree was issued " On Valuta Operations ". This categorically prohibited the use of old Russian currency or (except for foreign transactions) of foreign valuta as a means of payment. It confined transactions in foreign valuta to the Exchanges, thus restricting them to institutions and persons licensed by the special valuta commission. Holdings of

---

[1] *Sobranie Uzakonenii, 1922*, No. 28, art. 318.
[2] *Ibid*. No. 48, art. 604.   [3] *Ibid*. No. 65, art. 858.
[4] *Sobranie Uzakonenii, 1923*, No. 11, art. 133.

foreign valuta must be deposited on current account with Gosbank, which had a prior option to purchase them before they could be disposed of to any other institution or person.[1] These provisions, which gave Gosbank complete control over all holdings of foreign exchange and all foreign exchange transactions, were an example of one of the paradoxical consequences of NEP. The sweeping prohibitions which had been imposed under war communism in the name of socialist principles, but never systematically enforced because the means of enforcement were lacking, were replaced by specific regulations dictated by practical requirements. But these, though less onerous in form, were more rigorously applied, and concentrated in the hands of the central authorities a far more effective power than they had enjoyed in the earlier period. This tendency of NEP to negate itself by creating conditions which called imperatively for stronger centralized control first became apparent in the field of finance.

During the first six months of 1923, while all Soviet economic policy had marked time, no fresh ground was broken in the direction of financial reform. In March even Sokolnikov had a moment of hesitation. Writing in *Pravda*, he detected "symptoms of recovery" in the Soviet ruble, deprecated current comparison between it and the *assignats* of the French revolution, and declared that "our industry and trade need a firm Soviet power more than a firm valuta ".[2] Throughout the year a dual currency system was effectively maintained, the chervonets gradually coming more and more widely into circulation side by side with the Soviet ruble (known familiarly, and now somewhat contemptuously, as the Sovznak). The printing-press continued to work; and the amount of Sovznaks in circulation increased regularly by a quarter or a third each month. The total issue increased from just under two milliards of rubles (1923 pattern) on January 1, 1923, to four-and-a-half milliards on April 1, and nine milliards on July 1.[3] Sums were readily exchanged from one currency to the other at rates which reflected the progressive fall in value of the Soviet ruble or Sovznak. The rate of exchange between the two currencies was regularly quoted in the newspapers. But the

[1] *Sobranie Uzakonenii, 1923*, No. 15, art. 189.
[2] *Pravda*, March 10, 1923.
[3] L. N. Yurovsky, *Na Putyakh k Denezhnoi Reforme* (2nd ed. 1924), p. 84.

capacity of the printing-press to fill the gap in the exchequer was
now nearly exhausted.[1] The total value, in terms of chervontsy
and of purchasing power, of Sovznaks in circulation continued to
mount slowly from January to April 1923. Thereafter it fell into
a decline which the most feverish increases in the nominal amount
of the issue failed to arrest.[2] While, however, there was general
agreement that the two currencies could not continue to exist side
by side, the method by which the old currency would eventually
be eliminated or geared to the chervonets was still a matter for
controversy. In December 1922 the tenth All-Russian Congress
of Soviets had optimistically instructed VTsIK " in the very near
future " to set limits to the ruble note issue.[3] Narkomfin was
ready with a plan to stop the issue of Soviet rubles, stabilize them
at their current rate in terms of chervontsy, and so establish a single
stable currency.[4] Nobody, however, except the financial purists,
was prepared to face the consequences of the immediate abandonment of the issue of Soviet rubles as a source of revenue ; and the
twelfth party congress, with no practical solution of this difficulty
in view, passed over the question in silence.

Notwithstanding this set-back, the forces set in motion in the
previous year continued to work, and progress was made. Once
the postulate of a gold-standard currency had been accepted, it
was necessary to accumulate reserves of gold or stable foreign
currency as security for it ; for nowhere was the orthodox doctrine
of a gold reserve as the backing for currency more firmly believed
in than by those who directed the policy of Narkomfin. This
made Narkomfin a protagonist of the policy of an active trade
balance, which fitted in with the demand of the agriculturalists
to develop exports of grain; throughout this time Narkomfin
and Gosbank were strongly behind those who insisted on the

---

[1] Strumilin in an article in *Ekonomicheshaya Zhizn'*, March 22, 1923, accurately predicted that in a few weeks " the net ' profit ' from the note issue will
turn into a net loss not only for the economy and for the population as a whole,
but for the exchequer in particular ".

[2] L. N. Yurovsky, *Na Putyakh k Denezhnoi Reforme* (2nd ed. 1924), p. 86 ;
the value of the total Sovznak issue in terms of chervontsy rose from 113
millions on January 1, 1923, to 148 millions on April 1, and fell again to 118
millions on July 1 ; on January 1, 1924, it was 58 millions.

[3] *S"ezdy Sovetov v Dokumentakh*, i (1959), 236.

[4] Z. V. Atlas, *Ocherki po Istorii Denezhnogo Obrashcheniya v SSSR (1917–
1925)* (1940), p. 203.

conciliation of the peasant as the keynote of economic policy. But
the most important achievement of these months was that the
chervonets became familiar, was accepted in those business and
financial institutions to which its circulation was at first confined
as a useful and necessary medium, and began to have a stable value
in terms of prices. The original purpose of the issue of the
chervonets, in the words of the decree of October 11, 1922,
authorizing it,[1] had been to " strengthen the revolving funds of
Gosbank for its commercial operations ". At first chervontsy were
treated primarily as a unit of value for the opening of credits by
Gosbank for industrial or commercial concerns, and were not
intended to be used in current transactions.[2] But this limitation
soon threatened to defeat the purpose for which the new unit
had been created. On January 25, 1923, Narkomfin authorized
the acceptance of chervontsy notes for tax payments at the current
rate of exchange, thus conferring on them the character, not yet
of a regular legal currency, but of tax certificates; and in the
following month Narkomfin sanctioned the making of payments
by Gosbank in chervontsy, though only with the consent of the
customer.[3] Under these conditions the chervonets issue, though
not yet enjoying the status of legal tender, steadily expanded
throughout the first months of 1923. On January 1 notes to the
value of just over 1 million chervontsy had been " issued " (i.e.
transferred from the issue to the banking department of Gosbank),
of which only 350,000 chervontsy were in circulation. The issue
tripled in the next three months, and again in the three succeeding
months. On July 1 the total issue had risen to 9,600,000 chervontsy, of which 7 millions were in circulation.[4] Though its legal
status was unchanged, the chervonets had gradually become,
within the limits in which it circulated, a recognized and reliable
currency.

The basic function of the chervonets was to serve as a stable
unit of value. The original stipulation laid down to maintain
its stability was a 25 per cent cover in precious metals; and
throughout 1923 Gosbank made assurance doubly sure by holding

[1] See *The Bolshevik Revolution, 1917–1923*, Vol. 2, p. 358.
[2] As late as the autumn of 1923, 75 per cent of the chervontsy in circulation
were said to be held by the trusts (*Ekonomicheskaya Zhizn'*, October 1-2, 1923).
[3] L. N. Yurovsky, *Na Putyakh k Denezhnoi Reforme* (2nd ed. 1924), pp.
72-73.   [4] *Ibid.* p. 71.

a cover of 50 per cent, or almost 50 per cent, in gold or in gold-standard foreign currencies.[1] Thanks to this precaution and to the publicity given to it, the chervonets maintained its parity throughout the year, subject to minor fluctuations, with the pound and the dollar. Less satisfactory was its failure to maintain its purchasing power on the home market. This remained reasonably stable till May 1923 and then declined steeply between May and October, its value being substantially lower in terms of the retail price-index than of the wholesale price-index.[2] The fall was apparently due to the development of a serious sales crisis, a contracting market being no longer able to absorb the rapidly expanding chervonets issue. The value of the chervonets thus lagged further and further behind the value of the theoretical " goods ruble " — a factor which became important in the wages controversy.[3] During this period, therefore, internal prices rose in terms not only of the constantly depreciating Sovznak, but also (though of course in a far smaller degree) of the new and stable chervonets. This phenomenon puzzled financiers and economists, and led to a dispute reflecting the conflict of policy between Narkomfin and the industrialists. The spokesmen of Narkomfin attributed it, not without much show of reason, to the selfish policy of the trusts and syndicates in driving up prices. The spokesmen of industry laid the blame on the authorities of Narkomfin and Gosbank, who had rashly increased the issue of chervontsy at a more rapid rate than the state of the market justified.[4] This argument later received confirmation from the fact that, after October 1923, when the issue of chervontsy was restricted (being increased during the last quarter of the year by no more than 20 per cent), chervonets prices stabilized themselves and remained fairly constant over a long period. But the argument proved of little help to those

[1] The figures are in L. N. Yurovsky, *Na Putyahh k Denezhnoi Reforme* (1924), p. 74 ; as the issue increased, the holding of foreign currencies, and their proportion in the total cover, increased also.

[2] *Ibid.* p. 75 ; the disparity between the two indices reflected the fact that the margin between wholesale and retail prices was considerably greater than in 1913, the year on the basis of which the indices were calculated (see p. 12 above).

[3] See pp. 122-124 below.

[4] This charge was repeated by Preobrazhensky at the thirteenth party conference in January 1924 (*Trinadtsataya Konferentsiya Rossiiskoi Kommunisticheskoi Partii (Bol'shevikov)* (1924), p. 37).

who propounded it, since a restriction in the issue of chervontsy automatically brought with it the curtailment of credits to industry.

To crown the policy inaugurated by the introduction of the chervonets, however, it was necessary to overcome the system of the dual currency either by withdrawing the Sovznak or by stabilizing it in terms of the chervonets. This required in turn that the dependence of the treasury on issues of paper currency should cease, and that the budget should be balanced by reducing expenditure and expanding revenue. Under the first head, the reduction of staffs both in industry and in government departments was an obvious way of lightening the load on the budget. An instruction was issued in March 1923 to complete by May the working out of a scheme " tending towards the planned reduction of the general establishment of departments by as much as 25 per cent ".[1] But no such drastic measure was put into effect ; and a committee appointed by Sovnarkom to effect budget economies was unable to do more than reduce a budget deficit of 294 million rubles for the first half of the financial year 1922–1923 to 221 million rubles for the second half.[2] While constant exhortations to economy in public expenditure continued to be issued (*The Soviet Kopek will take care of the Soviet Ruble* was the title of a leading article in *Ekonomicheskaya Zhizn'* on April 22, 1923), it soon became clear that the curtailment of subsidies and credit for industry, which must result either in reduced production or in a lower level of real wages for the industrial worker, remained the only potential source of substantial budgetary economies.[3] On the revenue side new rates were issued in January 1923 for the tax on incomes introduced in the previous autumn, and showed a sharp grading for high salaries : the recipient of an income of over 5000 rubles (of the 1923 pattern) a month paid a tax of 1630 rubles on 5000 plus 80 per cent of the remainder. But these rates evidently proved too high and were drastically reduced in a further decree of May 1923.[4] Taxation of industry which in

---

[1] *Sobranie Uzakonenii, 1923*, No. 19, art. 237.

[2] *Ekonomicheskaya Zhizn'*, June 30, 1923.

[3] For the attempt to secure budgetary economies at the expense of industrial wages see pp. 72-79 below.

[4] *Sobranie Uzakonenii, 1923*, No. 4, art. 80 ; No. 43, art. 457 ; for the original introduction of income-tax see *The Bolshevik Revolution, 1917–1923*, Vol. 2, pp. 354-355. Sokolnikov in November 1923 described the tax as having

1922 amounted to only 3-4 per cent of net production was estimated to have risen in 1923 to 10-12 per cent.[1] But sources of fresh revenue were limited so long as general policy precluded any serious increase of the burden of taxation on the peasant.[2] Nor did public borrowing provide the possibility of bridging the gap between expenditure and revenue. In March 1923, following the successful precedent of the previous year, a " second internal state grain loan " of 30 millions of rye was announced, to be redeemed at the end of the year ; [3] but this was a device to facilitate

" a perfectly precise class structure " (*Tret'ya Sessiya Tsentral'nogo Ispolnitel'-nogo Komiteta Soyuza Sovetskikh Sotsialisticheskikh Respublik* (1924), p. 87) ; at that time it fell on incomes of 75 chervonets rubles a month and over — a limit far above the wages of the industrial worker.

[1] S. G. Strumilin, *Na Khozyaistvennom Fronte* (1925), pp. 225-226.

[2] A revenue-raising measure of this period which attracted more attention than any other, or than its intrinsic importance warranted, was a decree of January 1923 permitting the manufacture of potable spirit up to a strength of 20° in state factories and its sale in licensed shops and establishments (*Sobranie Uzakonenii, 1923*, No. 6, art. 100 ; the new vodka was affectionately dubbed *rykovka*, whether because Rykov was concerned with the execution of the decree or because he was credited with an addiction to alcohol). The abolition of the state manufacture and sale of vodka after the outbreak of war in 1914 was a much publicized and widely approved measure of the Tsarist government. For seven or eight years spirit almost disappeared from the countryside. Then, after the civil war and the famine, with the excellent harvest of 1922, the illicit distilling of home-made spirit (samogonka), from grain or potatoes, began on an extensive scale, both for consumption and for sale. (A graphic description of the process from a district in the province of Tver is given in A. M. Bolshakov, *Sovetskaya Derevnya za 1917-1924 gg.* (1924), pp. 84-90). When it became clear that heavy penalties were not an effective deterrent, it was natural that the financial authorities, in a desperate search for new sources of revenue, should have sought to revive the old vodka monopoly and draw revenue from a propensity which would otherwise be indulged illicitly and for private gain. Sentiment was, however, strongly against such a step. According to an uncontradicted statement in Trotsky's letter of October 8, 1923 (see p. 106, note 1 below), a majority of the Politburo desired a full restoration of the spirit monopoly, but was deterred by strong opposition in the central committee and in the rank and file of the party : the introduction of *rykovka* was a compromise. Some years later, Stalin stated that " the members of the central committee, including myself, had at that time a conversation with Lenin who recognized that, if we did not receive the indispensable loans from abroad, we should have to resort openly and directly to the vodka monopoly as a temporary measure of an exceptional character " ; this statement was made to foreign delegates and led up to the conclusion that "some share of responsibility for the vodka monopoly rests on our western European friends " (Stalin, *Sochineniya*, x, 232-234). There is no other evidence for Lenin's personal participation in the decision.

[3] *Sobranie Uzakonenii, 1923*, No. 24, art. 278 ; for the rye loan of 1922 see *The Bolshevik Revolution, 1917-1923*, Vol. 2, pp. 355-356.

and anticipate the collection of revenue rather than to augment it.[1]

In the summer of 1923 the expanding circulation and growing popularity of the chervonets, and the improvement in the budgetary situation, at length encouraged Narkomfin to embark on its long-prepared campaign to bring the financial reform to a final and logical conclusion. At the session of TsIK in July 1923, which ratified the constitution of the USSR,[2] Sokolnikov drew an optimistic picture of the national finances. " Ordinary " expenditure to a total of 1050 million gold rubles in the current budget year would be balanced by revenue from taxation and from state undertakings. " Extraordinary " expenditure to cover the deficit on transport (140 millions) and on industry (120 millions) and the needs of agriculture, to a total of from 320 to 350 millions, had still to be covered by currency emission. But on the assumption that the deficit on transport could be reduced next year to 50 millions and that, with increased and more efficient production, industry would be able to fend for itself, it now seemed possible to look forward to the day when recourse to the printing-press could be dispensed with. Relying on these calculations, Sokolnikov boldly proposed to fix a legal maximum for the issue of Sovznaks of 15 million rubles a month from August 1, 1923.[3] Preobrazhensky expressed scepticism about the prospect, and reiterated his familiar objection that currency stabilization was impossible without effective economic planning.[4] But there was no real opposition ; and TsIK adopted a resolution approving the efforts of Narkomfin " for the curtailment of unproductive expenditure and the reinforcement of economy in the expenditure of public funds, for the limitation of the note issue and the regularization of the fiscal system ", and deciding that the issue of Soviet rubles should be restricted as from May 1 to the value of 30 million gold rubles a month and from August 1 to the value of 15 million rubles a month. The budget for the financial year

[1] A. M. Bolshakov, *Sovetskaya Derevnya za 1917-1924 gg.* (1924), pp. 98-100, describes the heavy peasant demand for the 1923 loan (the 1922 loan had been taken up only by a few well-to-do peasants) ; the inducement was that the certificates could be used for tax payments.
[2] See *The Bolshevik Revolution, 1917-1923*, Vol. 1, p. 402.
[3] *Vtoraya Sessiya Vserossiiskogo Tsentral'nogo Ispolnitel'nogo Komiteta X Sozyva* (1923), pp. 107-118.　　　　[4] *Ibid.* pp. 161-162.

beginning October 1, 1923, was to be drawn up with strict regard
to this limit. A significant passage in the resolution attempted
to reconcile the divergent principles of planning and of a market
economy, and to prove that the financial reform was equally in
the interest of both :

> All these measures of a financial character should promote
> the introduction into the national economy of the Union of
> Soviet Socialist Republics of the indispensable elements of
> coherent planned development, and can exert a particularly
> powerful and prolonged influence on the extension of the trade
> of the country and of the market capacity of agriculture.[1]

The die now appeared to have been cast, and the course firmly
set. These decisions were hailed in the official economic journal
as giving " new strength to our financial department in the
struggle for a real budget and for the purification of our monetary
circulation ".[2] At the end of July further steps were taken
towards the establishment of the new currency. A decree was
issued which, while not yet making the chervonets sole legal tender,
made it possible not only to draw up contracts for major commercial transactions in chervontsy, but to enforce payment in
chervontsy on such contracts. Bills of exchange containing no
specific provisions about the medium of payment could be discharged either in chervontsy or in Soviet rubles at the option of
the debtor ; but bills providing for payment in chervontsy could
be discharged only in chervontsy.[3] The budget for 1923–1924
was to be drawn up, no longer (like the budget for January–
September 1922) in pre-war rubles or (like the budget for 1922–
1923) in gold rubles, but in chervontsy. Parallel with this change,
decrees were issued by Vesenkha in August and September 1923
instructing all trusts, syndicates and other institutions under its
control to keep their accounts exclusively in chervontsy and to
make their financial year begin on October 1 to coincide with the

[1] *Postanovleniya Vtoroi Sessii Vserossiiskogo Tsentral'nogo Ispolnitel'nogo Komiteta X Sozyva* (1923), pp. 16-18 ; the resolution was reprinted in the form of two decrees in *Sobranie Uzakonenii, 1923*, No. 66, arts. 636, 637.
[2] *Ekonomicheskaya Zhizn'*, July 5, 1923. A leading article, *ibid.* July 15, 1923, carried the heading : " Is it not time for the transition to a single uni-versally obligatory standard of value ? "
[3] *Sobranie Uzakonenii, 1923*, No. 90, art. 882.

fiscal year.[1] For the moment it seemed as if the efforts of Narkomfin, thwarted in the spring, to drive the Soviet ruble from the field and establish the chervonets as the sole and stable currency unit were to be crowned with success. But at this point the autumn crisis, itself due in part to the measures taken by Narkomfin, once more shattered these ambitions and brought a further postponement in the return to financial orthodoxy.

[1] *Sbornik Dekretov, Postanovlenii, Rasporyazhenii i Prikazov po Narodnomu Khozyaistvu*, No. 8 (11), August 1923, pp. 21-24; No. 9 (12), September 1923, p. 33.

CHAPTER 2

THE PLIGHT OF LABOUR

I T was only gradually that the industrial worker became conscious
of the lowered status which NEP conferred on him in the
Soviet economy. He had at the outset profited by the relaxation of tension and the general economic recovery which NEP
had initiated. He had been freed from the bogy of labour
conscription ; his wages rose steadily throughout the greater part
of 1922 ; and his standard of living, though wretched enough
even when compared with that of 1914, had risen well above the
starvation level of war communism. The adoption of NEP had
been a concession to the peasant. But it still seemed a needless
indiscretion to enquire at whose expense the concession had been
made ; assurances that what benefited the peasant *ipso facto*
benefited the whole economy were still plausible enough to be
believed. It was only in the winter of 1922–1923, when the
scissors crisis loomed on the horizon, when a balanced budget
and a stable currency became the lodestars of financial policy,
and concern for the peasant became the keynote of every official
speech of the principal leaders, that the industrial worker became
slowly conscious of his changed position. Everywhere acclaimed
under war communism as the eponymous hero of the dictatorship
of the proletariat, he was now in danger of becoming the step-
child of NEP. In the economic crisis of 1923 neither the defenders
of the official policy nor those who contested it in the name of the
development of industry found it necessary to treat the grievances
or the interests of the industrial worker as a matter of major
concern. The peasant had replaced him as the first preoccupation
of official policy. The eclipse of the industrial worker could in
the last analysis be traced back to the catastrophic decline in
industry and to the flight of the workers from city and factory
in the years of famine and civil war — the process of " the disintegration of the proletariat " whose first symptoms Bukharin had

detected as early as March 1918.[1] But in the period of economic revival which followed the introduction of NEP two specific causes had more directly contributed to weaken the position of the industrial worker : the increase in the authority and influence of the industrial managers, and the growth of widespread unemployment.

That the interests of the industrial worker should have been in a certain sense subordinated by NEP to those of the peasant was inevitable ; this was inherent in the nature and purpose of the new policy. What could not have been so easily foreseen was that NEP would weaken the position of the industrial worker, not only in relation to the peasant, but in relation to the directors and managers of industry ; indeed this seemed all the more anomalous since large-scale factory industry, which employed a high percentage of all industrial workers, suffered no change of status under NEP and remained in public ownership and administration.   Under war communism many of the old factory owners or managers had already reappeared in the guise of " specialists " and managers of nationalized industry.[2] But at that time bourgeois specialists were still regarded as a necessary evil and an unwelcome anomaly ; posts of formal responsibility and power were commonly reserved for unimpeachable proletarians, or at any rate for party members — a category to which the bourgeois specialist was at that time rarely admitted. With the coming of NEP this picture changed, gradually but fundamentally. Statistics collected from the major trusts and syndicates in the latter part of 1923 showed that, whereas in 1922 65 per cent of the managing personnel were officially classified as " workers " and 35 per cent as " nonworkers " (only one in seven of these being party members), a year later these proportions had been almost exactly reversed, only 36 per cent being " workers " and 64 per cent " nonworkers ", of whom nearly one-half were now party members.[3]

[1] See The Bolshevik Revolution, 1917–1923, Vol. 2, pp. 193-195.
[2] See ibid. Vol. 2, pp. 182-186.
[3] The figures are quoted in an article by Larin in Trud, December 30, 1923, from Torgovo-Promyshlennaya Gazeta, December 2, 1923 ; an obvious misprint in the tables has been corrected. The article concluded with a demand for trade union control over the appointment of managers. Another set of figures for 88

Two significant processes were thus at work : the management
of industry was passing back into the hands of former bourgeois
managers and specialists, and a higher proportion of these were
acquiring the dignity and security of party membership.

The rise in status and influence had its natural counterpart in
rising rates of remuneration. So long as the specialists in the
early days of war communism were subjected to a suspicion which
kept their influence within narrow bounds, their rates of remuneration, though they soared far above those of the ordinary worker
or employee, were also jealously watched and circumscribed.
Under NEP these limitations gradually disappeared. The introduction of NEP in industry encouraged a return to capitalist
modes of organization and ways of thought. By stressing the
need for independence and decentralization, and by substituting
trusts for *glavki* as the major units of organization, it helped to
transform those who managed and directed important industrial
concerns from bureaucrats into captains of industry. *Khozraschet*
was the order of the day ; and those who knew how to make
profits, emerging from the cloud of suspicion hitherto resting on
them, were once more held in honour.

The scandal of high salaries began to attract attention. In
August 1922, with the expressed purpose of preventing " ex-
travagance in the use of public funds " and also of bringing about
" a closer correspondence in the matter of remuneration between
those engaged in intellectual and in physical work ", a decree
was issued providing that maximum salaries should be fixed for all
those employed in state institutions or enterprises or enterprises
in receipt of state subventions ; but the payment of bonuses on
profits (*tantièmes*) above the maximum was not excluded.[1] Thereafter decrees were regularly issued fixing a monthly maximum
rate for salaries ;[2] and throughout 1923 the limit was raised

large trusts showed that on January 1, 1924, of presidents of boards of directors
of industry, 91 per cent were party members and 51 per cent were workers,
but that of all directors of industry only 48 per cent were party members and
35 per cent workers (*Trud*, June 27, 1924) ; the pressure to reserve posts for
party members and for workers was strongest at the top.

[1] *Sobranie Uzakonenii, 1922*, No. 49, art. 617.
[2] The maximum for January 1923 was 1500 rubles (1923 pattern) a month
(*Sobranie Uzakonenii, 1923*, No. 3, art. 41) ; the legal minimum monthly wage
for January 1923 varied from 44 to 22 rubles according to region and grade
(*Sbornik Dekretov, Postanovlenii, Rasporyazhenii, i Prikazov po Narodnomu*

D

month by month to take account of the falling value of the currency.[1] But these restrictions did not affect " personal " salaries sanctioned by STO, which were enjoyed by the highest specialists and about which detailed information was not disclosed.[2] Many stories were current of the extravagant pretensions of managers and specialists — the industrial counterpart of the nepmen in commerce.[3] Much difficulty was experienced in inducing specialists to take up posts in remote places,[4] and a decree of July 1923 offered special inducements to specialists taking up such posts.[5]

Already in the autumn of 1922 these processes had led to the emergence of a new feature in the NEP landscape — a loosely organized but influential group which came to be known as the " Red managers " or " Red industrialists ". In spite of their predominantly bourgeois origins and affiliations, they were now recognized members of the Soviet hierarchy; they had their modest place in the party; and they exercised an increasingly powerful voice not merely in industrial administration, but in

Khozyaistvu, No. 1 (4), January 1923, pp. 86-87). The effective wages of all skilled, and most unskilled, workers at this time far exceeded the legal minimum (see p. 61, note 5 below); but the discrepancy between wages and salaries was none the less striking.

[1] See, for example, Sobranie Uzakonenii, 1923, No. 12, art. 164; No. 23, art. 271; No. 31, art. 350. In June 1923 the limit was fixed in goods rubles at 150 a month (Sbornik Dekretov, Postanovlenii, Rasporyazhenii i Prikazov po Narodnomu Khozyaistvu, No. 6 (9), June 1923, p. 104); at that time 10 goods rubles was reckoned as the " standard " monthly wage of the worker (see p. 70 below).

[2] Ibid. No. 4 (7), April 1923, p. 107. Party members, being limited by the party maximum, were not supposed to receive these personal salaries; but the rule apparently broke down, since an attempt was made to re-enforce it in July 1924 (ibid. No. 10, July 1924, pp. 86-87).

[3] Mikoyan told the thirteenth party conference in January 1924 of a specialist who, on being offered a position in a factory in Kuban, had demanded, in addition to various financial bonuses in excess of the maximum salary, an apartment of four rooms fully furnished, with heating, lighting and a bath; a horse and carriage for himself and his family; two months' leave a year and a two-room summer lodging on the Black Sea for his family; and permission to keep a cow in the factory grounds. The cooperative which was running the factory agreed to these terms — but too late; for the specialist had in the meanwhile received a more attractive offer in Moscow. Such experiences were said to be quite normal (Trinadtsataya Konferentsiya Rossiiskoi Kommunisticheskoi Partii (Bol'shevikov) (1924), p. 79).

[4] This was a subject of complaint in an article by Lomov in Ekonomicheskaya Zhizn', April 20, 1923.

[5] Sobranie Uzakonenii, 1923, No. 69, art. 673.

decisions of industrial policy, the success of which depended largely on their efforts. The formation of the syndicates in the spring of 1922 [1] had been the first reaction of the " industrialists " to market conditions unfavourable to industry ; it was from the structure of trusts and syndicates built up by NEP that the new group derived its authority and prestige. Separate industries had recently revived the practice of holding congresses for the discussion of their problems and desiderata. In September 1922 a " temporary bureau " was set up, consisting of representatives of different industries, for the purpose of creating a common standing organ for industry as a whole — a " council of congresses ". The project had the blessing of Vesenkha, and it was decided to hold a conference before the end of the year to bring the " council of congresses " into being.[2] The end in view was described by *Trud* as being " the coordination of simultaneous political action by the Red industrialists and a more consistent attention to labour questions ". One of the functions of the new organization was apparently to present to the authorities the views of the industrialists on the labour code then in course of preparation.[3] It soon acquired sufficient authority to be able to denounce industrialists who failed to follow policies prescribed by it for " a breach of the front of industrial solidarity ".[4]

At this point the trade unions began to take alarm. Even in the days of war communism, the employment of bourgeois specialists had aroused constant suspicion in trade union circles ; and Lenin had had to use all his influence to impose the principle of " one-man management " in industry in the teeth of fierce opposition from the unions.[5] The improvement in the status of managers and specialists under NEP could only intensify this hostility. In August 1922 *Trud* opened a strong attack on the new " united front " of managers, which it accused of aiming at " a diminution in the rôle of the unions ", especially in the

[1] See *The Bolshevik Revolution, 1917-1923*, Vol. 2, pp. 314-315.
[2] *Trud*, September 13, 1922. Krasnoshchekov addressed the meeting as delegate of Vesenkha : it must have been one of his last public appearances.
[3] *Ibid*. September 29, 1922. For the labour code see *The Bolshevik Revolution, 1917-1923*, Vol. 2, pp. 330-331 ; among its noteworthy provisions was the wide power given to employers and managers to dismiss unsatisfactory workers.
[4] *Ekonomicheskaya Zhizn'*, October 15, 1922.
[5] See *The Bolshevik Revolution, 1917-1923*, Vol. 2, pp. 187-191.

engagement and dismissal of workers, and of wanting " ' free trade '
in matters of hiring and firing ". The article ended with a
rhetorical question :

> Have our managers so far entered into the rôle of " the
> masters " that they prefer unorganized workers to organized
> and disciplined members of trade unions ?

A few days later another article diagnosed a reversion among the
new managers to the traditional attitudes of employers towards
their workers : " our managers, even the best of them, have been
wonderfully quick in adopting the manners and tastes of our
former capitalist owners ".[1] The trade unions were caught in a
dilemma. To contest the authority of specialists and managers
was to fly in the face of party policy. To take sides with them was
to ignore the interests, and flout the prejudices, of the mass of
the workers. At first the tendency was to choose the second
alternative. *Trud* complained of " too much ' growing together '
at the top ", which led to " a divorce of the unions from the
masses ", and even noted " a special obstinacy " in resisting
workers' demands on the part of " managers who have recently
come from trade union work ".[2] The new developments in
managerial organization, coming at a moment when the unions
were for the first time threatened with the onset of mass unemployment, could not be allowed to pass without resistance. When the
industrialists held their conference in December 1922 to create the
standing " council of congresses ", the central council of trade
unions was also in session. Tomsky referred to a draft said to
have been drawn up by Mezhlauk for the conference of industrialists which declared *inter alia* that industry was " passing
through a grave crisis because it faces an offensive along the wages
line ", and that it was for this reason necessary to build up " an
industrial front " and " a corporate organization of industrialists ".
Tomsky angrily threatened " a trade union front against the Red
industrialists ", and reminded them that under the dictatorship
of the proletariat, not they, but the workers, were the factory
owners. Thus primed, the trade union council protested in
advance against any attempt " to change established forms of
mutual relations between the economic organs and the trade

[1] *Trud*, August 15, 17, 1922.   [2] *Ibid*. August 25, September 13, 1922.

unions in the direction of limiting the rights of the latter " ;   and
it passed a specific resolution on the proposed council of congresses :

> The trade union central council does not object to the creation
> under the presidium of Vesenkha of a council of congresses of
> industry, enjoying consultative functions, to prepare for in-
> dustrial congresses.
>
> But it categorically rejects the idea of creating a per-
> manently functioning council of congresses of industry, trade
> and transport, opposing itself as a " social-corporative organiza-
> tion ", on the one hand, to the organs of state administration
> and of the control of industry (Vesenkha, Narkomput'), and,
> on the other hand, to the trade unions, and thus basing its
> programme and tactics on fundamentally unsound principles.[1]

These emphatic protests seem to have produced little effect.
The " council of congresses of industry, trade and transport " was
duly created.[2]   The character of its activities may be judged from
a complaint which appeared in the official economic journal a
month later that " a lot of our Red industrialists are more inclined
to follow the line of least resistance, seeking to lower taxation or
reduce wages, than to undertake the meticulous and onerous work
of reorganizing the whole process of production ".[3]   The trade
union journal reiterated the time-honoured doctrine that in " the
transitional period from capitalism to communism "— while classes
still existed and class conflicts occurred — it was the duty of the
party, of the trade unions and of the Soviet state to espouse the
cause of the workers in their struggle against other classes.   It
even published a cartoon depicting a Red industrialist, with a cigar
in his mouth and all the attributes commonly ascribed by Soviet
art to the capitalist, sitting in a cart drawn by a worker and
complaining that " labour legislation " stood in the way of a
revival of industry.[4]   But the needs of industry were too im-
perative.   The authority of the Red industrialists was confirmed
by the decree of April 10, 1923, on the organization of the trusts,

[1] *Ibid.* December 26, 1922.

[2] An account of the foundation of the council and its early history is contained in an article by Smilga in *Ekonomicheskaya Zhizn'*, August 2, 1923 ;
during 1923 it published several numbers of a journal entitled *Predpriyatie*
(*The Enterprise*), which is quoted in *Trud*, January 3, 1924.

[3] *Ekonomicheskaya Zhizn'*, January 25, 1923.

[4] *Trud*, March 29, 1923.

which not only emphasized their independence, but made
specific provision for the payment of bonuses calculated as a
percentage of profits (*tantièmes*).[1]   A few days later the report
on industry submitted by Trotsky to the twelfth party congress
and unanimously approved by it, in a passage endorsing one-man
management in industry, defined the functions and duties of the
managers : they must be careful not to set the workers against
them by putting their demands too high, but also not to " take
the line of least resistance in questions of the productivity of
labour, wages, etc." The workers must be helped to understand
that " the director who strives to earn profits is serving the
interests of the working class in the same degree as the trade
union worker who strives to raise the standard of living of the
worker and to protect his health ". The director who " proves himself by the positive results of his work " should be able to count on
the unqualified " protection and support " of party organs.[2]   In a
resolution which paid scant attention to the demands of the workers
or of the trade unions the distribution of emphasis was significant.

One incidental change of the summer of 1923 provided evidence
of the rising status of the " Red industrialists ". When the USSR
was constituted in July, and Narkomtrud was reorganized as one
of the " unified " commissariats, the opportunity was taken to
reconstitute the collegium of Narkomtrud by " the introduction
of new members, chiefly representatives of industry " : this, explained Shmidt, was calculated to improve the relations between
the commissariat and the industrialists. One of the new representatives of industry was put in charge of the section of the
commissariat dealing with the labour market and the organization
of labour.[3]

The other and more decisive cause of the weakened position of
the industrial worker was the growth of widespread unemployment ; for the labour policy of NEP resembled that of a capitalist
economy in the way in which, consciously or unconsciously, it
made use of unemployment as an instrument for the discipline
and direction of labour. The causes of the spread of unemployment under NEP were manifold. Demobilization after the civil

---

[1] See *The Bolshevik Revolution, 1917–1923*, Vol. 2, p. 309.
[2] *VKP (B) v Rezolyutsiyakh* (1941), i, 484-486.   [3] *Trud*, July 13, 1923.

war brought a general dislocation of the structure of industry at a
moment when insistence on *khozraschet* and on the necessity of
earning profits, and the demand for governmental economies and
a balanced budget, set up everywhere strong pressures for the
dismissal of redundant workers.[1] Heavy industry had scarcely
recovered at all from the condition of collapse and disintegration
in which it had been left at the end of the civil war, and seemed
to have little prospect under NEP of the large-scale state support
which was indispensable to revive it. Consumer industries
suffered in the *razbazarovanie* crisis of 1921-1922, recovered under
the lead of the syndicates in the following year, but were again
overwhelmed by the " sales crisis " of the summer of 1923. From
the summer of 1922 onwards mass unemployment became endemic
in the Soviet economy. The far-reaching measures of state intervention which would have been necessary to remedy it would
have been difficult to reconcile with the spirit and policies of NEP
as they were at this time conceived ; and even less was done to
mitigate its hardships than in the western capitalist countries
which were facing a similar problem at the same period. Thanks
to the gravity of the unemployment crisis, the publication of labour
statistics was resumed at the end of 1922 ; and, though complete
figures are not available, the dimensions and course of the crisis
can be estimated with reasonable accuracy.[2] According to what
were afterwards accepted as the official statistics, the total of unemployed workers rose steadily from half a million in September
1922 to a million and a quarter at the end of 1923, and in 1924

---

[1] A calculation made in January 1924 showed dismissal through redundancy
as the cause of 47 per cent of all cases of unemployment (*Statistika Truda*,
No. 5, 1924, p. 6).

[2] Shmidt, when he first drew attention to the problem of unemployment at
the fifth trade union congress in September 1922, admitted that he had no complete figures (*Stenograficheskii Otchet Pyatogo Vserossiiskogo S"ezda Professional'-
nykh Soyuzov* (1922), p. 84). The (slightly irregular) monthly journal *Statistika Truda*, which had suspended publication at the end of 1919, reappeared
in December 1922 as the organ of " the bureau of labour statistics of the central
council of trade unions, the central statistical administration and Narkomtrud " ;
its unemployment figures for 1922 and 1923 were based on reports from 52
provincial capitals (including Moscow and Petrograd) and later from 70 labour
exchanges. More complete figures were published subsequently and accepted
as official : these were conveniently collected in *Voprosy Truda v Tsifrakh i
Diagrammakh, 1922-1926 gg.* (1927). All statistics are based on the records of
the labour exchanges which were at this time ill-organized and unreliable.
Complaints were frequently made that the registers contained the names of

was higher still.[1] The figures available at the time were appreci-
ably lower, and the Soviet leaders throughout 1923 were slow to
realize the magnitude of the problem. Rykov, who was president
of Vesenkha, confessed in January 1924 that he had just learned
to his surprise that there were " about a million unemployed ";
and Shmidt, the People's Commissar for Labour, repeated the
same estimate a few days later.[2]

One reason — or excuse — which at first encouraged the
Soviet leaders to watch the growth of unemployment without
undue concern was that it fell most heavily on two categories
which enjoyed little sympathy in official and trade union circles.
Of 540,000 unemployed registered at the labour exchanges on
December 1, 1922, 166,000 or one-third of the whole were "Soviet
workers " (i.e. clerical workers or other employees dismissed
from Soviet institutions), and 104,000 were unskilled manual
workers, male and female, representing largely the influx of

many persons who had never worked in the cities, or worked there only casually
(including former bourgeois temporarily employed in Soviet departments). On
the other hand, it is only too likely that the frequent attempts to purge the lists
of these " fictitious " entries sometimes resulted in the exclusion of *bona fide*
unemployed workers, and some unemployed appear not to have registered at
all. (An article in *Trud*, January 13, 1923, complained that, while the registers
of the labour exchanges were full of " fictitious unemployed ", unemployed
skilled workers applied direct to employers and managers for jobs and avoided
the labour exchanges.) The final figures may still underestimate the facts, but
sufficiently indicate the gravity of the crisis.

  [1] The quarterly totals for the period were :

September 1922	503,000	September 1923	1,060,000
December 1922	641,000	December 1923	1,240,000
March 1923	824,000	March 1924	1,369,000
June 1923	1,050,000	June 1924	1,341,000

(*Voprosy Truda v Tsifrakh i Diagrammakh, 1922–1926 gg.* (1927)). The slowing
up in the increase between June and September 1923 is explained by the usual
exodus of workers from the cities to the country during the harvest.

  [2] *Trinadtsataya Konferentsiya Rossiiskoi Kommunisticheskoi Partii (Bol'-
shevikov)* (1924), p. 13 ; *XI Vserossiiskii S"ezd Sovetov* (1924), p. 103. More
detailed figures for January published in June 1924 still showed only 111,000
unemployed registered in Moscow, 134,000 in Petrograd, and 780,000 in the
other labour exchanges from which information had been supplied (*Statistika
Truda*, No. 5 (14), 1924, p. 5). This fell well short of the total later admitted
of one and a quarter million. On the other hand, *Ekonomicheskaya Zhizn'*,
November 22, 1923, already put the number of unemployed on September 1,
1923, " according to the most cautious calculations ", at a million ; and on the
day on which Rykov made his speech *Trud* reported the number of unemployed
as having reached 1,200,000 on December 1, 1923.

casual peasant labour into the cities in the famine of 1921–1922.[1]
Among skilled industrial workers and regular factory workers in
general the incidence of unemployment was still comparatively
small.[2] The seriousness of the problem was for a long time
minimized with the argument that the unemployed were chiefly
petty bourgeois elements who had never, or only for short periods,
held jobs as industrial workers.[3] The argument was supported
by the fact that, in spite of the growth of unemployment, the
total number of workers in industry declined only very slightly
throughout 1923, and even increased in most of the major industries.[4] But this was not wholly convincing. In a society
where mobility between factory and countryside was far greater
than in the more developed and stratified capitalist economies,
and labour far less organized, rationalization and changes in the
industrial structure easily produced a situation in which new
recruits were drawn into industry from without while hitherto
employed workers were being laid off. The process was in part
a reversal of the flight from the cities and factories — the " disintegration of the proletariat " — which had marked the hungry
days of war communism.[5] The former urban worker, lured by
the easier conditions of NEP and the rise in industrial wages
throughout 1922, flowed back to the towns and added to the
congestion of a now inelastic labour market.[6]

[1] *Voprosy Truda*, No. 2, 1923, p. 24 ; according to *Statistika Truda*, No. 1,
December 1922, p. 2, 30 per cent of the unemployed in Moscow on November
1, 1922, were " Soviet workers " and more than 20 per cent unskilled workers ;
of the male unemployed 35 per cent were " Soviet workers ".

[2] On the basis of figures said to cover 90 per cent of trade union membership, the total of unemployed trade unionists was returned as late as July 1,
1923, as 381,000 (*Statistika Truda*, No. 9, 1923, p. 16) ; the total number of
unemployed at that time already exceeded a million.

[3] This argument was constantly repeated in official publications of the
period, e.g. *Trud*, July 4, 1923, where it was alleged that a substantial number
of the registered unemployed were " typical non-worker elements, engaged in
trade and speculation, who besieged the labour exchanges in order to obtain a
legalization of their position as workers " ; see also Shmidt's statement quoted
on pp. 50-51 below.

[4] *Statistika Truda*, No. 1 (10), pp. 1-4 ; even so, the number of workers in
industry was only just over half the total of 1914 (*ibid.* No. 6, 1923, p. 3).

[5] See *The Bolshevik Revolution, 1917–1923*, Vol. 2, pp. 193-195.

[6] " The influx from the village into the town " was one of the explanations
of the unemployment crisis given by Rykov to the fifth congress of Comintern
in June 1924 (*Protokoll: Fünfter Kongress der Kommunistischen Internationale*
(n.d.), ii, 538-539).

Throughout the first half of 1923 the crisis grew slowly in intensity. Even if the skilled industrial worker seemed largely immune, the unskilled casual worker still constituted so high a proportion of the total Russian labour force that his fate could not be wholly ignored. A contemporary press account of a typical scene at a labour exchange in the industrial suburbs of Moscow, where a vast mob of unemployed, men and women, fought and struggled for admission when the doors were thrown open, since only those first inside could hope for the few available jobs, reveals the crude dimensions of the misery of urban unemployment in the spring of 1923.[1] As the wave of prosperity in consumer industries which followed the creation of the trusts and syndicates in 1922 exhausted itself and gave way to the " sales crisis " of the summer of 1923, while no progress was made in the revival of heavy industry, large-scale unemployment spread rapidly to the factory worker. Trotsky's report on industry to the twelfth party congress in April and the resolution of the congress had admitted — the former explicitly, the latter by implication — that the rationalization of industry would entail extensive dismissals of redundant workers.[2] In June 1923 the trade union central council reported " a relative growth in unemployment among men as compared with women and an increase of unemployed skilled workers ".[3] A few weeks later the principal representative of Narkomtrud in the Ukraine wrote that " the increase of unemployment is falling on the industrial workers " and was likely to be intensified by the " unavoidable reorganization " of some of the trusts. The report continued :

Unemployment is becoming chronic ; its character is bound up with the condition of our economy, and it is unavoidable so long as we are unable to stimulate sufficiently the development of our industry.[4]

At the session of the trade union central council in September, Shmidt once more asserted that 62 per cent of the unemployed were either " bourgeois elements " or unskilled workers, and that women were in a majority in both categories : he repeated the allegation that the lists of the unemployed were swollen with " fictitious " claimants — " traders from the Sukharevka " and

[1] *Trud*, May 9, 1923.
[2] See pp. 22, 25 above.
[3] *Trud*, June 26, 1923.
[4] *Ibid.* July 20, 1923.

daily workers. But he admitted that the remaining 38 per cent formed " the real cadre of the unemployed, to which we must address all our attention ".[1] After the summer of 1923 the gravity of the unemployment problem might be minimized, but could no longer be ignored.

To deal with a crisis of this character the Soviet administrative machine of the NEP period was totally unequipped. Some conventional gestures were made. On December 15, 1922, Sovnarkom allocated 500 million rubles (1922 pattern) for public works to relieve unemployment.[2] A report covering the first quarter of 1923 recorded that 1½ million puds of rye and 1,600,000 rubles (1923 pattern, which divided the nominal value of the 1922 ruble by one thousand) had been allocated to the promotion of public works, and claimed that from 4 to 5 per cent of the total number of unemployed had been occupied on them.[3] But even this modest claim was apparently exaggerated, since the proportion of unemployed so occupied in Moscow and Petrograd in May 1923 was less than 1 per cent.[4] In Yaroslav the special commission on public works attached to the labour exchange was " temporarily unable to proceed owing to lack of funds ". In Petrograd it was said that an average of 1000 workers a day was employed on public works during the first half of 1923, but that in July the number had fallen owing to organizational difficulties to 666.[5] Nor were the rates paid such as to encourage the view that public works were anything but a makeshift form of outdoor relief. Taking the " standard " monthly wage of ten goods rubles as the basis, an instruction of Narkomtrud limited the wage of unskilled workers employed on public works to 40 per cent of this figure,

[1] *Ibid.* September 28, 1923 ; for a further attempt by Shmidt to distinguish between the different categories of unemployed see *Voprosy Truda*, No. 10-11, 1923, p. 19 In January 1924 he gave the figures as 38 per cent Soviet workers, 26 per cent unskilled workers from the country and only 24 per cent skilled workers (*XI Vserossiiskii S"ezd Sovetov* (1924), pp. 103-104) ; but one of these percentages — probably the last — is evidently wrong.

[2] *Voprosy Truda*, No. 2, 1923, p. 28; the decree does not appear in the official collection — generally a symptom that no major importance was attached to it.

[3] *Trud*, May 13, 1923. The rye was not intended for direct relief or for payment in kind : it was sold for 1,300,000 gold rubles, which were credited to the fund. These advances were treated not as grants, but as revolving credits to the economic organs concerned, due for repayment after periods ranging from six to eighteen months (*ibid.* October 24, 1923).

[4] *Ibid.* May 23, 1923.   [5] *Ibid.* March 9, July 15, 1923.

of skilled workers to 60 per cent and of workers with special skills to 80 per cent.[1] As early as May 1923 the trade union newspaper admitted that not much could be hoped for from public works and advocated an organized mobilization of the unemployed for the harvest.[2] Finally, in September 1923, at the central council of trade unions, Shmidt, the People's Commissar for Labour, who claimed that 4½ million gold rubles had been spent on public works to absorb 5 or 6 per cent of the total of unemployed, wrote off the whole scheme in unusually emphatic terms :

> It is impossible to do much about this owing to the grievous financial position of the state. . . . It is more practical to use the huge sums which the organization of public works demands for the support of industry. . . .
> We cannot organize public works of any kind, with the exception of communal works in Moscow and Petrograd, and it is therefore inappropriate to make public works into a system and take note of them in a resolution of the plenum of the trade union central council. We are not rich enough to carry them out.[3]

Rather more promising at the outset was the attempt to give support to *artels* or cooperatives of unemployed workers, since the *artel* had long been a characteristic feature of Russian economic life and seemed to represent a genuine measure of self-help. A report of October 1923, which distinguished between " productive " *artels* engaged in various forms of small industry and " workers' " *artels* hiring out the labour of their members, collected records from 42 cities of 116 " productive " *artels* employing 12,000 workers and 173 " workers' " *artels* employing 18,000 workers. But, far from solving the unemployment problem, these organizations themselves " flourish in time of economic prosperity and are subject to crises in time of depression ".[4] What success was enjoyed by the *artels* was achieved by undercutting the miserable wage rates of regularly employed workers. In July 1923 the president of the central committee of the builders' trade union protested energetically against workers' *artels* which, though fostered by the labour exchanges, represented " the crudest and most ruthless exploitation of the workers ", who enjoyed the protection neither of collective agreements nor of labour legisla-

---

[1] *Trud*, September 8, 1923 ; for the standard see p. 70 below.
[2] *Ibid.* May 23, 1923.   [3] *Ibid.* September 28, 1923.
[4] *Ibid.* October 24, 1923.

tion in general; and trade unionists complained about the same
time that the *artels* in Petrograd " inevitably degenerate into petty
private concerns to exploit the labour of the unemployed ".[1]
It was officially stated that one of the reasons for employing the
artels was that " this considerably cheapens production ".[2] A
little later the trade union newspaper referred once more to the
" deviations " which had occurred in *artels* of the unemployed
owing to the fact that they had been " captured by the market ",
but pleaded against their unconditional abandonment.[3] *Artels*
continued to exist, and continued to be looked on with suspicion
by the trade unions and by the organized workers. But as a
means of combating unemployment they were quickly discounted.

Social insurance against unemployment, in abeyance under
war communism, had been revived in the autumn of 1921. At the
end of the year a decree put the rate of benefit at from one-sixth
to one-half of current wage rates according to the qualification
of the worker, and left the maximum duration of unemployment benefit to be fixed by the People's Commissariat of Social
Security (Narkomsobes) in conjunction with Narkomtrud.[4] The
instruction issued by Narkomsobes on January 31, 1922, in
pursuance of this decree, required registration within seven days
of the beginning of unemployment, and from unskilled workers
and clerical employees (though not from skilled workers) proof
of previous employment for a period of three years. In the conditions of the time, few persons can have been able to comply
with this requirement if it was strictly enforced; and the purpose
of the instruction was apparently to limit unemployment benefit
to the small minority of skilled industrial workers.[5] Under the
labour code of November 1922 the duration of benefit was not
to be limited to a shorter period than six months, and discretion
was left to Sovnarkom to fix a minimum previous period of work
required to establish a claim to benefit, at the same time the

[1] *Ibid.* July 11, 15, 1923.   [2] *Ibid.* October 24, 1923.
[3] *Ibid.* December 14, 1923.
[4] *Sobranie Uzakonenii, 1922*, No. 1, art. 23 ; for the earlier decrees see *The
Bolshevik Revolution, 1917–1923*, Vol. 2, p. 322, note 1. A summary account of
the history and working of unemployment insurance down to 1924 is in *Sotsialisticheskoe Khozyaistvo*, No. 3, 1924, pp. 215-229.
[5] The instruction is quoted in *Sotsialisticheskii Vestnik* (Berlin), No. 3 (73),
February 11, 1924, p. 11 : the original text has not been available.

administration of unemployment insurance was transferred from
Narkomsobes to Narkomtrud — an indication that it was to be
treated as a specific labour problem rather than as a problem of
social welfare.[1]

With the growth of mass unemployment in the latter part of
1922, the idea that the total number of those vainly seeking
employment in the cities could be covered by insurance benefits
had to be dismissed as chimerical. Of the total number of
registered unemployed in January 1923, 26 per cent in Moscow
were in receipt of relief, 14 per cent in Petrograd and 11 per cent
in 12 other major industrial centres; outside them, the percentage
was no doubt lower still.[2] In the same month the Moscow
labour exchange undertook a re-registration of all unemployed on
its books with a view to the elimination of " fictitious claimants ".[3]
This example was followed by labour exchanges throughout the
country, and became one of the burning issues of 1923. Some
exchanges, according to a report in the trade union newspaper,
" interpreted re-registration as a temporary artificial reduction of
unemployment by means of the wholesale removal from the register
of all who could be ' got rid of ' "; and reductions of from 60
to 70 per cent were effected in some places, though these were
soon counterbalanced by fresh entries.[4] A complaint was heard
that the trade unions insisted on the registration of office workers
in industrial enterprises as " Soviet workers ", thus effectively
excluding them from benefit.[5] A fresh instruction of Narkomtrud
of June 11, 1923, slightly relaxed the conditions on which relief
was to be granted. " Intellectual workers of high qualifications
who have received a special education, such as engineers, agro-
nomists, doctors, teachers, etc.", were placed on the same footing

---

[1] Sobranie Uzakonenii, 1922, No. 70, art. 903, paras. 186-187; No. 81,
art. 1049.
[2] Statistika Truda, No. 3 (12), 1924, p. 7; according to Trud, December
13, 1923, 10·9 per cent of all unemployed were receiving relief in February 1923.
[3] Ekonomicheskaya Zhizn', January 18, 1923.
[4] Trud, April 14, 1923; the same article complained that the regulations
made by the labour exchange in Tsaritsyn were so complicated that none of
the unemployed there qualified for benefit. A later article drew attention to
the rapid turnover, and resulting inefficiency, of workers in labour exchanges :
" owing to the extremely onerous and nervous character of the work, and also
to the low rates of pay, they run away to other institutions at the first opportunity " (ibid. July 11, 1923).
[5] Ibid. January 26, 1923.

as skilled workers : they were entitled to relief without having
to demonstrate a continuous period of employment. Unskilled
workers became entitled in virtue of one year's continuous employment (instead of three).[1] These relaxations do not seem, however,
to have led to any substantial extension of the scope of relief.
The proportion of unemployed in receipt of it rose to 15 per cent
in April, and fell back to 12 per cent in July.[2] But, since the rise
was balanced by the vigorous purging of " fictitious claimants ",
it is doubtful whether a higher proportion of *bona fide* unemployed
in fact obtained relief.

What did substantially increase during the first six months of
1923 was the miserable pittance actually paid to recipients of
relief. In January 1923 the average payment was only 13 per
cent of the so-called standard wage of ten goods rubles, i.e. 1·3
goods rubles, though the rate for Moscow was higher than the
average. By June 1923 the average rate had reached 45 per cent,
i.e. 4½ goods rubles.[3] Higher than this figure, which was still
well below the commonly accepted subsistence level, it did not
go. When the social insurance scheme was reorganized in the
winter of 1921–1922, unemployment did not rank high among
the contingencies against which provision was made. The unemployment fund was originally financed by contributions from
" employers " (no contribution was exacted from workers)
amounting to 2½ per cent of wages paid; this compared with
contributions of from 6 to 9 per cent, according to the category
of enterprise, to the sickness and temporary disability fund.
and from 7 to 10 per cent to the pensions fund.[4] But difficulty
was evidently experienced in collecting these contributions.
In April 1923 defaulters were rendered liable to criminal pro-
secution; and shortly afterwards the rates were reduced to 2
per cent for the unemployment fund out of a total contribution

---

[1] *Ibid.* June 13, 1923, which also records the optimistic estimate of the
official in charge of the fund that the new instruction would increase the proportion of unemployed in receipt of relief to 30 or 35 per cent.

[2] *Ibid.* December 13, 1923 ; on January 1, 1924, 30 per cent of the registered unemployed in Moscow were reported to be in receipt of relief, 16 per cent
in Petrograd, and 11 per cent in 12 other major industrial centres (*Statistika Truda*,
No. 3 (12), 1924, p. 7) — percentages only slightly higher than a year earlier.

[3] *Trud*, September 28, 1923 ; average rates for the first eight months of
1923 are quoted, *ibid.* October 10, 1923.

[4] *Sobranie Uzakonenii, 1922*, No. 2, art. 34 ; No. 6, art. 65.

ranging from 12 to 16 per cent for enterprises owned or financed by the state and from 16 to 22 per cent for private enterprises.[1] Yet, whatever the shortcomings on the revenue side, the fact remains that throughout the unemployment crisis the resources of the unemployment fund were not seriously strained.[2] In January 1923, only 70 per cent of the revenues of the fund were being paid out in relief. But revenues continued to rise, presumably owing to improved methods of collection; and in June 1923, when the rate of relief had been largely increased, the proportion of out-goings to revenue fell to 60 per cent, and remained at or below that figure for the rest of the year.[3] During the first formidable unemployment crisis which the Soviet economy had had to meet, the fund created to meet such an emergency was drawn on only to the extent of rather more than half its total resources. Yet, when the crisis reached its height in the summer of 1923, no serious attempt was made either to increase the sum paid to the individual by way of relief or to extend the categories of individuals entitled to draw relief.

The reasons for this restraint must be sought in the field of general policy. The refusal to raise the rate of payment to the individual rested on the cogent ground that the pittance of $4\frac{1}{2}$ or 5 goods rubles a month already approached the lowest actual wage paid to the unskilled casual worker. Indeed, as Shmidt explained to the trade union central council in September 1923, the delays in the payment of wages to the miners in the Donbass had already produced a situation in which they were no better off than unemployed in receipt of relief.[4] The low rate of relief was

---

[1] *Sobranie Uzakonenii, 1923*, No. 27, art. 313 ; No. 31, art. 342. The complaint was still heard in January 1924 of the difficulty of collecting full contributions (*XI Vserossiiskii S"ezd Sovetov* (1924), p. 96) ; and in the following month, at the time of the financial reform, the total contribution for enterprises financed by the state was " temporarily reduced " to 10 per cent (*Sobranie Uzakonenii, 1924*, No. 32, art. 299).

[2] The statement in the report of the visiting British Labour Delegation in 1924, cited in *The Bolshevik Revolution, 1917–1923*, Vol. 2, p. 323, note 1, which attributed the shortcomings of unemployment relief to " the financial failure of the system of social insurance ", was incorrect.

[3] *Trud*, September 28, December 13, 1923.

[4] *Ibid.* September 28, 1923 ; in the same speech Shmidt claimed that the standard rate of relief at that time was 5 goods rubles for the skilled, and 3 for the unskilled, worker, with corresponding rates of 6 and 4 respectively in Moscow and Petrograd.

an index of the poverty of the economy as a whole. The trade
unions accepted this view, and pressed only for an increase in the
number of the unemployed to whom relief should be accorded.[1]
But this too was incompatible with the ruling policies of Narkomfin,
which, in pursuit of the strictest principles of orthodox finance,
made deflation and the curtailment of the currency issue its overriding aim. The compromise reached and put in practice throughout 1923 meant at best a strictly limited measure of relief (less
than the lowest wage of the unskilled worker) for a fairly high
proportion of skilled workers, especially in Moscow and Petrograd,
where the most important industries were still congregated and
where industrial discontent might have been politically dangerous ;
and this was reluctantly accepted by the trade unions, whose
members were at any rate in a better position than other workers.[2]

The sharpness of the distinction between the skilled worker
and the mass of casual unemployed was an accurate reflexion of
Russian labour conditions, where the peasant and the unskilled
urban worker were interchangeable entities with regular seasonal
fluctuations between the two groups, and where a large part even
of the skilled labour force was liable to disintegrate in unfavourable
conditions and return to the peasant mass out of which it had so
recently emerged. The distinction was stated with brutal frankness by Shmidt, who explained to the trade union central council
in September 1923 that the aim was " the preservation of the
skilled labour force which we cannot employ in the immediate
future " :

> Our industry [he went on] has been so contracted that our
> skilled workers have been thrown out of work. Unemploy-
> ment among this group is persistent. . . . Yet this labour force
> is necessary to us, because we must at all costs preserve it until
> such time as the possibility occurs of developing our industry.

[1] For the resolution of the trade union central council in September 1923
acquiescing in the view that an increase in the rate of relief was " impracticable
. . . owing to the existing level of the minimum wage " see *Trud*, October 2,
1923 ; as late as January 1924, Shmidt repeated that, while payments to the
unemployed, compared with payment to the sick and disabled, were extremely
" small ", it was " impossible in the immediate future to raise them " (*XI
Vserossiiskii S"ezd Sovetov* (1924), p. 94).

[2] At a time when only one-seventh of all unemployed were receiving relief,
one-half of unemployed trade unionists were receiving it (*Trud*, December 13,
1923).

E

All the other groups registered at the labour exchange cannot count on our help.

The resolution of the council demanded " a struggle with unemployment among skilled and auxiliary industrial workers and, at the same time, a further purging from the labour exchanges of the extraneous element ".[1]   A decision to refuse registration to new arrivals from the country [2] was met by an illegal enterprise of the newcomers, who began to organize a private labour exchange of their own.[3] But the policy of Narkomtrud remained clear and uncompromising. To support by measures of relief those unskilled workers who could easily be reabsorbed into the peasant mass until such time as a further demand arose for unskilled labour would have been pointless; it was necessary to support only those limited groups of skilled workers whose dispersal, even if there was no immediate call for their services, would be a long-term national disaster. What was striking about the official attitude was not so much the uninhibited admission that little or nothing could be done to relieve the evil of unemployment — in this respect, as in the overriding importance attached to financial considerations, the NEP economy of Soviet Russia displayed much the same characteristics as contemporary capitalist economies — but the tenacity with which, even in the midst of NEP, the long-term purpose of the development of industry was kept firmly in mind, and treated as outweighing any conceivable hardships or privations imposed on the mass of workers in the immediate future.

A curious by-product of the unemployment crisis was its effect on the régimes of the penal labour camps.[4] Hitherto prisoners in these camps had been regularly drafted to work in factories or other enterprises requiring labour. Now that jobs were few, the competition of this forced labour came to be keenly resented by free workers and by the trade unions. A decree of February 1923 provided that persons condemned to compulsory labour must in future as a rule " be allocated to work specially designed for places of detention or to economic enterprises attached to such places "; only if such work was not available were they to be

[1] *Trud*, September 28, October 9, 1923.   [2] *Ibid*. October 4, 1923.
[3] *XI Vserossiiskii S"ezd Sovetov* (1924), p. 105.
[4] For the institution of these camps see *The Bolshevik Revolution, 1917–1923*, Vol. 2, pp. 210-211.

sent elsewhere " to the most dangerous and hardest work for which there are no volunteers among the unemployed ". This would appear to have been the starting-point of the large-scale enterprises organized under the management and direction of the GPU for the employment of compulsory labour. But there was no absolute line of demarcation between the two types of enterprise ; in case of need unemployed free workers could be sent by labour exchanges to enterprises employing primarily compulsory labour.[1]

Of the consequences of the diminished weight of the industrial worker in the Soviet economy, the most conspicuous was the decline in the influence and prestige of the trade unions. The immediate result of NEP had been a sharp reduction in trade union membership, due in part to the growth of unemployment, but mainly to the new regulation making membership voluntary and conditional on the payment of dues.[2] Numbers fell from a high level of 8·4 millions on July 1, 1921, to 5·8 millions on April 1, 1922, and 4·5 millions on October 1, 1922 : the figures remained almost stationary for the rest of the year 1922, and then began to recover, probably owing to improved organization, reaching a total of 5·35 millions on July 1 and of 5·5 millions on October 1, 1923.[3] But a better index of the scope of trade union activity is provided by the numbers of workers covered by collective agreements, which under NEP replaced labour service as the normal form of engagement for industrial and clerical workers. On July 1, 1923, 81 collective agreements covering 2 million workers had been concluded by or with the sanction of the central trade union organization. This covered 41 per cent of all trade union members, but in widely different proportions in different occupations. All railwaymen (and 90 per cent of all transport workers), all teachers and all workers in the sugar industry were covered by centrally concluded collective agreements ; but only 41 per cent of workers in metal-working industries were so covered, 39 per cent of miners, 19 per cent of " Soviet workers " and 2 per cent of building workers.

---

[1] *Sobranie Uzakonenii, 1923*, No. 16, art. 202.
[2] See *The Bolshevik Revolution, 1917–1923*, Vol. 2, p. 328.
[3] *Statistika Truda*, No. 3, February 1923, p. 10 ; No. 4, 1923, p. 7 ; No. 2 (11), 1924, p. 19.

In addition to these agreements, 8430 collective agreements concluded locally and covering 1,400,000 workers (an average of
about 165 workers for each agreement) were recorded on July 1,
1923.[1] The further nominal membership of 2 millions (including
a substantial number of unemployed) not covered by any collective
agreement was no source of additional strength; and it is uncertain how far the trade union membership of workers covered
by local agreements, most of them employed in small and scattered
undertakings, was really effective.

More significant than the fluctuations in figures of trade union
membership was the changed status of the unions. In the period
of war communism the industrial workers, whatever burdens were
placed on them in the form of military or labour service, were the
privileged class on which Soviet policy hinged; and the trade
unions represented the workers within the state machine, of which
they were in all but name an integral and vital part. The trade
unions under war communism eclipsed in influence and importance both the managerial side of industry, which still suffered
from the active prejudice against former bourgeois " specialists ",
and the labour organ of the state, Narkomtrud, which became a
mere executive instrument of policies decided on by the trade
unions.[2] Under NEP these relations underwent a radical change.
In the industrial " triangle " formed by state, management and
labour, the trade unions soon found themselves relegated to the
subordinate position. The " Red industrialists ", freed from the
suspicions which had formerly clung to them, were now the main
pillars of NEP in industrial affairs. It was they, rather than the
trade unions, whose opinion counted in issues of industrial policy.
Now that the trade unions were financed, no longer by the state,
but by the contributions of their members, it became a common
and convenient practice to collect members' dues by arrangement
with the factory management, which deducted them from wages.
This practice was a subject of constant protest from trade union
headquarters. In February the trade union newspaper congratulated the trade union council of the Don region on starting

---

[1] *Statistika Truda*, No. 9, 1923, pp. 12-15 ; the resistance to the adoption
of collective agreements outside the large centres was referred to in an article
in *Trud*, May 3, 1923, which complained that local Soviets were refusing to
conclude such agreements with their employees.

[2] See *The Bolshevik Revolution, 1917–1923*, Vol. 2, pp. 201-202.

a campaign for the collection of dues by the unions themselves ; [1]
but there is no evidence of its success. In June 1923, on the
occasion of the congress of the metal workers' union, the complaint
was again heard that branches collected dues " through the office
of the enterprise " and that " the true relation of the worker to
the union is thus concealed ".[2] But reform proceeded " at the
pace of the tortoise ", and in October only 10 per cent of the
metal workers in Moscow were yet paying dues direct to union
collectors, though figures of from 30 to 60 per cent were reported
from other centres.[3] If this was the state of affairs in the powerful
and relatively well-organized metal workers' union with its membership of highly skilled workers, even less progress is likely to have
been made elsewhere.[4] The procedure of the automatic deduction
of dues from wages was too convenient to the unions to be lightly
abandoned ; but it threw a revealing light on the relation in which
the trade unions normally stood to the management.

Nor was the authority of the state machine any longer available
to uphold the interests of the trade unions in any conflict with the
managers. One of the results of NEP had been to deprive the
industrial worker of the direct patronage which he had enjoyed in
the preceding period from the state. The functions of the state
in regard to him were now confined under the labour code of
November 1922 to the safeguarding of certain minimum conditions of safety and welfare, the fixing of a minimum wage,
and the maintenance of labour exchanges through which the
engagement of labour was normally effected.[5] Wages were no
longer determined by the state, but by collective contracts concluded between employers and trade unions. In theory, the trade
unions were completely independent ; their functions were those

[1] *Trud*, February 21, 1923.   [2] *Ibid*. June 15, 1923.
[3] *Ibid*. September 21, October 18, 1923.
[4] *Sotsialisticheskii Vestnik* (Berlin), No. 10 (80), May 10, 1924, pp. 15-16,
described a system in force at the Sormovo works by which " collectors " of
trade union dues were elected by the workers, and received from the union a
percentage of the amounts collected ; by arrangement with the management
the collectors obtained possession of the metal discs which workers had to produce in order to obtain admission to the factory, and refused to hand these
over till the dues were paid.
[5] See *The Bolshevik Revolution, 1917–1923*, Vol. 2, pp. 330-331. The official
minimum wage was fixed monthly by Narkomtrud, from December 1922 to
October 1923 in Soviet rubles, and thereafter (*Sbornik Dekretov, Postanovlenii,
Rasporyazhenii i Prikazov po Narodnomu Khozyaistvu*, No. 11 (14), November

normally exercised by unions in a capitalist economy. In practice, their independence was a source of weakness rather than of strength; prohibited by the compulsion of party discipline on their leaders from delivering any direct challenge to governmental decisions, they paid for their formal independence by a removal from the centre of authority which made them less able to protect and further the interests entrusted to them. Narkomtrud not only resumed charge of the administration of social insurance,[1] but took once more the place in the governmental hierarchy from which the trade unions had ousted it in the days of war communism. The industrialists, now firmly entrenched in influential posts in the commissariat,[2] noted the development with satisfaction. " Instead of the creaking organ with insignificant functions of the period of war communism ", wrote *Ekonomicheskaya Zhizn'* in an article on Narkomtrud on July 17, 1923, " we have again a strong healthy organism responsible for the performance of very great and important tasks." Broadly speaking, the trade unions may be said, from 1923 onwards, to have accepted the full implications of NEP. They devoted themselves with success to the extension and improvement of their organization; they performed the necessary and often embarrassing function of acting as intermediaries between government and workers, inculcating on the workers the duty of loyally accepting governmental decisions and impressing on the government, sometimes with success, the need to alleviate the lot of the workers on specific points; but they no longer claimed a rôle in major decisions of policy.

Of the symptoms of the growth in the power of employers and managers at the expense of the workers in the winter of 1922–1923 the first and most obvious was the by-passing of the labour exchanges. Labour exchanges, originally set up in 1917, had become in the autumn of 1918 the sole legal medium for the hiring of workers. This system had been short-lived, and gave

---

1923, pp. 61-62) in chervonets rubles, the whole country being divided into three regions to which different rates were applicable. But the legal minimum lagged so far behind even the lowest wage fixed by collective agreement (for November 1923 it was only five rubles in the highest zone) that it played no part in wages negotiations or policy. On January 9, 1924, *Trud* solemnly predicted that, if not raised, it would become " an empty formality "; in fact it had long been.

[1] See *The Bolshevik Revolution, 1917–1923*, Vol. 2, pp. 328-329.
[2] See p. 46 above.

place under war communism to the direct recruitment of workers by public authority ; the labour exchanges had been transformed into organs of Narkomtrud with compulsory powers to mobilize and direct labour.[1] Under NEP the labour exchanges resumed their original function, and the labour code of November 1922 maintained the principle that all labour was to be engaged, whether by private employers or by state institutions and enterprises, through them. Even before this, however, the obligation to engage labour from the exchanges was evaded by the employers (a fruitless protest against this abuse had been registered by the fifth All-Russian Congress of Trade Unions in September 1922) ; and the code itself provided a generous schedule of exceptions in which the rule of engagement through the exchanges could be neglected. From this point the campaign against the labour exchanges gathered strength. The new authority exercised by the industrialist in labour questions was illustrated not only by the ample provisions for the dismissal of workers embodied in the new labour code,[2] but by a decree of January 1923 on the registration of unemployed at labour exchanges which stipulated that enquiries for workers must be satisfied " not by mechanical allocation of the unemployed in order of rotation, but by the strictest observance of the requirements expressed by the employer ".[3] A decree of February 1923 drew up detailed lists of workers who could be engaged directly : these included specialists, managers, book-keepers and all responsible clerical workers.[4] In a period when the supply of workers so far exceeded the demand, the employers were in a strong position to circumvent the exchanges when it suited their convenience to do so. In July 1923 a further decree dealing in detail with the functions and organization of labour exchanges reaffirmed the right of employers to choose workers from lists drawn up by the exchanges, and offered every loophole for employers to reject workers sent to them.

[1] See *The Bolshevik Revolution, 1917–1923*, Vol. 2, pp. 209-210.
[2] See *ibid.* Vol. 2, p. 331.
[3] *Sbornik Dekretov, Postanovlenii, Rasporyazhenii i Prikazov po Narodnomu Khozyaistvu*, No. 1 (4), January 1923, pp. 91-92 : six months later a further decree gave the employer a right of " direct selection of labour power from the list of workers registered at the exchange " (*Sobranie Uzakonenii, 1923*, No. 68, art. 655).
[4] *Sobranie Uzakonenii, 1923*, No. 13, art. 171 ; a protest against this extension of exemptions from labour exchange procedure appeared in *Trud*, March 10, 1923.

employed persons must be allocated to jobs " exclusively on the strength of their skill, experience or working capacity ", though as between two equally suitable candidates preference was to be given to a member of a trade union.[1] Two months later a circular of Narkomtrud set up a procedure of " consultation " between employers and labour exchanges in respect of all demands for more than ten workers or for workers of special qualifications.[2] All this constituted part of what *Trud* called " pressure by the industrialists on the labour exchanges in the form of an assault on their monopoly position in the labour market ".[3] These successive pronouncements gradually prepared the way for the disappearance of the labour exchanges as obligatory channels for the engagement of labour and their transformation into voluntary employment agencies maintained by the state. This process was completed at the beginning of 1925.[4]

A field in which the trade unions were at this time continually fighting a rearguard action to maintain their influence was the procedure for settling labour disputes. Under war communism, where the state was virtually the sole employer of labour, labour disputes in the ordinary sense of the term did not arise ; contested points were settled by Glavkomtrud, and obedience enforced by the " comradely courts of discipline ".[5] Under NEP, where labour was voluntary and the collective contract the usual form of engagement, the question of the handling of disputes was quickly reopened. The resolution on the trade unions drafted by Lenin and adopted by the party central committee on January 12, 1922, while guardedly conceding the admissibility of strikes against " bureaucratic perversions " or " survivals of capitalism ", relied in the event of conflicts on " the mediatory action of the trade unions ", which would either enter into negotiations with the economic organs concerned or appeal to the highest organs of state : the setting up by the trade unions of " conflict commissions " was

<hr>

[1] *Sobranie Uzakonenii, 1923*, No. 68, art. 655.

[2] *Trud*, September 29, 1923.

[3] *Ibid.* December 30, 1923 ; the same article recapitulated the old abuses in the labour exchanges — " the notorious ' purges ' . . ., quibbles about registration, cessation of registration of newcomers in order to ' diminish unemployment ' ".

[4] *Sobranie Zakonov, 1925*, No. 2, art. 15 ; the only restriction now remaining was that private employment agencies might not be set up.

[5] See *The Bolshevik Revolution, 1917–1923*, Vol. 2, p. 211, note 6.

recommended for dealing with disputes.[1]   In pursuance of this
resolution, it became customary to include in collective agreements
provisions for the establishment of so-called Assessment and
Conflict Commissions (Rastsenochno-Konfliktnye Komissii or
RKK) composed of representatives of employers and workers
(or of the trade unions acting on their behalf) to settle current
questions of relations between management and labour and dis-
puted points arising out of the agreement.   The procedure
remained voluntary on both sides ; and the assumption was that
the weapon of the strike remained in the hands of the workers as a
last resort, however much its use might in practice be discouraged.[2]

  Before long, however, the inadequacy of the RKK as a means
of dealing with the discontent of the workers became apparent ;
and a decree of July 18, 1922, marked a further attempt to face
the issue.   The RKK were left in being, but two new institutions
were superimposed on them as instances of appeal for disputes
which they had failed to settle to the satisfaction of both parties.
These were conciliation courts (Primiritel'nye Kamery) and
arbitral tribunals (Treteiskie Sudy).   The conciliation courts
differed in two respects from the RKK : they could deal not only
with disputes arising out of the collective agreements, but with
complaints against the provisions of the collective agreements,
which were beyond the competence of the RKK ; and the president of a conciliation court was appointed by Narkomtrud.   Since
the parties were equally represented and the president had no
vote and could exercise only powers of persuasion, the voluntary
principle was preserved, though decisions once agreed on were
legally binding.   On the other hand, the president of an arbitral
tribunal, who was also appointed, in default of agreement between
the parties, by Narkomtrud, had a casting vote ; and decisions
of the tribunal so constituted were legally binding.   Here, too, the
voluntary principle was in theory preserved, since disputes
(whether or not they had previously come before a conciliation
court) could be referred to an arbitral tribunal only by agreement

  [1] For this resolution see *The Bolshevik Revolution, 1917–1923*, Vol. 2,
pp. 326-327.
  [2] The status of the RKK was later confirmed and regulated by a decree
(*Sobranie Uzakonenii, 1922*, No. 74, art. 911) ; while their decisions could be
taken only by agreement, the execution of decisions once taken was obligatory
and legally enforceable.

between the parties. But a loophole for compulsion was found in a provision, apparently inserted by way of an afterthought, that, in disputes in state enterprises and institutions, the trade union could bring the issue before an arbitral tribunal without the assent of the management and thus force a decision.[1] This one-sided provision appeared to accord an exclusive advantage to the workers. But, with the rising power of the industrial managers, this privilege was short-lived, and was quickly turned into a weapon which could be wielded against the workers themselves. A month after the promulgation of the original decree, the procedure was amended by a further decree of August 23, 1922, providing that " disputes about the conclusion of a collective agreement " (though apparently not other disputes) could be referred by Narkomtrud to an arbitral tribunal " on the declaration of either one of the parties ".[2] There was, in fact, little doubt that the principle of compulsory arbitration once established would be applied indifferently to managements and to workers ; and Shmidt, the People's Commissar for Labour, had an ungrateful task in attempting to justify the new decree to the fifth All-Russian Congress in September 1922. He explained that he had himself been opposed to the decree, but that his objections had been overruled by Sovnarkom. The decree having left the initiative in the hands of Narkomtrud, he undertook that the arbitral procedure would be applied only to individual disputes, not to disputes involving a collective agreement, and that trade unions would in no circumstances be deprived of the right to strike.[3] It was a notable example of the laxity of Soviet and party discipline still prevailing at this time that a People's Commissar could make what was virtually a public promise to an interested party not to enforce an unpopular provision of a decree.[4]

---

[1] *Sobranie Uzakonenii, 1922*, No. 45, art. 560.

[2] *Ibid.* No. 54, art. 683.

[3] *Stenograficheskii Otchet Pyatogo Vserossiiskogo S"ezda Professional'nykh Soyuzov* (1922), pp. 86-88.

[4] Statistics for the second half of 1922 indicate the relative importance of the different procedures. The number of disputes increased from 588 involving 20,000 workers in July to 786 involving 105,000 workers in December ; the proportion of these dealt with by the RKK fell from 87 per cent to 79 per cent, the proportion referred to conciliation courts and arbitral tribunals rose from 9 to 12·7 per cent and 3 to 7·9 per cent respectively (*Statistika Truda*, No. 4, 1923, p. 18).

The enactment of the labour code of November 1922, which covered all three procedures for the settlement of disputes, once more blurred the situation in regard to compulsory arbitration. Having stressed the optional character of the RKK and the conciliation courts, the code prescribed that, " in the event of a dispute arising in a state enterprise or institution, Narkomtrud on the request of the trade union sets up an arbitral tribunal ", thus apparently restoring the unilateral initiative of the trade unions provided for in the decree of July 18. It added, however, that " in the event of grave disputes which may threaten the security of the state, the arbitral tribunal may be appointed by special order of VTsIK, Sovnarkom or STO ".[1] In such cases the initiative passed out of the hands of the trade unions and Narkomtrud, and compulsory arbitration in labour disputes could be imposed by the highest organs of the state; and, since both the labour code and the decrees made it plain that contravention of a decision by a properly constituted conciliation court or arbitral tribunal was a criminal offence punishable by the courts, the ultimate power of coercion was now firmly established. The next step was a decree of March 1923 which, while purporting to be no more than an implementation of the provisions of the labour code, added clarity and precision to the legal situation. It confirmed the status and powers of the conciliation courts and the arbitral tribunals. In principle the consent of both parties was still required for the constitution of an arbitral tribunal; even the one-sided right accorded to the trade unions by the decree of July 18, 1922, and maintained in the labour code, to bring disputes in state enterprises before an arbitral tribunal without the consent of the management was abandoned. But the emergency provision of the code on the right of VTsIK, Sovnarkom or STO to impose compulsory arbitration " in the event of grave disputes which may threaten the security of the state " was reaffirmed;[2] and this power was ultimately decisive. The effect of the decree was not only to provide powers of coercion against recalcitrant managers or employees, but to apply penal sanctions to breaches of labour discipline, and thus reconstitute in a slightly different form the disciplinary courts of the period of war communism.

[1] *Sobranie Uzakonenii, 1922*, No. 70, art. 903.
[2] *Sobranie Uzakonenii, 1923*, No. 24, art. 288.

Fear of unemployment, stern and ever-present though it was, did not by itself suffice to keep men at work in the harsh conditions of industrial labour in Soviet Russia in the early 1920s. But these provisions were not wholly one-sided. In July 1923 disciplinary courts were set up to deal with persons occupying responsible positions in state institutions or enterprises who might be guilty of negligence or irregularities in work. The penalties included reprimand, dismissal and the obligation to make good any damage or loss caused.[1]

The most striking symptom of the re-emergence of the capitalist element in the Soviet economy was, however, that the major issues of labour policy now turned once more on wages. Under war communism when labour had been recruited by compulsory mobilization, payment in kind, in the form of rations and other free services, largely replaced not only money payments but even the calculation of wages in monetary terms. The aim of NEP was to replace all forms of payment in kind by monetary transactions. The social services were placed on an insurance basis and made self-supporting, and payment was made obligatory for other services, including house rents, which had been supplied gratis under war communism.[2] It was not possible to discontinue at one stroke the issue of rations to workers. Here the changeover was gradual; transport workers, postal workers and workers in some of the nationalized industries were in receipt of rations for more than two years after the introduction of NEP.[3] The

---

[1] *Sobranie Uzakonenii, 1923*, No. 54, art. 531.

[2] See *The Bolshevik Revolution, 1917-1923*, Vol. 2, p. 329, note 1, p. 347, note 3. This order was, however, apparently ineffective as regards rents, since as late as June 1923 a further decree was issued re-establishing rent payments " for the purpose of maintaining houses in a good state of upkeep ". Persons living on unearned incomes and members of the free professions paid at the highest rates ; rent payments by workers were calculated as a percentage of their wages (less than 1 per cent except for the most highly paid) ; persons in receipt of insurance benefits, unemployed persons, families of Red Army men and students were exempted altogether (*Sobranie Uzakonenii, 1923*, No. 55, art 540).

A decree of February 1923 allocated 3,383,855 puds of grain to the wages fund, of which 270,000 were for transport, 190,000 for postal workers and 493,855 for nationalized industries (*Sobranie Uzakonenii, 1923*, No. 11, art. 132) ; in the same month 80 per cent of all wages were being paid in cash, the proportion having risen to 97 per cent in Moscow and 88 per cent in Petrograd

monetary value of the rations was debited to the wage rate fixed
by the collective contract of employment, so that all workers were
from the autumn of 1921 onwards in receipt of wages calculated
in money, even where the actual wages were still paid partly in
kind. It was clear, however, that the depreciating ruble currency
provided no basis for the fixing of wages. After the establishment
by Narkomfin in November 1921 of an official monthly rate of
exchange for the Soviet ruble in terms of a price-index based on
1913 prices — the so-called " pre-war ruble " or " goods ruble " [1]
— all wages were calculated in this new unit, though they continued to be paid in Soviet rubles at the current rate.

When in March 1922 Narkomfin abandoned the goods
ruble for the gold ruble, new difficulties arose ; for nobody was
at present prepared to abandon for purposes of wage-fixing a
standard which had the merit of being tied to the cost of living.[2]
The calculation of the value of the goods ruble in terms of
1913 prices was taken over by Gosplan, which worked on a price-
index of its own ; and the goods ruble of Gosplan was henceforth used in collective agreements as the basis for drawing up
wage schedules, this practice being formally sanctioned and recommended by a circular of the trade union central council of
October 1922.[3] The resulting situation was extremely complex.
To fix current wage rates from month to month in terms of the
goods ruble price-index was a matter of expert computation.
To fix the rate of exchange between the goods ruble and the
Soviet ruble in which payment would actually be made to the
worker involved another delicate and highly controversial calculation, in the course of which many devices were employed to force
down real wages below the rates agreed on and ostensibly paid.
For this reason official statistics for this period persistently over-
state real wages. The official rate of wages recorded in the
statistics was in practice often less important than the varying
rate of exchange at which the actual payment in Soviet rubles
was made, and the date on which it was made. The absence of a

(*Statistika Truda*, No. 5, 1923, p. 11) ; another estimate put the proportion of
wages still being paid in kind in March 1923 at 25 per cent (*Trud*, August 2,
1923). The last traces of payment in kind disappeared in the financial reform
of February 1924.
    [1] See *The Bolshevik Revolution, 1917–1923*, Vol. 2, p. 350.
    [2] See *ibid*. Vol. 2, p. 357.   [3] *Trud*, October 14, 1922.

wages policy combined with rivalry between departments to produce almost inextricable confusion. Narkomfin and Gosbank controlled the supply of rubles ; Narkomprod was responsible for payments in kind ; the trade union central council fixed the wage rates embodied in the collective agreements ; two or three inter-departmental commissions were concerned in the administration of the wages fund, in cash and in kind ; finally, Gosplan provided somewhat theoretical calculations of the total wages fund borne by the national budget. A supreme wages council sought to mediate between these various authorities, but lacked the power to overrule them.

According to the calculations now made in Gosplan, the wage of a Russian " worker of average qualifications " before 1914 was reckoned at 20 rubles a month. When independent calculations of wage rates in pre-war rubles were made in Gosplan early in 1922, it was found that monthly wages at the end of 1920, including payments in kind, had been equivalent to no more than 3 rubles 40 kopecks, which was probably made up by illicit receipts to the minimum subsistence level of 5-6 rubles. Under the impulse of NEP wages had risen steadily though unevenly throughout the year 1921. In January 1922 the ration issued by Narkomprod at this time to the heaviest workers was valued at 8·10 " goods rubles ", the ration issued to other manual workers at 6·78 and to the lowest category of workers at 4·76. Food constituted the major, almost the sole, item in the worker's budget ; and the total of real wages for this month, inclusive of the monetary payment, ranged from 8·78 rubles for the highest category of workers to 6·26 for the lowest.[1] In these conditions the statisticians of Gosplan took a hypothetical figure of 10 rubles, or half the monthly wage of 1913, as a standard or " target " figure for their calculations. Current estimates of real wages were made in terms of the cost of specified quantities of a group of essential commodities making up the monthly budget of a typical worker, which would in 1913 have cost 10 rubles in Moscow or in Petrograd or 7·40 rubles in average prices for the whole country. Statistics of real wages appeared in official publications as per-

---

[1] These calculations made in Gosplan and published in *Ekonomicheskaya Zhizn'* in February 1922 will be found in S. G. Strumilin, *Na Khozyaistvennom Fronte* (1925), pp. 74-79.

centages of this Gosplan price-index. On this basis the average
monthly wage of the industrial worker was shown to have increased
from 75 per cent in January 1922 to 142 per cent in December
1922, and 162 per cent in January 1923.[1] The reality was somewhat less encouraging. Throughout 1922 Narkomfin, refusing
to be bound by the Gosplan price-index and relying on quite
different calculations of its own, often failed to release sufficient
funds to honour the wage schedules of the collective agreements
in the industries dependent on state finance, with the result that
wages were either paid with the connivance of the trade unions
(the individual worker, confused by the constantly depreciating
currency, could not know what was due to him) at a lower rate
of exchange, or else fell into arrears.[2] In some of the consumer
industries, notably the food, tobacco and textile industries, the
practice, common in the days of war communism, of paying
workers in the products of the factories where they worked, for
them to sell or barter elsewhere, still lingered on, though now
admittedly an abuse,[3] so that here too an accurate computation
of wages actually paid was extremely difficult. But, when all
allowances have been made, it is reasonably certain that real wages
continued to rise steadily throughout 1922.

While the movement in the general wage level inspired a
qualified optimism, the specific problem of increasing differences
in industrial wages still defied solution. In September 1922 the
fifth trade union congress had demanded " the regulation of wages
and equalization of those which lagged behind as a result of the
unfavourable economic situation, those of the workers in large-
scale industry (mainly heavy industry) and transport ". In
another resolution it had cautiously raised the question of
principle :

The difference in the economic situation of different
branches of industry and the unplanned influence of the
market have created in their turn a disparity in the remuneration

[1] *Statistika Truda*, No. 5, 1923, p. 10 ; a detailed monthly analysis of the
wages of Petrograd members of ten leading trade unions in 1922 showed that
real wages almost exactly doubled during the year, and in December stood at
57 per cent of the pre-war level ; the peak was reached in November 1922
(*Petrogradskii Listok Truda* (a special supplement to *Trud*), March 8, 1923).

[2] S. G. Strumilin, *Na Khozyaistvennom Fronte* (1925), pp. 81-82.

[3] *Trud*, February 27, 1923.

of labour and a failure of rates of wages to conform to the specific weight and importance of different industrial sectors in the general system of the national economy.[1]

The wage situation in industry reflected one of the basic dilemmas of NEP, whose principles excluded direct state intervention in wage regulation. The relative prosperity of the consumer industries caused wages in these industries to soar above the levels current in the depressed heavy industries which were, from the standpoint of the general restoration of the economy and of the eventual victory of socialism, of far higher importance; moreover, higher wages were being paid in the sectors of industry where private enterprise predominated than in the nationalized industries which were directly dependent on the central wages fund of Narkomfin. In December 1922 " girl workers in tobacco factories packing cigarettes were getting more than a coal-hewer or a fitter ".[2] In April 1923 a speaker at the twelfth party congress declared that transport workers were so badly paid that 40 per cent of their budget came from illicit sources.[3] Only the persistent low level of employment prevented a general desertion by the workers of the nationalized, and from the national standpoint vital, sectors of industry. Such were the apparently unescapable results of the return to a market economy and insistence on the principles of khozraschet.

Before the end of 1922, therefore, wages policy had become on all counts a burning issue. Once the establishment of a stable currency — and therefore the balancing of the budget and the restriction of issues of paper money — had been accepted as a paramount aim, the pressure to reduce wages became very strong; not only did industrial wages represent a large item of public expenditure, but resistance to economies in this item was less powerful and influential than in many others. Gosplan, on the other hand, represented the opposing view that the productivity of the worker was in close relation to his standard of living, and that wages could not be reduced, or maintained indefinitely at

[1] *Stenograficheskii Otchet Pyatogo Vserossiiskogo S"ezda Professional'nykh Soyuzov* (1922), pp. 512, 527.
[2] *Trinadtsataya Konferentsiya Rossiiskoi Kommunisticheskoi Partii (Bol'shevikov)* (1924), p. 339.
[3] *Dvenadtsatyi S"ezd Rossiiskoi Kommunisticheskoi Partii (Bol'shevikov)* (1923), p. 339.

their existing low level, except at the cost of industrial efficiency.[1] It is significant that two government departments should have been the protagonists in the struggle, and one of them, rather than the trade unions, should have been the main champion of the interests of the industrial worker. The trade unions, being more directly subject to party instructions than the theorists of Gosplan, were readier to compromise with hard facts. A resolution on wages of the fifth trade union congress in September 1922 had already sounded a note of warning " against the illusion that it is possible in the very near future to raise wage rates to the level of the pre-war minimum standard " : all that it demanded was " a general unit of account which will guarantee wages against the continual fluctuations of market prices, and permit of the most simple comparison of the present level of wages with the pre-war level ".[2] Three months later, optimistically declaring that real wages had now reached one-half the pre-war level, the trade union central council, on instructions from the party central committee, called a halt to all further wage increases :

> The present economic situation makes objectively impossible a general rise in wages in industry. The council considers that the attention of the unions in the immediate future should be concentrated on maintaining the present level of wages and not permitting a reduction of real wages in future agreements.

At the same time it urged that some particularly low wages, notably those of transport workers, should still be levelled up.[3]

This quasi-official wages-stop remained in force throughout 1923, and encouraged an active offensive against industrial wages. The campaign waged by Narkomfin in the interests of economy and budgetary stability was now reinforced by the " Red industrialists ", themselves under heavy pressure from Narkomfin

---

[1] This view was strongly expressed in a report of Strumilin to Gosplan of March 1923 and in a resolution of Gosplan of July 1923 : both are reprinted in S. G. Strumilin, *Na Khozyaistvennom Fronte* (1925), pp. 87-92.

[2] *Stenograficheskii Otchet Pyatogo Vserossiiskogo S"ezda Professional'nykh Soyuzov* (1922), pp. 527-528.

[3] *Trud*, February 25, 1923 ; that the order came from the party central committee was freely stated by speakers at the thirteenth party conference a year later (*Trinadtsataya Konferentsiya Rossiiskoi Kommunisticheskoi Partii (Bol'-shevikov)* (1924), pp. 51, 84).

F

and anxious to find a scapegoat for the high prices of industrial goods. On January 16, 1923, *Ekonomicheskaya Zhizn'* declared that labour costs, including wages, social insurance and social services, were too high for industry to bear if it was to work at a profit; a further article in the same journal on January 25, written by a former textile magnate who was now one of the managers of the linen trust, alleged that wages and other services to the workers now accounted for 56 per cent of the costs of production as against 25 per cent before the war. *Trud*, in a reply on the following day, rashly claimed that " the question of wages stands *outside any relation to the productivity of the worker's labour* ". But this was certainly not the official line; [1] and a few weeks later the paper protested in a leading article against the idea that " the rôle [of the trade unions] as defenders of the interests of the working class consists of an unrestrained struggle to raise the wages of the workers irrespective of anything else ".[2] It is noteworthy that the trade unions, conscious of carrying little weight in the government machine, were at this time the strongest opponents of official regulation of wages : there were " neither reasons of principle nor practical reasons to revive the wage-fixing methods of the era of war communism ".[3] In March a compromise was recorded in a statement on wages issued jointly by the central council of trade unions and by Vesenkha. It noted that, while wages had risen to 50 or 60 per cent of their pre-war level, productivity had risen equally fast or faster; a reduction in wages " must be recognised as completely inadmissible ". It was still necessary to bring up wages in transport and heavy industry to the levels prevailing in light industry. But a general rise in wages must await more favourable conditions :

---

[1] At the central council of trade unions in April 1923 Andreev reaffirmed that " wages are the pure expression of what is given to the worker for his labour ", the moral being that only higher productivity could justify higher wages (*Trud*, April 14, 1923). At the session of the council six months later he expressed the same view more categorically : " Parallel with the indispensable increase in wages, we shall take a firm line in favour of achieving a rise in the productivity of labour : we are in favour of the rational utilization of the whole working day " (*ibid.* September 30, 1923).

[2] *Ibid.* February 25, 1923.

[3] *Ibid.* March 1, 1923 ; on the other hand, the organ of STO, which on such points represented the views of the industrialists, now advocated the " planned regulation " of wages by the state (*Ekonomicheskaya Zhizn'*, March 7, 1923).

The most important task of the economic organs and of the trade unions is to create the further economic conditions which would justify a rise in the remuneration of labour.[1]

What in effect was gained by the trade unions at this time was a levelling of wages between heavy and light industry. Trade union pressure, combined with the declining prosperity of the consumer industries, put an end to those wage discrepancies which had been a scandal in 1922. In spite of official assurances the process proved to be one of levelling down as well as of levelling up. But it had at least the advantage of counteracting the first effects of NEP and restoring a saner balance between wages in different sectors of industry.

Wages policy during the first three quarters of 1923 continued to exhibit an ever widening margin between theory and practice. According to the official statistics, real wages in industry, which stood in January at 153 per cent of the standard index figure, enjoyed a modest rise to 170 per cent in June, then fell back a little and recovered to 174 per cent in September; the real wages of transport workers remained constant throughout the same period at a little over 130 per cent.[2] These figures suggested a fairly stable wage level with an upward tendency and, apart from the continued lag in the wages of transport workers, corresponded accurately enough to the official prescription. The reality was very different. By the spring of 1923 it was apparent that the wages-stop of the previous December had, in fact, been the signal for an all round cut in wages. A leading article in *Trud* on March 11, 1923, under the title *Wages are, however, Falling*, diagnosed a general decline since December, referred to " the campaign of the industrialists for a gradual reduction in wages ", and complained of the passivity of " some " trade unions. In a resolution of April 14, 1923, on the eve of the twelfth party congress, the central council of trade unions admitted that wages were " falling in real terms " and called for action to arrest the decline.[3]

---

[1] *Trud*, March 24, 1923 ; Andreev at the next meeting of the trade union central council referred to the statement as " a document signed by Tomsky and Bogdanov in final settlement of the discussion about wages " (*ibid.* April 14, 1923).

[2] *Statistika Truda*, No. 1 (10), 1924, pp. 14-15.

[3] *Trud*, April 17, 1923.

By this time the discrepancy between the official wage rates and the rates actually paid was becoming notorious. The difficulty of reconciling the official policy of stable wages expressed in the collective agreements concluded with the trade unions and the inability or unwillingness of Narkomfin to provide the wherewithal to pay wages at these levels was met in a manner characteristic of the confusions and evasions manifested in all party and Soviet policy at this period. What precise legal authority originally attached to the Gosplan index is not clear. What happened was that local authorities everywhere began to ignore the Gosplan figures, and to draw up price-indices for themselves; and wages were, in fact, paid at these local and varying rates, which were adjusted not so much to prices on local markets (which was the theoretical justification for them) as to the extent of the funds actually available for wage payments. Calculations were thus made on what was to all intents and purposes a fraudulent price-index. By this device both the rates laid down in the collective agreements and the principle of the " stable unit " were in theory maintained, so that the workers did not easily discover what was happening to them, while arbitrary manipulation of the index kept actual payments within the limits resulting from the policy of Narkomfin. Since the factories were starved of funds, the choice often lay between paying wages at these cut rates or defaulting altogether. It need hardly be said that these procedures could not have been applied without the tacit connivance of the trade unions. Figures from the Donbass showed that the miners of that region lost 25 per cent of their real wages in January 1923 through the application of a local price-index and 37 per cent in March 1923.[1] In April 1923 an attempt was made to deal with the wages scandal in a decree which instructed the regional or provincial organs of Narkomtrud, together with representatives of other economic departments, to draw up and publish a weekly price-index based on the local market prices of a list of commodities prepared by Gosplan.[2] But this too proved ineffective. As the " sales crisis " deepened in the summer of 1923 the

---

[1] The practice was described with this and other examples in an article by Strumilin in the bulletin of Gosplan in May 1923 (S. G. Strumilin, *Na Khozyaistvennom Fronte* (1925), pp. 92-99) ; that it did not stop is shown by a further protest in October 1923 (*ibid.* pp. 99-102).

[2] *Sobranie Uzakonenii, 1923*, No. 31, art. 341.

consumer industries working for the market faced the same chronic shortage of funds which had hitherto mainly afflicted heavy industry. By the autumn the scandal had spread to the capital itself, and a price-index issued by the labour section of the Moscow Soviet for the calculation of wages in Moscow was attributed by Strumilin to " an ingenious miracle-worker who, like Joshua stopping the sun, appeared on the Moscow market, raised his hands to heaven and cried ' Prices, be still ' — and prices obediently stood still : some of them even receded in terror ".[1]

But the device of exchange manipulation, however shamelessly employed, still did not suffice in many cases to make both ends meet, and funds were not always available to meet wage requirements even at these adjusted rates. As early as the winter of 1921–1922 complaints had been heard of wage payments falling into arrears, especially in regions remote from the centre.[2] A decree of August 1, 1922, attempted to increase the authority of the supreme wages council. Wage payments in excess of the fixed rates were not to be charged to the state wages fund ; on the other hand, delays in wage payments were to be reported to the council, and irregularities investigated by the judicial authorities. The People's Commissariat of Workers' and Peasants' Inspection was also to keep a check on the proper distribution of wages.[3]

---

[1] S. G. Strumilin, *Na Khozyaistvennom Fronte* (1925), p. 100 ; the quotation is from an article entitled *New Juggling with the Index*. The practice was admitted by the light-hearted official apologist, Rykov : " Every institution had not only one, but several indices, which were brought into use according to convenience and necessity. Thanks to these indices nobody knew what he would receive or when, and why he received so much, and not more or less " (*Pravda*, January 4, 1924). The confusion introduced by these practices and by the multiplicity of authorities issuing statistics made impossible any accurate computation of real wages at this time. A table presented to the sixth All-Union Congress of Trade Unions in November 1924 purported to show a fairly steady and general rise in wages throughout 1923 ; but a speaker at the congress launched a vigorous attack on the central bureau of labour statistics (a joint organ of the trade union central council, Narkomtrud and the central statistical administration), alleging *inter alia* that its figures of wages were based on an unrepresentative sample of workers (*Shestoi S"ezd Professional'nykh Soyuzov SSSR* (1925), pp. 138-140, 293).

[2] S. G. Strumilin, *Na Khozyaistvennom Fronte* (1925), pp. 81-82 ; according to this account, which dates from February 1922, " hungry school-mistresses from the remote provinces are still sending information that for five months past they have received no issue either of rations or of wages ".

[3] *Sobranie Uzakonenii, 1922*, No. 48, art. 609.

But the decree was more eloquent as evidence of the prevailing chaos than as a promise of amendment. There seems no doubt that employers, and particularly the managers of nationalized concerns, took advantage of the time-lag and deliberately extended it wherever they dared, in order to benefit at the expense of the workers from the falling currency. Complaints of such delays, and attempts of the authorities to end this abuse, became a constant theme in the press of the winter of 1922–1923. The regular procedure under the collective agreements seems to have been to make the calculations at the rates ruling either on the 1st or (more favourably) on the 15th of the month for which the wage was due, but to make the payment only in the following month.[1] With a currency frequently depreciating by as much as 30 per cent in a month the loss to the worker involved in this time-table was already severe. But, in fact, the punctual observance even of this time-table was the exception rather than the rule. For the last three months of 1922 the workers in the Don were reported to have lost 34, 23 and 32 per cent respectively of their real wages through currency depreciation.[2] In January 1923 the trade union newspaper alleged that " cases of failure to pay wages in full for two or three months are more and more becoming a daily occurrence ".[3] In the Don mines, where conditions were always particularly bad, the February wages were paid in two instalments, 24 per cent at the end of March, the balance early in April; in July the wages for May and June were in arrears to an amount of 115 million rubles.[4] Variations in the degree of punctuality with which wages were paid caused " colossal differences " in the real wages of the same category of workers in different enterprises.[5] In June an article in *Ekonomicheskaya Zhizn'* apologetically explained that the delays in wage payments were due to divided responsibility, and claimed that the situation had now improved; [6] and in the same month a decree was issued

[1] For examples from Kharkov, the Don basin and Petrograd see *Trud*, February 21, February 27, March 8, 1923.
[2] *Trud*, March 14, 1923.   [3] *Ibid.* January 12, 1923.
[4] *Ibid.* June 3, July 18, 1923 ; at the beginning of August a joint protest was made by party, trade union and economic organizations in the Don, pointing out that during the past eight months the miners had lost 33·5 per cent of their wages through currency depreciation due to delays in payment (*ibid.* August 8, 1923).
[5] *Ibid.* July 28, 1923.   [6] *Ekonomicheskaya Zhizn'*, June 13, 1923.

to the effect that wages for the month should be paid not later
than June 25, and final accounts made up by July 5.[1] At the
same time the metal workers' union, which had taken the matter
to arbitration, obtained an award from an arbitral tribunal presided
over by Shmidt himself that half the monthly wage should be paid
on the 20th of the current month at rates of exchange ruling on
the 15th, and the balance not later than the 10th of the following
month at rates ruling on the 1st of that month.[2] But the improvement was at best partial. The chronic dilemma of a shortage of
ready cash, which was the immediate result of the attempt to
balance the budget and curtail currency emissions, could not be
circumvented even by the strictest regulations and supervision.
More than half the strikes occurring in the second half of 1922
were officially attributed to unpunctual payment of wages ; [3] and
the same cause was constantly alleged for the increasing wave of
strikes in 1923.[4]

While the plight of the industrial worker was still largely
unregarded in the controversy which engaged the attention of the
party leaders, unrest among the rank and file found an outlet in
two underground dissentient groups which were active in the
party on the eve of the twelfth party congress in April 1923.
The first and older of these groups called itself, after the name
of an illicit journal in which it launched its programme, the
" Workers' Truth ". It was composed mainly of intellectuals,
and professed allegiance to the ideas of Bogdanov, an old Bolshevik
whose unorthodox views had more than once brought him into
opposition to Lenin before the revolution. It had come into
being in the autumn of 1921, when the spirit of opposition, crushed
at the tenth party congress of March 1921 in the panic which
followed Kronstadt, began to revive ; and it gathered strength a
year later with the spread of industrial unrest. It treated NEP
as a return to capitalism pure and simple. In an appeal to " the
revolutionary proletariat and all revolutionary elements that
remain faithful to the struggling working class ", it dwelt on the

[1] *Sbornik Dekretov, Postanovlenii, Rasporyazhenii i Prikazov po Narodnomu
Khozyaistvu*, No. 6 (9), June 1923, p. 103.
[2] *Trud*, July 10, 1923.   [3] *Voprosy Truda*, No. 2, 1923, p. 17.
[4] See, for example, a leading article in *Trud*, March 17, 1923.

rift between the workers and the new " industrialists " and between the workers and the party :

> The working class ekes out a wretched existence, while the new bourgeoisie (responsible party workers, directors of factories, managers of trusts, presidents of executive committees, etc.) and nepmen live in luxury and revive in our memory the picture of the life of the bourgeoisie of all ages. . . . The Soviet, party and trade-union bureaucracy and the organizers of state capitalism live in material conditions sharply differentiated from the conditions of existence of the working class ; their very material prosperity and the stability of their general position depends on the degree of exploitation, and of the submission to them, of the toiling masses. All this makes inevitable a contradiction of interests and a rift between the communist party and the working class.

Worse still, NEP had driven the trade unions to concentrate on the wage demands and material conditions of the worker : this was a revival of " Economism "[1] and sapped the revolutionary spirit of the workers. The " once leading section of the proletariat, the Russian working class " had been " thrown back — perhaps for decades ".[2] The constructive parts of the programme were much less clearly defined, though the group explicitly dissociated itself from the Mensheviks, the SRs and the former " workers' opposition ",[3] and apparently desired to reform the party from within. Most of the same arguments were repeated more briefly in a manifesto to the twelfth party congress, in which the trade unions were accused of " converting themselves from organizations to defend the economic interests of the workers into organizations to defend the interests of production, i.e. of state capital first and foremost ".[4]

The second and bolder of the two opposition groups called itself simply the Workers' Group and was composed mainly of

[1] For " Economism " see The Bolshevik Revolution, 1917–1923, Vol. 1, pp. 10-12.

[2] The appeal was printed in the Menshevik Sotsialisticheskii Vestnik (Berlin), No. 3 (49), January 31, 1923, pp. 12-14 ; no copies of the journal of the group Rabochaya Pravda seem to have survived outside secret party or GPU archives, nor is it known how many issues appeared ; the first was dated September 1921. The working body, or " collective ", of the group is said not to have exceeded 20 (Pravda, December 19, 30, 1923).

[3] See The Bolshevik Revolution, 1917–1923, Vol. 1, pp. 196-197.

[4] Sotsialisticheskii Vestnik (Berlin), No. 19 (65), October 18, 1923, pp. 13-14.

workers. Its moving spirit was Myasnikov, the worker from the Urals who, immediately after the tenth party congress of 1921, had stirred up a revolt in the party in the name of " freedom of the press from monarchists to anarchists inclusive ", had been reprimanded by Lenin and, having refused to desist from his agitation, had been expelled from the party early in 1922.[1] In February 1923 Myasnikov joined hands with Kuznetsov, who had been expelled from the party at the eleventh congress in March 1922 as one of the ringleaders of the " appeal of the 22 " to IKKI,[2] and a party member named Moiseev, to draw up a " manifesto of the Workers' Group of the Russian Communist Party ", said to have been based on an earlier pamphlet of Myasnikov; the three constituted themselves as the " central organizing bureau " of the group, and set about surreptitiously to woo recruits among party and non-party workers.[3] The group occupied an out-and-out " Leftist " position and denounced all compromises with the bourgeoisie or with capitalism. Its economic policy was confused but significant. It was whole-heartedly opposed to the policy of concessions to the peasantry inaugurated by NEP as the expression of the famous " link " between peasantry and proletariat :

> The overcoming of NEP in Russia depends on how quickly the countryside can be conquered by the machine, on the victory of the tractor over the wooden plough. The organic link between town and country will be established on this basis of the growth of productive forces in both.

Even imports of machinery from abroad were unnecessary and harmful : they merely brought about " a link between our

[1] See *The Bolshevik Revolution, 1917-1923*, Vol. 1, pp. 207-208.
[2] See *ibid.* Vol. 1, p. 210.
[3] The main source for the Workers' Group is V. Sorin, *Rabochaya Gruppa* ("*Myasnikovshchina*") (1924), a party pamphlet issued with a preface by Bukharin ; it contains copious quotations from the manifesto and from statements subsequently made by members of the group when interrogated by the GPU. The manifesto circulated illegally in typewritten form in Russia, but was printed in Berlin in the summer of 1923, prefaced by an appeal from the group " to communist comrades of all lands " written after the twelfth party congress ; this has not been available, but I have used an abbreviated German translation of the appeal and the manifesto, *Das Manifest der Arbeitergruppe der Russischen Kommunistischen Partei*, published in Berlin in 1924 with comments by the KAPD and described as being " issued by the Russian section of the 4 International ".

agriculture and foreign merchants and a weakening of Russian industry ".[1] The ninth party congress of 1920 which had given its blessing to the employment of " specialists " had put the whole administration of industry on the wrong lines :

> The organization of this industry since the ninth congress of the RKP(B) is carried out without the direct participation of the working class by nominations in a purely bureaucratic way.
> The foundation of the trusts takes place in the same way, both as regards the appointment of the administration and the grouping of enterprises in the trusts. The working class does not know why this or that director is appointed, or why the factory belongs to this and not to that trust. Thanks to the policy of the ruling group of the RKP, it can take no part.[2]

The most successful phrase in the manifesto, which put the attitude of the group in a nutshell, was a quip that the letters NEP stood for " new exploitation of the proletariat ". The positive recommendations were in the old syndicalist tradition. Workers' control was to be restored in the factories ; " productive Soviets " were to replace the political Soviets (a degeneration of the original Soviet idea) as organs of government ; the People's Commissariat of Workers' and Peasants' Inspection was to be superseded by control exercised by " productive trade unions ".

It is not surprising that the party leaders in the spring of 1923, preoccupied by the importance of following the line laid down two years earlier and maintaining the uneasy compromise between worker and peasant, should have paid little attention to these proceedings. Both groups in their composition and in their programmes reproduced most of the Leftist movements which had arisen in the party, or on the fringes of it, since the seizure of power. Workers' control had been abandoned in the winter of 1917–1918 ; the battle for the employment of specialists had been fought and won under war communism ; the workers' opposition of 1920–1921 had attacked the evil of bureaucracy and the predominance of intellectuals in the party ; the project of vesting control of production in the trade unions had been ventilated and dismissed as syndicalism in the famous controversy which preceded

---

[1] *Das Manifest der Arbeitergruppe der Russischen Kommunistischen Partei* (n.d. [1924]), pp. 19-20.
[2] *Ibid.* p. 23.

the tenth party congress ; even the objection to a policy of imports
had been raised by Shlyapnikov a year later.[1] It was natural to
regard the two new manifestoes, which were widely known in
party circles, though the identity of the groups sponsoring them
was still undisclosed, as a farrago of old and discarded ideas propounded by discredited Leftist cranks. With the party leadership
in the throes of much more delicate problems and controversies,
they were not taken seriously or treated as a menace. What was
new about the two groups, and especially about the Workers'
Group, was that they attempted to appeal to the discontents of
the workers engendered both by the decline in real wages and the
increasing fear of unemployment and by the growing power of
managers and directors of industry, who showed little sympathy
for the interests of the workers. But these discontents were only
beginning to take serious shape in the first months of 1923 and
had not yet forced themselves on the attention of the party leaders.
At this stage those who challenged party policy in the name
of industry, and protested against the stepmotherly treatment
accorded to it since the inception of NEP, fell into two categories
— the " old Bolsheviks " who believed in capital investment in
heavy industry as the necessary first step in the building of
socialism, and the new " industrialists " who had wholeheartedly
embraced the commercial and capitalist aspects of NEP and
wished only to earn profits by the successful running of their
concerns. Neither group could easily cooperate with the spokesmen of labour, whose claims for increased benefits for the workers
were not immediately compatible either with rising profits or with
capital accumulation. Trotsky was the one potential leader and
focus of an " industrial " opposition. Yet his record as the
protagonist of the militarization of labour under war communism,
and as the champion of the " statization " of the trade unions,
made him particularly suspect in trade union circles. In the heat
of the trade union controversy in December 1920 he rallied to
the defence of bureaucracy on the score of the low political
and cultural level of the masses ; [2] and there was a wide gulf between his convictions as a centralizer and a planner in economic

[1] See *The Bolshevik Revolution, 1917–1923*, Vol. 2, p. 322.
[2] Trotsky, *Sochineniya*, xv, 422 ; it was this outburst which enabled Stalin
to taunt him later as the " patriarch of bureaucrats " (see p. 336 below).

organization and the quasi-syndicalist views of the promoters of the two " workers' " groups. Easily identified with these freak groups of the Left, the interests of the industrial worker found at this moment few responsible spokesmen in party circles.

This situation was reflected when the twelfth party congress met in April 1923. Zinoviev in his opening speech contemptuously dismissed the charge of the Workers' Group that NEP stood for the " new exploitation of the proletariat "; and Trotsky let fall the remark that the Workers' Truth should " be more correctly called the ' Workers' Untruth ' ".[1] Trotsky in his speech at the congress not only looked forward with relative equanimity to increased unemployment resulting from the rationalization of industry and the dismissal of redundant workers, but condoned the continuous downward pressure on wages as a necessary contribution to " socialist accumulation ".[2] The perfunctory section on wages policy in the congress resolution on industry dubiously claimed " a significant rise in wages during the past year for all categories of workers ", demanded " an equalization, more or less, of the average wage in all branches of industry " while maintaining the dependence of the individual wage on work done, and pointed out that real progress would be made only " on the basis of an expanding, i.e. profit-earning, industry ", so that rationalization was in the ultimate interest of the workers themselves.[3] These unimpeachable sentiments held out little hope of any early remedy for the grievances of the industrial workers or of escape from the under-privileged position into which NEP had thrust them. The insistence in every party and trade union pronouncement of the period of the supreme need for higher productivity was a continuous reminder of the unceasing drive for greater efficiency and intensity of labour.[4]

The plight of the industrial worker grew progressively graver through the spring and summer of 1923. It was part of the logic

[1] *Dvenadtsatyi S"ezd Rossiiskoi Kommunisticheskoi Partii (Bol'shevikov)* (1923), pp. 23, 316.

[2] See pp. 23-24 above.

[3] *VKP(B) v Rezolyutsiyakh* (1941), i, 483-484.

[4] At the end of 1922 the trade union central council set up a Central Institute of Labour, which attempted to popularize the slogan of " the scientific organization of labour " (NOT). Its methods were attacked by a group of trade unionists at the time of the twelfth party congress as savouring of " Taylorism " (*Pravda*, April 15, 1923) : the controversy continued throughout the year.

of NEP that the burden which had been partially lifted from the
shoulders of the peasant should have been transferred to those of
the worker, and that the managers and employers, struggling to
keep industry afloat in an unpropitious environment, should have
seemed those most concerned to place and keep it there. While
the standard of living of the industrial worker in 1923 was higher
than in the harsh years of war communism, there had been no
time since the revolution when discrimination was so overtly
practised against him, or when he had so many legitimate causes
of bitterness against a régime which claimed to govern in his
name. The insistent demand for greater efficiency in industry
expressed the overriding need of the Soviet economy, and until
it was met no serious progress was possible. Yet the two measures
through which greater efficiency could be attained — the concentration of industrial undertakings and increased personal productivity of the individual worker — both pointed to the same
immediate result, the dismissal of redundant workers to swell
the ranks of the unemployed; and with no general plan of industrial development, and no capital resources to make such a
plan feasible, the prospect of reabsorbing redundant labour was
still remote. Thus the long-term interests of the Soviet economy
— and, under a socialist régime which had abolished capitalist
exploitation, as party and trade union spokesmen were never tired
of explaining, the long-term interests of the workers themselves —
called for measures which in the short run imposed new and
intolerable hardships on the industrial worker, who could see
nothing in view but harder work, falling — or at best stationary —
real wages and ever increasing fear of unemployment. From
this vicious circle there could be no escape except through an
unremitting drive for greater production at lower cost ; and, since
the essence of NEP was the relaxation of past pressures on the
peasant, the intensification of such pressures on the far less
numerous industrial workers was the unescapable corollary. That
these should be the underlying economic realities of the so-called
dictatorship of the proletariat was a grim commentary on the
attempt, inexorably imposed by the victory of the revolution in
Russia and its failure in the advanced countries of the west, to
achieve the building of socialism by shock tactics in a backward
economy.

CHAPTER 3

THE CRISIS BREAKS

IN the late summer of 1923 the crisis at length came to a head and compelled the attention of the reluctant party leaders. Throughout the year 1923 emphasis had continued to be laid, especially in the pronouncements of Zinoviev, on the importance of conciliating the peasant. Since the twelfth party congress in April the anti-religious campaign had been moderated out of respect for his feelings. In August *Pravda* announced that " the muzhik's god " could be destroyed not by " scolding and ridicule ", but only by making the peasant feel that he was no longer helpless in face of the blind forces of nature : forcible methods would only create " fanatics ready to suffer for their faith ".[1] The large-scale agricultural exhibition first mooted at the end of 1921 [2] as a stimulus for the revival of Soviet agriculture was finally opened in Moscow in August 1923 under the title of the " first agricultural and rural industries exhibition of the USSR ", and used to symbolize the significance of the peasant in Soviet economic life.[3] But the idyllic picture of a predominantly peasant country painlessly evolving towards socialism under the gentle pressures of NEP was disturbed by the strained relations between the agricultural and industrial sectors of the economy, whose persistence still constituted the root of the trouble. It had been comfortably believed or hoped after the twelfth party congress that the price scissors would widen no further and the situation gradually right itself. The opposite happened. The disparity between industrial and agricultural prices continued to increase month by month.

[1] *Pravda*, August 18, 1923.
[2] See *The Bolshevik Revolution, 1917-1923*, Vol. 2, p. 286.
[3] The decree of August 1923 on the organization of the exhibition is in *Sobranie Uzakonenii, 1923*, No. 95, art. 938. A number of foreign delegations were invited to the exhibition, and the occasion was taken to found a so-called " Peasant International " (see p. 198 below).

On October 1 the scissors opened to what proved to be their widest extent. On that date retail and wholesale prices of industrial goods calculated in pre-war rubles stood respectively at 187 and 171 per cent of the 1913 level, and retail and wholesale prices of agricultural products at 58 and 49 per cent of that level.[1] By this time other unmistakable signs of a grave economic crisis had begun to appear. Throughout the summer sales of consumer goods had declined. The industrial trusts, relying on the strength of their financial position and of their monopoly sales organization, and on the market provided by the new " middle class " which NEP had created in the towns, continued to force up prices and were content to hold back goods, awaiting the moment when the harvest would put more money into the hands of the peasant : they were encouraged in this course by the Vesenkha circular of July 1923 reminding them of their primary duty to earn profits.[2] The economic crisis of 1923 clearly differed from the preceding crises through which the Soviet régime had passed since 1917. These had been crises of scarcity ; now the warehouses were over-stocked with consumer goods and the harvest had yielded substantial surpluses of agricultural products. The crisis was due primarily not to a failure to produce, but to a failure to establish terms and methods of trade to bring about a flow of goods from factory worker to peasant and vice versa.[3] It

[1] *Ekonomicheskaya Zhizn'*, October 1-2, 1923, published Trotsky's diagram of April 1923 brought up to date ; the diagram in *Trinadtsatyi S"ezd Rossiiskoi Kommunisticheskoi Partii (Bol'shevikov)* (1924), p. 396, prolonged the lines down to April 1924 when the scissors had once more almost closed. From the point of view of the peasant the proper comparison was between the retail prices of industrial goods and the wholesale prices of agricultural products, thus putting the disparity at its greatest. According to the calculation in S. G. Strumilin, *Na Khozyaistvennom Fronte* (1925), p. 220, the ratio of industrial prices to agricultural prices on October 1, 1923, stood at 323 per cent of the corresponding ratio for 1913.   [2] See p. 9 above.

[3] The controversy at the thirteenth party conference in January 1924 whether the crisis was, as Rykov asserted and Smirnov and Pyatakov denied (*Trinadtsataya Konferentsiya Rossiiskoi Kommunisticheskoi Partii (Bol'shevikov)* (1924), pp. 8, 69, 81, 86), a crisis of " over-production ", turned on the standpoint of the disputants. It was a crisis of over-production in the capitalist sense, which the party leadership sought to remedy by " capitalist " methods of financial pressure to liquidate stocks with the result of curtailing production. It was not a crisis of over-production from the standpoint of a planned economy, and prices should in the view of the opposition have been brought down by extended credit to expand production : whether this was a practicable policy in the existing state of resources is another matter.

had been assumed that the terms of trade would be automatically settled by NEP to the best possible advantage of all concerned; this, in classical theory, was bound to result from the removal of restrictions on trade. The sequel had conspicuously failed to bear out this expectation.

While, however, what happened in 1923 was in this sense a crisis of NEP — " the first crisis ", in Rykov's words, " which has driven a serious wedge between workers and peasants " [1] — it was in a profounder sense part of a struggle between agriculture and industry, between peasantry and proletariat, which dated back not to the beginning of NEP, and not to the Bolshevik revolution, but to the emancipation of the serfs. The meaning and purpose of the emancipation had been to pave the way for the industrial revolution in Russia. The maintenance of large landowners' estates and the introduction of some degree of efficiency in cultivation made possible a constantly increasing export of grain and other agricultural products, which made Russia an important supplier of foodstuffs to western Europe. These exports defrayed, however, only the interest on the capital invested in developing Russian industry; the capital investment itself had been provided by foreign loans. Nor was industrialization a spontaneous and unplanned process. It was the result of governmental decisions and governmental action dictated by a political motive — the strengthening of Russia's military might; and the state was always the most important customer of Russian heavy industry both for arms and munitions and for the development of transport. The Bolsheviks, when they took power in Russia in 1917, were committed up to the hilt to continue and intensify this planned and deliberate policy of industrializing Russia — not, indeed, in order to achieve military power but in order to build a socialist society. But they lacked the two resources which had carried forward the process successfully and rapidly in the two decades before 1914. The disintegration caused by the war and the break-up of the larger estates into peasant holdings ruled out any prospect of grain exports on a significant scale. The political revolution was fatal to the chance of foreign loans. Hence a resumption of the process of in-

[1] *Trinadtsataya Konferentsiya Rassiiskoi Kommunisticheskoi Partii (Bo'l-shevikov)* (1924), p. 84.

dustrialization would be possible only if capital for investment in industry could be drawn from the Russian economy itself, and, to a large extent, from its predominant agricultural sector.

Before the new régime had seriously begun to consider this problem the crisis of the civil war descended on it, compelling the concentration of all resources on the army and on the industry that served military needs ; and this meant — like industrialization, though in a much more extreme form — the taking of supplies from the peasant without a full equivalent return. When the civil war ended, the peasant was so exhausted and so restive that the continuance of the process, even in the milder form which a reasonable programme of industrialization would have required, became unthinkable. The essence of NEP was the timely recognition of this hard fact. Failing an influx of foreign capital — and this, as the experience of the next two years was to show, was a remote contingency — the expansion of industry, which was the golden road to socialism, depended on the accumulation of fresh capital within the national economy ; and this would scarcely be possible on any significant scale until such time as agriculture had been sufficiently restored, and the peasant sufficiently appeased, to provide a substantial part of this accumulation out of the agricultural sector of the economy. Until that time arrived, all that could be done would be to keep intact the " commanding heights " of nationalized industry and await the opportunity for renewing the advance. So long as this waiting policy was practicable, no point of doctrine arose, and the controversies in the party which had been silenced by the introduction of the temporary expedient of NEP could still be held in check. By the autumn of 1923, however, it was slowly becoming plain that NEP had created no stable or automatic equilibrium in which it was safe to take refuge so long as conditions were unpropitious for a fresh advance. What NEP had created was not the much vaunted " link " or " alliance " between the proletariat and the peasantry, but an arena in which these two main elements of the Soviet economy struggled against one another in competitive market conditions, the battle swaying sharply first to one side, then to the other ; and such a contest, which might be tolerable and even salutary in a rich and powerful country in the heyday of capitalism,

G

was necessarily disruptive of the enfeebled resources of the backward Russian economy. The state could not afford to allow the
battle of the scissors to be fought out to a finish, with the peasant
holding up the towns to ransom and the consumer industries
engaged on an uninhibited quest for maximum profits. Intervention would one day be required to set in motion once more the
process of industrialization and resume the advance on the road
to socialism. But intervention was required in the meanwhile
even to maintain the uneasy balance established by NEP between
agriculture and industry. NEP had been inaugurated two and a
half years earlier as a compromise, which, while keeping intact
the foundation of socialism in the nationalized industries, would
provide commercial incentives to the peasant to grow food for the
factories and towns. It was now apparent, however much the
harassed leaders might seek to evade or postpone the issue, that
this dual aim was no longer being attained through the release
and free interplay of economic forces.

It is not surprising that the complexity of these problems, and
the deep-seated character of the dilemma which confronted the
would-be builders of socialism in a backward peasant economy,
were not yet fully realized by the party leaders who set out to
grapple with the scissors crisis in the autumn of 1923.[1] The
two groups which now began to crystallize within the central
committee were both reluctant to admit the possibility of conflict
between the claims of agriculture and those of industry, since the
purpose and foundation of NEP had been precisely to make any
such conflict impossible; yet this was the one point which
emerged clearly from the discussions. The majority, impressed
with the material progress realized under NEP and with the
dangers of any renewal of those policies of pressure on the peasantry
which had nearly brought disaster under war communism, was
eager only to maintain the *status quo* established by NEP and let

---

[1] It is fair to say that the opinions of the economic and financial experts,
to whom the political leaders might naturally have turned for advice, were
equally confused and divided on the causes of the crisis : articles from the
contemporary press are quoted in M. H. Dobb, *Russian Economic Development
since the Revolution* (2nd ed., 1929), pp. 227-245. Preoccupation with the
anomaly of a double currency, and with the continuous depreciation of the
ruble, encouraged the superficial view that the scissors crisis was explicable in
terms of the monetary problem.

the socialist future take care of itself; and, since the scissors crisis
which at present threatened the *status quo* arose from what appeared
to be inflated prices charged for consumer goods by the industrial
trusts, it was difficult to contest the view that the peasant was
the victim, and industry the villain, of the piece, and that the
remedy lay in applying pressure to the trusts to reduce prices and
profits, and in bringing further relief to the peasant by increasing
grain prices through export and by reducing his taxation. The
troubles of industry were the result of its loss of the peasant
market, due mainly to the high prices of industrial goods. Meanwhile the revival of heavy industry must await more propitious
conditions.

The minority, soon to be distinguished as " the opposition ",
starting from the basic Marxist doctrine of the predominant importance of the proletariat and of industry in the socialist revolution, approached the scissors crisis from the standpoint of the need
to safeguard the interests of industry in general and, in particular,
to promote a revival of heavy industry as the foundation of a
socialist economy. Called on to defend the rise in industrial
prices and to propound a remedy, they explained the rise in terms
of increased costs due partly to increased taxation and increased
overheads over which industry had no control, such as transport,[1]
and partly to the admitted inefficiency of industrial organization,
and argued that the only proper way to bring down prices was
to increase the efficiency of industry by rationalization and concentration and by broadening its basis of production. On this
view the primary cause of the scissors was the failure of the
revival of industry to keep pace with the revival of agriculture,
and the remedy could only be to come to the aid of industry, and
primarily of heavy industry as its essential base. As Strumilin,
the economist of Gosplan, crisply put it :

---

[1] Bogdanov at the twelfth party congress estimated that half the overheads
of industry were accounted for by items which were outside the control of the
undertakings themselves — taxes, freights, interest on advances from Gosbank,
annual depreciation, etc. (*Dvenadtsatyi S"ezd Rossiiskoi Kommunisticheskoi Partii
(Bol'shevikov)* (1923), p. 332). According to S. G. Strumilin, *Na Khozyaistvennom Fronte* (1925), pp. 225-226, industry in 1913 paid 3 per cent of its net
production in taxes, in 1922 3-4 per cent, in 1923 10-12 per cent ; credit, which
cost 6 per cent per annum in 1913, cost 60 per cent in 1923 ; and freights,
which in 1922 were only one-third of their 1913 rates, were 25 per cent above
1913 rates in 1923.

If we wish to achieve maximum success in bringing the scissors together, we must, in reviewing the plans of production of our industry, first and foremost guarantee its most rapid possible expansion. A further increase in the working load and in the productivity of labour in our industry — there is the fundamental condition of a successful struggle with the disparity in prices. And all the rest — will be added unto you.[1]

This, however, involved, as Trotsky and the spokesmen of Vesenkha had perceived in the previous winter, a revised credit policy. While the first half of 1923 had seen a rapid expansion of credit to consumer industries, the natural result of a policy whose criterion was the earning capacity of the borrower in market conditions had been to discriminate against heavy industry, which had no prospect of escaping from the doldrums so long as this criterion was applied. Trotsky's speech at the twelfth party congress had dwelt on the contrast between the rapid progress of rural and light industry and the consumer industries generally and the stagnation of heavy industry, and pointed out the incompatibility of this state of affairs with an advance towards a socialist economy. The conclusion was obvious that heavy industry could be revived only in the conditions of a planned economy, and that a planned credit policy, which served specific ends and did not accept the criterion of earning capacity as final, was an essential part of such an economy. The minority in the central committee, while making no criticism of the credits extended to the consumer industries, demanded the extension of generous advances to heavy industry as a condition of its expansion, or even of its survival. The further the discussion was carried, the more profound appeared to be the gulf which separated these views from the opinion of the majority.

Three apparently unrelated events of August and September 1923 marked the ripening of the crisis and showed that some broad decisions of policy could no longer be avoided. The first was an outbreak of widespread strikes and disturbances among the industrial workers; the second was the decision of Gosbank to prevent any further widening of the scissors and force down

[1] S. G. Strumilin, *Na Khozyaistvennom Fronte* (1925), p. 229.

industrial prices by curtailing credits to industry; the third was
a monetary crisis involving the resumption of the printing of
Soviet rubles on a large scale in order to finance the harvest.

The strain on the worker, hitherto largely ignored in the
controversies engendered by the scissors crisis, had now reached
breaking-point. What was darkly referred to as " the wave of
unrest and strikes about wages which swept over some regions
of the republic in August." [1] was not reported at the time, and
the story can be told only in broad outline. The main troubles
occurred in heavy industry; the first mass strike recorded was in
the engineering works at Sormovo at the beginning of August
1923. All accounts agree that delays in wage payments were
the main cause, though the desire of workers to return to their
villages for the harvest is also mentioned. When the workers
of Sormovo protested in August against the delay in July payments, they were told that in the south and in the Urals the
workers had not yet received their wages for May and June. A
new grievance was the practice of paying a proportion of wages
in bonds of the gold loan; the workers at first accepted this
under the impression that the bonds could be cashed at their
nominal value, but soon discovered their mistake. [2] Coupons

[1] Stalin, *Sochineniya*, v. 356; Kamenev in his speech of December 11,
1923, spoke of " alarming occurrences in the working class in July and August "
and of strikes at Kharkov and Sormovo (*Pravda*, December 13, 1923). *Pravda*,
December 21, 1923, referred to " the events which occurred during July–
September in a number of big enterprises ", and thought that they " indicated
a definite divorce of the trade unions from the masses ". The fullest available
accounts of these occurrences were published in the Menshevik journal *Sotsialisticheskii Vestnik* (Berlin): circumstantial reports of strikes at Sormovo
appeared in No. 16 (62), September 16, 1923, pp. 14-15; No. 21-22 (67-68),
November 27, 1923, pp. 20-21; in the Donbass in No. 14 (60), August 16,
1923, pp. 15-16; No. 23-24 (69-70), December 17, 1923, p. 17; at Kharkov in
No. 1 (71), January 10, 1924, pp. 7-8. In the years between 1923 and 1927,
when authentic reports of untoward events no longer appeared in the Soviet
press, but could still be smuggled out of the country without too much difficulty,
this journal frequently published valuable and otherwise inaccessible material;
the anti-Soviet bias, which increased as time went on, has to be discounted.
Among its regular informants was Ryazanov, who travelled widely in Europe
on behalf of the Marx-Engels Institute.

[2] This practice, at first introduced without formal authorization (a protest
against it appeared in *Trud*, July 27, 1923), was later defended (*ibid.* September
1, 1923) as a necessary step towards financial stability, and sanctioned by a
decree of September 4, 1923 (see p. 100 below). This was one of the major
grievances recalled a year later by Tomsky at the sixth trade union congress
(*Shestoi S"ezd Professional'nykh Soyuzov SSSR* (1925), p. 71).

which could be cashed only in certain cooperative shops stocking unwanted goods were sometimes issued in part payment of wages.[1] The threat of dismissal or a lockout was the very effective weapon constantly used by managers to counter all forms of discontent or to force down wages. In theory, workers were entitled to notice and a month's wages on dismissal. But the number of causes for instant dismissal recognized in the labour code rendered this safeguard worthless. The position of the trade union organizers in these clashes was wholly unenviable. It need not be doubted that they exercised such pressure as they could on the financial authorities in Moscow to make punctual payment of wages due; and in this they often had the sympathy and support of the managers, who were as much concerned as anyone to avoid labour troubles. But trade union policy, closely conforming to the party line, was unconditionally opposed to strikes. Any threat of a workers' strike to enforce attention to their grievances was treated as a breach of trade union discipline and punished by exclusion of those responsible from the trade union, which meant automatic dismissal from the factory and inability to obtain another job.[2] In practice, therefore, the trade union representatives and the factory committees tended to find themselves in league with the managers and with the police to maintain discipline among the workers, to prevent strikes and to suppress disturbances. When stoppages of work occurred, the GPU at once intervened, at the request of the management and with the tacit or explicit assent of the unions, to arrest " ringleaders " and " instigators ". Protests and demonstrations by the workers were ruthlessly met with force. The industrial disturbances which reached their peak in August and September 1923 were a spontaneous and unorganized movement : there is no evidence to connect

[1] *Trud*, November 21, 1923.

[2] *Trud* in the first half of 1923, when strikes were freely reported, frequently recorded the exclusion of strikers from the unions as a penalty (e.g. *Trud*, February 18, May 19, June 29, 1923). Later this practice began to excite indignation : a leading article in *Trud*, November 27, 1923, protested against the eagerness of the trade unions to purge recalcitrant members, and a further article of December 15, 1923, complained that verdicts of expulsion were pronounced by the administrations of the unions without right of appeal to the membership. This grievance still rankled at the time of the sixth trade union congress of November 1924 (*Shestoi S"ezd Professional'nykh Soyuzov SSSR* (1925), pp. xv-xvi, xix-xx).

them with propaganda of the Workers' Truth or the Workers' Group or any other opposition faction. Larin, at the thirteenth party congress a year later, made one of the few sympathetic attempts to depict the state of mind of the workers at this time :

> You remember that the period before the autumn of 1923 was a period when on the one hand the broad mass of workers saw the growth of our economic achievements — industry was developing, the financial position of the state was improving, the railways were working better, we ourselves, at meetings and in the newspapers, were triumphantly proclaiming : we are going up, up, year by year we are going up ; and at the same time the mass of workers began to feel some bewilderment : well, we are going up, it is clear, but the nepmen too are going more and more on the spree and getting fatter and fatter. The mass of workers began to take offence : we are going up, but for us, the workers, there is a standstill in the improvement of our position.[1]

The proletariat had seized power ; the means of production belonged to it. Yet the revolution had brought it few material advantages. These had gone for the most part to the specialist and the nepman. The conditions were sufficiently similar to those prevailing in the factories in the worst days of the Tsarist régime to provoke wry reflexions on the fate of the workers under the " workers' state ".

In the economic controversies of the autumn of 1923 the discontent of the workers played only a minor part. The whole subject was too delicate for public discussion and was placed under the ban, not only by the majority, which was committed to defend the interests of the peasant even if this for the time being bore hard on the industrial worker, but by the minority, which represented the " employer " side of industry — the managers, administrators and planners — and, being itself hard pressed by official policies, was little disposed to look with sympathy on fresh demands by the workers or to condone proletarian breaches of industrial discipline.[2] There is sufficient evidence in what

---

[1] *Trinadtsatyi S"ezd Rossiiskoi Kommunisticheskoi Partii (Bol'shevikov)* (1924), p. 182.

[2] One of the incidents of the economic controversy in the autumn of 1923 had been a renewed campaign against the salaries of the specialists, due in part to the long-standing hostility of the trade unions, in part to the friction between Narkomfin and the industrialists on the issue of credits. On October

followed to show that the strikes and disturbances in factories in July, August and September 1923 had administered a shock to the party leadership, and had shown that a point had been reached where the burdens placed on the shoulders of the industrial worker both by NEP and by the policy of reorganizing and restoring industry could no longer be safely increased. The attempts to apply a less penurious and oppressive wages policy and the new campaign against the nepmen in the winter of 1923–1924 sprang from a realization of this fact.

The second factor which brought the crisis to a head was the restriction of credits to consumer industries by Gosbank. A cautious credit policy had from the outset been imposed on the directors of Gosbank by the canons of financial orthodoxy. The bank had always been unwilling to grant credits to traders,[1] and industry was therefore all the more dependent on credit to finance the sale of its products. With the rapid expansion of the chervonets issue in the first half of 1923, these credits were readily granted. Complaints of credit stringency at this time related to the refusal of the banks to make advances to heavy industry. The rate of interest on advances was still as high as 60 per cent per annum; but this compared favourably with the still higher rates of 1922.[2] These halcyon days ended with the continued widening of the scissors in the late summer of 1923. Any struggle between the conflicting interests of agriculture and industry found Narkomfin at this time whole-heartedly on the side of the peasant in its determination to bring down industrial prices. Early in July 1923, Sokolnikov, the People's Commissar of Finance, in

---

10, 1923, by what can hardly have been a coincidence, both *Trud* and *Ekonomicheskaya Zhizn'* carried articles attacking the system of *tantièmes* which encouraged directors of enterprises to declare profits that had not really been earned, or to raise prices and depress wages in order to inflate profits ; on October 17, *Trud* demanded a reduction in the remuneration of specialists ; on the following day *Ekonomicheskaya Zhizn'* once more attacked the system of *tantièmes*, which had been originally introduced to attract specialists " who would not work for ideological considerations ".

[1] Kutler, the effective professional head of Gosbank (see *The Bolshevik Revolution, 1917–1923*, Vol. 2, pp. 351-352), explained to a conference of merchants in January 1923 that " broad credits for trade, however desirable in themselves, cannot practically be granted in the immediate future " (*Ekonomicheskaya Zhizn'*, January 17, 1923).

[2] S. G. Strumilin, *Na Khozyaistvennom Fronte* (1925), p. 225 ; for the earlier rates see *The Bolshevik Revolution, 1917–1923*, Vol. 2, p. 349.

his speech to TsIK, reported that 100 million gold rubles had been advanced to industry by Gosbank, and 10 million gold rubles by Prombank, and issued a warning on the flow of credit to industry :

> If this credit is used not in order to expand the operations of industry, but in order to restrict sales and bring about a rise in market prices, this of course will not be a practical utilization of bank credit by industry, but an abuse of bank credit.[1]

Six weeks later action was taken on this warning. Gosbank, in agreement with Narkomfin, began suddenly and severely to restrict its credits to industry.[2] The measure, apart from considerations of price policy, could be justified or explained on monetary grounds. The fall in the purchasing power of the chervonets was plausibly attributed to an over-issue of the new currency due to too rapid an expansion of credit [3] But the measure was also construed, and rightly construed, as a deliberate intervention in the scissors crisis. The introduction of the chervonets had at first had highly favourable effects for the consumer industries. The granting of credits against stocks was one of the factors which had enabled these industries in the winter of 1922–1923 to surmount the *razbazarovanie* crisis of the previous year, and, under the lead of the syndicates, put the screws on the consumer. But, when this reversal of fortune led, in the first half of 1923, to a crisis of the opposite kind resulting from high industrial prices, voices were quickly raised to demand a restriction of the credit policy which had put industry in this strong position : [4] to withhold credit from industry was an obvious

---

[1] *Vtoraya Sessiya Vserossiiskogo Tsentral'nogo Ispolnitel'nogo Komiteta X Sozyva* (1923), pp. 114-115 ; for this speech see p. 36 above.

[2] *Ekonomicheskaya Zhizn'*, November 11, 1923, while defending the measure in principle, admitted that it had been applied " abruptly and roughly " ; the suddenness and violence of the contraction of credit was one of the items in the subsequent indictment of official policy by the opposition (*Trinadtsataya Konferentsiya Rossiiskoi Kommunisticheskoi Partii (Bol'shevikov)* (1924), pp. 70, 81). Since Gosbank was an autonomous institution with full powers over the use of its funds, this decision did not formally involve governmental responsibility ; " the self-sufficient character of our financial policy " and " the autonomy of Gosbank" also figured in the indictment (see p. 105 below).

[3] See p. 33 above.

[4] Kutler put the case against industry in *Ekonomicheskaya Zhizn'*, September 12, 1923 : " The sellers are not troubled by the fact that a rise in prices curtails the sale of their product. . . . Subsidies and credit come to their aid. The

way to force industrial goods on to the market at lower prices. Thus intervention by Gosbank in credit policy was approved even by those who, in other respects, wished to preserve the free interplay of market forces as the essential feature of NEP; and this opinion, which was equally agreeable to those who were primarily interested in the principles of financial orthodoxy and those who sought above all to uphold the interests of the peasant, far outweighed the protests of those who believed that industrial prices should be brought down through improved methods of production stimulated by a more generous credit policy.

The curtailment of credit was almost immediately effective in compelling the consumer industries to lower prices and liquidate stocks on a falling market. In the latter part of September 1923 the press was full of cries of distress from almost every branch of industry.[1] It was on October 1 that the price scissors widened to their furthest extent. From that date both a fall in industrial prices and a rise in agricultural prices set in.[2] The restriction of credit to industry, which was the most important act of economic policy since the twelfth party congress, could not be said to contravene any of the vague and eclectic resolutions of the congress. It could even be supported by recalling Lenin's surprising remarks at the eleventh party congress on the salutary properties of a financial crisis.[3] It also had the effect of ending the discrimination in credit policy in favour of consumer industries, and thus closed the gap which had arisen in the first years of NEP between the interests of the consumer industries and those of heavy industry. After the autumn of 1923 it was no longer possible to maintain a

goods pile up in the warehouses." In November 1923 Sokolnikov repeated the allegation that industry had " to a certain extent abused credit " (*Tret'ya Sessiya Tsentral'nogo Ispolnitel'nogo Komiteta Soyuza Sovetskikh Sotsialistícheskikh Respublik* (1924), p. 99) ; the textile industry in particular, having got credit in order to market its goods, had fixed its prices so high that the peasant refused to buy, and the financial authorities had retaliated by making a reduction in prices a condition of further credit (G. Y. Sokolnikov, *Finansovaya Politika Revolyutsii*, ii (1926), 93-95).

[1] See, for example, *Ekonomicheskaya Zhizn'*, September 19 (tobacco), 20 (oil), 21 (salt), 1923.

[2] From about the beginning of October wholesale prices also began to be regulated by official order (see p. 110 below). But it was the restriction of credit which struck the first blow, and, judging by previous experience, official price-fixing would have been ineffective without it.

[3] G. Y. Sokolnikov, *Finansovaya Politika Revolyutsii*, ii (1926), 93-94 ; for Lenin's pronouncement see *The Bolshevik Revolution, 1917-1923*, Vol. 2, p. 353.

system by which consumer industries working for the market obtained credit from the banks, while the basic industries on which the revival of the whole economy ultimately depended were starved of credit by Narkomfin on budgetary grounds. Henceforth the question of credits for industry would be treated as a whole, and as an item in industrial policy. To this extent the " anarchy " of the first years of NEP had been overcome.

The curtailment of credit for industry in August 1923, apart from its other implications, could be regarded as a further step to strengthen the chervonets and pave the way for the final stabilization of the currency. It was, however, quickly followed by a major monetary stringency which was the third factor in bringing the whole economic crisis to a head.[1] The weak point in the policy of Narkomfin was still the difficulty of meeting the requirements of public expenditure if the operations of the printing press were confined within the narrow limits laid down in the July decree.[2] Feverish efforts were made by Narkomfin to fill the gap by borrowing. The gold loan originally announced in October 1922 had been poorly received, in spite of the moral pressure to subscribe, and the use of the bonds in part payment of wages.[3] The bonds were endorsed " not negotiable and not quotable on the exchange ". But they were, in fact, bought and sold on the free market at a heavy discount, so that all incentive to normal subscriptions quickly disappeared.[4] Bonds were being deposited by unwilling holders at Gosbank which in August was advancing 60 per cent of the face value on them. The attempt to put the hard-pressed industrial worker under contribution and

---

[1] In an interview in *Ekonomicheshaya Zhizn'*, October 26, 1923, Kutler explained the curtailment of credits to industry by the need to finance the harvest. This inverts the order of events, and alleges a direct connexion which did not exist ; but both measures were part of the same policy of rectifying the scissors by pressure on industry and by aid to agriculture.

[2] See pp. 36-37 above.

[3] For the " moral pressure " see *The Bolshevik Revolution, 1917–1923*, Vol. 2, p. 356 ; Sokolnikov admitted at TslK in July 1923 that the floating of the gold loan had met with great difficulties, but thought that, like the rye loan, it would go better in a second year (*Vtoraya Sessiya Vserossiiskogo Tsentral'nogo Ispolnitel'nogo Komiteta X Sozyva* (1923), pp. 127-128). For the payment of wages in bonds see p. 93 above.

[4] G. Y. Sokolnikov *et al.*, *Soviet Policy in Public Finance* (Stanford, 1931), p. 263 ; the market value is said (*ibid.* p. 265) to have sunk as low as 40 per cent of the face value, but this seems to have been after extensive forced placings.

mitigate the currency shortage by paying a part of his often belated wages in bonds was justified in a curious advertisement in the form of question and answer which appeared in the official economic journal :

Question : How can real wages be increased ?
Answer : By stopping the depreciation of money.
Question : How can the depreciation of money be stopped ?
Answer : By mass purchase of bonds of the gold loan.[1]

The advertisement was more successful as an appeal to the makers of financial policy than to the workers. On September 4, 1923, a decree was issued authorizing the payment of a graduated percentage of wages and salaries in state bonds, varying from 3 per cent of the lowest to 20 per cent of the highest wages ; and on the following day another decree prescribed that payers of income and property taxes and applicants for trading licences were obliged to subscribe for state bonds in proportion to the amounts due from them. A fortnight later yet another decree placed a similar obligation on contractors or agents undertaking business for state institutions or enterprises.[2] Yet even these measures, which converted the loan into a forced levy, failed to produce the desired results ; and Sokolnikov was obliged to announce in November 1923 that only 75 million rubles out of the 100 millions budgeted for a year earlier had been subscribed.[3]

The failure of the loan was already apparent when Narkomfin was confronted with an inescapable monetary crisis. In pre-revolutionary days it was a regular and necessary procedure to expand credit and the note issue each autumn to finance the marketing of the harvest and to contract them when the operation had been completed. This procedure had fallen out of use since 1918. Under war communism the collection of the harvest had taken the form of direct requisition. In the first two years of NEP much of it had been absorbed by the tax in kind. Nor in

[1] *Ekonomicheskaya Zhizn'*, August 9, 1923.
[2] *Sobranie Uzakonenii, 1923*, No. 96, art. 960 ; No. 98, art. 978 ; No. 99, art. 981 ; the schedule of compulsory subscriptions from payers of income-tax was revised in a further decree of October 1923 (*Sobranie Uzakonenii, 1924,* No. 9, art. 58).
[3] *Tret'ya Sessiya Tsentral'nogo Ispolnitel'nogo Komiteta Soyuza Sovetskikh Sotsialisticheskikh Respublik* (1924), p. 85.

any of these years had any reluctance been shown to expand the note issue to meet any and every demand. In 1923, when the peasant had for the first time the option to pay a substantial part of the tax in cash, a far higher proportion of the harvest was likely to reach the free market than in any year since the revolution; for the first time since the revolution the grain market was reopened in the Moscow Exchange.[1] Experts who remembered the old days had foreseen the need of an expansion of the currency to finance the purchase of grain, and had early canvassed " the possible use of the Sovznak as an instrument of credit for this purpose ".[2] The July decree limiting the issue of Sovznaks, though a necessary step towards the financial reform, wilfully shut the door on this solution; and nobody had any other to propose. An expansion of the chervonets issue to finance the harvest was ruled out by all parties concerned. In the first place, it was assumed, rightly or wrongly, that the peasant would refuse to accept payment in an unfamiliar currency which had not yet been seen in the country-side;[3] secondly, it was feared that a large issue of chervontsy would jeopardize the stability of the chervonets itself.

The first acute symptom of monetary stringency came from another quarter. In July 1923 STO gave its approval to a proposal of Narkomfin and the People's Commissariat of Communications (Narkomput') for the issue of " transport certificates " to the value of 5 million gold rubles in denominations of from 5 to 25 rubles which would be legal tender for all transportation costs and would be redeemable in any event in March 1924; and transport certificates to the value of 24 million gold rubles were actually issued between September 1923 and March 1924.[4] Apart from

---

[1] *Ekonomicheskaya Zhizn'*, August 10, 1923.

[2] *Ibid.* May 24, 1923; attention was drawn to the same problem by Lezhava, president of Komvnutorg, who thought that it would be necessary to delay the collection of the tax until the harvest had been marketed (*ibid.* June 28, 1923).

[3] The assumption, though universally made, may not have been correct; the story was told that, after large consignments of Sovznaks had been sent to Turkestan to purchase the 1923 cotton crop, the peasants nonplussed the author-ities by demanding payment in chervontsy (L. N. Yurovsky, *Na Putyakh k Denezhnoi Reforme* (1924), p. 72).

[4] *Sobranie Uzakonenii, 1923*, No. 87, art. 842; *Sobranie Uzakonenii, 1924*, No. 13, art. 120; No. 16, art. 154; No. 47, art. 445. The motive of the issue of the transport certificates was " to strengthen the resources of Narkomput' at the period of the realization of the harvest " (minute of Narkomfin quoted

this official, though unavowed, addition to the currency — the first tentative experiment in creating a subsidiary medium of exchange on the basis of the chervonets — the currency shortage produced the usual assortment of substitutes in the form of notes or certificates issued by local Soviets, factories or cooperatives. But when it became necessary to finance the harvest, these devices proved plainly inadequate, especially since the peasant had elected to pay an unexpectedly high proportion of the agricultural tax in cash.[1] The situation now defied all expert advice. On July 31, 1923, *Ekonomicheskaya Zhizn'* carried an article proposing that credits should be given to the peasantry " primarily in the form of goods " — a belated and desperate cry for a return to a " natural " economy. On August 3, Katsenellenbaum, a financial expert of Gosbank, argued conclusively in the same journal that a further issue of Soviet rubles to finance the harvest could not be avoided. Ten days later a leading article reiterated that " the question of credit for the grain collection has become extremely acute ", and reported that delays had already occurred in the collection owing to lack of currency.[2] In September the logic of the situation was at length perforce accepted by the financial purists of Narkomfin. The attempt registered in the decree of July 7 to limit and reduce the issue of Soviet rubles was abandoned as hopeless and all restraint thrown to the winds. Without any fresh decree, or any public announcement of the change of policy, the printing of Soviet rubles without limit in the quantities required to meet any demand was resumed.[3] The monthly issue

in Z. V. Atlas, *Ocherki po Istorii Denezhnogo Obrashcheniya v SSSR (1917–1925)* (1940), p. 211) ; Sokolnikov explained in public that its purpose was to help to cover the deficit of Narkomput', which had amounted to 140 million rubles in the past financial year and which it was hoped to reduce to 50 million rubles in the current year (*Vtoraya Sessiya Vserossiiskogo Tsentral'nogo Ispolnitel'nogo Komiteta X Sozyva* (1923), p. 116).

[1] Narkomfin had reckoned on half the tax being paid in kind and half in cash, or bonds of the rye loan ; in fact, rather more than half was paid in cash, nearly a quarter in bonds and only a quarter in kind (*Tret'ya Sessiya Tsentral'nogo Ispolnitel'nogo Komiteta Soyuza Sovetskikh Sotsialisticheskikh Respublik* (1924), p. 85). This was a favourable symptom, but caused a larger immediate demand for currency. At the end of the year the option of payment in kind was withdrawn altogether (*Ekonomicheskaya Zhizn'*, December 20, 1923).

[2] *Ekonomicheskaya Zhizn'*, August 15, 1923.

[3] A decree of September 29, 1923 (*Sobranie Uzakonenii, 1923*, No. 102, art. 1024) authorized the issue of Soviet ruble notes in the denomination of 5000 rubles (1923 pattern) ; this decree merely authorized the issue of a new

of Soviet rubles suddenly rose from 3400 millions, 4200 millions
and 6000 millions in July, August and September 1923 respectively
to 39,000 millions, 46,000 millions and 110,000 millions for the
last three months of the year.[1] The effects of this step were less
far-reaching than those of the unlimited note issues of an earlier
period. On the one hand public accounts and the accounts of
major branches of industry were now kept in chervontsy; and
on the other hand the Soviet ruble was now so thoroughly discredited that the issue could no longer yield any substantial profit
to the treasury: the rise in prices now quickly overtook every
increase in the note issue.[2] But the resumption of the unrestricted
flow of paper money, while it solved on familiar lines the overriding problem of bringing grain to the market, was, on a longer
view, a defeat for the financial policies of the past twelve months.
It not only introduced a fresh period of uncertainty and currency
speculation, but confused the major issue of the scissors crisis by
overlaying it with the more conspicuous phenomenon of an un-
controlled inflation.

and higher denomination to take account of the falling value of the ruble,
but set no limit on the amount of the issue. In later literature this decision was
often represented (e.g. by Rykov in *Trinadtsataya Konferentsiya Rossiiskoi Kommunisticheskoi Partii (Bol'shevikov)* (1924), p. 85) as the counterpart of the restriction of credit to industry : credits (in chervontsy) were withheld from industry
and transferred (in the form of credits in Soviet rubles) to agriculture. In fact,
the two decisions do not appear to have been in any way interdependent. The
essential difference between the two currencies was that the chervonets was
used only for credit purposes, not for financing government purchases (*Tret'ya
Sessiya Tsentral'nogo Ispolnitel'nogo Komiteta Soyuza Sovetskikh Sotsialisticheskikh Respublik* (1924), p. 98) ; the grain transactions fell partly in the latter
category.

    [1] See the table in L. N. Yurovsky, *Current Problems and Policy of the Soviet
Union* (1925), p. 106 ; some of the figures in this table have apparently been
corrected from the original table in L. N. Yurovsky, *Na Putyakh k Denezhnoi
Reforme* (2nd ed , 1924), p. 84.

    [2] Throughout the period of war communism prices tended to rise more
rapidly than the volume of currency in circulation (see *The Bolshevik Revolution,
1917-1923*, Vol. 2, pp. 258-259). With the wave of prosperity resulting from
NEP this process was interrupted between the summer of 1922 and the summer
of 1923, during which time the rise in prices merely kept pace with the rise in
the note issue, or sometimes lagged behind it. From June 1923 onwards prices
began again to outstrip the note issue, and this process was intensified when the
unlimited note issue was resumed in September. Finally, in January and February 1924, when the note issue rose by 100 per cent monthly, the monthly
increase in prices reached 200 per cent (see the table in Z. V. Atlas, *Ocherki po
Istorii Denezhnogo Obrashcheniya v SSSR (1917-1925)* (1940), p. 160).

The existence of a serious economic crisis, with sharp divisions in the ranks of the party and of its central committee, could now no longer be disguised. Industrial labour was in a state of ferment, almost of revolt. The restriction of credits had been a crippling blow to the consumer industries ; and the plight of heavy industry was recalled in a memorandum signed by Rykov and Pyatakov as president and vice-president of Vesenkha, and submitted to the party central committee on September 19, 1923, protesting that " the running of the industry entrusted to us is becoming increasingly difficult in the present set-up ".[1] The forced resumption of the unlimited issue of Sovznaks to finance the harvest cast doubt on the prospects of the financial reform and weakened confidence in Narkomfin and in its policies. It was in these conditions, with fundamental problems of agriculture and industry, of labour and finance, jostling one another in inextricable confusion that the central committee of the party set up at the end of September 1923 three committees, one to report on the scissors crisis, one on wages and one on the internal situation in the party.[2] The scissors committee, which ended by eclipsing altogether the wages committee, emerged as a committee on economic policy, not unreasonably treating the " scissors " as the focal point of the whole crisis. It was composed of 17 members, and was intended to represent all shades of opinion in the central committee, though these had not yet crystallized into groups. But neither Trotsky nor any of the more prominent dissentients in the central committee were in Moscow when the decision to set up the committee was taken.[3] Trotsky declined membership on the ground of lack of time ;[4] Pyatakov was sent on a mission to Germany ;[5] and Preobrazhensky apparently boycotted the committee, so that the principal spokesmen of the opposition did not

[1] The memorandum does not appear to have been published, but was quoted in Trotsky's letter of October 8, 1923 (see pp. 105-106 below).

[2] The decision to appoint the committees was not published, but the three committees were referred to in the decision of the central committee of October 25, 1923 (*VKP(B) v Rezolyutsiyakh* (1941), i, 531 ; for the committee on internal party affairs see pp. 294-295, 304 below. [3] See p. 294 below.

[4] *Trinadtsataya Konferentsiya Rossiiskoi Kommunisticheskoi Partii (Bol'-shevikov)* (1924), p. 7. This is Rykov's account ; Trotsky's refusal to serve on the committee accorded with the tactics pursued by him, since Lenin's collapse in March, of refusing to bring into the open his differences with his colleagues in the Politburo. [5] See p. 219 below.

make themselves heard.[1] This left them with free hands to attack
the recommendations of the committee, but deprived them of an
opportunity to participate actively in the formulation of policy at a
moment when external pressures had evidently alarmed the party
leadership and made it amenable to some measure of conciliation.

But scarcely had the scissors committee begun its work when
Trotsky, betrayed by his own impatience or seeing the hopeless-
ness of further argument within the Politburo, took a momentous
step. On October 8, 1923, once more playing a lone hand and
apparently without consulting the group in the central committee
which broadly shared his views, he addressed a letter to the
central committee which was in effect an indictment of the policy
of the Politburo. Beginning with a reference to the reappearance
of fractional groupings within the party, Trotsky traced it to two
causes : " (a) the radically incorrect and unhealthy régime within
the party, and (b) the dissatisfaction of the workers and peasants
with the grievous economic situation, which has been brought
about as the result not only of objective difficulties, but of flagrant
radical errors of economic policy ". In spite of the injunctions of
Lenin and the resolution of the twelfth party congress, Gosplan
and the principle of planning had been thrust more and more into
the background. Decisions about economic policy were more
than ever being taken by the Politburo " without preliminary
preparation, out of their planned sequence ". Nationalized
industry had been sacrificed to " the self-sufficient (i.e. not subordinated to the economic plan) character of our financial policy ".
The price scissors, which destroyed the economic link between
industry and the peasant, were " equivalent to the liquidation of
the New Economic Policy ". But the policy of the scissors committee, which was attempting to solve the problem by arbitrary
price reductions, was ineffective.

The very creation of a committee to lower prices [wrote
Trotsky] is an eloquent and devastating indication of the way
in which a policy which ignores the significance of planned
and manipulative regulation is driven by the force of its own

[1] Stalin at the thirteenth party conference accused Preobrazhensky and other
members of the opposition of " ignoring the work " of the scissors committee
(*Trinadtsataya Konferentsiya Rossiiskoi Kommunisticheskoi Partii (Bol'shevikov)*
(1924), p. 150).

H

inevitable consequences *into attempts to command prices in the style of war communism.*

The right approach to the peasant was through the proletariat; in economic terms this meant that the rationalization of state industry was the key to the closing of the scissors.[1]

Emboldened by this initiative, 46 leading party members, including several members of the central committee, now drew up a policy manifesto which was issued on October 15, 1923, and came to be known as " the platform of the 46 "; it was signed, among others, by Pyatakov, Preobrazhensky, Antonov-Ovseenko, Osinsky, V. Smirnov, I. N. Smirnov, Kaganovich, Sapronov, Serebryakov and Rozengolts. The manifesto declared that " the casual, unconsidered and unsystematic character of the decisions of the central committee " had brought the country to the verge of a " grave economic crisis ", the symptoms of which were the currency crisis, the credit crisis, the sales crisis in industry, the low prices of agricultural products and wage inequalities. Having deplored the " absence of leadership " which had been responsible for these failures, the manifesto passed on from its economic diagnosis to a general attack on the dictatorial behaviour of the party machine, ending with the demand for an immediate conference to consider the situation.[2] About the time the platform of the 46 was handed in, Trotsky's colleagues in the Politburo replied to his letter of October 8; and this reply provoked a further letter from Trotsky, in which he once again asserted the issue of principle :

> I stood and stand on the point of view that one of the most important causes of our economic crisis is the absence of correct uniform regulation from above.[3]

But this further exchange between Trotsky and the Politburo moved over into the field of personal and political recrimination,[4] and contributed nothing new to the economic discussion, though

[1] Lengthy extracts from the letter were published in *Sotsialisticheskii Vestnik* (Berlin), No. 11 (81), May 24, 1924, pp. 9-10 ; the full text has never been published. For the political aspects of Trotsky's letter see pp. 295-297 below.

[2] For the political aspects of the platform see pp. 297-298 below ; for the full text see pp. 367-373 below.

[3] Extracts from the letter are in *Sotsialisticheskii Vestnik* (Berlin), No. 11 (81), May 24, 1924, pp. 11-12.

[4] For a further discussion of these letters see pp. 295-297, 299 below.

it made clear the acuteness of a crisis which turned largely on economic issues. Confronted with this situation, the party central committee (sitting jointly with the central control commission which was competent for the disciplinary issues involved [1]) passed on October 25, 1923, a resolution instructing the Politburo to hasten the work of the three committees set up by the central committee a month earlier, and to take any necessary action on them, reporting to the next session of the central committee in January 1924.[2] What might be crucial decisions were thus transferred into the safer hands of the Politburo. On November 1, 1923, *Ekonomicheskaya Zhizn'* discovered a crisis which " economically and politically threatens the very existence of the Soviet power " ; and on November 7, the anniversary of the revolution, following an article by Zinoviev, *Pravda* announced that its columns would be thrown open to spokesmen of the different trends and opinions which were dividing the party.[3]

The obscurity of the scissors crisis and the wide variety of the explanations offered to account for it compelled the scissors committee to range far and wide over the field of economic policy. The wages committee may presumably be held responsible for the somewhat more liberal wages policy adopted towards the end of 1923.[4] But no record exists of its work, and the only formal statement of the party attitude to wages at this juncture was a section included in the report of the scissors committee. The proceedings of the scissors committee were not reported. That Narkomfin was in an intransigent mood, and unwilling to brook any challenge to the main principles of economic and financial policy, was shown by an unusually outspoken speech made by Sokolnikov at a special meeting of the presidium of Gosplan on October 13, 1923. Sokolnikov reacted against the doctrine assiduously preached in Gosplan that the planning of credit was a necessary part of the planning of industrial production. Credit, he explained, was a matter of commerce and banking. In the

[1] For these issues see pp. 300-301 below.

[2] *VKP (B) v Rezolyutsiyakh* (1941), i, 531-532.

[3] For this article and the announcement see p. 301 below.

[4] The decision to resume the unlimited issue of Sovznaks, though taken for the benefit of the peasant, automatically eased the currency stringency which had been responsible for the delays in paying industrial wages. *Trud*, October 4, 1923, claimed that delays in payment were gradually disappearing, though " loss on exchange does still occur ".

words of a press report of the meeting, he " categorically protested against the introduction of obligatory planning into the work of credit institutions ". He maintained that " credit is not, like production, amenable to the compulsion of planning ", and that production must be brought into line with credit, not vice versa. In vain might Smilga reply that, if Gosplan could not plan credit, it could never advance towards a general plan for the economy ; in vain might Krzhizhanovsky protest against the subordination of Gosplan " to the spontaneous principles of the market ".[1] Never since the revolution had the doctrine of the supremacy of finance, as the stern executor of the laws of the market, been so openly proclaimed ; never had NEP been so uncompromisingly inter- preted as the victory of *laissez-faire* over planning. But the position of the critics was weakened by their close approximation to the views expressed in the platform of the 46 with its direct challenge to the policy of the central committee. On these fundamental issues the scissors committee was bound to range itself behind the official line, which was still the line of Narkomfin.

When it came, however, to the specific question of prices which the committee had been summoned to consider, the line no longer seemed so clear and impregnable. The theory of trade as originally developed under NEP had postulated a salutary sub- mission to the laws of the market ; communists were adjured by Lenin to " learn to trade ", to " adapt themselves " to the pro- cesses of buying and selling.[2] The state machine did not purport to regulate trade. With the progressive substitution of payment in money for payment in kind in the collection of the agricultural tax, and with the gradual disappearance of the system of payment, or part payment, of wages in kind, the buying and selling of agricultural products passed more and more into private hands ; and NEP left the peasant free to sell his " surplus " at whatever price he could get. Nationalized industries producing manu- factured goods had been instructed to work for a profit. The application of the principles of *khozraschet* left them free to fix wholesale prices for their output in accordance with the con- ditions of the market. An initial attempt to control prices in the autumn of 1921 had quickly been abandoned, and the commission

---

[1] The report of the meeting is in *Ekonomicheskaya Zhizn'*, October 16, 1923.
[2] See *The Bolshevik Revolution, 1917–1923*, Vol. 2, pp. 333-335.

for internal trade (Komvnutorg) set up in May 1922 became little more than a statistical office. Those were the days when Narkomfin publicly defended nepmen from the charge of being speculators, and argued that the regulation of prices was contrary to the principles of the market economy established by NEP.[1]

This confident belief in the virtues of *laissez-faire* did not survive the winter of 1922–1923, when industrial prices, bolstered by the newly organized syndicates, began to soar at the expense of the peasant and of the urban consumer. In the new conditions, Narkomfin whole-heartedly accepted the necessity of readjusting the balance in favour of the peasant, though it hoped at first to achieve this result by stimulating grain exports and without resort to direct intervention. The prejudice against price regulation, as against everything that savoured of the practices of war communism, died hard. At a conference of representatives of the newly established Exchanges in January 1923, Lezhava, the president of Komvnutorg, submitted a set of theses arguing that the " regulation of prices " should be concentrated in a single organ with the object of promoting a further extension of trade. But, when Lezhava went on to complain that " the establishment of prices has hitherto been purely spontaneous ", and hoped that the newly established Exchanges would help to lower prices by introducing improved conditions of marketing, Sokolnikov retorted that everything turned on achieving financial stability ; and the conference, though it apparently accepted Lezhava's theses in principle, ended with a resolution expressing no more than a pious wish for the reduction of industrial costs and prices.[2]

---

[1] See *ibid.* Vol. 2, pp. 343-344. According to a later reminiscence of Zinoviev, Komvnutorg was set up rather casually as the result of a telephone message from Lenin in order to " study the market " : in Zinoviev's words, " we marched against private capital light-heartedly, with a crutch " (*Trinadtsatyi S"ezd Rossiiskoi Kommunisticheskoi Partii (Bol'shevikov)* (1924), p. 91) Ekonomicheskaya Zhizn', December 13, 1922, complained that " there has not been a single case of refusal [by Komvnutorg] to confirm prices submitted by the syndicates from the standpoint of cost or of market conditions " ; as Bogdanov said at the twelfth party congress, " the attempt to influence the market by compulsory price-fixing was a fiasco " (*Dvenadtsatyi S"ezd Rossiiskoi Kommunisticheskoi Partii (Bol'shevikov)* (1923), p. 313).

[2] For Lezhava's theses and the approval of them by the conference see *Ekonomicheskaya Zhizn'*, January 11, 14, 1923 ; for the debate between Lezhava and Sokolnikov, *Trud*, January 17, 1923 ; for the final resolution, *Ekonomicheskaya Zhizn'*, January 19, 1923.

At the twelfth party congress in April 1923, Trotsky graphically diagnosed the crisis as a crisis of the prices at which industrial and agricultural products changed hands. But the obvious conclusion was not immediately drawn either by himself or by others. The resolution of the congress attributed the trouble to " *commercial incompetence* which cannot be justified by the conditions of the present extremely narrow market ", and made no proposal for price control, contenting itself with a conventional compliment to the cooperatives as " the trading apparatus which must in ever increasing proportions unite state industry with agriculture " and a conventional recommendation to all trading organs to cut down overheads and adapt themselves to the requirements of the consumer.[1]

By the autumn of 1923, when the scissors committee met, the argument that the state could not and should not intervene in the fixing of prices was discredited on all sides. In August *Ekonomicheskaya Zhizn'* had demanded an extension of the powers of Komvnutorg with a mandate to pass from a " passive " to an " active " rôle and stabilize prices of industrial goods in terms of the chervonets ; and *Trud* had followed suit a week later.[2] Down to October 1, 1923, the scissors continued to open ; and nobody could predict that they had reached the limit of the disparity. None of the indirect devices to compel industry to lower its prices had yet borne fruit. On October 3 Komvnutorg issued an order, in defiance of a protest from the textile syndicate, reducing the wholesale price of cotton cloth by some 20 per cent.[3] On the following day, in order to forestall similar action, the linen trust announced a reduction in prices " in order to satisfy general state interests ", and this was followed by further announcements of voluntary reductions in wholesale prices by other trusts.[4] The blow struck by the action of Gosbank in restricting credits was being driven home. The spokesmen of Narkomfin, who had the ear of the party leadership, swung round sharply to a policy of price control, however incompatible this might appear with the hitherto accepted assumptions of NEP. At the meeting of

[1] *VKP(B) v Rezolyutsiyakh* (1941), i, 482.
[2] *Ekonomicheskaya Zhizn'*, August 15, 1923 ; *Trud*, August 23, 1923.
[3] *Ibid.* October 4, 1923.
[4] *Ibid.* October 6, 1923 ; *ibid.* October 12, 1923.

VTsIK in November 1923 Sokolnikov stoutly maintained that the " state regulation of prices is indispensable as a means of struggling against the abuses of monopoly " ; [1] and to critics who attacked price regulation as a " violation of NEP " he retorted that, if this was true, then NEP was no better than " capitalist America ", where " the small peasant and worker is powerless against the trusts, against the Rockefellers, Morgans and the rest ".[2] Coming from Narkomfin this was new language ; and, though it was in the first instance only another move in the campaign of Narkomfin against the industrial trusts, it also showed how acutely the stresses set up by NEP were now beginning to affect every part of the economy.

The principle of the control of wholesale prices had thus secured general approval by the time the scissors committee met. But the control, of retail prices was a different matter. Retail trade had largely escaped control, in so far as it had survived at all, even under war communism, and to encourage it to flourish by the removal of restrictions had been one of the declared purposes of NEP. Private traders were responsible for 83 per cent of the retail trade of the country ; [3] and the vast majority of trading units were country pedlars or stall-holders in markets and bazaars ; [4] even in the towns the small shopkeeper predominated. If it had been impossible to stop " bagging " in the days of war communism, the notion of bringing this scattered private trade under control in the laxer conditions of NEP was at first dismissed as wholly utopian. But the popular argument that it was retail prices which concerned the purchaser, and that it was useless to reduce wholesale prices if this merely meant additional profit margins for the middleman, was difficult to rebut. The campaign against the nepmen gathered strength, and articles appeared in the press showing how the retail prices of articles of mass consumption were swollen by the number of hands through which they passed

---

[1] *Tret'ya Sessiya Tsentral'nogo Ispolnitel'nogo Komiteta Soyuza Sovetskikh Sotsialisticheskikh Respublik* (1924), p. 100.
[2] G. Y. Sokolnikov, *Finansovaya Politika Revolyutsii*, ii (1926), 97.
[3] See p. 11 above.
[4] Of the trading licences issued in 1923, 314,000, or 66 per cent of the total number, fell within the first two categories, i.e. pedlars and open markets (Rykov in *Pravda*, January 4, 1924) ; for the categories of licences see *The Bolshevik Revolution, 1917–1923*, Vol. 2, p. 337, note 2.

on the way from producer to consumer.[1]   In spite of these con-
tentions, however, it was not surprising that the scissors committee " hesitated for a very long time " before it decided to
include in its recommendations a control of retail prices.[2]   It
cautiously proposed that control should be limited in the first
instance to " products which are uniform in quality and which
we hold in great quantity " ; [3] and salt, paraffin and sugar were
selected for the first experiment.

The general regulation of wholesale prices and the regulation
of retail prices of selected commodities was the only important
innovation in the recommendations of the scissors committee.
The principle involved not only a substantial concession to the
critics, but a serious derogation from NEP, since it reintroduced at
a vital point the state control of trade which NEP had expressly
abandoned.   The ingenious and eccentric Larin, now converted
into a strong supporter of the official policy, declared that, in
superseding " commercial freedom " by " the compulsory fixing
of industrial prices by a single state centre ", the resolution paved
the way for the transition from " state capitalism " to " state
socialism ".   This was, he argued, the " historic significance "
of the recommendation of the scissors committee : it was not yet
socialism, but it marked " the real ending of the economic retreat ".

[1] This was demonstrated for salt and for textiles in *Ekonomicheskaya Zhizn'*,
October 5, 10, 1923.   Large variations in retail prices were also shown ; an
arshin of cotton cloth sold wholesale by the textile trusts at 32 kopeks was sold
at retail prices varying from 70 kopeks to two rubles.   Nogin, an influential
party member and director of a textile trust, a former worker, attacked the
middleman as the cause of inflated prices in *Pravda*, October 16, 1923.
[2] This was admitted by Rykov in his speech of December 29, 1923, reported
in *Pravda*, January 4, 1924 ; the gradual change of front can be traced in the
columns of *Ekonomicheskaya Zhizn'*.   A leading article of October 23, 1923, firmly
demanded " a lowering of wholesale prices of articles of mass consumption ",
but still hedged on the control of retail prices ; on November 15 a signed article
by Shekanov argued that the control of retail prices, however difficult, was
indispensable if the scissors crisis was to be overcome ; on November 18 a
leading article cautiously came out for the control of retail prices though still
insisting on its difficulty ; in the same issue Lezhava maintained that it was
easy to fix retail prices for standard articles like salt and kerosene, though
difficult for manufactured goods of variable quality.   A conference of " communist managers ", meeting on November 13, 1923, set up a commission to
draft a programme of desiderata for industry ; the programme included " the
establishment of retail prices for manufactured goods through state planning
organizations (Komvnutorg, Gosplan) " (*Pravda*, December 20, 1923).
[3] Kamenev in *Pravda*, December 30, 1923.

It was the first " unequivocal " and " correct " revision of one
of the most important aspects of NEP.[1] Nobody else was anxious
to raise these issues of principle, or to probe the relation of price-
fixing to NEP. For the moment the new proposal seemed an
obvious, if modest, contribution to solving the problem of the
scissors crisis. But it laid up new difficulties and new precedents
for the future.

The resolution drafted by the scissors committee and unanimously adopted by it was submitted to the Politburo some
time in December 1923.[2] While it reflected the ambiguities and
embarrassments inherent in NEP and made some concessions to
the critics, its main structure and outlook represented an unqualified victory for the party leadership. It opened with a long
introduction designed to throw into relief the predominant rôle
of peasant agriculture as the factor that must continue to govern
Soviet economic policy. This appeared to represent Lenin's last
injunction to the party, and was the most convenient vantage-
point from which Trotsky's criticism could be repelled and discredited. The scissors crisis, while admittedly acute and requiring
specific remedies, was not to be treated as a fundamental crisis
calling in question the validity of the policy pursued since the
twelfth party congress. Continuity of present official policy with
that of the past was emphasized by including in the introduction
a carefully pruned excerpt from the resolution on industry which
Trotsky had sponsored at the twelfth party congress. The first
sentence quoted was the one which had been inserted by the
majority of the central committee against Trotsky's opposition,
and insisted on the " primary significance " of agriculture " for
the whole economy of the Soviet power ". The following passage
in the congress resolution, in which Trotsky had argued that the
predominance of agriculture could be overcome only by the

---

[1] *Trud*, December 8, 1923 ; *Pravda*, December 30, 1923.

[2] This account was given by Kamenev in his speech of December 27, 1923,
reported in *Pravda*, December 30, 1923, and confirmed by Rykov at the thirteenth party conference (*Trinadtsataya Konferentsiya Rossiiskoi Kommunisticheskoi Partii (Bol'shevikov)* (1924), pp. 6-7, where it is expressly stated that the
work of the committee " proceeded with complete unanimity ") ; Pyatakov and
Preobrazhensky attacked the resolution at the conference, but made no reference to the proceedings of the committee.

development of heavy industry and of electrification and that the party must spare no efforts or sacrifices to bring this about, but that success depended not only on progress at home, but on the progress of the revolution " beyond the borders of Russia ", was omitted altogether. Then, passing over the opening words of the next sentence (which ran " Keeping the international prospect always in view "), the excerpt went on :

> Our party should at the same time, in appraising any step it takes, never forget or leave out of account for a moment the predominant importance in practice of peasant agriculture. Not merely neglect of this factor, but even insufficient attention to it, would be fraught with innumerable dangers both in the economic and in the purely political sphere, since it would inevitably shatter or weaken that alliance between the proletariat and the peasantry, that confidence of the peasantry in the proletariat, which for the present historical period of transition are among the fundamental bastions of the dictatorship of the proletariat.

Having thus cautiously revoked the April compromise by removing one of its two main pillars, the resolution of the scissors committee proceeded to attribute the current " sales crisis " to inadequate realization of the predominant importance of the peasant, to lack of coordination between different parts of the economy and, first and foremost, to the failure of state industry and commerce to make its way to the mass peasant market.[1] The introduction set the tone of the whole resolution, and was designed to mark a shift away from the moderate position which Trotsky had still been able to defend at the twelfth party congress. The body of the resolution reviewed each sector of the economy in turn and recorded " practical conclusions " for each. Agriculture (Rykov noted it as significant that this was the first occasion on which agriculture had been given pride of place in a party resolution [2]) was to be assisted by an extension of credit, by curtailment of taxation and the organization of grain exports. Industry, which

---

[1] *VKP(B) v Rezolyutsiyakh* (1941), i, 545-546, which contains the text of the resolution as amended by the thirteenth party conference, there being no amendments in this section ; comparison of the excerpt from the twelfth party congress resolution with the original text (*ibid.* i, 476) shows that the omission of the crucial passage quoted above is unmarked, but that marks of omission occur at a later point in the excerpt where no omission has, in fact, been made.

[2] *Pravda*, January 1, 1924.

lay under the imputation of pushing up prices and earning excessive
profits, was pointedly reminded that " *socialist* accumulation "
(the phrase popularized by Trotsky at the twelfth congress), while
it required that prices should cover costs and an " indispensable
minimum profit ", did not justify prices beyond the reach of the
mass of the population, and was adjured to adopt measures to
rationalize production, increase productivity and reduce overhead
costs. A gesture was made in favour of heavy industry. Now that
the fuel situation had improved, it had become " possible and
indispensable " to concentrate the attention of the party on the
metallurgical industry, which must now " be advanced to the
front rank and receive from the state support of all kinds, especially
financial, on a far larger scale than in the previous year ".[1] But
this statement of principle did not for the moment attract much
notice, and no corresponding recommendation appeared in the
summary of concrete proposals at the end of the resolution.

While, however, the resolution as a whole seemed to mark a
further victory in defence of the *status quo* and a defeat for the
planners, the element of compromise was not wholly absent. The
aim of wages policy was declared to be "a rise in wages corresponding to a rise in industry and in the productivity of labour ".
Low wages were to be brought up to the " average level "; the
" severest penalties " were to be imposed for any delay in the
payment of wages and the workers compensated for losses on
exchange due to such delays. The payment of bonuses was to
be sanctioned only where a net profit had been earned, and only
in individual cases for meritorious service, with the assent of the
trade unions.[2] Attention was now to be given to housing for the

------

[1] Gosplan had prepared in the summer of 1923 a " five-year plan " for the
development of the metallurgical industry (*Ekonomicheskaya Zhizn'*, August 9,
1923), and on December 1 was discussing " a five-year perspective plan " for
industry as a whole (*ibid.* December 4, 1923); but such plans were at this time
little more than academic exercises.

[2] The campaign against the salaries of specialists (see pp. 41-42 above) continued throughout the autumn. A decree of November 2, 1923, prescribed
that all agreements providing for " personal " salaries should be registered with
Narkomtrud (*Sobranie Uzakonenii, 1924*, No. 11, art. 90). Later the same
month an agreement was reached between Narkomtrud and the trade union
central council on specialists' salaries, which was recorded with satisfaction in a
leading article in *Trud* referring to " the capriciousness of individual salaries "
and " the present bacchanalia of ' rates for specialists ' " (*Trud*, December 1
1923).

workers.   These were tangible concessions to the dangerous
proletarian discontent.   The monopoly of foreign trade was to
be maintained intact and a favourable trade balance sought.   In
the sphere of internal trade, regulation of wholesale prices of
articles of mass consumption, especially for the peasant market,
was to be strengthened and extended to retail prices, pressure on
which would be exercised through state and cooperative trading
institutions and through credit policy; legal maximum retail
prices were to be fixed for salt, paraffin and sugar.   This section
of the resolution went surprisingly far to meet those critics who
had insisted on the need for action to counter the dangers of
NEP :

> The question of the relation between state capital and
> private capital in the economy is the most important question
> of the present moment, since it determines the question of the
> relation of the class forces of the proletariat, whose strength is
> based on nationalized industry, and of the new bourgeoisie,
> whose strength is based on the element of the free market. . . .
> One of the fundamental conditions of the strengthening of
> our positions against private capital is a price policy. . . . In
> order to subordinate the activity of private capital to the general
> direction of the economic policy of the Soviet power far-
> reaching measures must be taken to regulate the prices of
> fundamental objects of mass consumption.

The critics were to be appeased by turning the edge of the new
policy against the ever unpopular nepman.   It was recognized
that " private accumulation " should be controlled through fiscal
policy : " taxation of luxuries should be unswervingly carried out,
and the struggle with vicious speculators, etc. intensified ".
Finally, the transition to a stable currency, the crown of the whole
policy, was to be hastened by the balancing of the budget and the
curtailment of the issue of Sovznaks ;   credit was to be cheapened,
but with due regard to its " regulating rôle " in the economy, the
activity of Gosbank and other credit institutions being coordinated
" through Gosplan and STO with the organs administering
industry and trade ".   The resolution ended with the usual tribute
to the importance of planning and to the need to strengthen
Gosplan.

The resolution of the scissors committee was approved by
the Politburo, apparently without modification, on December 24,

1923. It was published in *Pravda* on the following day; but
some errors crept into the text, and it was reprinted in full in
Pravda of December 28, 1923 — a tribute to its unusual importance. The resolution as a whole was a conflation of different
and sometimes conflicting opinions. The sections on wages and
on internal trade bore witness to an attempt to maintain the
uneasy balance established at the twelfth congress. But its main
effect was a vote of confidence in the policy of the central committee and of the Politburo. It confirmed the peasant in his
commanding position as the main beneficiary of NEP and the
arbiter of the Soviet economy.

CHAPTER 4

THE CLOSING OF THE SCISSORS

WHILE the scissors committee pursued its deliberations in the last months of 1923, the grave economic situation which had prompted its appointment underwent a substantial change for the better. The harvest, the outcome of which was still the dominant factor in the Soviet economy, had been excellent for the second year in succession.[1] The resumption of grain exports, and the promise of their further expansion, brought about a recovery in agricultural prices at the same moment when the contraction of credit and other official pressures had begun to force down industrial prices. The scissors began to close. Agricultural prices which stood on October 1, 1923, at 49 per cent of the 1913 level for wholesale prices and 58 per cent for retail prices had risen by January 1, 1924, to 68 and 77 per cent respectively. Industrial prices fell during the same period from 171 to 134 per cent of the 1913 level for wholesale prices and from 187 to 141 per cent for retail prices.[2] Nor did these changes bring the disasters which had been predicted for industry. The process of concentrating industry, and especially heavy industry, in a smaller number of the more efficient units, which had been undertaken in the spring, and had received the blessing of the twelfth party congress,[3] though it had in the short run undoubtedly aggravated the problem of unemployment, was now bearing fruit in the form of increased efficiency and lower production costs.[4] In a report of December 1923 Rykov, the president

[1] *Ekonomicheskaya Zhizn'*, October 1-2, 1923, gave a figure of 2756 million puds for the grain harvest of 1923 against 2790 millions for 1922 ; the harvest had surpassed that of 1922 in the Ukraine but fallen short elsewhere.

[2] See the table in *Trinadtsatyi S"ezd Rossiiskoi Kommunisticheskoi Partii (Bol'shevikov)* (1924), p. 396.

[3] See pp. 10 and 25 above.

[4] A report on the results of concentration was published in *Ekonomicheskaya Zhizn'*, October 14, 1923 ; see also Bogdanov's report to VTsIK in November

of Vesenkha, claimed that the total production of industry during the past year had been double that of 1920 (the worst year of the recession), though the heavy industries still lagged behind the consumer industries ; coal-mining and the metallurgical industries had achieved 159 per cent of the 1920 total, textiles 320 per cent. But, though heavy industry as a whole had still reached only 34 per cent of the 1913 figure, recovery had begun even in this most recalcitrant sector of the economy.[1]

With production increasing all round, and the trend of prices which had produced the scissors crisis reversed, the " sales crisis " of the preceding summer was gradually resolved. When the harvest had been realized and the agricultural tax collected in kind or in cash, the peasant still had money which falling prices could tempt him to spend. From October onwards the market began slowly to expand. In December a report of Vesenkha somewhat grudgingly admitted that " the acutest symptoms of a monetary and commercial crisis have begun to be overcome since the middle of November ", and that there had been " some revival of buying in connexion with the fall in prices and the completion of the collection of the tax in kind ". The report went on to describe the position of industry as still " serious and precarious ", and to maintain that " a further reduction of prices is impossible ".[2] But for the moment the all-round improvement was undeniable. Its effects were far-reaching and important. It paved the way for the consummation of the long delayed currency reform ; and it stultified the case of the opposition which was fighting on an economic platform drawn up at the beginning of October, when the crisis was in its most acute stage and the economy could plausibly be depicted as standing on the brink of disaster. Nothing had occurred to affect the issues of principle

1923 (*Tret'ya Sessiya Tsentral'nogo Ispolnitel'nogo Komiteta Soyuza Sovetskikh Sotsialisticheskikh Respublik* (1924), pp. 47-48). For detailed figures see Y. S. Rozenfeld, *Promyshlennaya Politika SSSR* (1926), pp. 225-226 ; the most spectacular results seem to have been obtained in Petrograd, where the engineering trust was working in November 1923 at 80-90 per cent of capacity (against 11 per cent at the beginning of the year).
    [1] *Trud*, December 12, 1923. According to *Ekonomicheskaya Zhizn'*, October 1-2, 1923, output in heavy industry in 1922-23 had increased by 15 per cent over the preceding year, the number of workers employed by 8 per cent, the productivity of the individual worker by 10 per cent ; the corresponding increases in light industry were 57, 21 and 26 per cent.
    [2] *Pravda*, December 20, 1923.

at stake. But the economic climate had almost imperceptibly changed to the detriment of the critics and to the advantage of those who upheld the general soundness of the current line.

The new conditions had not been fully realized when the resolution of the scissors committee was endorsed by the Politburo on December 24, 1923. Its publication threw a fresh pebble into the already turbulent sea of party discussion.[1] It was hailed by the party leaders as a victory for the policy of the central committee, and attacked as such by the opposition. Kamenev expounded the resolution with cautious moderation in a speech to a gathering of party secretaries of the Krasno-Presnya district on December 27, 1923. There was nothing in it to justify the assertion of the 46 that the crisis had brought the country to the ɔrink of ruin or the assumption that a revision of " the very foundations of our economic policy " was in question. The text of the resolution was not to be treated as sacrosanct; perhaps the points about wages and the function of the trade unions might, in particular, be amended or supplemented. But in general it represented " the only true line " and " a continuation of the line indicated by Vladimir Ilich in his last articles ". In this restricted gathering no dissentient voice was raised, and the resolution was unanimously endorsed.[2]

Two days later Rykov reviewed the situation and the outlook in even more optimistic terms at a large meeting of Moscow party workers. But here the opposition put in an appearance, and Osinsky submitted in the names of himself, Preobrazhensky, Pyatakov and I. N. Smirnov, a long counter-resolution which remained the most detailed statement of the opposition case. It once more attributed the crisis to " the lack of a plan uniting the work of all sectors of the state economy "; in default of such a plan the attempt had been made " to regulate the economy from a financial centre ". Evidence of these errors was found in " the chaotic structure of our industry ", which should have been remedied by bringing the trusts under the more direct control of Vesenkha, and in a fluctuating credit policy, which had at first showered credit too generously on industry and then suddenly curtailed it. The statement attacked the policy of instructing the

---

[1] For the general discussion see pp. 308-322 below.
[2] *Pravda*, December 30, 1923, January 1, 1924.

trusts to aim only at an " indispensable minimum profit ". The correct policy was to base the state budget on profits earned by industry from the market ; and price reductions should be sought through an expansion of production. Finally, the policy of the financial reform and of the active balance in foreign trade was subjected to attack. Soviet Russia " cannot afford the luxury of going over from bank-notes to a gold currency " ; and " goods intervention " (defined as " partial importation from abroad of goods which we lack and of which the price has particularly increased ") was advocated, as well as the import of capital goods, if necessary by means of a foreign loan.[1] This, like every other, opposition platform regarded the development of industry, not the appeasement of the peasant, as the key to recovery, and rejected the supremacy of the market and of the financial mechanism in favour of an economic plan. To this extent it involved a challenge to the principles of NEP. But unity was lacking. Little was done to weld the forces of the attack into a coherent whole ; and the impression remained both of a captious eagerness to find fault with every item of the official policy and of the lack of any concrete alternative. These weaknesses made it easy for the party leaders to appeal in the name of party loyalty even to those who sympathized with the opposition on this or that point of its platform.

Apart from measures of persuasion and of party discipline, two steps were taken to commend the resolution of the scissors committee to a restive party opinion. The first was an active campaign against the nepmen, which fitted in logically enough with the decision to re-establish control over trade through price-fixing : the campaign also no doubt served as an outlet to relieve the feverish tension of the party discussion by turning the indigna-tion of the malcontents against a familiar scapegoat. At the end of December 1923, at the same moment as the publication of the resolution of the scissors committee, the GPU made a sweep of places of luxury entertainment and other resorts of prosperous traders and speculators, arrested several hundred of them and expelled them from Moscow, some to the provinces and some to

---

[1] Rykov's speech is in *Pravda*, January 1, 3 and 4, 1924, the opposition resolution in *Pravda*, January 1. Translations of both are in *Internationale Presse-Korrespondenz*, No. 13, January 28, 1924, pp. 111-122, 139-140.

I

concentration camps.[1] The number of those expelled was not
large enough to disrupt the trading community, but large enough
to serve as an example and to make an impression of a vigorous
party offensive against private capitalists. The nepmen continued to flourish, not least as an indispensable adjunct of the
nationalized sector of the economy. But the campaign took the
sting out of the opposition charge against the central committee of apathy in face of the growth of private capital under
NEP and of craven surrender to the spontaneous forces of the
market.

The other step taken at this time was an attempt, foreshadowed in Kamenev's speech of December 27, 1923, to appease
labour unrest and opposition by some concession on the wages
question. Throughout the autumn attempts had been made to
overcome the scandal of delayed wage payments and juggling
with the exchange; and on December 29, 1923, a decree was
issued prohibiting the practice, expressly sanctioned four months
earlier, of making part payment of wages in bonds of the state
loan.[2] But this no longer sufficed to allay the discontent of the
workers. A fresh problem had arisen of which no account had been
taken in the deliberations of the scissors committee. Since the
autumn a determined attempt had been made by Narkomfin to
bring about a change-over in the basis of wage payments from
the goods ruble to the chervonets. This move accorded with the
long established hostility of Narkomfin to the goods ruble as the
rival to the gold ruble or the chervonets, and with the desire to
prepare the way in all possible directions for the final establishment of the single gold currency. But it also had a special
significance at a time when labour unrest had brought into the

---

[1] *Izvestiya*, December 28, 1923, reported that 1000 " socially dangerous "
persons had been arrested and expelled, that a " cleansing operation " was in
process and that the arrests had caused " dismay and perplexity among the
nepmen ". *Sotsialisticheskii Vestnik* (Berlin), No. 1 (71), January 10, 1924,
p. 13, put the number at 2000 and gave further details ; Zinoviev, referring to
this account at the thirteenth party congress, did not question its accuracy, but
merely denied that the arrests meant " the end of NEP " (*Trinadtsatyi S"ezd
Rossiiskoi Kommunisticheskoi Partii (Bol'shevikov)* (1924), p. 94 ; cf. a further
reference *bid*. p. 96 to the " nepmen whom we expelled ").

[2] *Sbornik Dekretov, Postanovlenii, Rasporyazhenii i Prikazov po Narodnomu
Khozyaistvu*, No. 3 (15), December 23, p. 37 ; for the earlier decree see p. 100
above.

open the scandal of the delays in the payment of wages and of the juggling with the price-index, and had forced the abandonment or partial abandonment of these malpractices. As a result of the rise in chervonets prices, which was equivalent to the fall of the chervonets in terms of the price-index, the financial authorities, by substituting the chervonets for the goods ruble as the basis of calculation for the payment of wages, were able to provide themselves with another convenient device for a concealed reduction of real wages. The project was also supported by the industrial " council of congresses ", which had the ear of STO. In October 1923, when the collective agreements for the workers in the Donbass and for transport workers throughout the USSR came up for renewal, the transition was made from the goods ruble to the chervonets ruble at parity.[1] Early in November STO issued a decree converting the wages of all employees in People's Commissariats from a goods ruble to a chervonets ruble basis.[2]

The principle of conversion of wages to a fixed currency basis was difficult to resist. The trade union newspaper *Trud* attempted to fight a delaying action. *Need We Hurry?* was the title of its leading article on October 24, 1923. Two days later it published a table showing that the chervonets ruble, which had been worth 80 per cent of the goods ruble in January 1923, was now worth only 60 per cent, so that the effect of conversion at parity was to cut real wages by 40 per cent with the prospect of further depreciation. The campaign of protest slowly gathered force. At the beginning of December a conference on wages convened by the central council of trade unions demanded not only punctual payment of wages, an end of " artificial index-fixing " and the disappearance of payments in kind in lieu of wages, but also a guarantee against a fall in real wages as a result of conversion from the goods ruble to the chervonets ruble.[3] Shortly afterwards the announcement was made that the president of

---

[1] An article in *Ekonomicheskaya Zhizn'*, October 26, 1923, which reported these changes, attacked *Trud* for its opposition to them, and extolled the virtues of payment in a stable currency, evading the question of the exchange. A trade union official defended the agreement with the transport workers on the same ground, while admitting delicately that " the chervonets ruble has a tendency to lag behind the goods ruble " (*ibid.* November 2, 1923).

[2] *Trud*, November 10, 1923.   [3] *Ibid.* December 4, 1923.

TsIK had "handed over for fresh examination by Sovnarkom" a resolution of Sovnarkom and STO approving the conversion of wages, and had prescribed that "the decision must be changed in such a way as to prevent the transition to calculation in chervontsy leading to a real diminution of wages". But the effect of this statement was attenuated when it was subsequently explained that it referred only to wages of Soviet employees covered by existing wage agreements, and not to the conclusion of new collective agreements.[1] The resolution of the scissors committee, adopted by the Politburo without amendment on December 24, 1923, did not refer, in its rather perfunctory section on wages, to this now burning question. But feelings were running high when Kamenev admitted, in his speech of December 27, that this was one of the sections of the resolution which might still admit of amendment. On January 4, 1924, it was announced that the central control commission and Rabkrin would appoint a special commission to watch over and ensure the punctual payment of wages.[2] On January 6 Rykov addressed a meeting of party workers in the trade unions. After what was evidently a stormy discussion the meeting passed a resolution, without opposition but with two abstentions, endorsing the resolution of the scissors committee adopted by the Politburo, but affirming the necessity of "indispensable practical amendments and additions", the character of which was not further specified.[3] It was now clear that some concession was to be made on the chervonets rate, though this evidently encountered strong resistance, and the final decision was left to the party conference itself. A paradoxical feature of the situation, which must have been watched with cynical relief by the party leaders, was that the wages issue, on which the leaders knew themselves to be vulnerable, was not taken up either by Trotsky or by the "official" opposition led by Preobrazhensky and Pyatakov, and did not figure in any opposition platform. The failure of the opposition to make common cause with the industrial workers and to exploit their

---

[1] *Trud*, December 15, 1923.
[2] *Sobranie Uzakonenii, 1924*, No. 21, art. 214 ; as late as April 1924 complaints of unpunctual payment of wages were received from the Gomza works and from the Urals (*Trud*, April 8, 1924).
[3] *Ibid.* January 8, 1923.

deep-seated discontents was once more a revealing symptom of its weakness.[1]

The ground had thus been prepared for the full-dress discussion of the resolution of the scissors committee at the thirteenth party conference, which met in Moscow from January 16 to 18, 1924, in the week before Lenin's death. Trotsky was once more absent on grounds of health, having just left Moscow for a visit to the south, but chose the moment to issue a collection of recent articles, published and unpublished, under the general title of *The New Course*, with a preface in which he declared that the decisions of the twelfth party congress on planning had " until lately scarcely been applied at all ", and complained of sceptical judgments on various sides about Gosplan and about planned direction in general.[2] One of the hitherto unpublished articles summed up his views on the essence of the current controversy. Gosplan should " coordinate, i.e. unite and direct according to plan, all the fundamental factors of the state economy "; " the core of the work of Gosplan should be concern for the growth and development of state (socialist) industry "; and, within the complex of state economic organs, " the ' dictatorship ' should belong not to finance, but to industry ".[3] Trotsky thus shared the basic standpoint of the opposition, without openly identifying himself with it or accepting the details of its programme. It was an attitude which made the worst of both worlds, and exposed him to charges of not frankly defining his position.

When the conference met, the scissors committee resolution " On the Current Tasks of Economic Policy " was submitted to it for approval by Rykov, the president of Vesenkha, as the main resolution. Rykov in his speech drew the now familiar conclusion from the economic backwardness of Russia, with its 100 million peasants and five million industrial workers, of the need

[1] Shlyapnikov in an article in *Pravda*, January 19, 1924, argued that " there is no reason to separate comrade Trotsky in questions of policy from the other members of the central committee ", and that Trotsky, who merely wanted greater concentration of industry and more power in the hands of Gosplan, was indifferent to " the fate of the working class ".

[2] L. Trotsky, *Novyi Kurs* (1924), p. 4 ; for Trotsky's health and movements see pp. 331-332 below.

[3] Trotsky, *Novyi Kurs* (1924), p. 71.

to propitiate the peasant : the " political dictatorship of the workers " could not be turned into an " economic dictatorship of the factory ". He apologized for his error in having endorsed the Vesenkha instruction to industrial trusts of the previous July, drafted by Pyatakov, to earn maximum profits. He cheerfully accepted official estimates of a large rise in industrial wages throughout the past year ; and, while he admitted that a figure of a million unemployed was colossal, he minimized its significance by claiming that, with the growth of unemployment there had been a " parallel " growth of factory employment, and by repeating the old argument that " the greater part of the unemployed is made up of unskilled workers from the country and employees ". He poked fun at planning. How could one plan in a predominantly peasant economy where the harvest might depend on " a shower of rain " ? In any case it was absurd to suppose that a commission in Moscow could plan for the whole country " from Petrograd to Vladivostok, from Murmansk to Odessa ".[1] The speech was not merely an unqualified defence of the resolution of the scissors committee and of the Politburo : it was a general plea for confidence in the existing party leadership and in the soundness of the official line.

In Trotsky's absence Pyatakov was the chief spokesman of the opposition. He defended his own past record and the platform of the 46, and proposed a number of specific amendments to the resolution. An addendum to the introduction condemned " the line of least resistance " — by implication, the line of the central committee and of the Politburo — which encouraged " the commercial element, the element of NEP " instead of seeking to strengthen " the state economy and the cooperatives ". A new section was proposed on the administration of state enterprises ; instead of treating these on NEP principles as isolated units on a par with private enterprises, they should be welded into a planned whole and made the predominant element in the economy. A third amendment reasserted not only the theoretical importance of planning, but the practical possibility and necessity of making

---

[1] *Trinadtsataya Konferentsiya Rossiiskoi Kommunisticheskoi Partii (Bol'-shevikov)* (1924), pp. 6-20 ; a passage from Rykov's attack on planning has already been quoted in *The Bolshevik Revolution, 1917–1923*, Vol. 2, p. 374, note 3.

a start with it (in his speech Pyatakov had made an effective retort to Rykov's " shower of rain " attitude). A fourth amendment attacked price policy : a reduction of industrial prices was desirable, but should be achieved by broadening the basis and volume of industrial production (in other words, by further aid to industry) and not at the expense of the capital resources of industry. The last two amendments rejected the theory of an active foreign trade balance in favour of " a considered programme of imports " designed to " benefit our state industry first and foremost ", and dismissed as absurd the injunction to industry to earn " a minimum profit ".[1] Pyatakov's indictment of current policy and defence of the principles of planning was an impressive intellectual performance, and certainly enjoyed more sympathy in the party than was allowed to appear at the conference.[2]

In the ensuing debate, Pyatakov was supported in general terms (and without reference to his specific amendments) by Preobrazhensky and V. Smirnov. Pyatakov in his speech had sounded a note of alarm on the growth of private trade and of private capital in industry. Private undertakings were now not only " stronger in capital " (he presumably meant working capital) but " stronger in experience and knowledge of how to operate on the market " than state undertakings. Without rigorous organization and planning it could be predicted that, " in the struggle between the developing element of private capital and the state, or socialist, element, the state, or socialist, element will inevitably suffer defeat ".[3] Preobrazhensky estimated the profits of private trade and capital for the years 1922-1923 at 500 million gold rubles, and argued that this " NEP accumulation " threatened to outweigh any " socialist accumulation " which could be expected from the nationalized sector of the economy.[4] Smirnov devoted

[1] Pyatakov's speech is in *Trinadtsataya Konferentsiya Rossiiskoi Kommunisticheskoi Partii (Bol'shevikov)* (1924), pp. 20-31, the amendments *ibid.* pp. 219-233.
[2] Rykov admitted, or rather complained, that Pyatakov had " repeatedly " secured majorities for his amendments in party meetings in Moscow (*ibid.* p. 83).
[3] *Trinadtsataya Konferentsiya Rossiiskoi Kommunisticheskoi Partii (Bol'shevikov)* (1924), p. 21.
[4] *Ibid.* pp. 35-36. Rykov (*ibid.* p. 15) had tried to scale down the figure to 200 or 300 millions, but without much conviction : where Preobrazhensky appears to have been in error was not in over-estimating the profits of private capital, but in under-estimating the recovery of nationalized industry.

himself to the demand for more planning, and argued that even
the references to planning in the resolution of December 24
treated it, not as an essential ingredient of socialism, but as a
mere expedient to surmount a crisis.¹ Molotov, Kamenev and
Mikoyan attacked Pyatakov and defended the official line; and
Sokolnikov replied to Preobrazhensky who had expressed scepticism about the financial reform.   Krasin repeated his isolated
view that economic recovery depended entirely on obtaining
a foreign loan.   The official spokesmen followed Rykov in pok-
ing fun at planning.   Mikoyan described both the original resolution of the ninth party congress of 1920 on the " single
economic plan " and Trotsky's famous " Order No. 1042 " on the
repair of locomotives of the same year as " the height of utopia ".²
The programme of the opposition, it was hinted, pointed the way
back to war communism with its centralization and bureaucracy;
Pyatakov's ideas on organization were denounced as " glavkizm ".³
These were appeals to prejudice rather than to reason, but they
had the required effect on the well-packed audience of delegates.

It was left to Lutovinov, a former member of the workers'
opposition, and Kosior, a signatory of the platform of the 46,
both workers by origin and both members of the trade union
central council, to plead the cause of the industrial worker.
Both emphatically rejected Rykov's claim that real wages had
risen in 1923.   Lutovinov, who followed Pyatakov and appears
to have spoken with unusual brevity and restraint,⁴ deprecated

¹ *Trinadtsataya Konferentsiya Rossiiskoi Kommunisticheskoi Partii (Bol'shevikov)* (1924), p. 69.
² *Ibid.* pp. 48, 56, 76. Trotsky in his collection of articles published on the
eve of the conference had already replied to the attack on order No. 1042, of
which Mikoyan was probably not the originator, accusing his attackers of the
" renovation " and " falsification " of history (L. Trotsky, *Novyi Kurs* (1924),
pp. 59-74) ; the attack was taken up in greater detail by Rudzutak at the thirteenth party congress (*Trinadtsatyi S"ezd Rossiiskoi Kommunisticheskoi Partii
(Bol'shevikov)* (1924), p. 206). For Order No. 1042 see *The Bolshevik Revolution,
1917-1923*, Vol. 2, pp. 373-374.
³ *Trinadtsataya Konferentsiya Rossiiskoi Kommunisticheskoi Partii (Bol'-
shevikov)* (1924), p. 77 ; Sokolnikov similarly tried to discredit those who were
sceptical of the financial reform by attributing to them " relics of views which
gained a hold over us during the entirely peculiar period 1918-1921 " (speech
of December 5, 1923, quoted in S. S. Katsenellenbaum, *Soviet Currency and
Banking, 1914-1924* (1925), p. 139).
⁴ The impression is strong that his speech was abbreviated and toned down
in the record (*Trinadtsataya Konferentsiya Rossiiskoi Kommunisticheskoi Partii*

the conventional optimism expressed in the wages section of the resolution, and drew attention once more to past and current abuses in the calculation of wage rates. Claiming to speak on behalf of the party fraction of the central council of trade unions,[1] Lutovinov now asked that any further transition from the goods ruble to the chervonets as the basis of wage payments should be suspended, and that, where the transition had already taken place, adjustments should be made in the monthly wage payments on the basis of the goods ruble so that the level of real wages should not be impaired.

The careful organization of the selection of delegates to the conference by the party secretariat [2] was no doubt the main reason for the hopeless minority in which the opposition found itself. But the ease with which the party leadership triumphed over it was helped by the evident lack of sympathy between the leaders of the opposition and those who spoke for the workers. The official spokesmen, passing over in silence the substantial grievances of labour, turned the weight of their attack on Pyatakov and his tiny group. Thus overwhelmed, the opposition could do no more than fight a half-hearted rearguard action. Pyatakov predicted that the party would one day have to come to " the organization of our economy ". But he weakly disclaimed any desire " to set my line in economic policy against the line of the central committee ", and complained only that " the Politburo, in following a correct line in the matter of our economy, does not

(*Bol'shevikov*) (1924), pp. 32-33) ; it seems inconceivable that what was evidently an important speech should have been so short and so uniformly flat and factual. The record of Kosior's speech (*ibid.* pp. 50-52) is not obviously open to the same suspicion, though the record of Kosior's speech at the twelfth party congress in the previous April is known to have been cut (see p. 279 below). The text of the two speeches in the official record, however, corresponds closely to the text as it appeared in *Pravda*, January 18, 19, 1924.

[1] Lutovinov's rôle at the conference was somewhat obscure. It was natural that the decision to submit the question to the conference should have been taken not by the trade union central council (which was not a party organ), but by the party fraction in the council. But, though the recognized trade union leaders were members of the fraction, none of them chose to speak at the conference ; the invidious task of bringing up this awkward and embarrassing issue was left to Lutovinov, who was known as a *frondeur* and had no party reputation to lose. In May 1924, Lutovinov, disillusioned by events in the party, committed suicide : Bukharin and Trotsky paid tributes to him at the funeral (*Trud*, May 11, 1924).

[2] This is discussed on pp. 332-333 below.

yet put the questions which it is already time to put ".[1] He ended his reply to the debate with the remark that " future congresses " would show whether the point of view set forth in his amendments was not correct, and, when Orjonikidze tauntingly asked whether he did not demand a vote on them, could only answer, amid laughter, that he had " sufficient political experience to know that with the present membership of the conference they could not be accepted ". The amendments were none the less put to the vote and received three votes, with one delegate abstaining. The resolution was then referred to a drafting commission. What was on foot was shown by the inclusion of Lutovinov in the membership of the commission ; on the other hand, no representative of the opposition was included, and proposals to add Pyatakov and Kosior were rejected.[2] The commission, working behind the scenes on an issue which the conference had refrained from discussing, proposed two amendments to the wages section of the resolution. The first demanded that wages in industries and localities which lagged behind the general level should be brought up to it ; the second that, when wages were calculated in chervontsy, a bonus should be added at the end of each month to take account of any rise in the cost of living. These proposals, together with a few other amendments of minor consequence, were then submitted to the full conference, and the resolution carried unanimously in its amended form.[3] A step had been taken to appease the most pressing and dangerous grievances of the industrial workers. Price control had been tentatively decided on. But the opposition had been routed. The main structure of NEP and the insistence on the priority of the peasant remained intact. Neither the arguments of the critics nor the pressure of external events had proved the line of least resistance unworkable. The economic outlook seemed more promising than at any time during the past year. The conference marked the end of a long and acrimonious debate on economic policy, which was not reopened for many months.

The thirteenth party conference, by approving the resolution of the scissors committee, had endorsed the current line in

---

[1] *Trinadtsataya Konferentsiya Rossiiskoi Kommunisticheskoi Partii (Bol'-shevikov)* (1924), p. 31.   [2] *Ibid.* pp. 81-83, 91.   [3] *Ibid.* p. 187.

economic policy. Three decisions now required action through the governmental machine : the completion of the financial reform, the amendment on wages and the recommendation on the control of prices.

The accomplishment of the financial reform, which immediately followed the conference, marked the culminating phase in the stabilization of NEP. It resulted logically from what had gone before. The decision to resume the unlimited issue of Soviet rubles in September 1923 had been dictated by the need for currency to finance the collection of grain from the peasants ; and this decision in turn dictated the final solution of the currency problem. The Soviet ruble could now no longer be retrieved, and was not worth retrieving. By November 1923, four-fifths of the paper money in circulation, reckoned in terms of value, consisted of chervontsy notes, leaving only one-fifth for the dying Soviet ruble ; the chervonets had thus become, as the resolution of the scissors committee noted, " the basic currency of the country ".[1] Thanks to the grain exports and the policy of the active trade balance, reserves of gold and foreign currency had accumulated steadily during the year to provide for the chervonets a backing of unimpeachable integrity. The holdings of Gosbank in gold and foreign currency rose from 15 million gold rubles on January 1, 1923, to almost 150 million rubles — or more than half the total chervonets issue — on January 1, 1924.[2]

The one remaining weak point was the state budget, which had hitherto been balanced year after year by covering a large deficit with a fresh issue of paper money. But here, too, much had now been done to restore order. At the meeting of VTsIK in November 1923, Sokolnikov was able to congratulate himself that the estimates for the current quarter had for the first time been prepared before the beginning of the quarter, and that the whole budget for the current financial year (October 1923–October 1924) would be ready by the beginning of December. He claimed that two-thirds of the estimated expenditure would be covered this year by revenue, leaving only one-third to be covered by credit and currency issues ; with the steady expansion

[1] VKP(B) v Rezolyutsiyakh (1941), i, 552.
[2] Z. V. Atlas, Ocherki po Istorii Denezhnogo Obrashcheniya v SSSR (1917–1925) (1940), p. 196.

of economic activity, this did not seem an impossible task.[1]   The
conditions for the completion of the reform were slowly ripening.

The opposition, still mistrustful of the implications of the
reform for industry, but unable to come out openly against a
measure which had behind it all the authority of Lenin and of
the eleventh party congress, confined itself to sporadic expressions
of pessimism.   At the private meeting of VTsIK in November
1923, V. Smirnov had predicted that the chervonets would be dead
in three months, and was challenged by Sokolnikov to say whether
this was the official view of Gosplan.[2]   But there was force in the
argument used by Sokolnikov on this and other occasions that
a stable currency was a pre-condition of planning.   The only
questions still open were really whether to stabilize the Soviet
ruble in terms of the chervonets or to substitute a new issue of
notes in small denominations, and, in the latter event, whether
the issue was to be made by Gosbank as a part of the chervonets
issue or independently by the treasury.   During the winter, the
decision was taken in favour of a new issue of treasury notes
and token silver coinage in rubles and kopeks exchanging with
chervontsy at the par rate of 10 rubles to the chervonets.[3]   At
the thirteenth party conference Sokolnikov announced that the
time had come " to pass over to the stage of a stable treasury
currency issue, of a currency based on gold, of state treasury
notes expressed in terms of gold, playing the rôle of small change
in relation to the chervonets " : this he described as " building a
valuta bridge between town and country ".[4]   Preobrazhensky
grumbled once more that the carrying out of the financial reform

---

[1] *Tret'ya Sessiya Tsentral'nogo Ispolnitel'nogo Komiteta Soyuza Sovetskikh
Sotsialisticheskikh Respublik* (1924), pp. 79-81. Figures for the first nine months
of 1923 showed that the proportion of expenditure covered by currency emission
had fallen slowly throughout this time ; in the first four months it had fluctuated
round about one-third, then fallen to 14 per cent in August, rising again in
September (with the resumption of the unlimited issue of Sovznaks) to 21 per
cent (L. N. Yurovsky, *Na Putyakh k Denezhnoi Reforme* (2nd ed., 1924),
p. 102) ; in the last quarter of the year the proportion fell to 9 per cent (L. N.
Yurovsky, *Currency Problems and Policy of the Soviet Union* (1925), p. 124).

[2] G. Y. Sokolnikov, *Finansovaya Politika Revolyutsii*, ii (1926), 92.

[3] The whole plan was set forth by Sokolnikov in a detailed memorandum
of January 1924 translated in S. S. Katsenellenbaum, *Russian Currency and
Banking, 1914–1924* (1925), pp. 139-142, from a Russian pamphlet which has
not been available.

[4] *Trinadtsataya Konferentsiya Rossiiskoi Kommunisticheskoi Partii (Bol'-
shevikov)*, 1924, p. 72.

revealed " all the spontaneous character, the planlessness, of our economy ". But there was no serious criticism ; and Mikoyan could effectively taunt the opposition with being neither for nor against the reform.[1] The resolution of the scissors committee and of the Politburo endorsed by the conference hailed the completion of the financial reform as " one of the fundamental tasks of the Soviet power for the coming period ".[2]

The reform was brought into effect in several stages. The first was a decree of February 4, 1924, providing for the issue of treasury notes in denominations of 1, 2 and 5 gold rubles, which were legal tender for all transactions. The issue of treasury notes was limited to one-half the value of the chervonets issue of Gosbank, which thus remained the arbiter of the total note issue and the guarantor of its financial soundness.[3] The decree established no formal link between the new treasury gold ruble and the chervonets ruble. But since the chervonets was stable in terms of gold, no difficulty could arise ; and Gosbank issued on February 7, 1924, an announcement of its readiness to accept the new treasury notes at the equivalent of 10 rubles to 1 chervonets.[4] The next stage was a decree of February 14, 1924, announcing the cessation on the following day of the issue of Soviet rubles and the destruction of all unissued stocks.[5] A decree of February 22, 1924, provided for the issue of silver and copper coinage in denominations up to a ruble inclusive.[6] These measures prepared the way for the final stage, which was reached in a decree of March 7, 1924, under which Soviet rubles were to be redeemable as from March 10 at the rate of 50,000 Soviet rubles of the 1923 pattern (equivalent to 50,000 million pre-1921 rubles) for 1 gold ruble, and would cease to be legal tender after May 10.[7] A corollary of the financial reform was the disappearance not only of Soviet ruble notes, but of the hypothetical goods ruble or price-index ruble as a unit of calculation. A decree of STO of February 29, 1924, prescribed the translation into gold rubles of all contracts concluded in terms of the goods ruble, and

[1] *Ibid.* pp. 37, 77.   [2] *VKP(B) v Rezolyutsiyakh* (1941), i, 552.
[3] *Sobranie Uzakonenii, 1924*, No. 32, art. 288.
[4] S. S. Katsenellenbaum, *Russian Currency and Banking, 1914–1924* (1925), pp. 143-144.
[5] *Sobranie Uzakonenii, 1924*, No. 34, art. 308.
[6] *Ibid.* No. 34, art. 325.   [7] *Ibid.* No. 45, art. 433.

prohibited for the future the conclusion of contracts, or the quotation of prices, in terms of the goods ruble.[1]

The successive stages by which the reform was carried through were evidence of the anxiety felt in official quarters about its prospects of success. The necessary steps were taken separately and with a certain interval between them, as if to leave open as long as possible the chance to retreat if any part of the scheme failed at the last moment to work. But the most striking feature of the whole reform was its close conformity with western, and particularly British, canons of financial orthodoxy; none of the countries receiving advice at this time from British or League of Nations experts on the best way to maintain stable currencies applied more meticulously the precepts of the day regarding gold cover, a balanced budget, a prudent credit policy or correct relations between the treasury and the central bank. This ready acceptance of western models was rendered easier by the presence at Gosbank of the former Kadet minister Kutler [2] and of other experts trained in the orthodox tradition of nineteenth-century international finance. But it had also another significance. The establishment of a stable currency had become not only an end in itself, but a means of winning the confidence of the capitalist world and of securing the benefits of foreign trade and, ultimately perhaps, foreign loans, which, to others besides Krasin, seemed to offer the main hope of salvation for the Soviet economy. Kamenev put the point with complete frankness at the second All-Union Congress of Soviets :

> All Europe, which is struggling with a currency crisis, will recognize the economy of the country as sound if it has been able to achieve the results which we have achieved in the past year, if it creates a stable currency.[3]

A cartoon in *Izvestiya* depicted the chervonets as " the new *polpred* of the USSR in New York ".[4] An unexpected eagerness was shown to dwell on the similarities rather than the differences

---

[1] L. N. Yurovsky, *Currency Problems and Policy of the Soviet Union* (1925), p. 135. The only contracts for which the medium of the goods ruble was still in common use were the collective labour agreements concluded by the trade unions : for these see pp. 136-137 below.

[2] See *The Bolshevik Revolution, 1917–1923*, Vol. 2, pp. 351-352.

[3] *Vtoroi S"ezd Sovetov Soyuza Sovetskikh Sotsialisticheskikh Respublik* (1924), p. 94.   [4] *Izvestiya*, March 26, 1924.

between Soviet finances and those of the western world. Sokolnikov had long ago excused the irregularities of the Soviet budget by invoking a French precedent.[1] Now, at the climax of the return to sound finance, he drew a surprising moral from the measures taken almost simultaneously under western auspices to stabilize the currencies of Germany, Austria, Czechoslovakia, Poland, Latvia, Estonia and Lithuania :

> We, as members of a European whole, notwithstanding all the peculiarities of our political position, notwithstanding that with us a different class is in power, have been drawn into this European mechanism of economic and financial development.[2]

The currency reform had crowned the *rapprochement* between Soviet Russia and the capitalist world set in motion by NEP and by the Anglo-Soviet trade agreement. Most of all, however, the new financial policy expressed the desire for order and stability and the revulsion against revolutionary turmoil which had set in with NEP. It was still enough to damn any measure to suggest that it meant a return to the chaos and to the austerities of war communism. The leaders who controlled economic policy after Lenin's withdrawal seemed for the time being to have no other ambition than to mark time, to conserve and enjoy what had been gained and to strengthen their own tenure of the seats of power. So long as the economy continued to work without intolerable frictions or deficiencies, they were content to let it work with a minimum of interference : this end seemed most readily attainable by placing it under the guiding star of a gold standard currency functioning by the automatic and self-adjusting mechanism described by the classical economists. As Kamenev explained to the following party congress, a gold standard currency was " an excellent thermometer which can signal health or disease " : if at any time it indicated " morbid phenomena " that would be no reason for breaking the thermometer.[3]

The main purpose of the decision of the thirteenth party conference on wages, adopted as an afterthought by way of amendment

---

[1] See *The Bolshevik Revolution, 1917–1923*, Vol. 2, p. 145.
[2] *Sotsialisticheskoe Khozyaistvo*, No. 5, 1924, p. 6.
[3] *Trinadtsatyi S"ezd Rossiiskoi Kommunisticheskoi Partii (Bol'shevikov)* (1924), p. 392.

to the original resolution, was to compensate wage earners
for the rise in prices in terms of the new chervonets currency.
At the eleventh All-Russian Congress of Soviets [1] which immediately followed the party conference, the People's Commissar
for Labour, Shmidt, gave a modest account of recent efforts to
mitigate the plight of the workers. He claimed a rise " of small
dimensions " — about 3 per cent in all — in the wages of industrial
workers in the second half of 1923, alleging that wages in Moscow
had now reached 78 per cent of the pre-war level, and in Petrograd
68 per cent, though the wages of transport workers were still
only 50 per cent; 84 per cent of all wages were now paid in cash.
He then cautiously mooted the burning question of the conversion
of wage rates into chervontsy, admitting that the chervonets
had fallen during the last three months in terms of the goods
ruble :

> We must be very careful in approaching the question : Can
> we finally guarantee the level of wages under a system of cal-
> culation in chervontsy ? Here too there must be a certain
> measure of insurance. [2]

Bogdanov, the spokesman of Vesenkha, once more put the case
for the industrialists. He argued that the sales crisis of the past
four months was not yet over, and that prices could not be kept
down if wages rose without a corresponding increase in productivity. Increased productivity was the only way to " raise
wages painlessly without raising the price of goods ". He
advocated conversion of wage rates into chervontsy, and thought
that the workers must find compensation for any loss in a
strengthening of cooperation, which would bring about a reduction in the prices of what the workers had to buy. [3] But the issue
of principle had been settled by the resolution of the party conference, and nobody seriously proposed to reopen it. The
congress passed a resolution " On Measures for the Further
Improvement of Labour Conditions of the Workers ", demanding
that, where wages were calculated in chervontsy, the worker
should be entitled to a cost-of-living bonus by way of compensa-

---

[1] Narkomtrud, as a " unified " commissariat (see The Bolshevik Revolution,
1917-1923, Vol. 1, p. 404), was the concern of the RSFSR as well as of the USSR.
[2] XI Vserossiiskii S"ezd Sovetov (1924), pp. 97, 100.
[3] Ibid. pp. 117-119.

tion for any depreciation in the purchasing power of the chervonets.[1] Finally, on February 29, 1924, a decree of STO prescribed that all future collective agreements should be concluded in chervontsy, and wage rates under all existing agreements converted from goods rubles to chervontsy. The country was divided for this purpose into three zones ; and conversion was to be effected at rates varying, according to zone, from parity to a rate of 1·50 chervonets rubles to 1 goods ruble. Bonuses were to be payable in the event of a further rise in the cost of living in terms of the chervonets.[2] " The bonuses ", observed *Trud* ominously a few days later, " must be ' honest ', and be worked out in precise accord with the movement of market prices." [3]

This awkward and hard-won compromise proved to be of short duration. Once the transition to the fixing of wage rates and the payment of wages in chervontsy had been brought into effect, the principle of cost-of-living bonuses — the last relic of the discarded goods ruble — quickly came under attack. The completion of the financial reform and the stabilization of prices which accompanied it seemed to deprive the bonus system of its last justification. The rest of the economy was now geared to a stable gold-standard currency : it was logical that wages should follow suit. The argument was heard that the workers had already benefited so much from the payment of their wages at fixed rates in stable currency that further concessions to them were no longer required.[4] On April 4, 1924, " Circular No. 606 " was issued jointly by Vesenkha and by the trade union central council to all economic and trade union organizations. This began by explaining that the mixed system of wages based partly on a gold-standard currency and partly on a cost-of-living bonus

[1] *S"ezdy Sovetov RSFSR v Postanovleniyakh* (1939), p. 294 ; the resolution was also published in *Sobranie Uzakonenii, 1924,* No. 27, art. 262 — an indication of its mandatory character. Other paragraphs in it instructed the People's Commissar for Labour to prepare a scheme of public works for the unemployed and to raise the level of relief " for that part of the unemployed who represent a genuinely proletarian element and who must be drawn first of all into production when it expands " ; but nothing came of these well-worn admonitions.

[2] *Ekonomicheskaya Zhizn'*, March 1, 1924 ; *Trud*, March 1, 1924.

[3] *Ibid.* March 5, 1924.

[4] A leading article in *Trud*, April 13, 1924, admitted that, now that the worker had security, some decline in wages might be fair and inevitable.

K

had been adopted " for the moment of transition ". Now that the
new financial order had been firmly established, it was necessary
to " complete the reform in the computation of wage rates by
passing over to the conclusion of collective agreements for a
definite period with wages expressed in stable monetary terms
without any kind of cost-of-living supplements ". The new system
was to come into force as from April 1, except for workers in
transport, miners in the Don basin and workers in Yugostal, the
steel trust of the Ukraine : these were to enjoy the benefits of the
mixed system for a further month. By way of sugaring the pill,
salaries of specialists covered by " personal " agreements were to
be cut by 20 per cent as from April 1.[1] It can hardly be supposed
that the decision was received with enthusiasm by the workers
or by the trade unions ; and complaints of the victimization of
the workers were current for some time to come. " Circular
No. 606 " was vigorously attacked a month later at the thirteenth
party congress by a trade union delegate as an infringement of the
decisions of the Politburo and of the thirteenth party conference.[2]
But, thanks to the unexpected recovery in the purchasing power
of the chervonets and its stability throughout the year 1924, the
change was effected without much opposition or resentment.[3]
With memories of the fluctuations and uncertainties of the past
few years still vividly alive, and at a time when unemployment
was still rife, the worker in employment was not blind to the
unwonted advantage of receiving fixed wages in a currency of stable
purchasing power. Not the least of the merits of the financial
reform was that it put an end to the juggling with rates of exchange
on wage payments which had been the crying scandal of the
preceding period. In the next period the emphasis was to fall

---

[1] *Trud*, April 5, 1924. The decrees now issued prescribed a reduction of
10 per cent in salaries from 100 to 150 rubles a month, of 20 per cent in salaries
above 150 rubles (*Sobranie Uzakonenii, 1924*, No. 53, art. 525 ; No. 64, art.
646) another decree reiterated the requirement (see p. 115, note 2 above) that
such agreements should be registered with Narkomtrud, and recommended a
model form of contract drawn up by Narkomtrud (*ibid.* No. 53, art. 526).
[2] *Trinadtsatyi S"ezd Rossiiskoi Kommunisticheskoi Partii* (*Bol'shevikov*)
(1924), p. 173.
[3] The transition from the goods ruble to the chervonets as the basis of wage
rates was recalled at the sixth trade union congress in November 1924, but as a
grievance of the past rather than of the present (*Shestoi S"ezd Professional'nykh
Soyuzov SSSR* (1925), pp. 71-72).

on another aspect of the labour question : the relation of wages to productivity.

The third decision taken by the thirteenth party conference on the basis of the report of the scissors committee — the decision to control both wholesale and retail prices — required no specific legislation, since the necessary powers seem to have been already vested in Komvnutorg. But it was followed by a flood of decrees on prices issued by different authorities. A resolution of STO of February 22, 1924, empowered Komvnutorg to control the prices of " all goods circulating on the internal market at all stages of their commercial circulation " ; and a circular of Vesenkha of the same date warned the trusts that, under the new régime of a stable currency, it was no longer justifiable to include in their prices the element of " insurance against depreciation of Sovznaks ".[1] During the following week, Komvnutorg issued orders fixing the price of bread in Moscow and Leningrad, and drawing up a list of sixteen commodities of mass consumption the prices of which must be publicly displayed by retail traders outside their establishments.[2] The decree of STO of February 29, 1924, recording the compromise on wages,[3] also contained, doubtless by way of compensation for any potential decline in monetary wages, instructions to local organs of Komvnutorg throughout the country to reduce retail prices and to secure the publication by retail traders of prices of commodities of mass consumption. How far the attempt to force down prices by administrative order was successful is more than doubtful. Six weeks later a resolution of the party central committee not only recognized the necessary limitations of such an attempt, but appeared to retreat to the more cautious ground taken by the scissors committee in the previous December :

The fixing of retail prices should be extended to private trade in cases where it is possible to guarantee saturation of the market by state organs in specific commodities which are *de facto* subject to a state monopoly, e.g. paraffin, salt, matches, etc.[4]

[1] *Pravda*, February 26, 1924.
[2] *Ekonomicheskaya Zhizn'*, February 23, 26, 1924.
[3] See p. 137 above.   [4] *Trud*, April 24, 1924.

The stabilization of wholesale and retail prices which was achieved in the spring of 1924 was due far more to the success of the currency reform than to direct governmental control of prices. But the legacy of the scissors crisis remained. The doctrine that, even under NEP, price-fixing was a proper and necessary function of government had been clearly established, and was not again contested.

The new attitude to internal trade led to a long-overdue institutional readjustment : this brought to a head and ended an interdepartmental rivalry which had been a marked feature of the last two years. The growing authority of Narkomfin and Gosbank, which reflected the new importance attached to financial policy, had been one of the striking administrative consequences of NEP. Under war communism the two most powerful economic departments of state had been Vesenkha, which controlled industry, and Narkomprod, which handled the products of agriculture, with STO to exercise a supervisory and coordinating rôle. The functions of both these departments were radically affected by the coming of NEP. Vesenkha retained the management of industry, though its direct control was weakened by the substitution of trusts and leased enterprises for *glavki* and centres which, together with the introduction of *khozraschet*, narrowed the scope of its authority. But other organs also began to encroach on its position. The financing of industry, which (so far as it was possible to speak of finance under war communism) had hitherto been conducted through Vesenkha, now passed into the hands of Gosbank, which enjoyed the complete confidence of Narkomfin. Trotsky at the twelfth party congress pointed out that " the financial apparatus is . . . the fundamental apparatus of the administration of industry " and that " Vesenkha will indubitably remain a fifth wheel of the coach so long as it does not have in its hands the apparatus for financing industry ".[1] The establishment of Prombank [2] was an imperfect compromise ; the last word still lay with Gosbank. Nor could it well be otherwise in an economy where finance served as the ultimate regulator, and direct state intervention in the operations of the market was a contravention

---

[1] *Dvenadtsatyi S"ezd Rossiiskoi Kommunisticheskoi Partii (Bol'shevikov* (1923), p. 304.

[2] See *The Bolshevik Revolution, 1917–1923*, Vol. 2, pp. 356-357.

of accepted principles. On the other side, Vesenkha found its monopoly of power undermined by Vneshtorg and Komvnutorg, which claimed, though not very effectively, to exercise an overriding authority in operations of foreign and domestic trade respectively. Narkomprod, the equal partner of Vesenkha under war communism, was subject to still stronger pressures from the same two sides. The initial innovation from which NEP began — the substitution of a tax for a requisition — already brought Narkomfin into a field which had been under war communism the exclusive and all-important preserve of Narkomprod; for, while the collection of the tax remained in the hands of Narkomprod so long as it was paid in kind, the transition to money payments was soon to transform the tax-gatherer from an agent of Narkomprod into an agent of Narkomfin. The corresponding substitution of wage payments in money for rations and payments in kind made Narkomfin the ultimate arbiter of wages policy; and, finally, the growing importance of grain exports introduced a new factor into the peasant economy in the shape of Vneshtorg. Between 1921 and 1923 Narkomprod was shedding one by one all the dominant functions which it had exercised under war communism.[1]

The first attempt at readjustment came from Vesenkha, which about the time of the twelfth party congress mooted a project to combine Vesenkha, Vneshtorg and Komvnutorg into a single commissariat of industry and trade which would also be responsible for the collection and purchase of grain, thus bringing all the major sectors of the economy under unified control.[2] This far-reaching scheme was too reminiscent of Vesenkha's old ambitions to become the supreme and comprehensive organ of economic control to have any chance of acceptance. The first institutional change undertaken was a reform in the constitution of Vesenkha itself. Under war communism industry could be administered as a single whole. Under NEP industry was divided into two sectors : state industry and leased or privately owned industry. The functions of Vesenkha therefore fell into two categories : the direction of policy and the framing of legislation for industry as a whole, and the administration of state

[1] See also *The Bolshevik Revolution, 1917–1923*, Vol. 2, p. 338.
[2] The project was mentioned, but not supported, by Trotsky at the congress, and supported and elaborated by Bogdanov (*Dvenadtsatyi S"ezd Rossiiskoi Kommunisticheskoi Partii (Bol'shevikov)* (1923), pp. 304, 333-334).

industry, now organized in trusts under the decree of April 10, 1923.[1] The organization proved unequal to the strain; and the failure of Vesenkha to foresee and avoid the sales crisis of the summer of 1923 was attributed to neglect of its more general function.[2] In September 1923 Vesenkha was split into two major departments corresponding to these two functions. Rykov remained as president of Vesenkha with Bogdanov and Pyatakov as his deputies; Pyatakov was placed at the head of the administration of state industry.[3] Immediately after the reform, however, Pyatakov, whether by coincidence or design, was despatched on a mission to Germany; [4] and he afterwards complained bitterly that during his absence nothing was done to organize the direction of state industry as a single whole.[5] A further reorganization took place after Lenin's death. Rykov, who became president of Sovnarkom, was succeeded as president of Vesenkha by Dzerzhinsky, first head of the Cheka, and since 1921 People's Commissar for Communications; and this, combined with the revival of industry from 1924 onwards, gave Vesenkha a new lease of life. But Vesenkha never succeeded in reasserting its authority beyond the industrial sphere. At the beginning of February 1924, the State Universal Store (GUM) and its branches, an emanation of Vesenkha, were transferred to Komvnutorg, which thus obtained a direct foothold in retail trade.[6] The new attempt to control prices demanded the creation of an organ with greater powers and prestige than Komvnutorg; but this organ could not be specifically associated with industry.[7] The decision now shaped

[1] See *The Bolshevik Revolution, 1917–1923*, Vol. 2, p. 309.

[2] This view was propounded by its former president, Bogdanov, at TsIK in November 1923 (*Tret'ya Sessiya Tsentral'nogo Ispolnitel'nogo Komiteta Soyuza Sovetskikh Sotsialisticheskikh Respublik* (1924), p. 53).

[3] Accounts of this reform are given by Bogdanov, *ibid.* pp. 52-54, and more cursorily by Molotov in *Trinadtsataya Konferentsiya Rossiiskoi Kommunisticheskoi Partii (Bol'shevikov)* (1924), pp. 43-44; it was formalized in an order of TsIK of November 12, 1923 (*Postanovleniya Tret'ei Sessii Tsentral'nogo Ispolnitel'nogo Komiteta Soyuza Sovetskikh Sotsialisticheskikh Respublik* (1923), pp. 130-134).

[4] See p. 219 below.

[5] *Trinadtsataya Konferentsiya Rossiiskoi Kommunisticheskoi Partii (Bol'shevikov)* (1924), pp. 22-24.

[6] *Ekonomicheskaya Zhizn'*, February 5, 1924; for GUM see *The Bolshevik Revolution, 1917–1923*, Vol. 2, p. 336.

[7] G. I. Krumin, *Puti Khozyaistvennoi Politiki* (1924), pp. 39-41, assuming the principle of the creation of a commissariat of internal trade, argues strongly

itself almost automatically. In May 1924 decrees were issued creating a People's Commissariat of Internal Trade, which superseded Komvnutorg and took over what was left of the machinery of Narkomprod.[1] The People's Commissariat of Foreign Trade (Vneshtorg) remained independent, with Krasin still at its head.

An unexpected sequel of these arrangements, and of the victory of the party leadership at the thirteenth party conference, was a certain reaction against the contemptuous attitude of the majority, especially typified in the utterances of Rykov and Kamenev at the conference, towards the principle of planning. In the reshuffle of appointments which followed the death of Lenin, Krzhizhanovsky was succeeded as president of Gosplan by Tsyurupa, who was also one of the deputy presidents of Sovnarkom. Perhaps the most significant point about this combination of functions was that it had been proposed by Trotsky more than a year earlier and at that time rejected.[2] Kamenev now went out of the way to explain that its effect would be " to draw Gosplan nearer to the government, to increase its authority ".[3] In April 1924 the central control commission and Rabkrin turned their attention to Gosplan, defined its task as being " to establish a general perspective plan of the economic activity of the USSR for a number of years (five or ten) ", declared that a financial plan, of which the state budget would form part, was also required, and recommended the setting up of a labour section of Gosplan.[4] Though it was long before effective progress was made towards a comprehensive machinery of planning, the trend was symptomatic. More immediately important was a return, apparently as a result of Dzerzhinsky's appointment to Vesenkha, to the hitherto neglected recommendation of the scissors committee for increased financial aid to the metallurgical industry. Dzerzhinsky was

---

against its association with Vesenkha and, rather less strongly, against its association with Vneshtorg : this pamphlet, published after the thirteenth party conference, may be taken to represent the official view.
    [1] *Izvestiya*, May 11, 1924 ; *Sobranie Uzakonenii, 1924*, No. 50, art. 473; No. 62, art. 620. The decision was taken in the party central committee early in April (*Trud*, April 9, 1924).
    [2] See *The Bolshevik Revolution, 1917–1923*, Vol. 2, p. 380.
    [3] *Vtoroi S"ezd Sovetov Soyuza Sovetskikh Sotsialisticheskikh Respublik* (1924), p. 127.
    [4] *Ekonomicheskaya Zhizn'*, April 25, 1924; *Trud*, April 25, 1924.

instructed to look into the question, and reported that 100 to 200 million gold rubles would be required for the revival of heavy industry over the next five years.[1]

When the thirteenth party congress met in May 1924, economic issues no longer occupied the centre of the stage. On the eve of the congress the official economic journal in a leading article described the Soviet economy as resting on " a qualitatively new basis, a solid, healthy basis, showing clearly and sharply defined characteristics of recovery, of progress, of growth ".[2] The crisis seemed to be over, and nobody was eager to reopen the settlement in matters of economic policy which had been approved by the thirteenth party conference four months earlier and completed in the interval. Trotsky, in his one rather short speech to the congress, said little about economic issues, though he emphatically reiterated his demand for more planning and regarded it as " established without qualification " that " the party, in the person of its directing apparatus, does not approach the tasks of planned direction of the economy with the energy which is indispensable ". Preobrazhensky, the only other member of the opposition to speak, drew the same moral, pointing in particular to the shortage of capital in industry and to an unemployment figure which had now reached 1,300,000, apart from " colossal concealed unemployment in the countryside ".[3] Zinoviev, reporting Dzerzhinsky's conclusions on the sums required to give effect to the resolution of the thirteenth party conference on support for the metallurgical industry, rhetorically declared that " it is now the turn for metal, the turn for an improvement in the means of production, the turn for a revival of heavy industry ". Though pre-war levels of production could scarcely be expected in the next year or two, it was " *time to begin to leave the pre-war ideal behind* ". The congress resolution repeated the injunction to concentrate attention on " the production of the means of produc-

---

[1] *Trinadtsatyi S"ezd Rossiiskoi Kommunisticheskoi Partii (Bol'shevikov)* (1924), pp. 91-92.
[2] *Ekonomicheskaya Zhizn'*, May 23, 1924.
[3] *Trinadtsatyi S"ezd Rossiiskoi Kommunisticheskoi Partii (Bol'shevikov)* (1924), pp. 164, 204.

tion ".[1] On the question of unemployment Zinoviev, sharing the
pessimism still commonly current in capitalist countries, non-
chalantly replied that " we have still heard no practical propositions
in this field ".[2] But the main economic symptoms were still too
favourable for serious anxiety. The scissors had been steadily
closing for the past six months, and the pre-war relation between
agricultural and industrial prices had now been restored; industry
had made progress towards recovery; the fall in wages had been
arrested, and the scandal of unpunctual payments cleared up;
and some steps had even been taken to curb the predominance of
private capital and the nepman in trade. Above all, to Trotsky's
reiterated insistence on planning, Kamenev could triumphantly
reply that " the plan which our party has carried out in the last
two months . . . is contained in two words : currency reform ".
And this plan had been carried out against the wishes of the
opposition, which had demanded planning in all its resolutions.[3]

The congress discussed at length, though without revealing
any novel standpoints, the topical question of internal trade.
Zinoviev in his main speech repeated that " freedom of internal
trade is the foundation of NEP ".[4] Kamenev, who reported on the
subject, quoted Lenin's famous injunction, " Learn to trade ", but
observed rather ingenuously that " this slogan, launched two and
a half years ago, changes its concrete content in the course of our
economic work, and our task consists in defining exactly at any
given concrete moment how this slogan of Vladimir Ilich should
be understood and how it should be applied ". The essential
need was " to adapt the rate of development of our industry to the
strength of the peasant economy " and " to seek in the mass of the
peasantry the economic base on which the development of state
industry must rest ". But he spoke strongly in favour of the
control of industrial prices, and quoted the closing of the scissors
as proof that a policy of price control had been right and necessary.[5]
The general resolution of the congress noted that " the new
economic policy conducted by the party had fulfilled the tasks
which the party set before it ", and saw " no grounds for a
revision of the new economic policy ", on the basis of which it

[1] *Ibid.* pp. 91-92 ; *VKP(B) v Rezolyutsiyakh* (1941), i, 567.
[2] *Trinadtsatyi S"ezd Rossiiskoi Kommunisticheskoi Partii (Bol'shevikov)*
(1924), p. 253.
[3] *Ibid.* p. 220.   [4] *Ibid.* p. 95.   [5] *Ibid.* pp. 382-397.

was necessary to carry on " systematic work to strengthen the socialist elements in the general economy ".[1] The special resolution on internal trade declared that " the fundamental methods for the conquest of the market must be not measures of administrative intervention, but a strengthening of the economic positions of state trade and of the cooperatives ". But this equivocal declaration of principle was negatived by a precise direction that the newly established People's Commissariat of Internal Trade should exercise " the right of regulating all internal trade, of establishing fixed prices ".[2] The empirical character of NEP had been vindicated. Uncompromising fidelity to its principles was loudly proclaimed. But the principle that internal trade should be freed from state interference, or subject to interference only in the guise of financial policy, had given way under the strain of the scissors crisis. The control of prices by the state was restored in response, not to any doctrinal scruples, but to the pressures of a grave economic emergency.

No party congress held at this period and under Zinoviev's leadership could fail to pay its tribute to the primary importance of the peasant. But a note of uneasiness crept into the pronouncements of the official spokesmen on the subject. Zinoviev admitted that " the party is still too much an urban party, we know the country too little ". But he had no difficulty in establishing, by unusually copious quotations from party and non-party authorities, what was the crucial problem of the moment :

> The fundamental point affecting the countryside — the point about which all our ears have lately been buzzing — is the process of differentiation. Vladimir Ilich told us many times that the countryside was being levelled out. Now something new is beginning : as the result of NEP the countryside is undergoing a process of differentiation.

He admitted that there was increasing talk of *kulaks*, and dwelt on the appearance of " the nepman-usurer, the shop-keeper, the still-owner, the big trader ". Every prosperous peasant must not be dubbed a *kulak*. Nevertheless it was a disquieting symptom that the régime was most in favour in the " prosperous *kulak* sector ". But the moral was far from clear :

[1] *VKP(B) v Rezolyutsiyakh* (1941), i, 566.
[2] *Ibid.* i, 582-583.

What is required is not to squeeze the " *kulak* " at all costs into insensibility, but to support the middle peasant, to support the poor peasant.[1]

These generalities did not go much beyond the conventional conclusion registered in the congress resolution of " the unchanging task of the party to strengthen and reinforce the confidence of the peasantry in the proletarian state ".[2] For light on the differences which underlay these routine pronouncements it was necessary to turn to other speakers.

Kalinin, who made the main report to the congress on rural questions, began by quoting Lenin's pronouncements at the eighth party congress of 1919 on the need to conciliate the peasant, and especially the middle peasant. He recognized the increase under NEP of the difference between the poor peasant and the middle peasant on one side and the *kulak* on the other. A defence could, however, be found for this state of affairs :

> At the present moment the general well-being of the peasantry is rising. The condition of the poor peasant is perhaps being raised indirectly. Many, for example, are hiring themselves out to work. This is not socialism, but it is a direct improvement. . . . In proportion as the well-being of the peasantry increases, differentiation within it also increases.

After painting a rosy picture of the agricultural communes (which enjoyed the advantage over the Soviet farms that the labour code did not apply to them [3]), Kalinin returned to the individual peasant and declared that " equalization ", which he coupled with a " natural economy ", would be a step backward. The production of crops for the market was the road to socialism. In such conditions little or nothing could be done to alter " *kulak* tendencies ", though " it does not follow that the workers' and peasants' authority will take no measures at all of an administrative character against big racketeers and swindlers, who live by ruining the peasantry ". Kalinin then broached what was perhaps a

[1] *Trinadtsatyi S"ezd Rossiiskoi Kommunisticheskoi Partii (Bol'shevikov)* (1924), pp. 100-102.
[2] *VKP(B) v Rezolyutsiyakh* (1941), i, 566.
[3] For agricultural communes and Soviet farms see *The Bolshevik Revolution, 1917-1923*, Vol. 2, pp. 155-156. Agricultural communes were voluntary groups of individuals pooling their production, Soviet farms state institutions employing hired labour : hence their different status under the labour code.

question of symbolical rather than real importance, but turned out to be the most contentious issue of agrarian policy at the congress — the future of the peasant committees of mutual aid. The committees, originally created to supervise the distribution of relief during the great famine of 1921–1922, had since languished with an indeterminate mandate to assist the needy peasant. Bold spirits in the party now suggested that these committees should be reorganized as committees of middle and poor peasants, and used as an instrument to curb the growing power of the *kulak*, in short, to perform functions similar to those exercised under war communism by the short-lived " committees of poor peasants ".[1] Kalinin emphatically opposed this view. He wished to retain them as organs for assisting individual peasants in case of misfortune, and not to transform them into political instruments for improving the lot of the poor peasant as a class.[2]

Krupskaya followed Kalinin and, without directly refuting him, set a different tone with her opening quotation from a speech of Lenin in 1920 :

> The class war in the countryside has become a fact. It has now penetrated into the depths of the country ; there is now not a single village where it is impossible to distinguish between *kulaks* and poor peasants.

She sought to attenuate the impression left by Kalinin's speech of official indulgence for the *kulak*. The committees of mutual aid might serve as a form of union between the middle peasant and the poor peasant ; unless such a union was achieved, " the *kulak* will gain the upper hand, and the peasantry follow the line, not of cooperation, but of capitalist development ".[3] Rykov summed up in favour of Krupskaya's view. The task was " to separate the poor and middle peasant from the *kulak*, to organize him separately, and thus to strengthen our base among the middle and poor peasants against the *kulak* " ; the committees of mutual aid should " not only play a, so to speak, charitable rôle, but form the rallying-point for the forces of the poor and middle peasantry in the struggle against the rich peasantry and the *kulak*, and become the foundation of our power and influence in the

[1] See *The Bolshevik Revolution, 1917–1923*, Vol. 2, pp. 53-55.
[2] *Trinadtsatyi S"ezd Rossiiskoi Kommunisticheskoi Partii (Bol'shevikov)* 1924), pp. 458-471.   [3] *Ibid.* p. 478.

countryside ".[1] Notwithstanding these authoritative pronouncements, however, the *kulak* evidently had powerful protectors in
the party, who saw in him the best guarantee of increased agricultural production. Both Kalinin and Rykov made the unusual
admission that the congress resolution on the functions of the
committees lacked " clarity " and " definiteness ", and Kalinin
specifically added that " the formulation on this point is a compromise between two lines ".[2] The resolution, which bore the
general title " On Work in the Country ", was in conventional
terms. Its main emphasis was on the development of cooperation
of all kinds as the goal of party endeavour, and the best antidote
to capitalism in the countryside. It commended the committees
of mutual aid as organs for the assistance and organization of the
poorer peasants, but refrained from any attack on the *kulaks* or
encouragement of class war in the villages. Thanks largely to the
efforts of those who, if the point were pressed, might easily be
branded as *kulaks*, prosperity was still rising. The cities were
being fed, and grain was even being exported. The dangers of
a revival of capitalism in the countryside did not seem for the
moment either formidable or imminent. The symptoms of dis-
quietude manifested at the thirteenth congress about the ultimate
implications of NEP for Soviet agriculture were still no more than
a faint and distant warning of troubles to come.

[1] *Ibid.* p. 500.
[2] *Ibid.* pp. 470, 504; according to an article in *Sotsialisticheskii Vestnik*
(Berlin), Nos. 12-13 (82-83), June 20, 1924, p. 8, " a battle flared up " on this
question in the commission of the congress (the proceedings of the commissions
were not published). The full text of the resolution is in *VKP(B) v Rezolyu-*
tsiyakh (1941), i, 589-598.

PART II

THE CAPITALIST WORLD

CHAPTER 5

THE OCCUPATION OF THE RUHR

THE year 1922 had been on the whole a successful and re-assuring period for Soviet foreign policy. At Genoa, at The Hague, at Lausanne Soviet delegates sat side by side with those of other Powers on equal, or almost equal, terms. The Rapallo treaty, and the economic and military arrangements that lay behind it, constituted, if not an alliance, at any rate an *entente cordiale* with an important Power, and gave Soviet Russia for the first time the opportunity of making her weight count in European affairs. Not all the omens were favourable. In spite of the improvement in the diplomatic situation, the Soviet Government was recognized *de jure* by only twelve countries, of which only one could count as a great Power: Germany, Austria, Poland, Finland, Estonia, Latvia, Lithuania, Bulgaria, Turkey, Persia, Afghanistan and Outer Mongolia. Six more had accorded *de facto* recognition : Great Britain, Italy, Czechoslovakia, Norway, Sweden and China.[1] The rest of the world still declined any form of official relations. The ambition of the Soviet leaders to attract foreign capital on terms which would not be too onerous had been disappointed. Dictatorship in the new and disturbing guise of Fascism had seized power in Italy. In Great Britain, power had passed to a Conservative government under Bonar Law, in France, to Poincaré's national bloc, both openly proclaiming their distaste for the Soviet régime. In Germany the Wirth coalition government which had concluded the Rapallo treaty resigned in November 1922, and was succeeded by a government of a more markedly Right complexion than the Weimar republic had yet known — a so-called " business-men's government " headed by Cuno, a director of the Hamburg-Amerika line ; Germany became, in the

[1] *Dvenadtsatyi S"ezd Rossiiskoi Kommunisticheskoi Partii (Bol'shevikov)* (1923), p. 9.

current popular phrase, "a republic without republicans".
Above all, the fourth congress of Comintern in November 1922
had confirmed the diagnosis, originally made by the third congress,
of a general ebb in the revolutionary tide. Consolation could,
however, be felt for the postponement of the European revolution
in the increasing strength and stability of the Soviet Government,
which now at last seemed secure not only against internal, but also
against external, attack. Gradual progress had diminished the
eagerness for spectacular achievement. Tranquillity and consolidation were the order of the day.

This comfortable picture, which held out to Lenin's harassed
deputies the hope that no major decisions of foreign policy would
be called for in the near future, was shattered by the French
occupation of the Ruhr on January 11, 1923, as a reprisal for
shortcomings in German reparation payments. It was an operation in every way distasteful to the Soviet Government. It carried
with it the incalculable menace of another European upheaval;
it weakened Soviet Russia's only important ally and, by striking
at a vital spot, reduced that ally to the verge of collapse; and,
apart from these general results, it brought to a standstill a branch
of German industry which was a large supplier, or potential
supplier, of Soviet requirements. The fact that France had undertaken this step in defiance of British objections and with the sole
support of Belgium among the western countries only aggravated
the danger. For, if the operation was successful, France, with
her eastern satellite, Poland, would dominate Europe; and no
Power had been so consistently and uncompromisingly hostile to
the Soviet Government as France. The chances of successful
resistance in Germany were slender. But two days after the
French incursion the Cuno government issued an appeal to the
population of the Ruhr for "passive resistance" and non-coopera-
tion with the occupying authorities. The call was enthusiastically
received and, at the outset, generally obeyed. The industry of the
Ruhr ceased to work.

The French occupation of the Ruhr had found the German
Communist Party (KPD) in a chastened mood. Like communist
parties elsewhere, it was marking time and gathering strength
for the future: "the conquest of power as a practical task of the
moment", Radek had said at the fourth congress of Comintern,

" is not on the agenda ".[1]   But this did not mean that it was
inactive. Following the prescriptions of the fourth congress of
Comintern,[2] it was busily promoting a general campaign against
the Versailles treaty. A week before the occupation a conference
of delegates of all the western European communist parties had
been held in Essen and had passed a resolution denouncing the
Versailles treaty and the imperialist policies of the western Powers
towards Germany.[3] The Ruhr occupation let loose a flood of
protests. On the very day of the occupation the *Rote Fahne*
published a proclamation by the Zentrale of the KPD. Two days
later TsIK in Moscow adopted a resolution of protest to the
peoples of all countries ; [4] this was followed by a similar protest
from IKKI ; [5] on January 17, the *Rote Fahne* published a protest
signed in Berlin by Zetkin, Radek and Newbold on behalf of
Comintern and by Heckert on behalf of Profintern.[6] The keynote of all these documents was to depict the French adventure
as the culmination of the criminal policy of oppression and
exploitation of Germany initiated four and a half years earlier at
Versailles.

> The sovereignty of the German people [ran the resolution
> of TsIK] is infringed. The right of the German people
> to self-determination is trodden underfoot. Germany's dis-
> organized economy has suffered a new and shattering blow.
> Cruel poverty and unprecedented oppression threaten the
> working masses of Germany, while all Europe will witness an
> increase in economic dislocation. The world is again thrown
> into a state of eve-of-war feverishness. Sparks are flying in the
> powder-cellar created by the Versailles treaty.

Little or nothing was offered in the way of positive advice, though
the joint manifesto of Comintern and Profintern, which was
addressed " To all workers, peasants and soldiers ", spoke of " the
solution of union with Soviet Russia ".

[1] *Protokoll des Vierten Kongresses der Kommunistischen Internationale* (1923),
p. 318.
[2] See *The Bolshevik Revolution, 1917–1923*, Vol. 3, pp. 454-455.
[3] *Die Rote Fahne* (Berlin), January 9, 1923.
[4] *Izvestiya*, January 14, 1923 ; English translation in *Soviet Documents on
Foreign Policy*, ed. J. Degras, i (1951), 368-370.
[5] *Internationale Presse-Korrespondenz*, No. 11, January 15, 1923, p. 75.
[6] The text is also in *Die Rote Gewerkschaftsinternationale*, No. 1 (24),
January 1923, p. 82.

The weakness of all these documents was that they evaded the pressing practical question of the attitude to be adopted by the KPD towards the Cuno government which had proclaimed " passive resistance " to the French occupation. When Cuno asked the Reichstag on January 13, 1923, for a vote of confidence in his " passive resistance " policy, the members of the KPD demonstrated and voted against him. Frölich, who spoke for the party in the debate, attacked the past policy of " fulfilment " of the treaty as an attempt to sacrifice " a hungry, mortally sick and dying proletariat " for the benefit of the bourgeoisie, but none the less declared that " in this hour of danger from without, we must attack our bourgeoisie from within ", and demanded the overthrow of the Cuno government.[1] The *Rote Fahne* throughout this period continued to treat Poincaré and Cuno as twin enemies against whom its shafts were equally directed : in its issue of January 23, 1923, under the banner headline " Smite Poincaré and Cuno on the Ruhr and on the Spree ", it published a further proclamation of the party Zentrale demanding a struggle both against " the robber plans of Poincaré " and against " Stinnes, Thyssen and Krupp and their understrappers in the Cuno government ".[2] Frölich, who belonged to the Left wing of the KPD, described the " war in the Ruhr " as a joint struggle of French and German communists — " the first international action of the communists " — against Poincaré and against Cuno, and deprecated any attempt to face communists with the dilemma " *either* against Poincaré *or* against Cuno ".[3] Those responsible for the conduct of Soviet foreign policy must have been aware that the Cuno government was offering the only practicable, and partially

[1] *Verhandlungen des Reichstags*, ccclvii (1923), 9429-9434.

[2] The story in R. Fischer, *Stalin and German Communism* (Harvard, 1948), p. 264, that, on the day after the headline quoted above appeared in the *Rote Fahne*, Radek " fired the two men responsible for it " (one of them being Ruth Fischer's brother), and changed it to "Against Cuno on the Spree, on the Ruhr against Poincaré ", is inaccurate in every particular that can be checked. The original headline was not " rhymed " and is incorrectly quoted ; it was not " changed " for the simple reason that the *Rote Fahne* never repeated its headlines, and this one did not reappear in any form. Brandler subsequently quoted the slogan in the form, "Against Poincaré on the Ruhr and against Cuno on the Spree " (*Protokoll : Fünfter Kongress der Kommunistischen Internationale* (n.d.), i, 226).

[3] *Internationale Presse-Korrespondenz*, No. 29, February 14, 1923, pp. 214-215 ; No. 43, March 9, 1923, p. 319.

effective, opposition to the French plan and was to this extent working in the Soviet interest. Radek, at any rate, knew better than to suppose that a German government of the Right was a less reliable ally for Soviet Russia than a German government of the Left : the Rapallo policy and the secret military agreements were as safe in the hands of Cuno as in those of Wirth, and far safer than they would have been in the hands of Ebert or Scheidemann. But such considerations did not at this time enter into the formation of the policies of Comintern. Radek showed his usual agility in keeping in separate compartments his activities in Germany as agent of Comintern and as agent of the Soviet Government ; nor is there any evidence of serious pressure from Moscow on the leadership of the KPD except for the purpose of maintaining party unity. Nothing is more remarkable in the story of events in Germany in 1923 than the lack of any apparent attempt to coordinate the policies of Comintern and of the Soviet Government, and the acceptance by the German Government of the distinction between them.

The peace between the Right and Left wings of the KPD, which had been patched up at the fourth congress of Comintern [1] in the previous November, had no lasting quality, and the old battles were fought out once more at the eighth congress of the KPD, which opened in Leipzig on January 28, 1923. The only change was that Meyer, who had spent the latter part of 1922 at Comintern headquarters in Moscow,[2] was superseded as leader of the party, and of its Right wing, by Brandler, over whom Radek now cast the mantle of his support. Both sides continued to assert their loyalty to the Comintern slogans of the " united front " and of the " workers' government ". But the interpretation of the slogans differed widely in practice. The Right, led by Brandler and Thalheimer, sought to apply united front tactics by concluding agreements with the leaders of other Left parties as well as by agitating among their members, and interpreted the call for workers' governments as an invitation to enter coalition governments with social-democrats (a possibility which had already been mooted in Saxony and Thuringia); the Left, led

---

[1] See *The Bolshevik Revolution, 1917–1923*, Vol. 3, pp. 452-454.
[2] *Bericht über die Verhandlungen des III (8) Parteitags der Kommunistichen Partei Deutschlands* (1923), p. 58.

by Maslow, Ruth Fischer and Thälmann, preached the united front " from below " as a means of seducing members of other Left parties from their allegiance to corrupt leaders, and regarded no workers' government as worthy of the name which was not led and dominated by communists. The accusation of the Left against the Right was that it neglected the ultimate goal of revolution for the sake of immediate objectives and the tactical manœuvres necessary to secure them. These controversies absorbed the congress, which failed altogether to make any pronouncement on the Ruhr occupation. The Left did indeed propose that " the political situation and the tasks of the KPD " (meaning the Ruhr crisis) should be placed at the head of the agenda. But the Right treated the proposal as a motion of no confidence in the party leadership, and voted it down by a majority of 122 to 88.[1] Brandler's major speech at the congress was a long plea for the policy of seeking a united front with other workers' parties, and contained a specific offer to enter a coalition government with the social-democrats in Saxony.[2] The theses of the Right on the united front and the workers' government were adopted, and those of the Left rejected, by a majority of 118 to 59.[3] But for the outside world, as well as for the KPD itself, the most conspicuous feature of the conference was its failure to make any significant pronouncement on the decisive question of the hour. The Left attributed the failure to the bankruptcy of the Right leadership of the party, and indulged in rhetorical calls to action which the Right denounced as demagogy.[4] Radek, true to the Comintern line at this time, exerted himself to avoid the danger of a split in the German party and had insisted on the inclusion of three members of the defeated Left in the newly elected central committee.[5] The party, in spite of bitter recriminations, had held

---

[1] *Bericht über die Verhandlungen des III (8) Parteitags der Kommunistischen Partei Deutschlands* (1923), pp. 186-187.   [2] *Ibid.* p. 328.
[3] *Ibid.* p. 375 ; for the text of the theses as adopted see *ibid.* pp. 415-424.
[4] The views of the Left were summed up by Ruth Fischer after the Leipzig congress : " The Communist Party is lost as a revolutionary party if it confines itself to mere propaganda. It must be active, it must act. It must not only enter with all its forces into current mass movements, it must continually and always attempt to set the masses in motion " (*Die Internationale*, vi, No. 3 (February 1, 1923), pp. 90-91).
[5] R. Fischer, *Stalin and German Communism* (Harvard, 1948), p. 229, and P. Maslowski, *Thälmann* (1932), p. 42, both record Radek's appearance at a

together. But the Leipzig congress had scarcely added to its laurels or dissipated the doubts of those who questioned its efficiency as a revolutionary organization.

The Ruhr crisis brought into the open an embarrassment long latent in the history and policies of the KPD : the equivocal relation between German communism and German nationalism. The protests of the KPD and of Comintern against the French occupation of the Ruhr had been geared to the national campaign of protest against the Versailles treaty, making them at once topical and more intense. The vocabulary of denunciation employed by communists began to coincide more and more noticeably with that employed by the nationalists ; German nationalism, it seemed, could not be treated on the same footing as French nationalism or British imperialism as an unconditionally hostile force. In February 1923 Thalheimer, now the chief theorist of the Right leadership of the KPD, endeavoured to find a doctrinal basis for a more indulgent view. In the Ruhr conflict, he argued, " the rôles of the French and German bourgeoisies are not identical in spite of the identity of their class essence " ; the German bourgeoisie had acquired " an objectively revolutionary rôle . . . in spite of itself ". He invoked the precedent of Bismarck who had played the part of a " revolutionary from above " after 1848, and recalled the verdict of Marx and Engels that Bismarck's rôle had become " openly reactionary " only after Sedan. The defeat of 1918 had once more reversed Germany's position, and made German nationalism a potentially revolutionary factor. The logical conclusion followed : " the defeat of French imperialism in the world war was not a communist aim, its defeat in the war in the Ruhr is a communist aim ". Thalheimer's article appeared anonymously in the theoretical journal of the KPD.[1] It set a fashion. Radek, writing an article in celebration of the twenty-fifth anniversary of the foundation of the Russian

secret session of the congress to bring about this result. Radek, who was staying illegally in Germany, did not appear at the open sessions. According to Ruth Fischer a year later, " the factional struggle, the hatred between the two groups was so bad that only the intervention of the representative of IKKI at the last moment succeeded in averting the split " (*Die Lehren der Deutschen Ereignisse* (Hamburg, 1924), p. 51).

[1] *Die Internationale*, vi, No. 4 (February 15, 1923), pp. 97-102; a translation of the article, bearing Thalheimer's signature and the date February 13, appeared in *Kommunisticheskii Internatsional*, No. 25, June 7, 1923, cols. 6857-6864.

party, paid tribute to the current mood in an unexpected comparison of Bismarck with Lenin :

> When one reads his first reports, when one follows his policy step by step, one must ask oneself : " Whence this understanding of the whole European reality in a landowner ? " The same thought always comes to one when one thinks of the history of our party, of the history of the revolution and of Ilich.[1]

This new tenderness for German nationalism did not escape the notice of communists in neighbouring countries. A Czech communist, Neurath, wrote an article in a Czech communist publication directly attacking Thalheimer's position as an example of the corruption of the workers' movement by patriotic sentiments (such as had occurred in 1914), and challenged him to pursue his argument to its logical conclusion, i.e. that the German proletariat should support the German bourgeoisie against the French bourgeoisie. In the journal of the KPD another Czech communist, writing under the name of Sommer, denounced Thalheimer's thesis as " a magnificent flower of national Bolshevism ", and maintained that there was no distinction between 1914 and 1923. The obligation of the proletariat to fight against its own national bourgeoisie remained unchanged : " there can be no understanding with the enemy within ". Finally, Thalheimer in a reply seized on this point and attempted to justify the distinction between 1914 and 1923.[2]

The political forces making for cooperation between communists and nationalists in Germany in the summer of 1923 proved more compelling than the theoretical arguments advanced for or against this course. But the controversy did nothing to

---

[1] *Internationale Presse-Korrespondenz*, No. 45, March 12, 1923, p. 337.

[2] Sommer's article appeared in *Die Internationale*, vi, No. 7 (April 1, 1923), pp. 207-211 ; both Neurath's and Sommer's articles were reprinted in *Kommunisticheskii Internatsional*, No. 25, June 7, 1923, cols. 6865-6880, after Thalheimer's original article, and were followed by his reply, *ibid.* cols. 6879-6888. According to R. Fischer, *Stalin and German Communism* (Harvard, 1948), p. 282, Neurath and Sommer wrote their articles with the encouragement of Zinoviev, who used them as his " pawns " in his controversy with Radek. This antedates Zinoviev's intervention in KPD affairs and commitment to the Left ; the printing of all these articles in the journal of Comintern is evidence only of the toleration still accorded at this time to divergent views. Nor is there any ground for regarding Thalheimer as a " pawn " of Radek.

clarify party policy. While the continuance of passive resistance and the struggle against the occupying forces brought increasing political unrest and increasing dislocation to the German economy, the KPD had no plan to exploit the emergency, and no fresh directives were issued by Comintern. At the end of January 1923 a joint announcement appeared in the name of Comintern and Profintern of the creation of an " action committee against Fascism ", and in March a committee under the same name was established in Berlin under the presidency of Klara Zetkin and proclaimed an " anti-Fascist week ".[1] In March an attempt was made to pursue united front tactics by summoning an international conference at Frankfurt to which the parties of the Second International and the Amsterdam trade unions were also invited. A few social-democrats attended, but a large majority of the participants were communists.[2] Brandler, Zetkin and French and British delegates all denounced the Versailles treaty and the Ruhr occupation ; but Lozovsky, who came from Moscow to represent Profintern, seems to have been the dominant figure. The main resolutions of the conference were directed against " the danger of war " and " international Fascism ".[3] Denunciation of the German Government and demands for its overthrow were relegated to the background ; and to this extent the conference represented a success for the Right wing of the KPD. But in the ranks of the KPD in the Ruhr itself it was the more aggressive Left which predominated. A regional party conference meeting at Essen at the end of March attacked the tacit support given by the party to passive resistance, declared that " the propaganda and the preparations of the nationalists are the framework of counter-revolution ", and proposed " to save the German proletariat from endless grey enslavement by fighting for political power ".[4]

[1] *Internationale Presse-Korrespondenz*, No. 19, January 29, 1923, pp. 123-124 ; No. 48, March 14, 1923, p. 378 ; No. 55-56, March 28, 1923, p. 456.
    [2] The membership of the conference was described in detail by Bukharin in *Dvenadtsatyi S"ezd Rossiiskoi Kommunisticheskoi Partii (Bol'shevikov)* (1923), p. 265.
    [3] The proceedings of the conference were recorded in a pamphlet entitled *Der Internationale Kampf des Proletariats gegen Kriegsgefahr und Faszismus* (1923).
    [4] *Bericht über die Verhandlungen des IX Parteitags der Kommunistischen Partei Deutschlands* (1924), p. 132.

This incitement to revolution, which recalled the grim blunder of the March action, seriously perturbed the party Right. " History ", wrote Radek after the Essen conference, " is at present galloping like a frightened horse." [1] Local communists organized almost continuous disturbances in the Ruhr. An unsuccessful communist *putsch* occurred in Mühlheim in the middle of April, and serious disturbances in Gelsenkirchen in May. By way of keeping up the morale of the workers, the Soviet trade unions organized the despatch of two shiploads of grain to the Ruhr; these were intended not merely as a symbolical gesture of support, but as an indication of Soviet willingness to come to the aid of a victorious German revolution if it were subjected to measures of blockade and starvation from the west.[2] But by this time IKKI was thoroughly alarmed. It summoned representatives of the party Zentrale and of the Berlin and Hamburg organizations (which were the stronghold of the Left opposition) to a meeting in Moscow on April 22, 1923.[3] Here IKKI engaged in another of its attempts at compromise and conciliation. A resolution was adopted which admitted errors committed by the Right as well as by the Left. Some of the pronouncements of the central committee in favour of a united front had gone too far, though its line had been " in general and on the whole correct ". To start revolutionary action in the Ruhr would be dangerous " so long as no revolutionary movement can be detected in the unoccupied part of the territory and in the French working masses ". In Saxony, communists should pursue the policy of a united front with the social-democrats, but not to the point of accepting responsibility for their policy; the demand should be put forward for an " all-German workers' government ". Meanwhile members of the Berlin and Hamburg organizations were

[1] *Kommunisticheskii Internatsional*, No. 24, April 5, 1923, col. 6349.
[2] The arrival of the first consignment was reported in *Die Rote Fahne* (Berlin), March 30, 1923; the arrival of the second was described by a trade union delegate who accompanied it in *Die Rote Gewerkschaftsinternationale*, No. 5-6 (28-29), May–June, 1923, pp. 484-492. Radek used the occasion for a bitter article recalling the refusal by the SPD and the USPD of the offer of Soviet grain in November 1918 (*Internationale Presse-Korrespondenz*, No. 47, March 14, 1923, pp. 362-363).
[3] The text of Zinoviev's letter is in *Material zu den Differenzen mit der Opposition* (1923), a KPD pamphlet containing a number of opposition resolutions and declarations.

instructed not to carry on their agitation outside their own districts.[1] The essence of the compromise was revealed only after the return of the delegates to Germany. The central committee of the KPD decided to enlarge its membership to 25 and to coopt four " Leftists ", including Thälman and Ruth Fischer.[2]

During the first four months of the Ruhr occupation, it would be erroneous to attribute either to the Russian Communist Party or to Comintern any considered policy for dealing with the emergency or any desire to intervene in German affairs. In general terms both were concerned to strengthen the German Communist Party and to promote the cause of revolution in Germany. But, where the KPD itself was acutely divided on the means of attaining this end, the greatest reluctance still reigned in Moscow to take sides. This reluctance was no doubt partly due to the " marking time " mood which governed all the deliberations of the Politburo in the period of Lenin's incapacity. But it could also be pointed out that Lenin's last appearance in the affairs of Comintern had been designed to smooth over the difference between Right and Left in the KPD and to refuse to decide between them.[3] The almost continuous presence of Radek in Berlin during this time [4] may have given the impression that Comintern supported the party Right. But this impression was removed every time the issue was taken to Moscow, and the indications are that the Right would have commanded a majority in the German party even without Radek's support. The lessons of the March action had never been forgotten. In the aftermath of that tragic fiasco Radek had not unfairly described the traditional rôle of the KPD as that of " a power which held back the proletarians from unnecessary clashes, organized and enlightened the masses, and led it into great struggles only when no danger existed that it would be defeated and isolated ".[5] In the spring of 1923, divided counsels in the KPD and, more generally, among

---

[1] *Kommunisticheskii Internatsional*, No. 25, June 7, 1923, coln. 6845-6856.

[2] *Internationale Presse-Korrespondenz*, No. 84, May 18, 1923, pp. 709-710.

[3] See *The Bolshevik Revolution, 1917–1923*, Vol. 3, p. 453.

[4] According to R. Fischer, *Stalin and German Communism* (Harvard, 1948), p. 261, he had offices in the Soviet Embassy, in the Soviet trade delegation and in the *Rote Fahne*, and moved constantly between them ; he was certainly ubiquitous, but she probably exaggerates his influence.

[5] *Protokoll des III. Kongresses der Kommunistischen Internationale* (Hamburg, 1921), pp. 456-457.

the German workers made revolutionary action, even in the present desperate plight of the German nation, seem almost hopeless. Whether Radek, in supporting the attitude of the Right, was influenced by the desire to base Soviet policy on amicable and intimate relations with the German Government, whatever its political complexion, and whether this consideration consciously or unconsciously influenced members of the Politburo in taking their decisions, are questions which cannot be answered in default of evidence, and which, perhaps, are by their nature not susceptible of a precise answer. What can fairly be said is that, down to the middle of May 1923, the attitude of Comintern and its agents towards the German question can be explained without invoking the hypothesis of a specific Soviet interest in the decisions taken. Thereafter, a sharp turn in the international situation caused a new and dramatic departure in Comintern policy.

CHAPTER 6

THE CURZON ULTIMATUM

THE picture of Soviet reactions to western Europe in the first weeks of the Ruhr occupation was dominated by one preoccupation : the fear that it might be the prelude to a fresh European war. Whatever advantages the Bolshevik leaders might hope to reap from the occasion, whether through the reinforcement of German national resentments against the Versailles treaty or through the hastening of the process of world revolution, the desire to fish in troubled waters was outweighed by apprehension of a general war which might expose the Soviet frontiers to attack from the west.

> The complete domination of Germany [wrote *Izvestiya* on January 21, 1923] represents a grave menace for the Soviet republic. It would give Poincaré control over a territory reaching from the Seine to the Vistula, and, Poland being the ally of France, from the Vistula to the Soviet frontier.

In particular, the threat of the penetration of French armies into the heart of Germany seemed to portend the overthrow of the Rapallo treaty and, as Kamenev afterwards said, " a shattering of those foundations of stability and balance in the world position on which the Soviet republic rests." [1] In the middle of February 1923 Chicherin, back in Moscow from the Lausanne conference, attempted a more reassuring diagnosis of the French action. The progressive development of international cartels was the significant factor in the contemporary capitalist world. He argued that " a

---

[1] *Vtoroi S"ezd Sovetov Soyuza Sovetskikh Sotsialisticheskikh Respublik* (1924), p. 66. Stresemann some time later told D'Abernon that, " if Poincaré had carried through his policy, Germany would have formed a coalition with Russia, and together they would have swept over Europe " (D'Abernon, *An Ambassador of Peace*, iii (1930), 146) — one of the few occasions on which Stresemann tried to frighten the western Powers with the bogy of a Soviet-German alliance.

new world war is at any rate not near "; that " the Ruhr adventure is in the last resort only an episode in the process of cartel-building by the two industries [of France and Germany] "; and that " the intervention of England and, still more, a common intervention by England and America would at once lead to reconciliation ". Meanwhile Russia could congratulate herself on her growing importance in world politics.[1] But brave words did not remove current anxieties. The interest of Soviet Russia in peace became a constant theme of Soviet publicity. Kamenev, as deputy president of Sovnarkom, told Ransome, the correspondent of the *Manchester Guardian*, that Soviet Russia was now at peace and that, " so far as we are concerned, we shall do our utmost to make it last for ever ". Events in western Europe were menacing. " But whether we become involved depends entirely on Poland ", since a Polish mobilization against Germany " would in the long run be directed against us ".[2] Ten days later Ransome secured an interview with Trotsky, who tried to answer the delicate question " why we do not greet the French invasion of the Ruhr as a revolutionary stimulus ". He explained that " it is not at all to our interest that the revolution should take place in a Europe exhausted and drained of blood ". War might mean " the bleeding and destruction primarily of those generations of the working class which are the bearers of the future ". This would lead to " a most severe lowering of European culture over a long period " and " the postponement of revolutionary perspectives ".[3] Hence Soviet Russia was " vitally interested in the preservation of peace "; Trotsky expressed confidence that " the hypothesis of a Polish attack [on Germany] will remain merely an hypothesis ".[4]

Opportunities for acrimony in Soviet relations with the western Powers were, of course, never lacking and were rarely neglected. In January 1923 the Lithuanian Government, tired of long and fruitless discussions with the allies about the future of

---

[1] *Izvestiya*, February 15, 1923 ; a translation appeared in *Internationale Presse-Korrespondenz*, No. 37, February 26, 1923, pp. 263-264.

[2] *Manchester Guardian*, February 19, 1923 ; Radek argued about the same time that, if Poland became involved in war against Germany, " she will not wish to have Soviet Russia in her rear, and will march against us " (*Izvestiya*, February 17, 1923).

[3] Trotsky had expressed the same apprehension on the outbreak of war in 1914 (see *The Bolshevik Revolution, 1917-1923*, Vol. 3, p. 567, note 2).

[4] *Manchester Guardian*, March 1, 1923.

Memel, seized the port by a military coup ; and on February 16 the allied governments took the line of least resistance by recognizing Lithuanian sovereignty over it. This made it easier for them to compound with their consciences by officially recognizing the existing eastern frontier of Poland — a step hitherto delayed by the unending disputes over Vilna and Eastern Galicia. Recognition was now accorded by a formal act of the Conference of Ambassadors in Paris of March 15, 1923. While the Memel decision scarcely affected the interests of Soviet Russia, and the Polish decision did no more than recognize the existing frontier, these proceedings evoked the usual series of protests from the Soviet Government.[1] A similar protest was directed to the Finnish Government against its attempt to refer the Karelian question to the " so-called League of Nations ".[2] But in January 1923 the People's Commissar for Health, Semashko, for the first time appeared at Geneva to attend meetings of the League health organization ; [3] and, when in March 1923 an invitation arrived from the League to be represented at a projected naval disarmament conference in Rome, the reply, while reserving Soviet objections of principle to the " so-called League of Nations " (the formula was usual at this period), was an acceptance of the invitation.[4] There was nothing here to suggest an imminent crisis in relations with the west.

The even tenor of these relations was, however, soon to be broken from the other side. The advance into the Ruhr had increased the prestige and self-confidence of France and her

---

[1] Klyuchnikov i Sabanin, *Mezhdunarodnaya Politika*, iii, i (1928), 233-234, 235-238.

[2] *Ibid*. iii, i, 235.

[3] Representatives of the RSFSR and of the Ukrainian SSR had attended a European health conference convened under the auspices of the League of Nations in Warsaw in March 1922 (*League of Nations : Records of the Third Assembly* (1922), ii, 64-65). The body attended by Semashko in January 1923 was officially described, in order to soothe Soviet susceptibilities, as an " international commission " meeting concurrently with the League Health Committee ; but Semashko himself brushed aside these niceties, explaining that " the presence of a People's Commissar of the Soviets at a meeting of the Health Committee need not cause any surprise . . . and did not change in any way the attitude of the Government of the Soviets towards the League of Nations " (*League of Nations Health Committee : Minutes of the Fifth Session* (C27.M13, 1923), iii, 31-35).

[4] *Pravda*, March 4, 1923 ; Klyuchnikov i Sabanin, *Mezhdunarodnaya Politika*, iii, i (1928), 238-239.

allies, all of them implacable enemies of Soviet Russia; and the
rise of Curzon to undisputed control of British foreign policy
brought a progressive deterioration in Anglo-Soviet relations.
Lloyd George, remarked Kamenev in the interview already
quoted, " realised that he was living in the 20th century, though
he had not always the courage to make the necessary deductions
and act on them "; Curzon, on the other hand, " is determined
that, if this is not the 19th century, he will behave as if it were ".[1]
Curzon had been in no way mollified by Chicherin's hostile
thrusts at the Lausanne conference.   On March 30, 1923, the
British chargé d'affaires in Moscow, Hodgson, handed a polite
but curt note to Narkomindel containing a " pressing and final
appeal " that the death sentence recently passed on Butkevich, a
Catholic priest accused of espionage, who was a Soviet citizen,
should not be carried out.   On the following day a reply was sent
from Narkomindel, signed by the head of its western department,
Vainshtein.   It rejected this intervention in the domestic affairs
of " an independent country and a sovereign state ", quoted some
alleged remarks of a " representative of the Irish republic in
France " on " the hypocritical interference of the British Government ", and concluded that British behaviour in India and Egypt
did not make a British appeal " in the name of humanity and
sanctity of life " particularly convincing.   Hodgson's refusal to
receive a note couched in these insulting terms provoked a
further reply signed by Vainshtein on April 4.   The report was
afterwards current that Vainshtein had despatched these notes
in Chicherin's absence and without his approval; and Chicherin
on other occasions certainly showed greater finesse both in dealing
and in parrying blows.   Whether the report was correct or not,
the notes would not have been sent if it had been realized that
they would give Curzon the opportunity for which he was waiting.
A vigorous anti-Soviet propaganda campaign spread through the
British press.   Then, on May 8, 1923, after a month of reflexion,
the Foreign Office instructed Hodgson to hand to the Soviet
Government a long memorandum in twenty-six paragraphs, known
in history as " the Curzon ultimatum ".   Beginning with a
mention of the Vainshtein notes, it embarked on a general complaint about the character of Soviet policy towards Great Britain

[1] *Manchester Guardian*, February 19, 1923.

since the conclusion of the Anglo-Soviet trade agreement in March 1921. Its first three sections related to the anti-British activities of Shumyatsky and Raskolnikov, the Soviet envoys in Teheran and Kabul respectively, to propaganda in India, and to the work of Comintern generally ; abandonment of these activities and apologies for them were demanded. The fourth and fifth sections were devoted to claims arising out of the death of one British agent and the imprisonment of another (their status was apparently not contested, though the charges against one of them were described as false) as long ago as 1920, and out of the recent detention of two British trawlers ; immediate settlement of these claims was demanded. The final demand was for the " unequivocal withdrawal " of the two Vainshtein notes. If these demands were not met within ten days the trade agreement would be denounced and Hodgson was instructed to leave Moscow.[1]

The ultimatum came as a severe shock to Moscow, being stronger than anything that had been expected. At the twelfth party congress in the middle of April, Zinoviev had speculated a little light-heartedly on the possibility of a " new intervention ".[2] Now the danger seemed imminent. On the next day a notice was sent out postponing the impending session of the enlarged IKKI till June 10 on account of " the danger of war ".[3] The consternation in Moscow was reinforced by two unfortunate coincidences. On May 2, 1923, Foch had arrived in Poland on a much advertised ceremonial visit, and had spent more than a week there attending military parades and visiting military units. The impression that the Polish army was being groomed for another war against Soviet Russia was inevitable in Soviet minds, especially when Foch's visit was followed a week later by one from the British Chief of the Imperial General Staff. The other coincidence was a senseless crime. When the adjourned Lausanne conference met again in April 1923 the Soviet Government appointed Vorovsky, now Soviet representative in Rome, as its delegate. Since the negotiation of the Straits convention had

---

[1] *Correspondence between His Majesty's Government and the Soviet Government respecting the Relations between the Two Governments*, Cmd. 1869 (1923), pp. 5-13 ; *Anglo-Sovetskie Otnosheniya (1921-1927 gg.)* (1927), pp. 30-39.

[2] *Dvenadtsatyi S"ezd Rossiiskoi Kommunisticheskoi Partii (Bol'shevikov)* (1923), p. 15.

[3] *Internationale Presse-Korrespondenz*, No. 77, May 11, 1923, p. 666.

M

been completed [1] there seemed no further reason for the attendance of a Soviet delegate. But, after an initial attempt to deny Vorovsky courier facilities,[2] he was admitted as an observer. While at Lausanne on this mission he was assassinated by a " white " Russian on May 10, 1923, on the day on which Foch completed his Polish visit and two days after the delivery of the Curzon ultimatum.

In an atmosphere of intense alarm and apprehension the Soviet Government made haste to buy off what appeared to be the most pressing danger. The situation closely resembled that which had arisen at the time of Curzon's last major protest against Soviet misdeeds in September 1921. The British Government could have afforded, with the support of a large section of British opinion, to denounce the Anglo-Soviet trade agreement and break off relations, and was unlikely to withdraw its demands; the Soviet Government could not afford a breach and was therefore obliged to give ground.[3] On May 11, 1923, three days after the " Curzon ultimatum ", Litvinov signed a reply drafted more in sorrow than in anger and promising virtually unqualified acceptance on all points but one. Compensation was offered, though without formal admission of responsibility, for the treatment of the two British agents; the trawlers were released, the fines imposed on them remitted, and negotiations proposed on the issue of principle; and the Vainshtein notes were explained away and declared to be non-existent. Only on the remaining question of Soviet activities directed against British interests in Asia were the controversies of 1921 renewed with the polite exasperation of weary familiarity. The independence of Comintern from governmental authority was reasserted. As regards the information from secret agents on which the British Government relied, every government had in its possession " materials of a similar character "; if these were used as a ground of conflict " peaceful relations between any two states could scarcely exist ". The British Government had once again weakened its case by quoting unverified and highly improbable secret reports (this time, that Sokolnikov, the People's Commissar of Finance, was a

---

[1] See *The Bolshevik Revolution, 1917-1923*, Vol. 3, p. 489.
[2] Klyuchnikov i Sabanin, *Mezhdunarodnaya Politika*, iii, i (1928), 243.
[3] See *The Bolshevik Revolution, 1917-1923*, Vol. 3, pp. 344-346.

member of the committee of Comintern concerned with the disbursement of funds to foreign communist parties). But the tenor of the Soviet argument was conciliatory, and the basic contention not wholly unreasonable. British and Russian agents in Asia had conducted subversive activities at one another's expense for fifty years before the Soviet Government had existed, or before Comintern had been thought of. The rules of the game were well known : agents who were found out by the other side were disowned by their employers. It was no excuse for changing the rules that the Russian agents now wore the guise of communist agitators. The British protests, declared the Soviet note, " give reason to suppose that, in the opinion of the British Government, the Russian republic ought in general to have no policy of its own, but everywhere to support British aspirations "; and " such an obligation ", it concluded, " the Russian Government has never assumed ".[1]

The despatch of this reply was accompanied by the release of a flood of propaganda. On the following day a monster demonstration was held in the Bol'shoi theatre in Moscow to protest against the murder of Vorovsky and the Curzon ultimatum. Chicherin was the principal orator and, having spoken of the murder of Vorovsky, turned to " the extreme reaction " prevailing in other parts of the world, " and notably in Great Britain ". Lenin's illness had filled the enemies of Soviet Russia with " naïve confidence that the Soviet power is deprived of its firmness and can be overthrown by pressure from without ". He concluded with a gesture of defiance at the Curzon ultimatum : " We firmly await our enemy before our threshold, and we believe that he will not have the courage to attack ". Trotsky repeated the defiance, but was also eloquent on the Soviet desire for peace :

> In the present tense situation in Europe this would be a life-and-death struggle ; it would be a struggle which would last for months, perhaps years, which would swallow up all the resources and forces of our country, which would interrupt our economic and cultural work for years. That is why we say : " May this cup pass from us ".[2]

---

[1] *Anglo-Sovetskie Otnosheniya* (1917–1927 gg.) (1927), pp. 40-47.
[2] L. Trotsky, *Kak Vooruzhalas' Revolyutsiya*, iii, ii (1925), 87 ; all the speeches were reported in the Moscow press of May 13, 1923.

Bukharin also spoke, and Gallacher, a prominent member of the British Communist Party, was present as " the ambassador of the English proletariat ".[1] The trade union central council held a special meeting and issued an appeal to the British Left against " the instigation of a new imperialist war " : it was addressed comprehensively " to the general council of trade unions, to the Labour Party, to all the toilers of Great Britain, to the parliamentary fraction of the Labour Party, and to all members of trade unions ".[2] Two days later a protest was issued jointly in the name of IKKI and of the bureau of Profintern against Vorovsky's murder ; [3] and this was followed by an extremely stiff note from Chicherin to the Swiss Government holding the latter " responsible for the behaviour of the Swiss authorities which made this crime possible " and demanding " full and exhaustive satisfaction ".[4]

The British Government was sufficiently impressed by the mildness of the official Soviet reply to extend the time-limit of the ultimatum for further negotiations. These were now entrusted on the Soviet side to Krasin in London. It was an excellent choice. At the recent party congress Krasin had made a strong plea — which was ill received — for a more conciliatory foreign policy ; [5] and he understood British politicians and British opinion better than any other Bolshevik. A note from Krasin of May 23, 1923, repeated the substance of the Litvinov note in briefer and more business-like form, and proposed direct negotiations with Chicherin on the propaganda issue. A British reply of May 29 rejected negotiations, but proposed a new formula, supplementary to that in the Anglo-Soviet trade agreement, about propaganda ; and this in turn was accepted by the Soviet Government, which now bound itself " not to support with funds or in any other form persons or bodies or agencies or institutions whose aim is to spread discontent or to foment rebellion in any part of the British Empire ". The promise was given to remove Raskolnikov, the

[1] *Internationale Presse-Korrespondenz*, No. 84, May 18, 1923, pp. 695-697, 697-698.

[2] *Trud*, May 13, 1923.

[3] *Internationale Presse-Korrespondenz*, No. 83, May 17, 1923, p. 694.

[4] Klyuchnikov i Sabanin, *Mezhdunarodnaya Politika*, iii, i (1928), 267-268.

[5] *Dvenadtsatyi S"ezd Rossiiskoi Kommunisticheskoi Partii (Bol'shevikov)* (1923), pp. 117-119.

Soviet representative in Kabul, whose zeal had been particularly compromising. On June 16, 1923, a final note from Chicherin wound up the correspondence.[1] The dispute with the Swiss Government arising out of the murder of Vorovsky proved more stubborn. The Swiss reply was patient, but obstinate, expressing regret but admitting no responsibility; and on June 20, 1923, after further recriminations, VTsIK and Sovnarkom issued a joint decree instituting a boycott of Swiss citizens (other than workers) and of Swiss goods as a reprisal for " the unheard-of actions of the Swiss Government ".[2] But this counted for little in comparison with the successful appeasement of Great Britain. For the rest of the year official Anglo-Soviet relations were once more uneventful. Krasin was transferred to Paris in the hope of breaking the deadlock in Soviet relations with France, and was succeeded in London by Rakovsky. The announcement of Rakovsky's appointment and its acceptance by the British Government early in July was followed by a noisy campaign in the press and Parliament against an anti-British speech delivered by him at the time of the Curzon ultimatum, and later published as a pamphlet; and his arrival was postponed at the request of the Foreign Office for some weeks. The storm blew over, and Rakovsky took up his post at the end of September, though Chicherin afterwards complained that, since no British minister had received the Soviet envoy, he himself could meet Hodgson, the British representative in Moscow, " only in the houses of third parties ".[3] But these mutual discourtesies were no more than the small change of diplomacy. The reaction against the Lloyd George policy had spent its force. Other influences were preparing the way for the new phase which would begin when a Labour government took office in Great Britain early in 1924.

[1] *Anglo Sovetskie Otnosheniya (1917-1927 gg.)* (1927), pp 47-59; *Further Correspondence between His Majesty's Government and the Soviet Government respecting the Relations between the Two Governments*, Cmd 1890 (1923).
[2] Klyuchnikov i Sabanin, *Mezhdunarodnaya Politika*, iii, i (1928), 268-272; the decree is also in *Sobranie Uzakonenii*, 1923, No. 57, art. 563.
[3] Interview in the *Manchester Guardian*, December 24, 1923.

CHAPTER 7

COMMUNISM AND GERMAN NATIONALISM

THE series of shocks experienced by Soviet diplomacy in May and June 1923, coinciding with a progressive intensification of the German crisis, led to a reconsideration and readjustment of the policies both of the KPD and of Comintern in Germany. No radical new decisions were taken. But greater emphasis now fell on the revolutionary potentialities of the German situation. In everything that was done by the KPD and by Comintern in Germany in the critical months of May, June and July 1923 Radek appears to have been the initiator. He was momentarily successful in uniting the two wings of the German party more closely than at any recent time; and till the very end of July he did nothing that failed to win the endorsement of IKKI. The May Day slogans of the KPD, issued before the international crisis matured, included the usual denunciation of Fascism and the call for a " workers' government ".[1] On May 13, 1923, public demonstrations were organized in Berlin to protest against the Curzon ultimatum and the murder of Vorovsky ; [2] and on May 17 the *Rote Fahne* contained an article by Radek entitled *The Proletarian Bulwark Round Russia* summoning the workers of the world to rally round the Soviet republic. When the congress to reunite the Second and Two-and-a-half Internationals [3] was held in Hamburg in the latter part of May, the " action committee against the danger of war and Fascism " [4] invited the Hamburg congress to join in " a proletarian united front against the new war danger, against the strengthening of

---

[1] *Die Rote Fahne* (Berlin), April 29, 1923.
[2] *Ibid.* May 12, 1923.
[3] See *The Bolshevik Revolution, 1917–1923*, Vol. 3, p. 412.
[4] For the committee see p. 161 above ; the title had been extended to meet the current emergency.

the bloody beast Fascism ", and proposed itself to send delegates to the Hamburg congress — an offer which was unceremoniously rejected.[1] One of the rare successes in united front tactics was achieved at a congress in Berlin of the International Transport Workers' Federation, which embraced both western and Soviet trade unions; a joint protest against the danger of war and Fascism was signed jointly by Robert Williams, the British president of the federation, Fimmen, the secretary of IFTU, Lozovsky and Andreev.[2] But the more aggressive tactics of the KPD Left were also not neglected. A joint proclamation of the party Zentrale and of a national committee of factory councils attacked the Cuno government under the slogan, " Down with the government of national shame and national treason " ;[3] and on June 1 the *Rote Fahne* appeared with the headline " The Workers Mobilize ".

While the communists moved feverishly from one approach to another, the most conspicuous feature of the events of May in Germany had been the growing strength and organization of those groups of the extreme Right to which the new label of Fascism was indiscriminately applied by their opponents — the nationalists, members of the numerous illicit military formations, former members of the Freikorps that had fought in the Baltic, members of Hitler's recently founded National Socialist Party. The attitude of communists to these groups had for some time been a matter of discussion in party circles. As early as February 1923 the same number of *Die Internationale* which carried Thalheimer's article on German nationalism [4] also printed an article under the title *The Middle Class, Fascism, National Bolshevism and the Party*, which described Fascism and national Bolshevism (the two were treated as equivalents) as movements against the big German capitalists and foreign capital, and argued that, while communism rejected both movements, a new kind of

---

[1] *Die Rote Fahne* (Berlin), May 20, 1923 ; *Internationale Presse-Korrespondenz*, No. 89, May 28, 1923, pp. 754-757.

[2] *Die Rote Fahne* (Berlin), May 26, 1923. The central council of Profintern at its session at the end of June 1923 issued a protest against alleged attempts by IFTU and " reformist " trade unions to break the united front of transport workers achieved at this congress (*Internationale Presse-Korrespondenz*, No. 119, July 18, 1923, pp. 1047-1048).

[3] *Die Rote Fahne* (Berlin), May 29, 1923.   [4] See p. 159 above.

propaganda was needed to overcome them.[1]   The article provoked
no immediate reaction.   But on May 17, when the crisis was
reaching an acute stage, the central committee of the KPD
adopted a long resolution which, besides much that was familiar
and hackneyed, contained some novel points.   The international
situation was defined as an attempt by Great Britain to unleash
a new war against Soviet Russia, and an attempt by French and
German heavy industry to form a new Franco-German trust.
The Cuno government was described as " Stinnes's prisoner " ;
a workers' government and an alliance with Soviet Russia were
the way to salvation.   The most striking part of the resolution
was, however, an attempt to divide the Fascists into two categories,
one consisting of those " directly sold to capital ", the other of
" *misled nationalistic petty bourgeois* " who do not realize that the
national disgrace can be overcome only when the proletariat " has
taken the future of the German people into its hands ".   The
resolution concluded with a new directive :

> We have to go to the suffering, misled, infuriated masses
> of the proletarianized petty bourgeoisie to tell them the whole
> truth, to tell them that they can defend themselves and the
> future of Germany only when they have allied themselves with
> the proletariat for a struggle with the real bourgeoisie.   The
> way to victory over Poincaré and Loucheur lies only through
> victory over Stinnes and Krupp.

The last sentence suggested the possibility of combining the
attempt to split the Fascist movement with a concession to the
views of the Left wing of the KPD on the relative importance
of the internal and external struggle.[2]   The extreme nationalists
had meanwhile reacted to the crisis by intensifying their campaign
of sabotage and assassination.   On May 26, 1923, the French
authorities shot a young nationalist and former member of the

---

[1] *Die Internationale*, vi, No. 4, February 15, 1923, pp. 115-119.

[2] *Die Rote Fahne* (Berlin), May 18, 1923. The resolution, which was signed
by the principal members of the central committee, both Right and Left, was
drafted by Radek (*Protokoll: Fünfter Kongress der Kommunistischen Internationale* (n.d.), ii, 713) ; since Radek had just come from Moscow, where he
had spoken on May 11 on the assassination of Vorovsky, it is possible that he
had obtained approval there for the line adopted.   It is interesting to note that
the so-called " Schlageter line " made its first appearance a week before
Schlageter's execution and a month before Radek's " Schlageter " speech in
IKKI.

Freikorps named Schlageter, caught red-handed in an attempt to blow up a railway line. The nationalists needed a hero and a battle-cry. The name of Schlageter was elevated into a symbol of the revival of German national honour and a spur to fresh deeds of violence against the French aggressor.

Such was the situation when the regular session of the enlarged IKKI met in Moscow on June 12, 1923. Zinoviev's opening report paid no great attention to the German question. He referred briefly to the conference in Moscow in April which had dealt with " tactical differences affecting the German Communist Party ", and later made an oblique criticism of the leadership of the KPD, which did not " stress with sufficient force the so-called national factor in its communist interpretation ".[1] Radek, speaking in the debate on Zinoviev's report, devoted a significant last paragraph to the theme that the " national question " in Germany had a particular meaning of its own. A recent article in a National-Socialist journal, Gewissen, had described the KPD as " a fighting party . . . which day by day becomes more ' national-Bolshevik ' ". Radek no longer rejected the label :

> National Bolshevism meant in 1920 an alliance to save the generals, who would have wiped out the communist party immediately after the victory. Today national Bolshevism means that everyone is penetrated with the feeling that salvation can be found only with the communists. We are today the only way out. The strong emphasis on the nation in Germany is a revolutionary act, like the emphasis on the nation in the colonies.[2]

The argument was the counterpart, in terms of German internal politics, of Bukharin's argument at the fourth congress that the Soviet state was now " great enough " to conclude an alliance

---

[1] *Rasshirennyi Plenum Ispolnitel'nogo Komiteta Kommunistīcheskogo Internatsionala (12-23 Iyunya, 1923 goda)* (1923), pp. 20-21, 32-33. The session of the enlarged IKKI was also fully reported in *Internationale Presse-Korrespondenz*, No. 103, June 21, 1923, No. 105, June 25, 1923, No. 111, July 3, 1923. The substantial divergences suggest that the Russian and German records of the speeches were made independently and not collated : they are mainly differences of style and phrasing, but passages which occur in one version are sometimes missing in the other. It is difficult to assign priority to either version, but the Russian is generally fuller.

[2] *Internationale Presse-Korrespondenz*, No. 103, June 21, 1923, p. 869 ; this passage does not appear in the Russian version.

with a bourgeois state.[1] What, on this view, distinguished the situation from that of 1920 was that the communists could now strike a bargain with the nationalists in the conviction that they were the stronger partner and could utilize the partnership for their own ends. Zinoviev, in his reply to the debate, without dissenting from Radek's diagnosis, cautiously played down the hypothesis of an imminent revolutionary situation in Germany :

> Germany is on the eve of revolution. This does not mean that revolution will come in a month or in a year. Perhaps much more time will be required. But in the historical sense Germany is on the eve of the proletarian revolution.[2]

Any ripples which may have been stirred by this discussion died away ; and, when two days later Radek made his main report to the enlarged IKKI on the international situation, the Ruhr occupation received only conventional treatment as one of the four main items which contributed to the current tension in the capitalist world.[3] This time, however, Neurath intervened in the discussion, and, without referring to Radek, repeated his already published attack on Thalheimer's February article. Böttcher defended the standpoint of the party Right. Radek in his closing speech accused Neurath of " tilting at windmills ", and went on :

> Its [i.e. the French Government's] victory in the Ruhr would immensely strengthen it ; its defeat on the other hand would shatter the Versailles system and become a fact which would play a revolutionary rôle. In virtue of these circumstances, the German party should say to itself : Yes, the German working class, like the working class of the whole world, including the French working class, is interested in the defeat of Poincaré.

And he insisted once more that " what is called German nationalism is not only nationalism, but a broad national movement having a great revolutionary significance ".[4] Critics were eager to point out

[1] See The Bolshevik Revolution, 1917–1923, Vol. 3, p. 447.

[2] Rasshirennyi Plenum Ispolnitel'nogo Komiteta Kommunisticheskogo Internatsionala (12-23 Iyunya, 1923 goda) (1923), p. 103.

[3] Ibid. pp. 105-127 ; the other items were the Anglo-American debt agreement, the Lausanne conference, and the British decision to construct a naval base at Singapore.

[4] Rasshirennyi Plenum Ispolnitel'nogo Komiteta Kommunisticheskogo Internatsionala (12-23 Iyunya, 1923 goda) (1923), pp. 129-130, 131-132, 139-142.

that the policy of Radek and of the KPD in 1923 meant the abandonment of Lenin's thesis of 1914–1917 that the imperialist Powers were equally guilty and that the duty of the proletariat in every country was to work for the defeat and downfall of its own national government. But nobody recalled that it was also a return to the attitude of Marx, which Lenin had discarded as no longer appropriate before 1914.[1]

In spite, therefore, of the airing given to the well-known differences in the German party, and of Radek's conversion to the catchword of "national Bolshevism", nothing in the first few days' proceedings in IKKI foreshadowed any dramatic contribution to German policy. This came independently at a later stage, in the debate on Fascism introduced by Klara Zetkin. Zetkin denounced Fascism as "an extremely dangerous and terrible enemy" and "the strongest, most concentrated, classic expression of the general offensive of the world bourgeoisie". At the same time it was a result of the loss of faith by the workers in their own class, a "refuge of the politically homeless".

> We must not forget [Zetkin went on] that Fascism . . . is a movement of the hungry, the poor, of men torn from their background and disillusioned. We must strive either to win them over to our side in the struggle, or at any rate to neutralize these social forces which have succumbed to the embraces of Fascism.[2]

These generalities went little or no further than what had been said a dozen times before. But, when Radek intervened in the debate on the next day, his speech gave a new twist to the theme and made history. Striking a note of studied pathos, he declared that throughout Zetkin's speech he had had before his eyes " the corpse of *the German Fascist*, our class enemy, condemned to death and shot by the lackeys of French imperialism ". He hailed Schlageter as " the brave soldier of the counter-revolution " and — borrowing the title of a popular nationalist novel — " the wanderer into nothingness ". Schlageter had fought against the Bolsheviks in the Baltic and against the workers in the Ruhr; Ludendorff had spoken in his honour at his funeral in Munich.

---

[1] See *The Bolshevik Revolution, 1917–1923*, Vol. 3, p. 559.
[2] *Rasshirennyi Plenum Ispolnitel'nogo Komiteta Kommunisticheskogo Internatsionala (12-23 Iyunya, 1923 goda)* (1923), pp. 207, 211, 227.

But now that he was dead, his comrades in arms had still to answer the vital question.

Against whom do the German nationalists want to fight : against Entente capital or the Russian people ? With whom do they want to ally themselves ? With the Russian workers and peasants to shake off together the yoke of Entente capital or with Entente capital to enslave the German and Russian people ?

Radek invoked the historic example of Scharnhorst and Gneisenau who, after the humiliation of Jena, had perceived that the emancipation of the peasant was a condition of the liberation and restoration of Prussia.[1] The liberation of Germany from the chains of Versailles could be achieved only through the emancipation of the workers. The KPD " is not the party merely of the struggle for the industrial workers' loaf of bread, but the party of struggling proletarians who fight for their freedom, for *a freedom which is identical with the freedom of their whole people, with the freedom of all who work and suffer in Germany* ".[2]

It is unthinkable that on such a matter Radek should have spoken on his own responsibility. He afterwards stated without contradiction that he had obtained " not only the tacit, but the written assent " of Zinoviev to his speech, and that Zinoviev afterwards described his Schlageter articles as " correct and good ".[3] What is clear is that the overture seemed less dramatic, less novel and less fateful to those who heard it in Moscow than it appears in retrospect to the student of history. According to the record of the session, it was received with " general applause ". Zetkin, who wound up the debate on Fascism immediately afterwards with comments on the various speeches, remarked without special emphasis that the speech of Radek had " deeply moved " her. The resolution on Fascism drafted before Radek spoke was not modified : the call for an out-and-out struggle against Fascism in all countries did not seem to be in any way attenuated by the

---

[1] This was a favourite theme of Radek at this time : in a leading article in *Pravda*, September 13, 1923, he quoted Gneisenau's eulogy of the French revolution for having " awakened all forces [in France] and given to every force its proper field of action ".

[2] *Rasshirennyi Plenum Ispolnitel'nogo Komiteta Kommunisticheskogo Internatsionala (12-23 Iyunya, 1923 goda)* (1923), pp. 237-241.

[3] *Protokoll : Fünfter Kongress der Kommunistischen Internationale* (n.d.), ii, 713.

casual remark that " those revolutionary elements which, confusedly and unconsciously, are found in the Fascist ranks should be drawn into the proletarian class struggle ".[1] Nobody reverted to Radek's proposal during the last two days' proceedings ; and Zinoviev in his concluding speech did not mention Germany at all.[2] Whatever view may have been taken of Radek's policy, it was not treated as a radical new departure. It was conceived, not as an attempt to bring about a working alliance with German Fascists against the Versailles treaty, but as an attempt to split their ranks by proving that effective opposition to the Versailles treaty could in the long run be offered only by the communists ; it could therefore be logically reconciled with the continuation of a vigorous campaign against Fascism. Nevertheless Radek's comparison of the new emphasis on German nationalism with the policy of support for national movements in colonial countries foreshadowed the appearance in Germany of the same embarrassments which had already arisen in Asia, and were bound to arise wherever local communist parties were required to give their support to an ideological programme ultimately incompatible with the aims of communism.[3]

The launching of the " Schlageter line " at IKKI created a sensation in German politics and was followed by an extensive public debate. The *Rote Fahne* printed Radek's speech in full in its issue of June 26, and ten days later published a further article by Radek defending it against the denunciations of *Vorwärts*. Meanwhile Moeller van den Bruck, the intellectual of the Nazi movement, commented on Radek's speech in *Gewissen*, offering to communists on behalf of the nationalists the leadership which the proletariat could not supply.

---

[1] *Kommunisticheskii Internatsional* n *Dokumentakh* (1933), pp. 379-383.

[2] Germany was also not mentioned in a long account of the proceedings of IKKI given by Zinoviev to the party organization in Moscow on July 6, 1923 (*Internationale Presse-Korrespondenz*, No. 125, July 30, 1923, pp. 1089-1098).

[3] Radek, in a speech at the bureau of the Communist Youth International on July 13, 1923, defended the new line in Germany with a caution which suggests that his audience was not enthusiastic about it. He explained that, " if Fascism was not split into several parts, it would already have been victorious in Germany ", and described the policy as follows : "A united front of the proletariat, proletarian hundreds to defend the proletariat with armed force against the Fascists and, if necessary, to attack them, but at the same time a broadening of the basis of our agitation " (*Kommunisticheskii Internatsional*, No. 26-27, August 24, 1923, cols. 7171-7174).

A majority cannot lead itself. Only consciousness can lead, a consciousness such as Schlageter possessed. . . . Marxism will always be confined to the manual workers : it will win over no brain workers. But it is the intellectual workers who will lead the cause of the people as their own.[1]

Radek, once more in the columns of the *Rote Fahne*, retorted that " Fascism represents, not a clique of officers, but a broad, though contradictory, popular movement ", and reproached *Gewissen* with the vagueness of its political programme. Reventlow intervened in his journal, the *Reichswart*, to reassert the nationalist standpoint :

We know no classes and want no classes. We regard all internationalists and the internationally minded as the enemy within.

And Frölich, on behalf of the KPD, replied that the real " enemy within " was capitalism, an international force which trampled on national interests. These five articles together with Radek's speech were published in July 1923 as a pamphlet which quickly ran through two editions.[2] Nationalist and communist speakers appeared side by side on common platforms and trimmed their speeches carefully enough to win applause from mixed audiences.[3] These proceedings reached their culminating point early in August 1923 when the German political crisis was at its height. On August 2 Remmele, a member of the Zentrale of the KPD, addressed a large Nazi meeting in Stuttgart which is said to have

---

[1] These views were strikingly similar to those propounded to Radek by Rathenau in 1919 (see *The Bolshevik Revolution, 1917–1923*, Vol. 3, p. 316).

[2] K. Radek, etc., *Schlageter: Eine Auseinandersetzung* (1923). A third and much enlarged edition was issued in October 1923 : this also included further articles by Moeller van den Bruck, Reventlow and Frölich, and ended with a long summing-up by Radek under the title *Communism and the German Nationalist Movement* which originally appeared in three sections in *Die Rote Fahne* (Berlin), August 16, 17, September 18.

[3] The most serious embarrassment was the anti-Semitism in which nationalist speakers were prone to indulge. How far communists compromised with their principles on this question can only be guessed. An attack on Jewish capitalists was frequently quoted from a speech of Ruth Fischer (" he who denounces Jewish capital . . . is already a warrior in the class-war, even though he does not know it ") ; but the speaker has stated that her remarks were distorted (R. Fischer, *Stalin and German Communism* (Harvard, 1948), p. 283). *Sotsialisticheskii Vestnik* (Berlin), No. 21-22 (67-68), November 27, 1923, p. 12, quoted from an alleged KPD proclamation the phrase, said to have been carried in heavy type : " *Jewish* capitalists grow fat on the exploitation of the *German* people ".

been heavily packed with KPD supporters, and won loud applause by denouncing capitalism, the Versailles treaty and the Entente Powers and by demanding " a workers' and peasants' government " to liberate Germany. On August 10 a still larger meeting was organized by the KPD and was attended by representatives of the National Socialist Party (the SPD also received an invitation, which was declined). Remmele once more attacked the Versailles treaty and " the democratic German republic ". The Nazi speaker called for a national, not an international, socialism ; communism could never be national " so long as the communists are led by Radek-Sobelsohn and whatever the other Jews are called ". But a truce between Nazis and communists could be declared till the common enemy and the destroyer of Germany, democracy, had been overthrown. Remmele countered with an attack on anti-Semitism and a demand for an alliance for the overthrow of capital ; and the Nazi representative ended on the note of " honourable enmity ". But the experiment had by this time begun to embarrass the Nazis even more than the communists. On August 14, 1923, the Nazi leadership placed a ban on further cooperation, announcing that there could never be legitimate grounds for common action with communists.[1] This ban, together with the increasing acuteness of the German internal crisis, put an end to the short-lived episode of the " Schlageter line ". The breach coincided with the overthrow of the Cuno government and the accession of Stresemann to power. In the struggles of the autumn of 1923 Fascists and communists went their separate ways.[2]

Understanding of the somewhat tortuous tactics adopted by Comintern and by the KPD under Radek's inspiration in the summer of 1923 has been obscured both by a popular confusion of these tactics with the old programme of " national Bolshevism "

[1] These particulars are taken from a pamphlet issued by the KPD, *Sowjetstern oder Hakenkreuz? Deutschlands Weg — Deutschlands Rettung : Ein Waffengang zwischen Faschisten und Kommunisten* (Berlin, 1923) ; an article in *Internationale Presse-Korrespondenz*, No. 151, September 26, 1923, p. 1304, hailed the ban on further cooperation as proof of the embarrassment caused in Fascist quarters by the communist tactics.

[2] According to W. Krivitsky, *I was Stalin's Agent* (1939), pp. 59-60, communists fought side by side with nationalists and with the German police against the Rhineland separatists in a demonstration in Düsseldorf in September 1923.

and by the hindsight derived from knowledge of much later events in Germany. The programme of national Bolshevism was, as its name implied, an amalgam of nationalist and Bolshevik aims; from the nationalists it took the call for a union of all Germans to liberate the nation from the yoke of the imperialist Powers, from the Bolsheviks it took the conception of revolution, shorn, however, of its international framework. Critics had been quick to point out that national Bolshevism implied both a cessation of the class war in Germany and a national war against the proletariat of other countries. Radek had attacked it vigorously,[1] and now, in his reply to Moeller van den Bruck, briefly restated the grounds of his objection :

> In the year 1919 Laufenberg proposed a farrago (*Kuddel-muddel*) of communism and nationalism. We declare frankly that one cannot play tricks with ideas and make mixtures out of ideas.[2]

The " Schlageter line " represented no sort of compromise with Fascist doctrine or Fascist policy, which continued through this time to be an object of fierce hostility and denunciation in the communist press. The issue of the *Rote Fahne* of June 26, 1923, which printed Radek's Schlageter speech on its front page, also carried conspicuously reports of attacks on the workers by Fascist gangs ; and Radek once more expounded the line with complete frankness in his reply to the criticisms of *Vorwärts*, the social-democratic newspaper :

> It is the duty of German communists, if necessary, *to struggle with arms in their hands against the Fascist insurrection*, which would be a calamity for the working class, a calamity for Germany. But at the same time it is their duty to do everything *in order to convince the petty bourgeois elements of Fascism which*

[1] For national Bolshevism and Radek's articles denouncing it see *The Bolshevik Revolution, 1917–1923*, Vol. 3, pp. 312, 319.

[2] K. Radek, etc., *Schlageter : Eine Auseinandersetzung* (3rd ed., 1923), p. 20. Reventlow in his further reply just as emphatically rejected national Bolshevism in its original form from the nationalist side : " Three years ago the danger of a ' national Bolshevism ' among us was for a time very great. . . . At that time in national and nationalistic (*völkisch*) circles a mood of despair often existed : Nothing is any use, we shall become Bolsheviks, Bolshevism is coming, we will try to nationalize it in Germany and save Germany with its help. *That wave is past* ' (*ibid.* p. 35).

struggle against impoverishment that communism is not their enemy but the star which shows them the way to victory.[1]

In theory, the " Schlageter line " might be considered as a move to the Right; it implied that Germany was not yet ripe for a proletarian revolution, and was in the position of a " colonial country where one could march together with a bourgeois national government ".[2] In practice it was more favourably received by the Left wing of the party than by the Right.[3] The " Schlageter line " was defensible only as a tactical manœuvre leading up to an early attempt to seize power, and thus fitted in with the call of the Left for immediate revolutionary action. On the other hand, the appeal to the nationalists could only weaken the appeal of the KPD to the social-democrats which was the essence of the policy of the Right. But the issue was one of tactics rather than of doctrine, and as such the line was accepted without question throughout the party.[4] The end in view was to seduce the rank and file of the rival party by convincing it that the communists alone were capable of fulfilling its desires and ambitions and, for this purpose, to enter into a temporary agreement with the leaders for defined and limited objectives. The policy was subject to the same ambiguities and embarrassments as Lenin's injunction to British communists to " support the Hendersons and the Snowdens as the rope supports the man who is being hanged ", and to enter into an electoral pact with the Labour Party while retaining full liberty to attack it.[5] It may fairly be said that both sides embarked on the project with their eyes open and with full appreciation of the aims of their partners. In the long run the

[1] *Ibid.* p. 15; the article as originally published in *Die Rote Fahne* (Berlin), July 7, 1923, carried the date-line " Moscow, July 2 "

[2] It was attacked on this ground a year later, when denigration of Radek had become the rule, by a KPD delegate who had not been associated with the policy (*Protokoll: Fünfter Kongress der Kommunistischen Internationale* (n.d.), ii, 665); but this criticism was not heard at the time.

[3] According to Radek, " comrades Ruth Fischer and Remmele carried on this agitation arm in arm with me " (*Die Lehren der Deutschen Ereignisse* (Hamburg, 1924), p. 18); Remmele later belonged to the Centre group.

[4] Brandler in his defence of it formulated a significant priority: " Now that the KPD has successfully won the proletarian masses for the overthrow of the bourgeoisie, it is faced by the new important task of winning also the hesitating petty bourgeois strata " (*Die Internationale*, vi, No. 15 (August 1, 1923), pp. 419-421).

[5] See *The Bolshevik Revolution, 1917-1923*, Vol. 3, p. 179.

N

Fascists perhaps showed more skill in using the communists to serve their ends than the communists in using the Fascists. But this was scarcely true of the temporary cooperation between them in the summer of 1923.

It did not therefore portend any change of front when, early in July 1923, the KPD decided to organize an " anti-Fascist day " with street demonstrations in the larger German cities on Sunday, July 29. The strains imposed on the German economy by passive resistance had by now become intolerable; the mark was in headlong collapse; the prospects of disorder were serious everywhere. On July 11 the Zentrale of the KPD warned the party of the danger of a " Fascist rising " and predicted that " we are approaching decisive struggles ".[1] The proceedings in Berlin were to culminate in a monster procession to Potsdam, and similar demonstrations were arranged in other cities. Then on July 23, 1923, the Prussian Government issued a prohibition on all open-air processions and street demonstrations on the " day ". The prohibition at once opened the rift in the KPD between the Left, which preached action at all costs, and the Right, which believed that the situation was not yet ripe for a revolutionary challenge to authority. The party leadership called off the Berlin demonstration in defiance of the predominantly Left Berlin group of the party.[2] The issue was carried to Comintern headquarters, and produced there the first open disagreement on the German question. Zinoviev and Bukharin, who were absent from Moscow on holiday, telegraphed their encouragement to let the demonstration go forward. Radek, who hurried to Moscow, telegraphed in agitation to Zinoviev and Bukharin that their policy " would mean that Comintern is pushing the party into a July defeat " — the words being chosen to suggest the unhappy precedent of the " March action ".[3] Trotsky, who was also absent on holiday, was consulted, but refused to express an opinion in default of fuller

[1] Die Rote Fahne (Berlin), July 12, 1923.
[2] Die Lehren der Deutschen Ereignisse (Hamburg, 1924), p. 55.
[3] The main source for this episode is a statement by Zinoviev to the thirteenth party conference in January 1924; the date of Radek's telegram to Zinoviev and Bukharin is there given as June 12 — an obvious slip or misprint (Trinadtsataya Konferentsiya Rossiiskoi Kommunisticheskoi Partii (Bol'shevikov) (1924), pp. 168-169).

information. Stalin shared Radek's cautious scepticism, and was moved to one of his rare pronouncements on Comintern affairs. In a letter to Zinoviev and Bukharin he made an unfavourable comparison between the German situation of the moment and the Russian situation of October 1917, and thought that " if power in Germany were, so to speak, to fall to the street and the communists picked it up, it would end in failure and collapse ". The bourgeoisie and the social-democrats would " turn this demonstration into a general engagement for the sake of the lesson . . . and destroy the communists". The conclusion was that "the Germans should be restrained and not spurred on ".[1] On July 26, with Zinoviev and Bukharin still absent from Moscow, a telegram was sent from the presidium of Comintern to the Zentrale of the KPD :

The presidium of Comintern advises the abandonment of street demonstrations on July 29. . . . We fear a trap.

The main authors of the decision would appear to have been Stalin and Radek. Zinoviev sourly recorded afterwards that " some of our comrades, relying on Radek, supported him in this matter ".[2]

The verdict of the presidium of Comintern was mandatory for the KPD. The procession was called off ; and in Berlin the anti-Fascist day was celebrated only by indoor meetings, though in cities where the writ of the Prussian Government did not run outdoor demonstrations were held. It was explained in the *Rote*

---

[1] The Russian text of the letter has not been published. A German translation is in A. Thalheimer, *1923 : Eine Verpasste Revolution?* (1931), p. 31, an obviously faulty English translation in L. Trotsky, *Stalin* (N.Y., 1946), pp. 368-369. The letter was quoted by Zinoviev at a meeting of the party central committee in August 1927 : Stalin in his reply, while stating that he had no copy, and could not check the textual accuracy of Zinoviev's quotation, admitted the authenticity of the letter and described it as " absolutely correct from end to end " ; he added that he opposed " the demonstration of communist workers " because he believed that " armed Fascists were trying to provoke the communists to a premature action ", and did not want the communists to " fall into the provocation " (Stalin, *Sochineniya*, x, 61-62). The letter is not included in Stalin's collected works, and cannot be precisely dated. Thalheimer places it " at the beginning of August ", Trotsky simply " in August ", and Stalin himself " at the end of July or the beginning of August " ; but the mention of " this demonstration " seems to prove that it belongs to the controversy which preceded the anti-Fascist day of July 29, 1923.

[2] *Trinadtsataya Konferentsiya Rossiiskoi Kommunisticheskoi Partii (Bol'-shevikov)* (1924), p. 169.

Fahne that " the workers were not sufficiently prepared ", and that " we *not only cannot offer a general battle*, but should *avoid* everything that might give the enemy the chance to destroy us piecemeal ".[1] This cautious counsel was wise, if unheroic. But the episode had further deepened the split in the party ranks. A meeting of the central committee of the KPD on August 5-6 went over the old ground and aired the old dissensions without coming any nearer to a solution. Brandler looked forward to the impending collapse of the bourgeois régime, but thought it premature to proclaim the proletarian dictatorship, and believed that a section of the social-democrats could still be won over by propaganda. Ruth Fischer once again contested Brandler's and Radek's conception of the united front, wanted a decisive lead by the KPD and thought that " the intermediate stage of the workers' government is becoming in practice ever more improbable ". A resolution was adopted by a majority demanding " the overthrow of the Cuno government, the prevention of any new coalition government, and the formation of a workers' and peasants' government ". The dual character of the policy to be adopted towards Fascism was again emphasized.[2] The somewhat dismal impression remained that the KPD had exhausted its repertory of words and ideas, and was not equipped, or not ready, for action. Its mood seemed accurately to reflect the situation of the German workers who, since 1918, had rallied easily to revolutionary slogans and had every provocation to revolt, but shrank back half-heartedly, when the moment came, from the decisive step.

At the moment when the impotence of the KPD was being so ominously demonstrated, the Cuno government was already in the throes of its last convulsions. The currency depreciated from hour to hour and was almost valueless ; the economic situation not only of the workers, but of the whole middle class, had become intolerable ; and " passive resistance " was breaking down everywhere in the occupied territory. On August 10, 1923, the Cuno government was hit in its most vulnerable point by a strike of the printers of currency notes. On the following day a general strike broke out in Berlin and quickly spread to other industrial centres : and Cuno resigned. Neither the KPD nor any other party showed

---

[1] *Die Rote Fahne* (Berlin), July 30, August 2, 1923.
[2] *Ibid.* August 7, 8, 9, 10.

any eagerness to take power, whether by legal or by illegal means. The strike, having lost its *raison d'être* with the resignation of the government, fizzled out. Out of this bewildering void Gustav Stresemann emerged as the strong man. He was one of the leaders of the German People's Party, the party of the industrialists, and a friend of Stinnes. He represented the view of the Ruhr industrialists that the Cuno policy of passive resistance was bankrupt and must be abandoned. No party had the courage to contest this view; no other party had the courage to take practical steps to give effect to it. This courage, combined with a certain geniality and flexibility in negotiation, was Stresemann's major asset. He quickly gathered round him a government of all parties ranging from his own on the Right to the SPD on the Left — the so-called " great coalition " ; only the parties of the extreme Right and the KPD were excluded. Radek, in an unusually tentative article in the *Rote Fahne* of August 19, described Stresemann as the spokesman of the middle bourgeoisie and predicted that he would seek an agreement with France. An entirely new situation had arisen in Germany. It took some time for all concerned, both at home and abroad, to find a new orientation.

CHAPTER 8

BULGARIA AND THE PEASANT

BY a coincidence which played its part in the history of Comintern, the Bulgarian crisis came to a head at the same moment as the German in the summer of 1923. A few days after the French troops marched into the Ruhr in January, local elections in Bulgaria, conducted on strictly party lines, confirmed the verdict of the last parliamentary elections in 1920, and upheld the precarious authority of Stambulisky's peasant government which had been in power since 1919. The Peasant Union secured 437,000 votes or rather less than half the total poll; next came the Bulgarian Communist Party with 230,000;[1] the bourgeois parties taken together could muster only 220,000, and the " broad " (or Right) socialists no more than 40,000. A week after these elections the standing council of the Bulgarian Communist Party endorsed the slogan of a " workers' and peasants' government " propounded by the fourth congress of Comintern two months earlier;[2] if there was any country in Europe where this new variant of the united front was applicable, that country was certainly Bulgaria, where the peasants formed more than 80 per cent of a total population of under 5 millions. Unfortunately the endorsement carried so many reservations, and so much emphasis was laid on the interpretation of the united front as coming " from below ", that it was almost tantamount to rejection. In its resolution of January 22, 1923, the party council declared that " the workers' and peasants' government cannot today in Bulgaria be realized through a coalition of the communist party

---

[1] The membership of the party, at the time of its suppression in September 1923, was put at 39,000 (*From the 4th to the 5th World Congress* (CPGB, 1924), p. 44); the proportion between party members and voting sympathizers was about the same as in Germany.

[2] *Die Internationale*, vi, No. 9 (May 1, 1923), pp. 272-273; for the decision of Comintern see *The Bolshevik Revolution, 1917–1923*, Vol. 3, p. 453.

with the Peasant Union or through a peasant government resulting
from such a coalition ". The Peasant Union and its government
were denounced not only as defenders of the interests of the
Bulgarian *kulak*, of the rural bourgeoisie, against the small and
landless peasant, but also as " a blind tool of the Entente im-
perialists ". The Bulgarian Communist Party would struggle
for " a union of the broad masses of workers and the masses of
small peasants under its banner "; and it would do everything
to hasten the moment when, with the support of these masses, it
would seize power. An official commentary by the party leader
Kabakchiev drove home this declaration of war on the Peasant
Union :

> The idea and the possibility of a united front or coalition
> between the communist party and the Peasant Union are com-
> pletely excluded. . . . The workers' and peasants' government
> can be created only through the revolutionary struggle of the
> masses, i.e. through the independent struggle of the urban
> proletariat and of the small and landless peasant.[1]

In a general election of April 1923 the Peasant Union increased
the number of its votes to 500,000 and, by skilful manipulation,
secured 210 out of 246 seats in the chamber. The Bulgarian
Communist Party came next with 210,000 votes and 17 seats.[2]

Such was the situation when on June 9, 1923, the parties of
the Right in Bulgaria, reduced to parliamentary insignificance
but supported by the army and by Macedonian and other malcontents, carried out a *coup d'état* against the Stambulisky government. The Bulgarian Communist Party, imitating the official
attitude of the KPD in the similar circumstances of the Kapp
putsch,[3] announced its neutrality in what it regarded as a struggle
between two sections of the bourgeoisie. On the day of the
rising the party council issued a statement denouncing equally
the Stambulisky government and any bourgeois government

---

[1] The resolution is in *Internationale Presse-Korrespondenz*, No. 57, April 3,
1923, pp. 464-465, the commentary *ibid.* pp. 459-464; the resolution also
appeared in *Kommunisticheskii Internatsional*, No. 26-27, August 24, 1923, cols.
7323-7328.
[2] The results are reported with the usual allegations of " white terror " in
Internationale Presse-Korrespondenz (Wochenausgabe), No. 20, May 19, 1923,
pp. 420-471.
[3] See *The Bolshevik Revolution, 1917-1923*, Vol. 3, p. 172.

which might succeed it, and offered no positive guidance.[1] The
coup was completely successful. Stambulisky was murdered and
a military régime under Tsankov established. An article in the
communist party journal defined the party line :

> The Bulgarian Communist Party can in no case support the
> new government of the Right parties, since this brings with it
> only increased misery, new tax burdens, and a continuation of
> the terror and of the repression of every revolutionary movement.
> The Bulgarian Communist Party can also not help the govern-
> ment of Stambulisky to return to power.[2]

And Kabakchiev recorded that " the masses of urban workers
regarded the *coup* indifferently or even with a certain relief ".[3]
A further statement issued by the party council on June 15
boasted that in the "armed struggle"which was now "approaching
its end " communists had " maintained their full independence ".[4]

When the regular session of the enlarged IKKI opened in
Moscow on June 12, 1923, the fate of the Bulgarian *coup* was still
in the balance. As the disquieting news began to come in,
Zinoviev repeated the current rumours — that Stambulisky was
arrested, that Stambulisky was dead, that Stambulisky was march-
ing on Sofia at the head of 20,000 peasants — as well as a report
which unfortunately appeared certain : the communists at Plevna
had risen spontaneously against the " whites ", but had been
sharply ordered by party headquarters to remain neutral. Zinoviev was clear about the moral of these events. The slogan of the
united front must be not only proclaimed, but " clothed in flesh
and blood ". The Bulgarian communists " must ally themselves
with the peasantry and even with the hated Stambulisky in order
to organize a common struggle against the whites ".[5] When it

[1] *Internationale Presse-Korrespondenz*, No. 102, June 30, 1923, pp. 858-859.
[2] *Ibid.* (Wochenausgabe), No. 24, June 16, p. 574.
[3] *Ibid.* No. 105, June 25, 1923, p. 886.
[4] *Ibid.* No. 107, June 27, 1923, pp. 916-917.
[5] *Rasshirennyi Plenum Ispolnitel'nogo Komiteta Kommunisticheskogo Internatsionala (12-23 Iyunya, 1923 goda)* (1923), pp. 101-102 ; Zinoviev's opening
speech had contained a qualified eulogy of Stambulisky (see p. 197 below).
According to G. Besedovsky, *Na Putyakh k Termidoru* (Paris, 1931), i, 74
(the English translation of this work under the title *Revelations of a Soviet
Diplomat* (1931) was apparently made from a much abbreviated and inaccurate
French version), Goldenstein, the Comintern representative in Vienna who
looked after the Balkans, had tried in vain to persuade the Bulgarian Communist Party to support Stambulisky.

became clear at a later stage of the session that the Bulgarian party had behaved in a manner entirely contrary to these prescriptions, Radek intervened to sound a note of criticism. His speech was a plea rather than an indictment, though at one point, throwing aside his usual caution, he declared that it was the duty of a party with the masses behind it to fight " even at the risk of being beaten ".[1] A proclamation " to the Bulgarian workers and peasants ", issued in the name of IKKI at the end of the session on June 23, 1923, while it attributed the Bulgarian *coup* to " the scum of the European counter-revolution ", to " Fascist bands " and to the complicity of the Bulgarian social-democrats, none the less recognized that " the split between workers and peasants " was a predisposing cause.[2] Soon, however, the criticism became more outspoken. On June 28, 1923, the presidium of IKKI issued a statement signed by Zinoviev to all " sections of Comintern " on *The Lessons of the Bulgarian Coup*. Peasant parties in general, it argued, were no doubt rightly regarded with suspicion as " political cannon-fodder for the bourgeoisie ". But it must be admitted that Stambulisky had at the outset made some attempt at a peasant policy directed against the bourgeoisie. The Bulgarian Communist Party was condemned for its " dogmatic-doctrinaire approach "; a " waiting policy combined with a gesture of neutrality betokens in such a situation a political capitulation ".[3] Meanwhile the central committee of the party met in Sofia in the first week of July, endorsed the attitude adopted by the party council at the time of the *coup* as " the only possible one ", and dismissed the IKKI proclamation of June 23 (Zinoviev's later statement had apparently not yet been received) as based on inadequate information ; in any case it would now be a grievous error for the party " to restore to the agrarian leaders, those traitors to the interests of the working rural population, the influence which they have lost ".[4] This was open defiance. But the disciplinary powers exercised by IKKI at this time were weak, and great reluctance was still shown

[1] *Rasshirennyi Plenum Ispolnitel'nogo Komiteta Kommunisticheskogo Internatsionala (12-23 Iyunya, 1923 goda)* (1923), pp. 254-262.

[2] *Ibid.* pp. 300-304.

[3] *Kommunisticheskii Internatsional*, No. 26-27, August 24, cols. 7341-7354 ; *Internationale Presse-Korrespondenz*, No. 115, July 9, 1923, pp. 1007-1010.

[4] *Ibid.* No. 120, July 18, 1923, pp. 1051-1053.

to use them. The Bulgarian party was probably saved from formal censure by the severe reprisals inflicted on it at home : the comparatively tolerant régime of Stambulisky had been succeeded by a dictatorship which made the persecution of communists an important part of its policy. But opinion throughout the communist world was mobilized against it. Rakosi was employed to write an article fiercely condemning its attitude.[1] A resolution of the central committee of the KPD at the beginning of August described the Tsankov régime as an alliance of big capital, monarchists and Fascists against the proletariat and the peasantry, and argued that in a peasant country like Bulgaria the communist party could not be indifferent to an attack on the peasants whatever the attitude of the Stambulisky régime to the communists.[2]

What effect was produced by these admonitions in the Bulgarian party is not certain. But Kabakchiev, who was held responsible for the errors of the June policy,[3] was now eclipsed in the party leadership by Kolarov and Dimitrov, who showed themselves more amenable to the promptings of Comintern and were prepared to seek an alliance with Stambulisky's followers against the Tsankov régime. Preparations for an insurrection seem to have been in progress [4] when the government decided to strike first. On September 12, 1923, leading communists were arrested throughout Bulgaria, and party offices raided and closed.[5] This step forced the party into a hasty and ill-prepared rising, which began on September 22 in western and north-western Bulgaria with a certain amount of local support from the peasants.

[1] *Internationale Presse-Korrespondenz*, No. 120, July 18, 1923, pp. 1053-1054.
[2] *Die Rote Fahne* (Berlin), August 10, 1923.
[3] It is noteworthy that Kabakchiev was allowed to write in the official journal of Comintern a long article replying to criticisms and defending the earlier line (*Kommunisticheskii Internatsional*, No. 28-29, December 1, 1923, cols. 7679-7754) ; the days of such toleration were nearly over.
[4] The extent of these preparations was probably afterwards exaggerated both by government spokesmen in justification of the ensuing reprisals and by party historians in the interests of Dimitrov, whose participation in the September rising of 1923 was his first important achievement ; contemporary evidence is slender.
[5] This " policy of provocation " was the subject of an immediate protest by IKKI (*Internationale Presse-Korrespondenz*, No. 149, September 21, 1923, p. 1285).

It never enjoyed any prospect of success. Order was restored after a week of guerrilla warfare in outlying districts. The mild reprisals after the June *coup* now developed into a regular " white terror " ; the party was crushed out of existence or driven completely underground. The reaction in Moscow was, however, quite different from that of three months earlier. While the defeat could not be disguised, Zinoviev in a leading article in *Pravda* now praised the Bulgarian Communist Party for its courage and resolution. It might have seemed that, as in June the party had failed to act in time, so now it had acted prematurely. But no such verdict was passed. Communists, Zinoviev declared, could not " shrink from the struggle, when a Fascist government had decided on the annihilation of the communist party ". What had been achieved was that " the peasantry almost to a man is ready to follow the communist party ". The party had " made good its doctrinaire errors " and paved the way to future victory.[1] The tone of the article in which these sentiments were expressed suggested, however, that the writer was more concerned to lend encouragement to the imminent German insurrection than to analyse the fate of its ill-omened Bulgarian prototype.

The summer and autumn of 1923 was marked by one event which, though it left no lasting results, was symptomatic of the period : the foundation in Moscow of a Peasant International. When the civil war in Russia ended it was clear that the victory of the revolution had been due to the steadfastness of the peasant, and that peasant discontent was the one serious threat to its consolidation. The introduction of NEP meant the recognition of the preponderant weight of the peasant in the Soviet economy. At first this seemed to have no ideological consequences — least of all in the international field. But when the controversy about NEP became active in the winter of 1922–1923 the defenders of the official policy found themselves more and more constrained to extol the importance of the peasant ; and it was in this atmosphere that Comintern, at its fourth congress in November 1922, had given its blessing to a " worker-peasant government " as one

---

[1] *Pravda*, October 9, 1923 ; a translation appeared in *Internationale Presse-Korrespondenz*, No. 161, October 15, 1923, pp. 1371-1372.

of the theoretically acceptable forms of preparation for the victory of the proletariat.[1] The argument was even heard, especially when the prospects of the German revolution were discussed, that a successful socialist revolution in an industrial country would be exposed to the imminent danger of blockade by the capitalist world, and might easily be starved out if it were not supported by a sympathetic revolution in neighbouring agrarian countries. Just as the support of the Russian peasant had been essential to victory in October 1917, so the support of the European peasant was a condition of a victorious European revolution. The revolutionary movement would have the greatest prospects of success if it were first to seize power in peasant countries such as Rumania, Bulgaria and Yugoslavia, then spread to semi-industrialized countries like Italy and Austria, and only then reach a typically industrial country like Germany.[2] This doctrine, however, still seemed paradoxical to good Marxists, and failed to obtain any serious footing in Comintern. The twelfth party congress in April 1923 brought renewed emphasis on the peasant, especially from Zinoviev. But this found as yet no reflexion in Bukharin's report on Comintern affairs, which devoted some attention to the " hundreds of millions of colonial and semi-colonial slaves " of the east, and specifically recommended " a bloc between the working class and the peasantry " in Japan,[3] but continued to ignore the rôle of the peasant in Europe.

The issue was brought to a head by the Bulgarian *coup* of June 9, 1923, when the powerful Bulgarian Communist Party stood aside while Stambulisky's peasant régime was overthrown by military force. At the enlarged session of IKKI a few days later the peasant question was a major theme of Zinoviev's opening speech. The material was limited but he made the most of it. The Polish Socialist Party had recently been appealing to the agrarian discontents of the peasantry ; Zinoviev exhorted Polish communists to follow this example and to abandon the " old-fashioned views " still held by some of them on the rôle of

---

[1] See *The Bolshevik Revolution, 1917–1923*, Vol. 3, p. 453.

[2] According to a circumstantial account in G. Bessedovsky, *Na Putyakh k Termidoru* (Paris, 1931), i, 101–102, this view was being propounded by a minority group in Comintern in the spring of 1923.

[3] *Dvenadtsatyi S"ezd Rossiiskoi Kommunisticheskoi Partii (Bol'shevikov)* (1923), pp. 228, 245.

the peasant in the socialist revolution.[1] Stambulisky, the news of whose downfall was not yet confirmed, was praised for his efforts to constitute a " Green International ". The decision to create a Farmer-Labor Party in the United States — its founding congress was held at Chicago on July 3, 1923 — was noted with approval. The example of the successful tactics of the Russian revolution was invoked to justify the new teaching :

> The slogan " a worker-peasant government " is the *way* to the dictatorship of the proletariat, and in no sense a denial of the dictatorship of the proletariat.[2]

Nobody else contributed to the subject except Varga, the Hungarian economist of Comintern, who thought it essential to draw a distinction between " working peasants " and " exploiting peasants " ; [3] and the plenum passed a long resolution citing the resolutions of the second and further congresses of Comintern on the agrarian question and concluding that what was required to give expression to the correct relation of workers and peasants was " the political formula of a worker-peasant government ".[4] The condemnation of the Bulgarian Communist Party for its failure to ally itself with Stambulisky's peasant régime fitted into this tactical framework.

Notwithstanding Zinoviev's efforts, the attempt to rescue the peasant from the subsidiary place to which Marxist doctrine had consigned him continued to hang fire. The lessons of Russian experience seemed to have little validity in the international sphere. They had no application in the industrial countries of

[1] *Internationale Presse-Korrespondenz*, No. 107, June 27, 1923, pp. 914-915, carried an account of proposals for agrarian reform introduced into the Polish Diet by two deputies of a peasant group affiliated to the communists

[2] *Rasshirennyi Plenum Ispolnitel'nogo Komiteta Kommunisticheskogo Internatsionala (12-23 Iyunya, 1923 goda)* (1923), pp. 36-43.

[3] *Ibid.* pp. 47-48 ; in an article written after the session Varga called the resolution on a worker-peasant government " the most important event of the session of the enlarged IKKI ", but thought it should be restricted to " poor " and " middle " peasants (*Internationale Presse-Korrespondenz*, No. 104, June 22, 1923, p. 884). In a further article (*ibid.* No. 116, July 11, 1923, pp. 1020-1021) Dombal attacked Varga's view as " an attempt to win the west for the slogan of ' the village poor ' which had failed to justify itself in Russia ", and " an unnecessary narrowing of the basis of our work " ; the campaign should appeal to " the broad masses of the peasantry ".

[4] *Kommunisticheskii Internatsional v Dokumentakh* (1933), pp. 368-373.

western Europe, and the attempt to force American political combinations into this pattern was farcical. In the Asiatic countries the problem of the peasant was merged in the wider issue of national liberation. Only in one part of the world — in eastern and central Europe — were conditions partly analogous to those in Russia ; only here had peasant political parties risen to power. In the summer of 1923 a Polish communist of peasant origin and a former deputy in the Polish Diet, Dombal by name, who had just been released from a Polish prison in an exchange for Polish prisoners in Soviet Russia, put forward a proposal to constitute a peasant International. Unlike several earlier projects of the same kind, Dombal's plan aimed at organizing the International under communist auspices.[1] By a fortunate coincidence the Soviet agricultural exhibition, originally planned for 1922 and then postponed to the following year, opened on August 15, 1923, in Moscow.[2] The presence of visiting delegations from peasant organizations abroad helped forward the project ; and what was officially called the " first international peasants' congress " assembled there on October 10, 1923. More than 150 delegates represented the peasants of forty nations (including in this total several of the republics and autonomous republics of the Soviet Union).

The proceedings were conventional and of little interest. Dombal opened them and played a prominent rôle throughout. Kalinin brought greetings in the name of TsIK and of the government of the USSR. Zinoviev appeared only on the third day with a message of greetings from the Communist International. Klara Zetkin, in a rhetorical appeal, explained that " we do not dream of wanting to incorporate the broad working peasant masses in the ranks of the communist party " : all that was needed was

---

[1] The only precedent for Dombal's scheme was a proposal made by Osinsky at IKKI in March 1922 to convene a conference in Moscow of the agricultural sections of communist parties ; IKKI approved the proposal and appointed a committee to give effect to it (*Die Taktik der Kommunistischen Internationale gegen die Offensive des Kapitals* (1922), pp. 135, 163). But nothing more seems to have been heard of this. Dombal was exchanged with twenty-one other Polish communists in March 1923 for a group of Poles arrested in Soviet Russia (*Pravda*, March 18, 20, 1923) ; he appeared as a fraternal delegate of the Polish Communist Party at the twelfth congress of the Russian party in April 1923 (*Dvenadtsatyi S"ezd Rossiiskoi Kommunisticheskoi Partii (Bol'-shevikov)* (1923), p. 77).   [2] See p. 86 above.

an alliance " for the common struggle against capitalism ".   A
resolution against war was enthusiastically adopted.   Varga expounded at length the hopeless position of the peasant under
capitalism.   Teodorovich, the People's Commissar for Agriculture
of the RSFSR, described the position of the peasant in the Soviet
Union, whose only trouble was now the low price of his products
compared with the high price of industrial goods.   It was decided
to set up an International Peasant Council, with a presidium of
twelve, as a standing institution, and to hold further peasant
congresses every two years.   An agrarian institute would be
established in Moscow.   Nobody hinted at the dissensions in the
Russian party which reached an acute stage while the congress
was in session.   Events in Bulgaria were lightly touched on to
point the moral of cooperation between peasant and industrial
worker.   Nobody mentioned the political situation in Germany
except Bukharin and Radek, both of whom spoke at a final
ceremonial meeting in the Bol'shoi theatre.   Here Bukharin
remarked that the working masses in Germany were confronted
with " an enemy armed to the teeth, who can crush them if the
proletariat and peasantry of Germany do not march together " ;
and Radek, declaring that " Europe is on the eve of great disturbances ", appealed to the French and German peasants to put
pressure on their respective governments to avert the danger of
war.[1]

Immediately after the congress the International Peasant
Council held its first, and mainly formal, session, elected its
presidium and appointed A. P. Smirnov, a veteran Russian party
official, as its secretary-general with Dombal as his deputy.   The
council, or the presidium on its behalf, continued for a number of
years to issue manifestoes from time to time on current events.
The only conspicuous episode in its career occurred when, in June
1924, Radić and Kosutič, two leaders of the Croat Republican
Peasant Party, visited Moscow and applied in the name of the
party to join the Peasant International.   The application was
enthusiastically granted at a meeting of the presidium on July 1,
1924 ; and the impression momentarily prevailed in Moscow

---

[1] The records of the congress, giving the resolutions in full and the speeches
in a much abbreviated form, are in *Protokoll vom Ersten Internationalen
Bauernkongress* (1924).

that a great political success had been achieved.[1] The sequel
failed to justify these hopes. Radič, who appears to have taken
an unfavourable view of all Soviet politicians with the single exception of Chicherin, returned to Yugoslavia convinced that " from
the point of view of peasant interests the Soviet régime is the
most unpropitious known to history ".[2] His visit to Moscow
proved a useful card to play in the game of Yugoslav internal
politics. After some hard bargaining Radič achieved a reconciliation with the Serb-Croat-Slovene Government and accepted
a portfolio in it ; and nothing more was heard of Croat interest
in the Peasant International. Of the institutions set up by the
congress of October 1923 only the agrarian institute had some
vitality, and continued to exist for many years ; no further
international congress was held.

[1] The relevant documents for all these events are in *Die Bauerninternationale*,
i (1924), 160-186 ; *Pravda*, July 22, 1924.
[2] G. Besedovsky, *Na Putyakh k Termidoru* (Paris, 1931), i, 72-73 ; according to this source Radich's visit to Moscow was arranged by Goldenstein
(see p. 192, note 5 above), who was a personal friend of Radich.

CHAPTER 9

THE GERMAN FIASCO

THE news from Germany of the collapse of the Cuno government and of the establishment of a broad coalition government under Stresemann caused an immediate sensation among the Soviet leaders, then dispersed on vacation. Six months later it was easy to diagnose this event as " an ebb in the high tide of revolution "[1] which had been flowing steadily in Germany for the past six months. But few people, inside Germany or outside, took this view at the time, or had any confidence in the ability of the Stresemann government to weather the storm. The political barometer seemed set more certainly than ever for revolution. On August 15, 1923, Zinoviev wrote from the Caucasus that " the crisis is approaching " and that " a new and decisive chapter is beginning in the activity of the German Communist Party and, with it, of Comintern ".[2] Brandler was hastily summoned from Berlin for consultation. Zinoviev, Bukharin and Trotsky all hurried back to Moscow, where an extraordinary meeting of the Politburo was summoned on August 23, 1923, attended in addition to the members of the Politburo by Radek, Pyatakov, Shmidt and Tsyurupa.[3] Radek reported on the situation. The attitudes adopted by the leaders were important and characteristic. Trotsky had from the first been

[1] *Die Lehren der Deutschen Ereignisse* (Hamburg, 1924), p. 41.

[2] *The Errors of Trotskyism* (CPGB, 1925), p. 347.

[3] The only published record of their meeting is in B. Bazhanov, *Stalin* (German translation from French, 1931), pp. 122-126. The author, a member of Stalin's staff, was employed as secretary to the Politburo, to which he had been recently transferred from the Orgburo (the decision transferring him is reproduced *ibid.* p. 5). He writes from memory and in melodramatic style, and his judgments are of little value ; but his facts generally fit in with what is otherwise known. Zinoviev, referring to this meeting a few months later, explained that whereas, while Lenin was active, the Russian workers in Comintern " took counsel with comrade Lenin personally, and that was enough ", it had become necessary after his withdrawal " to replace the leadership of Ilich with the leadership of the collective " ; it thus came about that

O

more profoundly convinced than any of his colleagues — Lenin,
perhaps, at certain moments excepted — that the destinies of the
Russian and German revolutions were irrevocably linked : for
him it was an emotional, as much as a rational, belief. An article
written in New York immediately after the outbreak of the
February revolution had contained an imaginary dialogue between
a critic and himself :

> " But what will happen if the German proletariat fails to
> rise ? What will you do then ? "
> " You suppose, then, that the Russian revolution can take
> place without affecting Germany ? . . . But this is altogether
> unlikely."
> " Still, if this none the less happened ? "
> " Really, we need not rack our brains over so implausible
> a hypothesis." [1]

His attitude at Brest-Litovsk was governed by this overmastering
belief. Nor did the failure of the assumption to work at that
moment persuade him that it was false. Its realization was merely
postponed. Trotsky, alone perhaps of the principal Bolsheviks,
continued sincerely to believe that the chance of a victorious
proletarian revolution in Europe had been missed in 1919 only
because no organized communist parties yet existed to lead it.[2]
Throughout the spring and summer of 1923 he watched with
keen excitement the mounting tension in Germany. In August
he became convinced that the missed opportunity had provi-
dentially returned. The expected advent of the proletarian revolution in Germany could now — he thought — only be a matter
of weeks ; and he argued eagerly in favour of staking everything
in order to support it. Zinoviev demurred to so much optimism,
and thought it safer to reckon in months than in weeks, but

the party representatives in Comintern had discussed " the question of the
German revolution in all its details " with the Politburo (*Trinadtsataya Konferentsiya Rossiiskoi Kommunisticheskoi Partii (Bol'shevikov)* (1924), p. 167).
This, incidentally, confirms the supposition that the Politburo did not discuss
the " March action " of 1921 (see *The Bolshevik Revolution, 1917–1923*, Vol. 3,
p. 338).

[1] Trotsky, *Sochineniya*, iii, i, 20.

[2] " In the most critical year for the bourgeoisie, the year 1919 ", he had
written two years later, " the European proletariat could undoubtedly have
conquered state power with the smallest sacrifices if there had been at its
head a genuine revolutionary organization, . . . i.e. a strong communist party "
(L. Trotsky, *Pyat' Let Kominterna* (n.d. [1924]), p. 224).

broadly agreed with the proposed policy. Stalin was more cautious still. He saw no revolution in Germany now or in the autumn : it might come in the spring, but even that was dubious. But doubts and hesitations were quickly overcome. The Politburo, while not committing itself to Trotsky's enthusiasm, decided to support revolutionary movements in Germany by all available means, and appointed a standing committee consisting of Radek, Pyatakov, Unshlikht, now vice-president of the GPU, and Shmidt (to whom Krestinsky, the Soviet Ambassador in Berlin, was afterwards added), to supervise the operation.[1] An argument which probably weighed strongly with the Politburo, now or later, was the fear that Stresemann intended to give German policy a western orientation and turn his back on Rapallo. The assumption that Germany and Soviet Russia, whatever else divided them, had a common interest in resisting the domination of the western Powers seemed under serious challenge from the German side.

The new line approved by the Politburo called for fresh activity both on the international and on the diplomatic front. On August 27, 1923, a proclamation issued jointly by IKKI and the central council of Profintern declared the German proletariat to be in danger and invited workers of all countries to protest against the occupation of German territory.[2] In the September issue of the journal of Profintern Lozovsky set to work to fan the flames :

> Revolution is knocking at the door in Germany and demanding admittance. . . . We cannot fix the date of the German revolution. Judging, however, from the present state of things, it is only a question of months.

And the article ended by looking forward to the moment when " the world revolution will form a territorial block from Vladivostok to the Rhine ".[3] On August 31 the Zentrale of the KPD announced that the decisive moment was " no longer far off ",

[1] Stalin referred four years later to the appointment at this time of a " German commission of Comintern " consisting of Zinoviev, Bukharin, Stalin, Trotsky, Radek, and " several German comrades " to prepare for the seizure of power (*Sochineniya*, x, 63) : there appears to be no contemporary record of such a commission.

[2] *Die Rote Fahne* (Berlin), September 2, 1923 ; according to an oral statement to the author by Brandler, this proclamation was issued on Trotsky's initiative.

[3] *Die Rote Gewerkschaftsinternationale*, No. 9 (32), September 1923, pp. 785-786, 789.

and ended a proclamation with the appeal : " Arise for the struggle — then victory is sure ".[1] The issue of the *Rote Fahne* which published the IKKI-Profintern proclamation also carried an article by Radek written to conform with the new line : it accused Stresemann of seeking to turn Germany, like Austria, into " a colony of the Entente ", and insisted that only Soviet Russia was the true friend of the German masses. Even Radek momentarily shed his habitual scepticism. In an address to future Red Army commanders at the Moscow military training school he proclaimed that " the coming revolution in Germany will be only part of a series of great world conflicts that are approaching, and the cause of these conflicts is the utter bankruptcy of the bourgeoisie, not only of Germany, but of all Europe ".[2]

The decision of the Politburo to support the German revolution, if and when it broke out, was unequivocal. What had not been decided was whether active steps should be taken from Moscow to hasten and instigate the outbreak of the revolution. Brandler had been in Moscow since the middle of August waiting for the Bolshevik leaders to make up their minds. The leaders of the Left in the KPD, Maslow and Ruth Fischer, were now also summoned to Moscow to play their part in the decision and in the preparations to carry it out. What followed afterwards became the occasion of so much recrimination and so many attempts at self-justification that the precise attitude adopted at the time by those concerned remains in part conjectural. A fairly clear picture can, however, be drawn. The Left wing of the KPD, represented in the Moscow discussions by Maslow, Ruth Fischer and Thälmann, believed that the German situation was ripe for an immediate proletarian revolution, which would take the form of a seizure of power by the party, as the Bolsheviks had seized it in October 1917. What was important was to fix an early date to strike the blow ; the preliminary manœuvres leading up to it were a matter of secondary importance. This view was also taken by Trotsky and, somewhat less enthusiastically, by Zinoviev and by the majority of the Politburo. The position of Brandler was more equivocal. In public, bowing to the claims of party loyalty, he accepted what was clearly the majority view.

[1] *Die Rote Fahne* (Berlin), September 1, 1923.
[2] *Izvestiya*, September 19, 1923.

At a meeting of the executive committee of Profintern, he proclaimed the seizure of power in Germany to be " a fully practicable task ".   To retain power would be " more complicated and difficult " owing to the doubtful attitude of Poland and Czechoslovakia and a possible shortage of food supplies ; but here, too, " we have taken all that into account and say that the time is ripe to act ".[1]   In private, on the other hand, he continued to nurse doubts whether the party was as yet sufficiently prepared, either politically or technically, for the seizure of power ; it was necessary, he argued, before taking the final step, to see what attitude the workers in general would adopt to Stresemann's coalition government in which the SPD was represented.   This view, which was also that of Radek, appears to have been secretly shared by Stalin, at any rate to the extent of believing that the situation in Germany was not yet ripe for revolution.   But Stalin at this time neither had, nor claimed to have, any profound knowledge of European affairs ; and he had no inclination to separate himself from the majority of his colleagues on an issue on which he felt himself out of his depth.   He acquiesced in the general view.[2]

The most stubbornly contested issue was the fixing of a date for the seizure of power : this was the point on which a verbal compromise between Right and Left wings of the German party was most difficult to attain.   At a secret meeting at the end of September 1923 the Politburo decided, on Trotsky's insistence and with characteristic attention to the Russian precedent, to fix the date of the German revolution for November 7.[3]   When,

[1] *Trud*, September 22, 1923.   According to Kuusinen a year later, " comrade Brandler succumbed to fantastic revolutionary visions ", and " the seizure of power now appeared to him as an easy and certain matter " (*The Errors of Trotskyism* (CPGB, 1925), p. 348) : it is questionable whether Brandler ever held this view.

[2] Zinoviev said later : "All [the party leaders] estimated the position to be that the revolution in Germany was a question of weeks.   All our information pointed to that.   The difference between the most pessimistic judgments and the most optimistic was that pessimistically inclined comrades expected the revolution *two, three or four weeks* later.   That was the biggest divergence which we found " (*Trinadtsataya Konferentsiya Rossiiskoi Kommunisticheskoi Partii (Bol'shevikov)* (1924), p. 166).   Stalin himself in a speech of 1927 claimed that he had " stood decisively and definitely for the immediate seizure of power by the communists " (*Sochineniya*, x, 63).

[3] B. Bazhanov, *Stalin* (German translation from French, 1931), pp. 129-130.   A by-product of this controversy was an article by Trotsky which appeared in *Pravda*, September 23, 1923, and was reprinted as a special issue

however, this was proposed to Brandler, he obstinately resisted the fixing of this or any other date; and the issue was evaded by an agreement to leave the date of the German revolution to be fixed by the German communists.[1] On this basis, which appeared to leave the ultimate decision in his hands, Brandler allowed himself to be drawn into discussions of the preparations for revolution.

The immediate question of tactics related to the proposed entry of the KPD into a coalition government with the SPD in Saxony. This question had first arisen informally during the fourth congress of Comintern in November 1922, when the Saxon elections gave the SPD and KPD together an absolute majority over all other parties in the Landtag and a coalition between them was desired by many on both sides. The project was supported by the Right leaders of the KPD both in Germany and in Moscow, but abandoned on the insistence of IKKI,[2] leaving the SPD in Saxony to form a coalition with bourgeois parties. This coalition quickly broke down. Since early in 1923 a social-democratic government with Zeigner as Prime Minister had ruled in Saxony with the support of communist votes in the Landtag; and it was understood that the KPD could claim its share of ministerial posts if it so desired. It was now proposed that communists should join the government in Saxony (and in Thuringia where the same situation existed) as a spring-board for the German revolution. Among other advantages it was hoped that participation in the state governments would enable the communists to

---

of *Internationale Presse-Korrespondenz*, No. 152, September 26, 1923, under the title *Can a Counter-Revolution or a Revolution be fixed for a Definite Date?* The article argued that Mussolini, the " Bulgarian Fascists ", the Jacobins in 1789 and the Bolsheviks in 1917 had all set a date for their respective *coups*, and that this was a necessary step for any party claiming to exercise leadership in a revolution ; to adopt a " waiting attitude " in face of " the growing revolutionary movement of the proletariat " was Menshevism. The article was couched in theoretical terms and did not mention Germany. It was reprinted in L. Trotsky, *Pyat' Let Kominterna* (n.d. [1924]), pp. 575-580.

[1] R. Fischer, *Stalin and German Communism* (Harvard, 1948), pp. 316-317 ; Zinoviev afterwards stated that Radek also opposed the fixing of the date (*Die Lehren der Deutschen Ereignisse* (Hamburg, 1924), p. 60).

[2] *Ibid.* pp. 50, 64-65 ; *Protokoll: Fünfter Kongress der Kommunistischen Internationale* (n.d.), i, 192 ; Trotsky notes that there were " doubts and hesitations in the party ", but that the question was decided in the negative (L. Trotsky, *Pyat' Let Kominterna* (n.d. [1924]), p. 555).

lay hands on stocks of arms.[1] The somewhat confused programme of action was afterwards summarized by Radek in the following terms :

> The proletariat leads off (*marschiert auf*) in Saxony, taking its start from the defence of the workers' government, into which we enter; and it will attempt in Saxony to use the state power in order to arm itself and to form, in this restricted proletarian province of Middle Germany, a wall between the southern counter-revolution in Bavaria and the Fascism of the north. At the same time the party throughout the Reich will step in and mobilize the masses.[2]

But even on this programme whole-hearted agreement could not be reached between the KPD leaders. The Left apparently regarded these manœuvres with mixed feelings,[3] but accepted them as a step on the road to the seizure of power. Brandler, however, while in theory not opposed to limited measures of co-operation with the SPD, proved almost as reluctant to fix a time-table for the entry of the communists into the Saxon Government as for the outbreak of the revolution itself. The time, he argued, was not yet ripe, and the situation on the spot must be allowed to mature. The masses must first be mobilized.[4] But on this point, too, he allowed himself to be overruled; and on October 1, 1923, a telegram signed by Zinoviev on behalf of IKKI was despatched to the Zentrale of the KPD :

> Since we estimate the situation in such a way that the decisive moment will come in four, five, six weeks, we think it necessary to seize at once every position which can be directly utilized. The situation compels us to raise in a practical form the question of our entry into the Saxon Government. On the condition that the Zeigner people [i.e. the social-democrats] are really prepared to defend Saxony against Bavaria and the Fascists, we must enter. Carry out at once the arming of

---

[1] A. Thalheimer, *1923 : Eine Verpasste Revolution?* (1931), p. 25.

[2] *Die Lehren der Deutschen Ereignisse* (Hamburg, 1924), p. 5.

[3] According to Ruth Fischer (*Stalin and German Communism* (Harvard, 1948), p. 328), Thälmann " returned from Moscow with a new enthusiasm for the strategy of the coalition " ; this implies that she and Maslow did not share the enthusiasm.

[4] *Bericht über die Verhandlungen des IX Parteitags der Kommunistischen Partei Deutschlands* (1924), p. 246.

50,000 to 60,000 men, ignore General Müller. The same in Thuringia.[1]

Klara Zetkin afterwards described the decision not unjustly as " the result of a compromise between party leaders of two opposed tendencies, not the crown of a unified mass movement ".[2]

Another *contretemps* marred these ill-starred preparations. Trotsky took alarm at the evident lack of accord and sympathy among the leaders of the KPD, which augured poorly for the success of the enterprise. His conversion to the policy of revolutionary action in Germany had not shaken his personal loyalty to Brandler or tempered his mistrust of the Left leaders in the KPD.[3] He made the proposal to retain Maslow and Ruth Fischer in Moscow. After a stubborn contest, in which Trotsky and Zinoviev played the leading parts for and against the proposal, a compromise was reached. The case against Maslow was strengthened by the fact that Lenin had wished in the previous year to give him an assignment in Russia in order to keep him out of mischief in Germany, and by his past association with the workers' opposition.[4]

[1] *Die Lehren der Deutschen Ereignisse* (Hamburg, 1924), pp. 60-61 ; according to Brandler (*ibid.* pp. 24-25), Radek shared his objections and tried in vain to get the telegram modified. Zinoviev afterwards gave an illuminating account of the motives which inspired the instruction to " ignore " Müller. Following the proclamation of martial law on September 26, General Müller had just been appointed commander of the Reichswehr for Saxony. " I remember ", went on Zinoviev, " the example of Kronstadt in 1917, when the Provisional Government appointed as commissar the Kadet Pepelyaev, though power was really in the hands of the Kronstadt Soviet, and the Kronstadt Soviet ignored Pepelyaev and made him ridiculous, and then in our own good time we arrested him " (*Trinadtsataya Konferentsiya Rossiiskoi Kommunisticheskoi Partii (Bol'-shevikov)* (1924), pp. 167-168).

[2] *Bericht über die Verhandlungen des IX Parteitags der Kommunistischen Partei Deutschlands* (1924), p. 88.

[3] Trotsky, since the discussion of the " March action " at the third congress of Comintern in 1921, when he had appeared as a leading defender of the official policy (see *The Bolshevik Revolution, 1917–1923*, Vol. 3, pp. 383, 396-397), had been regarded in the KPD as a supporter of the Right ; in an article of January 1923 Ruth Fischer contrasted the " theorists of the offensive " with the " Trotskyists " as the two main groups in the KPD (*Die Internationale*, vi, No. 3 (February 1, 1923), p. 87). This impression was confirmed by the close association at this time between Trotsky and Radek, as well as by the personal support given by him to Brandler in spite of his conversion to the policy of immediate action.

[4] See *The Bolshevik Revolution, 1917–1923*, Vol. 3, p. 413; it had just been ascertained that the Workers' Group (see pp. 80-82 above) had sought to draw Maslow into its " foreign bureau " (V. Sorin, *Rabochaya Gruppa* (1924), p. 112), though there is no evidence that the bureau was ever constituted.

It was decided to hold him in Moscow while charges against his party record were investigated by a commission of Comintern, but to allow Ruth Fischer to return.[1]

The political issues debated in Moscow were, however, perhaps less important than the preparations for the military organization of the insurrection, which were now for the first time seriously taken in hand.[2] Few military preparations had been made for the March action in 1921 ; and such as were made resulted from spontaneous local initiative, not from any planning at the headquarters of the KPD — or, much less, in Moscow. But this fiasco had shown the futility of sporadic and uncoordinated risings against the disciplined forces of the police and the Reichswehr. When Brandler was in Moscow in the summer of 1922 Trotsky offered to send an officer of the Red Army to advise the KPD on questions of military organization. The offer was accepted, and in the autumn Skoblevsky, a Lett by birth, arrived in Germany in this capacity.[3] During the winter of 1922–1923, the proliferation of illicit political armies of the Right, and the scarcely disguised power and influence which they exercised, somewhat tardily convinced the communists of the need to emulate them.[4] It is said to have been at the moment of the Ruhr occupation that a group of five or six Soviet intelligence officers were

---

[1] Few references to this episode exist in party literature ; the passage relating to it in Zinoviev's speech to the presidium of IKKI on January 11, 1924 (" I will admit that during the October discussions Radek was with me and Bukharin against Trotsky, who demanded the elimination of Ruth Fischer, etc."), appears in *Die Internationale*, vii, No. 2-3 (March 28, 1924), p. 44, but was omitted from the official version of the speech in *Die Lehren der Deutschen Ereignisse* (Hamburg, 1924). Kuusinen, in his indictment of Trotsky two years later, also mentions only Ruth Fischer and ignores Maslow (*The Errors of Trotskyism* (CPGB, 1925), pp. 350-351). Maslow dilated on the incident in his trial before a Prussian court for treason in 1925 (his evidence was reprinted in a KPD pamphlet, *Der Fall Maslow* (1926), p. 19) ; and R. Fischer, *Stalin and German Communism* (Harvard, 1948), pp. 322-323, gives a highly personal account.

[2] According to R. Fischer, *Stalin and German Communism* (Harvard, 1948), p. 312, the discussions were " devoted principally to military strategy rather than politics ".

[3] Oral information from Brandler ; Brandler spoke of these questions in general terms at the fifth congress of Comintern (*Protokoll : Fünfter Kongress der Kommunistischen Internationale* (n.d.), i, 221-222).

[4] In an article of February 1923 in the party journal an anonymous member of the Zentrale argued that " the national-socialist movement forces upon us, and creates a favourable pre-supposition for, the transition from demanding

sent to Germany, and set to work to create within the KPD three forms of secret organization : an intelligence service working in close touch with the corresponding Soviet organ ; a sabotage and terror unit ; and a military organization to create the nucleus of a fighting force — the rank and file of a German revolutionary army.[1] The army was to be built up on the basis of units of 100 men — the so-called " Red hundreds " or " proletarian hundreds ", composed of workers, but not necessarily party members ; and stocks of arms, with which the black market of the day was liberally supplied, were accumulated. The stiffening was to be furnished by " groups of ten " of tried party members. These measures of military organization went on throughout the summer of 1923, while Germany plunged more and more deeply into chaos. The proposed strategy was apparently to mobilize the Red hundreds throughout Germany when the moment arrived and concentrate them in Saxony and Thuringia, the com-

armed detachments of workers to forming them ", and went on to advocate detachments composed not only of communists, but of social-democrats and non-party workers ; in default of sufficient arms, they were to be trained in ju-jitsu (*Die Internationale*, vi, No. 3 (February 1, 1923), pp. 75-76). This confirms that the military organization of the KPD was virtually non-existent till the Russians took it in hand.

[1] Evidence on these matters comes in the main from those who later left the party and were prepared to divulge its secrets, and must therefore be regarded with some caution ; the above facts, however, as stated in W. G. Krivitsky, *I was Stalin's Agent* (1939), pp. 55-58, may be taken as approximately correct. E. Wollenberg, *Der Apparat* (Bonn, 3rd ed., 1952), pp. 10-11, lists the six regional commands into which the military organization was divided, each with a Russian general attached : the author was in command of one of these units. Much detailed information about the terror organization, mainly for the period after January 1924, is provided in W. Zeutschel, *Im Dienst der Kommunistischen Terror-Organisation* (1931). This depicts the terror organization as being under direct Russian supervision : the KPD leadership used it, especially for the murder of traitors and spies, but disowned responsibility for it in cases of mishap — the normal attitude of governments to their own secret organizations. All accounts of this kind, whether from Russian or from German sources, tend for obvious reasons to exaggerate Russian responsibility and to represent German communists as docile pupils ; in the early and middle 1920s secret terror organizations and " political " murders were too familiar in all circles in Germany to require the stimulus of foreign inspiration. Among the alleged projects of the communist terror organization was a plot to assassinate Seeckt (*ibid.* pp. 65-66) ; according to J. Valtin, *Out of the Night* (1941), pp. 58-59, terror units organized by Skoblevsky planned the assassination of Seeckt and Stinnes, but " Radek through Brandler ordered that the plans to kill von Seeckt be dropped ". A nationalist plot to assassinate Seeckt was unmasked in January 1924 (J. W. Wheeler-Bennett, *The Nemesis of Power* (1953), p. 109).

munist strongholds which would serve as the base for the revolutionary campaign.[1]

The preparations seem to have suffered from a multiplicity of authorities. Skoblevsky was in charge of military operations with the assistance of a directorate composed of seven members of the central committee of the KPD. But Guralsky, who had accompanied Bela Kun to Berlin in March 1921,[2] and had since played an active part in German affairs under the *alias* of Kleine, was concerned with the military organization of the party, and was reinforced by a number of Red Army technicians, and foreign communists trained in the Red Army, who were charged with the task of equipping and training German units.[3] But this elaborate organization produced meagre results. The vaunted Red hundreds scarcely existed outside the Ruhr.[4] An estimate said to have been given by Brandler in Moscow that 50,000 to 60,000 men could be armed and mobilized in Saxony proved to be without foundation; the total number of rifles in the hands of the party amounted to no more than 11,000.[5] The verdict passed later by the presidium of IKKI erred, if anything, on the side of leniency:

> The technical preparations, the mobilization of the party apparatus for the struggle for power, the equipment and moral discipline of the hundreds were on a low level. The too brief and over-hurried technical preparation yielded in practice nothing; in the technical sense it mobilized the party

[1] W. G. Krivitsky, *I was Stalin's Agent* (1939), p. 60.

[2] See *The Bolshevik Revolution, 1917-1923*, Vol. 3, p. 335.

[3] J. Valtin, *Out of the Night* (1941), p. 48, describes the formation of Red hundreds in Hamburg in September 1923 with five or six " young Soviet officers " smuggled in from Russia to train them

[4] A. Thalheimer, *1923: Eine Verpasste Revolution?* (1931), p. 19.

[5] *Die Internationale*, vi, No. 18 (November 30, 1923), p. 524 ; Zinoviev used these miscalculations at the sessions of the presidium of IKKI and of the thirteenth party conference in January 1924 in order to place the blame of the defeat on the KPD leadership (*Die Lehren der Deutschen Ereignisse* (Hamburg, 1924), p. 60 ; *Trinadtsataya Konferentsiya Rossiiskoi Kommunisticheskoi Partii (Bol'shevikov)* (1924), p. 170) ; according to Brandler, he learned from Guralsky on his return from Moscow that no progress had been made during his absence in the collection of arms (*Protokoll: Fünfter Kongress der Kommunistischen Internationale* (n.d.), i, 231). A Soviet work published in 1931 and quoted in *Voprosy Istorii*, No. 11 (1948), p. 6, puts the numbers of Red hundreds as high as 800, of which more than a third were in Saxony ; this must have been the official figure and had little relation to reality.

membership for action, but failed to reach the great proletarian masses.[1]

No Russian schooling could at short notice have made the military detachments of the KPD a match for the disciplined forces of the Reichswehr or even for the experienced illegal armies of the Right. The military preparations and calculations of those responsible for the planning of the German insurrection of October 1923 can easily be made in retrospect to appear ridiculous. The efforts of amateur conspirators, possessed of none of the necessary qualities except audacity and self-confidence, were pitted against the cool hard-headed determination of the professionals of the Reichswehr. The struggle was so patently unequal that it could never have been undertaken but for two basic miscalculations which were more or less completely shared by all the responsible leaders, German and Russian.

The first of these miscalculations related to the Reichswehr itself. The fidelity of the officers and men of the Reichswehr to the republic was notoriously equivocal ; some of them were believed to be infected with the vague aspirations of " national Bolshevism " ; and the leaders of the Reichswehr attached a high value to their secret cooperation with the Red Army. On the strength of these facts, fantastic hopes seem to have been entertained in Moscow of the complicity of a section of the Reichswehr in a potential communist rising. In a speech in Moscow on the eve of the projected insurrection, Trotsky spoke of the Reichswehr as containing " working class elements which at a decisive moment will not defend the bourgeoisie very stoutly ".[2] Throughout the troubles of the summer of 1923 cases occurred of local fraternization between communist demonstrators and members of the police and of the Reichswehr.[3] At a higher level secret contacts were undoubtedly established between the communist military organization and certain Reichswehr officers. But how far these contacts were

[1] Die Lehren der Deutschen Ereignisse (Hamburg, 1924), p. 102.

[2] Izvestiya, October 21, 1923.

[3] W. Zeutschel, Im Dienst der Kommunistischen Terror-Organisation (1931), p. 12, speaks of " great sympathies even in the ranks of the police and the Reichswehr for the KPD " ; Schleicher at this time, with the approval of Seeckt, was busy promoting " a new spirit of social consciousness in the Reichswehr ", and the sentimental idea of " a community of comradeship between soldiers and workers " was fashionable " among the younger officers " (J. W. Wheeler-Bennett, The Nemesis of Power (1953), pp. 110-111).

with genuine sympathizers and how far with agents detailed to keep
the authorities informed of what was on foot in communist circles,
can no longer be guessed. What is clear is that the leaders of the
Reichswehr, whatever their attitude to the Weimar republic or to
the desirability of a working alliance with Soviet Russia, were
never at any time prepared to tolerate the growth of communist
power in Germany, and that sentimental sympathies among the
rank and file were never strong or widespread enough to undermine Reichswehr discipline. Any calculations based on the supposed acquiescence of a part of the Reichswehr in a German
communist seizure of power were wholly mistaken.

The other basic miscalculation of the leaders of the KPD —
and, still more, of the Politburo in Moscow — related to the
attitude of the German working class ; and this miscalculation
was shared in common by the Left, who believed that the party
had only to strike on an appointed day for the masses to follow
it, and by the Right, who believed that the active support of a
large part of the SPD could be secured by preliminary political
manœuvres. It was a repetition of the illusion which had
dominated the political thinking of the Bolshevik leaders and of
so many Germans since November 1918 — that Germany was
ripe for a proletarian revolution. The workers' movement,
probably the best organized in the world, had passed through the
school of Marxism ; its pronouncements were couched in the
language of Marxism. In the Germany of 1918–1919 every predisposing condition seemed to favour revolution. When it failed
the conclusion was drawn that its success had been merely postponed. The fiasco in March 1920, and again in the March action
of 1921, was attributed to faulty tactics, not to a fundamentally
false diagnosis. In the autumn of 1923 the German situation
was more desperate than at any time since 1919, the misery
greater, the prospect apparently more hopeless. This time the
masses could not fail to rise at the call of revolution. It was in
this firm belief that the decisions were taken, and plans laid, in
Moscow and in Germany. Nobody seriously supposed that the
victory could be won by a simple military *coup*, or that the Red
hundreds were a match for the Reichswehr in a pitched battle ;
and a verdict that the failure was due to the inadequacy of the
military preparations would be irrelevant. These preparations

were designed to put the match at the critical moment to highly inflammable material. There is no reason to suppose that they would not have served this purpose if the right material had been present. The preparations for the German rising in the autumn of 1923 were governed, as so many decisions taken in Moscow since 1917 had been governed, by the illusory belief that the proletariat of western Europe, and of Germany in particular, was ripe for the proletarian revolution.

The prevalence of these illusions also helps to explain one of the most puzzling features in the Soviet attitude towards the German crisis of 1923 — the absence of any attempt to resolve the apparent contradiction between the policy of Rapallo and of the secret agreements with the Reichswehr and the policy of all-out aid to the KPD and to the proletarian revolution in Germany. This contradiction reflected in unusually dramatic form the inherent and ineradicable duality of Soviet relations with the outside world. It was impossible to abandon the long-term belief in the world-wide revolution of the proletariat or to neglect measures likely to hasten it in particular countries. It was equally impossible to abandon the short-term expedients necessary to promote the security and stability of the isolated Soviet Government in the interval before the revolution spread to other major countries. The contradiction could be resolved only on the assumption, universally held by the Bolshevik leaders when the dual policy had been slowly and half-consciously elaborated in the period of Brest-Litovsk, that the victory of the revolution in other countries could be expected in weeks or months. The discrepancies in Soviet policy in Germany in the autumn of 1923 are explicable only in terms of the belief, universally held or professed by those responsible for framing it, that the German proletarian revolution was bound to occur within the next few weeks. Once that hypothesis was accepted, the need to support the coming revolution and the need to bridge over the brief interval by measures which would strengthen the Soviet Government and ward off the danger of an attack on it from the west — the only contingency which might stifle the German revolution at birth — became equally obvious. The contradiction disappeared in the light of faith in the imminent victory of the revolution. To arm the KPD and at the same time to assist in

arming the Reichswehr made sense if one believed that the
Reichswehr would, in fact, never use its arms against an organized
communist rising, or if one believed that the revolution was bound
to occur long before the policy of assisting the Reichswehr could
yield any tangible result.   These illusions alone justified the dual
policy as applied to Germany in 1923, and the dual policy made
the illusions psychologically necessary to the Bolshevik leaders. To
hold them was the only way to make sense of what was being done.

Notwithstanding the prevailing optimism, a sense of embarrassment was clearly visible in the fluctuations of official policy.
While the programme of unofficial Russian support for the
German communist rising was elaborated in the greatest detail,
the official policy of the Soviet Government was veiled in an
obscurity due not so much to diplomatic reticence — a quality
less honoured now than later — as to indecision in the highest
quarters.   In the first period of the Ruhr crisis bold spirits had
from time to time canvassed the prospect of intervention by the
Red Army.   At the twelfth party congress in April 1923 a delegate
had complained of a leading article in *Pravda* which had conveyed
the impression that " we were offering Germany active support,
almost in the form of a military alliance ".[1]   In the same month
a delegate of the central committee of the KPD paid a visit to
Tukhachevsky's military headquarters at Smolensk, where he
found the Red Army men eager " to march with arms in their
hands to the aid of the German and Polish proletariat ", and the
general staff full of confidence that " the Russian army will sweep
aside like chaff any Polish barrier which attempts to separate it
from the German proletariat in the decisive hour ".[2]   But the
scare of the Curzon ultimatum put an end to these provocative

---

[1] *Dvenadtsatyi S"ezd Rossiiskoi Kommunisticheskoi Partii (Bol'shevikov)*
(1923), p. 134 ; no such article has been identified. Zinoviev at the congress
said : " We tell the gentlemen of the German bourgeoisie . . . if you really want
to struggle against the occupation, if you want to struggle against the insults of the
Entente, nothing is left for you but to seek a rapprochement with the first proletarian country, which cannot help supporting those countries which are now in
servile dependence on international imperialism " (*ibid*. pp. 12-13).

[2] *Die Rote Fahne* (Berlin), April 22, 1923. Plans for a military offensive
against Poland were undoubtedly canvassed at this time ; Frunze and Voro-
shilov, who had once advocated the military reconquest of Bessarabia (see *The
Bolshevik Revolution, 1917-1923*, Vol. 3, p. 346), are said to have favoured them.
But there is no evidence that they were taken seriously outside military circles.
Such ideas were particularly popular in the Ukraine ; G. Besedovsky, *Na*

utterances. When the German crisis ripened in August and September 1923, it was clear that there could be this time no question of repeating the experiment of 1920 and using the Red Army in an attempt to bring the revolution to a head; and the keynote was struck in a much publicized interview given by Trotsky to a distinguished American visitor to Moscow, senator King :

> We want peace before all and above all. We shall not send a single Red Army man beyond the frontiers of Soviet Russia unless we are compelled by force to do so. . . . We do not want war. . . . We remember only too clearly that war between us and Poland would mean an all-European conflagration which would wipe the remnants of European civilization from the face of the earth.[1]

And the issue of *Izvestiya* which published the interview drove home the moral in a leading article entitled *The Phantom of Soviet Aggressiveness* :

> Whether the revolution is victorious in Germany or Bulgaria will depend in the first instance on how far the toilers of these countries have the will to fight and to win.

On the other hand, the Soviet leaders were preoccupied by the probability that, in the event of a successful proletarian revolution in Germany, Poland might be induced by French pressure to intervene, and were prepared in this event to threaten action by the Red Army against Poland. The essence of official Soviet policy was to neutralize Poland, but not otherwise to intervene in the German crisis.[2]

Official caution was reflected in a series of three speeches made

Putyakh k Termidoru (Paris, 1931), i, 62-65, describes a project worked out in the summer of 1922 by Ukrainian diplomats in central Europe, but rejected by party headquarters in Kharkov and subsequently by the Politburo in Moscow.

[1] The interview appeared in both *Pravda* and *Izvestiya* on September 30, 1923, and is reprinted in L. Trotsky, *Kak Vooruzhalas' Revolyutsiya*, iii, ii (1925), 114-117.

[2] According to B. Bazhanov, *Stalin* (German transl. from French, 1931), pp. 123-124, Trotsky at the meeting of the Politburo on August 23, 1923, predicted that the allies would intervene to stifle the German revolution, and proposed that the Red Army should be mobilized in full force to defend it. But this contradicts the cautious attitude usually adopted by Trotsky where military action was in question ; and no other authority suggests that action was seriously contemplated except in the event of intervention by Poland.

by Trotsky, on the eve of the crucial moment in Germany, in his
capacity both as People's Commissar for War and as the strongest
supporter among the Bolshevik leaders of the German revolution.
The first was delivered to the metal workers' trade union on
October 19 :

> They say that war with Poland is inevitable. This is not
> so. There are many reasons for thinking that there will be no
> war with Poland. . . . We do not want to fight, and are bound
> to do, and will do, everything possible to avoid war. We are
> wholly on the side of the German workers. We would eagerly
> stretch out a hand to them over the head of Poland in order
> to encourage them where necessary. The German workers do
> not need military support in their domestic struggle. It is a
> bad look-out for a revolution which cannot conquer by its own
> power.

But the German workers, he went on, would need Soviet grain ;
and the Soviet Union needed German industrial products.

> The geographical key to this exchange of goods is in the
> hands of Poland. Poland can serve as a bridge or become a
> barrier.

He concluded by saying that the chances were 51 per cent for
peace and 49 per cent against it. Next day he struck the same
note in a speech to the transport workers' union. Having predicted the seizure of power in Germany by the workers " in the
immediate future ", he canvassed the possibility that France and
Poland might then intervene, and went on :

> Poland can be either a bridge or a barrier between Germany
> and us. . . . We do not want war, we are prepared for a
> bargain to keep out of war ; but we will not isolate ourselves
> from the European market.

And on the following day, October 21, which turned out to be
the decisive turning-point in events in Germany, he repeated
the same theme without substantial variation to a conference of
political workers in the Red Army.[1] These utterances reflected
what appears to have been Trotsky's sincere conviction at this
moment : that the communist attempt to seize power would

[1] The three speeches which were widely publicized at the time are reprinted
in L. Trotsky, *Kak Vooruzhalas' Revolyutsiya*, iii, ii (1925), 120-125, 126-145,
146-172.

P

succeed as surely as the Bolshevik *coup* had succeeded in November 1917, and that the point of danger would come when the allied countries instituted a blockade of communist Germany in an attempt to starve out the new régime.[1] The question was not how to bring the German revolution to birth, but how to prevent the infant from being strangled by the wicked neighbours. By way of counteracting this danger Soviet trade missions in Europe were instructed to build up " a reserve of gold and grain to help the German proletariat ". At the same time arrangements were made to accumulate 60 million puds of grain at Petrograd and other frontier points to be rushed to Germany at the critical moment.[2]

The same conviction inspired the only diplomatic action known to have been taken by the Soviet Government at this time, which Kamenev later described as " the best expression of our policy in these months ".[3] Kopp, the first Soviet representative to the Weimar republic, who had returned to Moscow on Krestinsky's appointment as ambassador in Berlin, was despatched in the middle of October on a special mission to the Baltic states and to Poland. His purpose was to obtain assurances that, should trouble arise in Germany, these countries would not intervene in German affairs and would not interfere with traffic between the Soviet Union and Germany " irrespective of political changes and changes in the social order which might take place there ". The question of ways and means of preventing Polish intervention to crush a successful communist revolution in Germany was a matter of serious concern in Moscow, and it was recognized that neither threats nor diplomatic representations at Warsaw might alone suffice. The ingenious Radek, with the approval of the Politburo, had a conversation with Knoll, the Polish representative in Moscow, in which he suggested that the Polish Government should

---

[1] This apprehension was evidently based on the experience of the allied blockade of Germany in the first world war.

[2] G. Besedovsky, *Na Putyakh k Termidoru* (Paris, 1931), i, 123.

[3] *Vtoroi S"ezd Sovetov Soyuza Sovetskikh Sotsialisticheskikh Respublik* (1924), p. 66. Kamenev's speech of January 1924, from which this quotation is taken, is one of the few official Soviet utterances which betray some embarrassment over the dual policy pursued in Germany in 1923. Having described " the strengthening of friendly relations with Germany " as one of " the foundations of our policy ", he explained that " we could not remain indifferent " to the October–November crisis, which he ascribed to French imperialism and German Fascism : the KPD was not referred to at all (*ibid.* pp. 65-66).

agree to recognize a future communist régime in Germany in return for the cession of East Prussia to Poland; the Soviet Government would in such conditions recognize the "freedom of action" of the Polish Government in East Prussia. Such a proposal, if it became known in Berlin, would clearly have had the worst possible effect on Soviet relations with the German Government. For reasons of secrecy, therefore, it was decided to exclude these negotiations from the scope of Kopp's official mission, and entrust them to an agent named Raevsky, who would arrive in Warsaw via Dantzig simultaneously with Kopp.[1] These complicated moves were, however, overtaken by events. Scarcely had Kopp started on his mission when catastrophic developments occurred in Germany.

Early in October the KPD leaders other than Maslow had set off from Moscow on the return journey to Berlin to execute the agreed plan. A delegation of Comintern was appointed to proceed to Germany and direct the proceedings; Radek was in charge of party relations; Pyatakov exercised general supervision over military affairs in conjunction with Skoblevsky and Guralsky, who were already on the spot; Shmidt was to establish contacts with trade unions.[2] During the six weeks of deliberation in Moscow, the situation in Germany had lost none of its tenseness. The depreciation of the currency continued; the first step

---

[1] The main sources for the Kopp mission are a long statement in *Pravda*, November 17, 1923; Kamenev's speech at the second All-Union Congress of Soviets in January 1924 (*Vtoroi S"ezd Sovetov Soyuza Sovetskikh Sotsialisticheshihh Respublik* (1924), pp. 65-66); L. Fischer, *The Soviets in World Affairs* (1930), i, 459-460, quoting the annual report of Narkomindel for 1923, which has not been available; and G. Besedovsky, *Na Putyakh k Termidoru* (Paris, 1931), i, 139-143 (the author was at the Soviet mission in Warsaw at the time). *The Times*, October 24, 29, 1923, reported Kopp's movements. The Radek-Knoll conversation is reported in *The Times*, October 29, 1923 (from its Warsaw correspondent, who evidently had it from Polish sources), by Besedovsky, and by Fischer (the last implausibly attributing it to Knoll's initiative); the rôle of Raevsky is reported only by Besedovsky, but fits in with the obvious desire of the Soviet Government to be able to disclaim official responsibility for such a project.

[2] R. Fischer, *Stalin and German Communism* (Harvard, 1948), p. 323, omits Pyatakov; W. G. Krivitsky, *I was Stalin's Agent* (1939), p. 61, names Pyatakov, and incorrectly includes Bukharin. Radek afterwards stated that the delegation remained unanimous throughout the proceedings (*Die Lehren der Deutschen Ereignisse* (Hamburg, 1924), p. 5).

towards stabilization in the form of the creation of the Rentenmark had not yet borne fruit. Passive resistance had been officially terminated on September 26, 1923. This act had been followed by a strike in the Ruhr, and by hostile demonstrations from the nationalists who denounced it as a crowning national disgrace. The Zentrale of the KPD also protested against the " capitulation of the Stresemann-Hilferding government " in a proclamation ending with the words, " Long live the mass strike, Long live the struggle ! " A leading article by Radek in *Inprekorr* struck the familiar note of appeal to national sentiment by declaring that the bourgeoisie had ceased " to defend the independence of the nation ", and that the leadership in this task now devolved on the proletariat.[1] The Stresemann government displayed the courage of despair, proclaimed martial law and charged Seeckt and the Reichswehr with the maintenance of public order. The threat to order came quite as much from the nationalists as from the Left. But, in accordance with precedent, it was against the Left that the main measures of repression were directed. As early as September 4 the *Rote Fahne* had been suspended for a week ; it was suspended once more from September 24 to October 9 and then, after only two further issues, from October 11 to October 20. The initiative was beginning to pass into the hands of the government.

This was the atmosphere when Brandler arrived back in Germany on October 8, 1923.[2] The negotiations in Saxony were now far advanced. On October 10 the Zentrale of the KPD formally announced its approval of the entry of three party members, Brandler, Böttcher and Heckert, into a Saxon "government of proletarian defence " ;[3] and the new coalition was constituted two days later. Meanwhile the Berlin section of the KPD instituted conversations with the SPD which dragged on for a week without result.[4] Radek, on his way from Moscow to Saxony via Prague, halted at Warsaw, where he apparently revealed

[1] *Internationale Presse-Korrespondenz*, No. 153, September 28, 1923, p. 1318 ; No. 155, October 2, 1923, pp. 1327-1328.

[2] *Die Lehren der Deutschen Ereignisse* (Hamburg, 1924), p. 24.

[3] *Internationale Presse-Korrespondenz*, No. 162, October 12, 1923, p. 1370. Similar approval was expressed in Moscow ; *Izvestiya*, October 18, 1923, carried a photograph of the three communist ministers.

[4] *Die Lehren der Deutschen Ereignisse* (Hamburg, 1924), p. 63 ; G. Zinoviev, *Probleme der Deutschen Revolution* (Hamburg, 1923), p. 72.

to officials of the Soviet mission his low estimate of the revolutionary potentialities of German social-democrats and his pessimism
over the outcome of the impending struggle.[1] But by this time
the German Government and the Reichswehr felt strong enough
to make an issue of the inclusion of the communists in the Saxon
coalition. On October 20 an ultimatum was sent to it to dissolve
the " proletarian hundreds " in Saxony, and when this was refused
the order was given to march. The *Rote Fahne* reappeared on the
day of the ultimatum in time to carry an article by Brandler
expressing the conviction that the workers of Germany " will not
allow the Saxon proletariat to be struck down ", and concluding :
" This time everything is at stake ". The Reichswehr had done
what Brandler had shrunk from doing. It had fixed the date on
which the communists must either act or confess their impotence.

All over Germany the communist militant organizations were
put on the alert and awaited the signal for the rising. True to his
belief that the necessary prelude to a successful revolution was
to secure the cooperation of the Left wing of the SPD, Brandler
spent Sunday, October 21, in a conference of workers' organizations in Chemnitz, where he called for a general strike to resist
the impending Reichswehr invasion. The speech was received
without enthusiasm by the non-communist workers. One of the
social-democratic ministers in the coalition government threatened
to withdraw from the conference if the proposals were pressed.
The Saxon social-democrats had no stomach for a civil war against
the Reichswehr, and the Saxon communists no faith in their
capacity to act alone. The demand for a general strike was
politely buried by a resolution to set up a commission to examine
the proposal.[2] Brandler drew the logical conclusion and called

---

[1] G. Besedovsky, *Na Putyakh k Termidoru* (Paris, 1931), i, 130-135.
Radek was accompanied by Larissa Reisner, the young and beautiful wife of
Raskolnikov, the hero of the Soviet raid on Enzeli in May 1920 (see *The Bolshevik
Revolution, 1917-1923*, Vol. 3, p. 243) and later Soviet Minister to Afghanistan ;
she had come to Radek in Moscow in September 1923 and asked for his assistance in obtaining active party work in Germany, travelled with him to Saxony,
and was his wife or mistress till her sudden death in 1927 (K. Radek, *Portrety
i Pamflety*, i (1933), 59-71). She has left an impressionistic sketch of events in
Hamburg in the autumn of 1923 (L. Reisner, *Sobranie Sochinenii* (1928), ii,
5-77).
[2] A brief account of the Chemnitz conference is in *Internationale Presse-
Korrespondenz*, No. 164, October 22, 1923, p. 1398, a fuller and later one in
A. Thalheimer, *1923: Eine Verpasste Revolution?* (1931), pp. 26-27 ; Brandler

off the projected insurrection. Radek and the other Comintern delegates were not present at Chemnitz, but accepted the decision.[1] Couriers, who had been waiting to carry to expectant communists throughout Germany the order to act, were despatched to countermand the preparations. By a tragic blunder which has never been satisfactorily explained, two members of the party central committee, Thälmann and Remmele, left Chemnitz before the conference ended under the impression that its success was assured, and, arriving in Hamburg on the evening of October 22, gave the word for the rising to begin. Early next morning, while the Reichswehr was advancing on Dresden without resistance to depose the coalition government, a few hundred Hamburg communists attacked and occupied several police stations, seizing their stocks of arms, remained masters of a part of the city for forty-eight hours, and fought with desperation against the police and the troops that quickly arrived to crush this puny insurrection.[2] In Saxony Radek was still calling in vain for a general strike.[3] *Pravda* on October 24, 1923, continued to predict a general strike in Germany, and on the following day belatedly proclaimed that " the sixth anniversary of October coincides with the eve of the October days in the centre of Europe ". Undeterred by these bold prognostications, the Reichswehr arrested Zeigner, deposed his government and installed a commissioner to govern Saxony. The communist leaders escaped to Berlin. Thus ended the German October revolution. The *Rote Fahne* was again suspended, and the KPD shortly afterwards declared illegal. But reprisals were not very serious. The leaders lay low and remained

afterwards stated that the workers, " not only social-democrats, but also communists ", were against action (*Protokoll: Fünfter Kongress der Kommunistischen Internationale* (n.d.), i, 232-233).

[1] *Die Lehren der Deutschen Ereignisse* (Hamburg, 1924), p. 5 ; *Trinadtsatyi S"ezd Rossiiskoi Kommunisticheskoi Partii (Bol'shevikov)* (1924), pp. 356-357, adding the detail that the delegates refused to accept Brandler's offer to resign. According to H. von Dirksen, *Moskau, Tokio, London* (Stuttgart (n.d.) [? 1949]), p. 63, Radek at the time of the Saxon crisis was staying under an assumed name at a Dresden hotel.

[2] A detailed account of the Hamburg rising is in *Voprosy Istorii*, No. 11, 1948, pp. 13-23. According to this account, the rising was carried out by fighting detachments of party members, numbering 1300 in all, with a few dozen old pistols. There were 15 " Red hundreds " in Hamburg, but these had virtually no arms, and their training was " very weak " ; they apparently took no serious part in the fighting.

[3] *Die Lehren der Deutschen Ereignisse* (Hamburg, 1924), pp. 6-8.

at liberty. A few days later Hitler staged his famous *putsch* in Munich and secured the temporary support of Ludendorff. This proved a graver menace to authority than all the efforts of the KPD. But the Reichswehr, after some waverings, proved equal to the strain on its loyalties. By the middle of November order had been restored throughout Germany. Seeckt was master of the situation.

The abortive communist rising in Germany had had some repercussions in Poland. A few days before it took place a mysterious explosion occurred in the fortress at Warsaw ; [1] an insurrection broke out in Cracow; and a wave of strikes, including a railway strike, spread over much of the country.[2] On October 28, 1923, before the excitement had died down, Kopp arrived in Warsaw. His mission had enjoyed an unqualified success in Reval and Riga : the Estonian and Latvian Governments had given the

---

[1] The origin of this and other bomb outrages in Warsaw in 1923 has never been satisfactorily explained. According to a somewhat confused account in G. Besedovsky, *Na Putyakh k Termidoru* (Paris, 1931), i, 103-106, 125-129, they were engineered by the agent of the GPU in the Soviet mission in Warsaw. On the other hand, they could hardly have been undertaken without organized Polish participation. In a period of acute and violent factional struggle between the supporters of Pilsudski and the Polish national-democrats (the president of the republic, Narutowicz, was assassinated in December 1922 by a national-democrat), the GPU may conceivably have cooperated with the underground organization of one or both of these factions in planning outrages. The Polish Communist Party, or at any rate its leaders at this period (Warski, Walecki and Kostrzewa, whose outlook and policy resembled that of Brandler in Germany and was strongly opposed to terror), do not appear to have been involved ; an attempt is said to have been made to recruit 300 Polish communists " to form a military detachment ", but " responsible Polish communists, members of the central committee ", protested that the GPU agent in Warsaw (Loganovsky, also a Pole) " is demoralizing the Warsaw party organization by drawing it into his criminal plots ", and that " it is very naïve to suppose that one can provoke a terrorist struggle between Polish bourgeois parties by such methods " (*ibid.* pp. 105-106). A further complication was that Dzerzhinsky, the president of the GPU, and Unshlikht his deputy were both Poles ; Dzerzhinsky, who upheld the existing leadership of the Polish Communist Party, was opposed to terrorist activities, which were supported and directed by Unshlikht. After the fiasco of October 1923, this difference of opinion came before the Politburo, which appointed a committee of enquiry (*ibid.* pp. 116-117, 131-132). Radek shared the views of Dzerzhinsky.

[2] At the fifth congress of Comintern in June 1924 Zinoviev accused the Polish party of having remained passive at the time of the Cracow rising in October 1923 : the Polish spokesman replied that this rising had been wholly unexpected, and claimed that the ensuing general strike had been proclaimed " under our influence " (*Protokoll: Fünfter Kongress der Kommunistischen Internationale* (n.d.), i, 100, 285-286).

fullest possible guarantees of their disinterestedness in events in Germany and of their willingness to facilitate the transit of goods between Germany and the Soviet Union. By the time Kopp reached Warsaw, however, the German revolution was in the throes of defeat. For some days the situation remained obscure; and the conversations between Kopp and Seyda, the Polish Vice-Minister for Foreign Affairs,[1] proceeded in a cordial atmosphere, perhaps because there was no longer any real issue to discuss. Seyda disclaimed any intention on the part of the Polish Government to intervene in German affairs or to interfere with the ransit of goods between the Soviet Union and Germany, but saw no reason to give any formal written undertaking. Meanwhile Raevsky apparently had private talks about the future of East Prussia, which promised well, with national-democrat politicians. But before any conclusion had been reached, it became clear that the collapse of the German communists was complete and irretrievable. Revolution in Germany was no longer on the agenda. The basis of the conversations had disappeared, and Kopp was suddenly recalled to Moscow. To keep up appearances, Seyda's vague verbal assurances were hailed as the fruits of a successful diplomatic mission.[2]

The historian who is called on to explain the discrepancy between the policies pursued by the Bolshevik leaders through Comintern and the KPD and those pursued through the agency of the Soviet Government may be struck at this point by an equally disconcerting anomaly. The events of the year 1923 revealed a curious contrast, which may well have puzzled the Soviet leaders, between Soviet-German relations and relations with the western world. The western Powers, especially Great Britain, were highly sensitive to every suspicion of propaganda or intrigue designed to discredit and undermine their authority, and loudly and publicly held the Soviet Government responsible for the nefarious activities of Comintern. German diplomacy remained throughout 1923 outwardly indifferent not only to the most outspoken denunciations of the German Government by influential person-

---

[1] Dmowski, the national-democrat leader, had become Minister for Foreign Affairs on the eve of Kopp's arrival, and did not himself take part in the conversations.

[2] For the sources for the Kopp mission see p. 219, note 1 above.

alities in Moscow, but to the incitement and active preparation of insurrection in Germany by agents of Comintern. Some perfunctory protests were made by the German Ambassador in Moscow against Radek's illegal visits to Germany, and met with equally perfunctory denials.[1] There the matter was allowed to rest. The quiescence of the German authorities, when compared with the irritability of the British, could hardly be explained by a greater sense of security. However confident the Reichswehr may have been of its ability to quell a communist rising, the Bolshevik threat to the stability of the régime in Germany in 1923 both seemed and was greater than the threat to British power in central Asia or in India. The difference lay primarily in the fact that, whereas the western Powers saw little benefit to themselves in maintaining relations with Soviet Russia (the United States still had no official relations of any kind, and a strong party in Great Britain would have been glad to see relations under the trade agreement of 1921 broken off), Germany had compelling moral and material motives for keeping the Rapallo policy intact, and was therefore equally ready with the Soviet Government to accept the convenient fiction of a divorce between the official behaviour of that government and the surreptitious plottings of Comintern and the KPD. Something must also be allowed for other more pressing anxieties in the Germany of 1923, and for the notorious divisions and jealousies within the German governmental machine. The Reichswehr, which probably knew most about underground communist plots, was also the organ most keenly interested in friendly relations with the Soviet Government; and the Reichswehr had a way of taking its own decisions and securing compliance with them. Thus it was that, while Comintern was busy planning the proletarian revolution in Germany in the autumn of 1923, Brockdorff-Rantzau as German Ambassador in Moscow was establishing close and intimate relations with Chicherin, and building up for himself an important diplomatic position; and Krestinsky, the Soviet Ambassador in Berlin, who was actually a member of the Politburo committee

---

[1] G. Besedovsky, *Na Putyakh k Termidoru* (Paris, 1931), i, 136-137, where the well-established fact of the protests is embroidered with some improbable anecdotes; for other German-Soviet diplomatic exchanges at this time see G. Hilger and A. G. Meyer, *The Incompatible Allies* (N.Y., 1953), pp. 124-125.

for preparing the German revolution, none the less remained at his post for seven more fruitful years. Krasin was present at a brilliant reception at the Soviet Embassy in Berlin to celebrate the anniversary of the Bolshevik revolution on November 7, 1923, which was attended by a large company of German officials, bankers and industrialists.[1] The abortive communist rising a fortnight earlier is unlikely to have provided a topic of conversation at the reception ; nor perhaps was anyone present, except the ambassador himself, aware that this was the very day fixed by the Politburo six weeks earlier for the outbreak of the German revolution. Throughout the year 1923 the secret Soviet-German arrangements were getting into their stride : a leading Russian chemist, an " expert " in the service of the Soviet Government, records a month's visit to Berlin in the autumn of 1923, and the visit of a German communist to Moscow in the same year, in connexion with German projects to establish a factory for the manufacture of poison gas in Soviet Russia.[2] The line of demarcation between the different levels on which Soviet-German relations were conducted — the diplomatic, the military and the revolutionary — seems, in this chaotic period, to have been almost as easily accepted by the German as by the Soviet Government.

It was some time before the magnitude of the German defeat was brought home to the rank and file of the German party, who had been unaware of the extravagant hopes nourished, and the ambitious decisions taken, in Moscow. No immediate conclusions were drawn from the fiasco of the " German October ", since it was not regarded as such; and even the leaders seemed for the moment likely to escape grave censure. The delegates of Comintern had equally strong reasons to postpone the inquest.[3] On November 3, 1923, Brandler made a report to the central committee of the KPD. He admitted that the calling off of the insurrection, " for which I, first and foremost, bear and accept the responsibility ", had caused " something of a shock to the

[1] L. Krasin, *Leonid Krasin: His Life and Work* (n.d. [1929]), pp. 220-222.
[2] V. Ipatieff, *The Life of a Chemist* (Stanford, 1946), pp. 381-386 ; see also *The Bolshevik Revolution, 1917–1923*, Vol. 3, p. 437.
[3] Radek admitted this (*Die Lehren der Deutschen Ereignisse* (Hamburg, 1924), p. 12).

party ". He advocated " a reorientation of the party " (since it
was now exchanging a legal for an illegal status), and spoke of
" the coming struggle ", and of the dictatorship of the proletariat
as the only alternative to " the dictatorship of Fascism ". The
theme of a resolution drafted by himself and Radek [1] which he
presented to the committee was " the victory of Fascism over
the November republic ", the main significance of the events of
the past fortnight being found in the defeat and bankruptcy of the
SPD as the champion of the Weimar republic rather than in that
of the KPD. The resolution ended with the conventional appeal
for " the preparation of the struggle for the proletarian dictatorship ". It was carried by 40 votes to 13. The Left wing remained
irreconcilable, but was still unable to shake the authority of
Brandler and Radek.[2] Further reflexion proved, however, less
indulgent to the failures of the past A break came in the central
committee of the KPD, where the attacks of the Left began at
length to tell, and a new central group formed which joined
the Left in criticizing Brandler and the Right leadership. Once
the attack was opened, the dilemma was difficult to evade. If the
decision not to give battle in October was correct, then the policy
of the united front as applied by the KPD leaders for the past two
years under the authority of Comintern had been a failure. If the
contrary view prevailed that an unprecedented opportunity to
make a successful revolution had been missed in October through
faltering leadership, then the weight of responsibility falling on
Brandler and the Right was heavier still. On December 7, 1923,
Brandler and Thalheimer appealed for a discussion in the party
to bring about unity on the basis of the resolution of November 3.[3]
But it was too late. The authorities in Moscow, hitherto anxious
only to plaster over the cracks in the German party, had now
decided, for reasons of their own, to bring the issue to a head.

During the critical weeks in Germany, other anxieties had

---

[1] According to Zinoviev, Radek " began to invent a whole philosophy " to
justify the " opportunist behaviour " of the Right (*Trinadtsataya Konferentsiya
Rossiiskoi Kommunisticheskoi Partii (Bol'shevikov)* (1924), p. 171).

[2] The fullest account of the session and the text of Brandler's speech are
in *Die Internationale*, vi, No. 18 (November 15, 1923), pp. 516-530 ; the text
of the resolution is in *Internationale Presse-Korrespondenz*, No. 172, November
7, 1923, pp. 1457-1460.

[3] *Die Internationale*, vii, No. 2-3 (March 28, 1924), pp. 135-136.

weighed heavily on the Kremlin. In the same month of October which saw the culmination and collapse of the German revolutionary movement, Trotsky's two letters to the Politburo and the platform of the 46 had suddenly brought to the surface the acute dissensions in the Russian party ranks. The great party debate was opened. But nobody — not even Trotsky — was yet prepared to inject into it the question of responsibility for the German defeat; and this attitude of cautious self-restraint continued throughout the month of November 1923. The diagnosis in Moscow of the German fiasco of October 1923 was, however, so deeply involved in the crisis of the Russian party that objective pronouncements quickly became impossible, and the whole subject was soon surrounded by a maze of controversy and confusion through which the historian must cautiously pick his way.

Broadly speaking, two views could be taken of the German defeat : that the German proletariat had not been ripe for revolution when the call was made, or alternatively that the conditions were present for a successful revolution, but had been missed or spoiled by faults of leadership. The first view was that apparently taken by Stalin before the October failure, and by Radek and Brandler both before and after it. This view denied the validity of the comparison between the situation confronting the KPD in October 1923 and that in which the Bolsheviks found themselves six years earlier. Such a denial was implicit in Stalin's letter of July on the anti-Fascist day,[1] and was later made explicit by Brandler when he observed, in his defence at the fifth congress of Comintern, that there had been no " labour aristocracy " in Russia.[2] The conclusion to be drawn from this view was that the principal blame rested not on the leadership of the KPD, which had counselled caution, but on the Russian Politburo, which had decided for revolutionary action. Since Radek and Brandler had accepted, however unwillingly, the decision to act, and had been the main agents in attempting to carry it out, their position was now extremely weak. Stalin, who had taken no stand against the decision of the majority at the time, had now

---

[1] See p. 187 above ; for Stalin's attitude in the August-September discussions see p. 205 above.

[2] *Protokoll : Fünfter Kongress der Kommunistischen Internationale* (n.d.), i, 228 ; for the " labour aristocracy " see *The Bolshevik Revolution, 1917-1923*, Vol. 3, pp. 182-184.

even less inclination to set himself against the prevailing opinion ; and he remained silent during the period when the party line was in doubt.

The second view found its most outspoken champion in Trotsky, who had also been the most enthusiastic advocate of revolutionary action. Trotsky maintained that a revolutionary situation had existed in Germany from May, or at any rate from July, 1923 till November, when Seeckt finally consolidated his power. The decision of the Politburo had therefore been perfectly correct. The fault lay elsewhere :

> If the [German] Communist Party had promptly changed the tempo of its work, and fully and unreservedly utilized the five or six months offered to it by history to make political, organizational and technical preparation for the seizure of power, the *dénouement* could have been quite different from what we witnessed in November. . . . The proletariat ought to have seen a revolutionary party in action, marching directly to the conquest of power. Instead, the party in general continued its former propaganda policy, only on a larger scale.[1]

In his later and more famous article of September 1924, *Lessons of October*, Trotsky described the occasion as " a demonstration in a classical style . . . how it is possible to let slip an exceptional revolutionary situation of a universal historical character ".[2] This view stressed the parallel between October 1917 and October 1923 in order to convict the leaders of the KPD of having missed a unique opportunity for action. The curious feature about Trotsky's position was that, in spite of his view of the causes of the failure, he remained personally attached to the Right leadership of KPD, and especially to Brandler, and hostile to the Left wing whose opinions, both before and after the events of October, far more nearly approximated to his own. While he differed fundamentally from Radek's diagnosis of the German situation, he agreed with Radek on one important practical question : he saw nothing to gain by deposing the Right leadership of the KPD in favour of the Left.

---

[1] L. Trotsky, *Novyi Kurs* (1924), p. 42 ; the article containing this passage was not published in the press, and appeared for the first time in the middle of January 1924.

[2] Trotsky, *Sochineniya*, iii, i, p. xii.

Faced with this division of opinion, Zinoviev, now the un-challenged master of Comintern, found some difficulty in taking up a clearly defined position. The discussion in Moscow before October had revealed his antipathy to Radek and Brandler. But he had no ready alternative to propose; and the exigencies of the party struggle made him disinclined to accept Trotsky's diagnosis. Between October 12 and November 1, 1923, a series of ten articles appeared in *Pravda* from Zinoviev's pen under the general title *Problems of the German Revolution*. They were con-ventional in tone and content, and portended no change of attitude. The first six were written and published before the crisis in Saxony came to a head. The first optimistically hailed the impending German revolution :

> Only a short space of time, and it will become clear to everyone that the autumn months of 1923 were a turning-point not only in the history of Germany, but through it also for the whole of mankind. With trembling hand the German prole-tariat turns the most important page in the history of the world struggle of the working class. The hour strikes. A new chapter in the history of the world proletarian revolution has begun.

The fifth article argued that, in spite of difficulties, " the German proletariat will maintain itself in power " — an allusion to Lenin's famous pamphlet of September 1917, *Will the Bolsheviks Retain State Power?* The sixth discussed " the Achilles' heel of the German revolution ", the danger of foreign intervention, but, conforming to the line of official Soviet policy, offered no hint of military aid from the Soviet Union. The seventh, written on October 22 (the day after the collapse of the Chemnitz conference), asserted that " there is not the slightest doubt that the German Communist Party has by and large applied the tactics of the united front with great success ", and that " the objections of the ' Left ' communists . . . miss the mark ". Not till the tenth and last article, published on November 1 with the sub-title *No Illusions*, was any reference made to the disasters in Saxony and in Hamburg. The diagnosis was that " the SPD opened the way for the Fascists to a ' peaceful ' conquest of power "; the coalition government in Saxony had " not been able to carry out " the tasks assigned to it owing to the obstruction of the social-democrats. This was a confirmation of the line taken at the

time by Brandler and the Right wing of the KPD. No censure
of the KPD leadership was suggested either in the articles or in
the preface, written on November 2, for a German translation
to be published in Germany as a pamphlet.[1]

As, however, the magnitude of the disaster was gradually
revealed, a critical mood developed in Moscow as in Berlin. Its
first symptom was a letter from the presidium of IKKI to the
central committee of the KPD, which accused the leaders of
having failed to use the situation in Saxony as the starting-point
for armed action, and " converted participation in the Saxon
Government into a banal parliamentary combination with the
social-democrats ".[2] In November Zinoviev publicly repeated
this criticism in a postscript hastily added to the German translation of his *Pravda* articles, and referred to " the error of the
party ". It was an oblique announcement that Zinoviev was
separating himself from Radek and Brandler. But for the moment
an open attack was avoided, and the effect of the criticism was
attenuated by the concluding reflexion that " the unity of the
German party must *in all circumstances* be assured ".[3] Zinoviev's
new line may by a plausible conjecture be connected with Maslow,
who had been detained in Moscow throughout the events in
Germany. The examination of Maslow's record by a party commission, which was the excuse for his detention, seems to have
been perfunctory. Though it was still formally in progress,
" the atmosphere suddenly changed " in November, when Zinoviev " treated Maslow in a friendly fashion, consulting with him

---

[1] The pamphlet appeared as G. Zinoviev, *Probleme der Deutschen Revolution*
(Hamburg, 1923). The German translation of the articles was also printed in
Internationale Presse-Korrespondenz at various dates between October 19 and
November 12, 1923 ; the preface appeared *ibid.* No. 51, January 15, 1924, pp.
33-34.

[2] The letter was quoted by Zinoviev at the thirteenth party conference in
January 1924 (*Trinadtsataya Konferentsiya Rossiiskoi Kommunisticheskoi Partii
(Bol'shevikov)* (1924), pp. 170-171) ; he made play with the fact that both
Trotsky and Klara Zetkin had approved it. Its exact date cannot be determined,
but according to Zetkin it was sent " before we had detailed reports, when we
had nothing " (*Die Lehren der Deutschen Ereignisse* (Hamburg, 1924), p. 62).

[3] G. Zinoviev, *Probleme der Deutschen Revolution* (Hamburg, 1923), pp.
105-109. The date of the postscript is uncertain, but on internal evidence it
can be placed later than the preface of November 2 ; it was not published in
Pravda or in *Inprekorr*, but appeared together with the last three articles in
Kommunisticheskii Internatsional, No. 28-29, December 1, 1923, cols. 7511-7514.

often on German politics ".[1] It was about this time that Maslow wrote an article on *The Saxon Experiment and Its Lessons* which, though not published till two months later, was doubtless known to Zinoviev. It was an out-and-out attack on the entry of KPD leaders into the coalition Saxon Government, and reached the verdict that " a party, no longer young, underestimated a revolutionary situation, did not succeed in bringing its own strength to bear, and mistook the German·Social-Democratic Party for a revolutionary party, or at any rate a party susceptible of being revolutionized ".[2] The merit of Maslow, from Zinoviev's point of view, was that, belonging to the Left wing of the KPD, he was the sworn enemy of Brandler and therefore of Radek, but that he was also the enemy of Trotsky. Conversely, Zinoviev was the only Russian leader (since Stalin played no independent rôle in the German question) to whom Maslow could appeal for support.

For some time Zinoviev continued to temporize. In an article in *Pravda* on November 23 he unreservedly adopted the Maslow line. He directly attacked the formula incorporated in the KPD resolution of November 3 under Radek's inspiration, which summed up the events of October as " the victory of Fascism over the November republic ". Seeckt, he now argued, was no Fascist, but " the German Kolchak ". Just as Kerensky's so-called " revolutionary democracy " had " sold power piecemeal to the military reaction in the persons of Kornilov, Alexeev and Kolchak ", so the German social-democrats had sold power to Seeckt. The " dictatorship of Seeckt " and the " November republic ", far from being opposites, were the two faces of the same coin. The social-democrats, far from being defeated, had only come out in their true colours. On the following day an

[1] R. Fischer, *Stalin and German Communism* (Harvard, 1948), pp. 360, 363. Zinoviev's failure to intervene in the commission, here attributed to fear of Stalin, is more likely to have been due to Zinoviev's own indecision ; he did not finally commit himself till the middle of December, and meanwhile tried to keep all lines open. The preface to G. Zinoviev, *Probleme der Deutschen Revolution* (Hamburg, 1923), p. v, contains a reference to " one of our old comrades from Germany ", who described the Saxon affair as " a great and perhaps fatal mistake " : this was no doubt Maslow.

[2] This article was incorporated in a longer article published in the official journal of Comintern in January 1924 with a footnote stating that it was written " at the beginning of November 1923 " (*Kommunisticheskii Internatsional*, No. 1, 1924, cols. 469-490).

unsigned leading article in *Pravda* accused the German social-
democrats of allying themselves with the " Kolchak régime " of
Seeckt against the communist workers. The moral of this
diagnosis clearly emerged. The KPD was not to be allowed to
mask its own defeat as a defeat of the " November republic ",
and the short-sightedness of those who advocated the alliance
with the social-democrats was branded as the cause of the disaster.[1]
But Zinoviev stopped short of the demand for a change of leadership in the KPD ; and, frightened perhaps at his own boldness,
he attempted a few days later to cover up his tracks. On December
1, 1923, *Pravda* printed a long article by him entitled *The Second
Wave of the International Revolution*. Its main purpose was to
excuse the leaders of Comintern for their error in over-estimating
the prospects of the German revolution. This was achieved by
quotations from Lenin, who in the autumn of 1918 had believed,
like his successors five years later, that " history had quickened its
step " along the path to world revolution. The article breathed
a conventional and unconvincing optimism, and suggested no
criticism of the KPD or of its existing leadership. Thus the
month of December 1923 opened with Zinoviev and Stalin both
uncommitted on the German question. Both were waiting to
see how this awkward and delicate issue could best be utilized
in the Russian party struggle, now approaching its acute stage.
But, while Stalin masked his hesitation in a dignified and enigmatic
silence, Zinoviev betrayed himself in a flood of emphatic, in-
decisive and sometimes contradictory utterances. According to
Radek, Zinoviev considered as late as December 7, when the
Comintern delegation returned from Germany to Moscow, that
no change should be made in the central committee of the
KPD.[2]
   What brought matters to a head was a discovery which was

---

[1] A translation of Zinoviev's article of November 23 appeared in *Internationale Presse-Korrespondenz*, No. 182, December 20, 1923, pp. 1540-1542,
with an immediately following rejoinder by Thalheimer, who attempted to
refute the comparison of Seeckt with Kolchak and to restore the line of the
November 3 resolution.
[2] *Trinadtsatyi S"ezd Rossiiskoi Kommunisticheskoi Partii (Bol'shevikov)*
(1924), p. 357 ; Zinoviev later defended himself against the reproach of having
" suddenly " disowned Brandler by arguing that, if he had delayed further, a
split in the KPD would have been inevitable (*Protokoll: Fünfter Kongress der
Kommunistischen Internationale* (n.d.), i, 97).

Q

henceforth to play an important and demoralizing rôle in the affairs of Comintern. It had suddenly become apparent that foreign communist parties, indissolubly linked with Moscow through the organs of Comintern, were unlikely to disinterest themselves in the dramatic dissensions in the Russian party, which could no longer be concealed from their view; and, if this was so, it was equally obvious that divisions within foreign communist parties (such as those in the German party, the most important of them all, on the subject of the October fiasco) might be exploited to the advantage of one side or other in the Russian domestic struggle. Zinoviev did not hold the initiative in this discovery. On December 13, 1923, Radek, recently returned from Germany, made a speech at a party meeting in Moscow, in the course of which he remarked that, if the majority of the central committee of the Russian party turned against Trotsky, a majority of the German and Polish parties would turn against the majority of the central committee.[1] About the same time a letter from the central committee of the Polish Communist Party appeared to confirm this diagnosis so far as the Polish party was concerned. The crucial passage ran :

> The central point in the present crisis inside the Russian Communist Party consists of the differences of opinion between the majority of the RKP and comrade Trotsky. We know that these differences are connected with complicated problems of the building of socialism, and we are not in a position to judge these differences so far as economic policy is concerned. Only one thing is quite clear for us : the name of comrade Trotsky is for our party, for the whole International, for the whole revolutionary world proletariat, indissolubly bound up with the victorious October revolution, with the Red Army, with communism and world revolution.
>
> We cannot admit the possibility that comrade Trotsky could find himself outside the ranks of the leaders of the RKP and of the International. Nevertheless, we are perturbed by the thought that the disputes may go beyond the framework of the concrete problems under discussion, and some public

---

[1] The speech never appears to have been published, but was referred to by Zinoviev in a speech at IKKI on January 6, 1924 (*Internationale Presse-Korrespondenz*, No. 20, February 15, 1924, p. 225), and on other occasions in the subsequent controversy ; the date is given in A. Thalheimer, *1923 : Eine Verpasste Revolution?* (1931), p. 11.

utterances of responsible leaders of the party give reason for
the gravest anxieties.[1]

The Russian leaders took alarm. If Trotsky and the opposition
were to receive support from sections of foreign communist
parties, it was urgently necessary to seek allies in the same quarter
for the official line. From the middle of December onwards all
restraints were thrown aside and the campaign against Trotsky
gathered momentum.[2] Developments in the KPD, perhaps
stimulated directly or indirectly from Moscow, invited intervention. The balance in the party now definitely shifted against the
Right; and a majority of the Zentrale, representing a Centre group
which claimed to stand between the Right leadership and its
extremer critics of the Left, drafted a set of theses sharply
criticizing the policy and outlook which had been responsible for
the " October retreat ".[3] The demand for a change of leaders
became irresistible; and all groups, Left, Right and Centre, were
invited to send representatives to Moscow at the end of December
to meet the presidium of IKKI.

The Russian party crisis now entirely dominated the German
quarrel. Whatever chances Brandler and his associates might
have had of an indulgent verdict in Moscow were destroyed by
the support which they received from the opposition in the
Russian party. Zinoviev, still cautious in his handling of Trotsky,

---

[1] This extract is quoted in J. A. Regula, *Historja Komunistycznej Partji
Polski w Swietle Faktow i Dokumentow* (1934), pp. 105-106, from a Comintern
publication, *Sprawa Polska na V Kongresie Kominternu*, which has not been
available; it is here not more precisely dated than " December 1923 ", but a
reference to it in the later Polish declaration to IKKI (see p. 240 below) shows
that it was received in Moscow before December 18. At the fifth congress of
Comintern in June 1924 the spokesman of the majority of the Polish delegation
admitted that the letter of December 1923 had been " an opportunist error "
(*Protokoll: Fünfter Kongress der Kommunistischen Internationale* (n.d.), i, 283);
and the congress passed a resolution condemning Warski, Kostrzewa and
Walecki, the party leaders responsible for it (*Kommunisticheskii Internatsional
v Dokumentakh* (1933), p. 463).
[2] See pp. 315-318 below.
[3] *Internationale Presse-Korrespondenz*, No. 185, December 28, 1923, pp.
1564-1566. These theses bear no date; according to Zinoviev, they were
adopted " a few days after the departure of the representative of Comintern
i.e. Radek] from Germany " (*Die Lehren der Deutschen Ereignisse* (Hamburg,
1924), p. 75). Counter-theses issued respectively by the Right and by the
Left were published in *Internationale Presse-Korrespondenz*, No. 5, January 15,
1924, p. 40; No. 6, January 18, 1924, pp. 51-52.

could now at one and the same time pay off old scores and further weaken Trotsky's position by demolishing Radek. On December 27, 1923, the Politburo adopted (presumably in Trotsky's absence) the following resolution :

> Comrade Radek directs his course entirely to support the *Right* minority of the central committee of the KPD and to disown the Left wing of the party — which objectively threatens a split in the German party — whereas the Politburo of the central committee of the RKP bases its policy on support of the great majority of the central committee of the KPD and on collaboration with the Left, while criticizing the errors of the Left and upholding what is correct in it, and at the same time criticizing the gross errors of the Right.
>
> The general view of comrade Radek on the course of the further struggle in Germany arises from an incorrect assessment of the class forces in Germany : an opportunist over-estimation of the differences within Fascism and an attempt to base the policy of the working class in Germany on these differences.[1]

Radek, failing to realize the strength and determination of the forces ranged against him, was unabashed and irrepressible, and is said to have reminded his opponents that he was responsible for his actions in Germany, not to the central committee of the Russian party, but to the world congress of Comintern [2] — evidence of a touching belief in the doctrine of the overriding authority of the Communist International over all the parties composing it, including the Russian party.

This belief was soon to be put to the test. The debate in the presidium of IKKI with numerous representatives of the three factions of the KPD, which began on January 11, 1924, took place under the shadow of the deepening crisis in the Russian party, of which all present were acutely conscious. Zinoviev alone spoke for IKKI, and neither Trotsky nor any of the other party leaders was present. Radek opened with a report made in his capacity as chief delegate of Comintern in Germany during the events under discussion. Ever since 1919 Radek had, at the bottom of his heart, taken a pessimistic view of the prospects of

---

[1] *VKP(B) v Rezolyutsiyakh* (1941), i, 534.
[2] *Trinadtsataya Konferentsiya Rossiiskoi Kommunisticheskoi Partii (Bol'-shevikov)* (1924), p. 173.

revolution in Germany; and it was in the light of this diagnosis that
he now sought to absolve the leadership of the party from blame.

What now exists in the German proletariat is a reflexion of
the general position in Germany, of the collapse of political
activity, of an extraordinary political passivity in all social
classes with the exception of the army. . . . Although a good
workers' party, we are still nowhere a good communist party.
And that is the most important thing which I see in the whole
situation. It is not true, comrades, that the leadership did
not want to fight, and that the masses arc everywhere raging.
It did not happen like that.[1]

Radek ended by presenting theses which he described as " drafted
by comrades Trotsky and P[yatakov] and by myself "; these
defended the October retreat against Left criticisms as a necessary
and justifiable step, and ascribed to " panic " the demand for a
change in the Zentrale of the German party.[2] Brandler arrived
only after the proceedings had begun, having been detained by
delays in Moscow in providing him with a passport.[3] He,
Remmele and Ruth Fischer spoke for the Right, Centre and Left
groups in the KPD respectively, reiterating the well-worn arguments; the Centre in effect made the same criticisms as the Left,
but expressed them in less dogmatic terms and with less personal
bitterness towards the Right leaders.[4]

[1] *Die Lehren der Deutschen Ereignisse* (Hamburg, 1924), pp. 10, 13; this
volume appears to be the only, and evidently much abbreviated, published
version of the proceedings. Stalin later quoted a " stenographic record of the
fifth meeting of the presidium of IKKI with representatives of the KPD "
(Stalin, *Sochineniya*, x, 64); but no trace has been found of its publication. A
fuller record was current at the time in KPD circles, since passages not found in
the published version were quoted in *Die Internationale* (see p. 209, note 1 above).

[2] *Ibid.* p. 23; the theses have not been published, but quotations from
them (no doubt carefully selected) appear in an article by Kuusinen in *The
Errors of Trotskyism* (CPGB, 1925), pp. 340, 343-345, 345. They do not
represent Trotsky's view of the fundamental causes of the failure, in which he
differed from Radek (see p. 229 above; the article there quoted was first published a few days after the submission of the theses to IKKI); but, whatever
the faults of the past, he saw nothing to gain by deposing Brandler and transferring the leadership of the KPD to Maslow and Ruth Fischer.

[3] Oral statement by Brandler; the suspicion that Zinoviev would have
been glad to keep him away is plausible.

[4] The speeches are in *Die Lehren der Deutschen Ereignisse* (Hamburg,
1924), pp. 24-57; the theses submitted by the Centre in *Die Internationale*, vii,
No. 2-3 (March 28, 1924), pp. 47-51, and in *Bericht über die Verhandlungen des
IX Parteitags der Kommunistischen Partei Deutschlands* (1924), pp. 112-116; the
theses of the other groups do not appear to have been published.

On the following day, Zinoviev summed up against Brandler and Radek in language which undoubtedly owed something of its asperity to their association with Trotsky, though he cautiously refrained from whole-heartedly endorsing the view of the Left and cast the mantle of his approval over the Centre group. He described the attitude of the three leaders who had been ministers in the Saxon Government as " a symptom of rottenness ". To call the October events " a victory over the November republic " and not a victory over the working class was " either nonsense or opportunism ". The leadership of the KPD must be changed; his advice was that it should pass to " the present majority in the Zentrale together with the Left of the party ". The speech was frequently interrupted from the Right, Radek and Pieck at one point accusing Zinoviev of trying to " disrupt the Zentrale ".[1] But, in the absence of Trotsky, nobody had the authority or courage to resist Zinoviev, who conducted the proceedings in his own way. The commission set up to draft a resolution consisted of Maslow and Thälman for the Left of the KPD, Remmele and Koenen for the Centre, and Pieck for the Right, with Kuusinen as Comintern representative; a proposal to include Radek and Brandler was voted down, only Zetkin and Radek supporting it. The resolution detailed the mistakes committed by the KPD during the past year, declared that recognition of these mistakes was a condition of future progress, and ended with a call for party unity.[2] It was clearly designed as a vote of censure on the past leadership of the KPD and an appeal for a change of leaders.

Meanwhile important moves had been taking place elsewhere. The central committee of the Russian party, meeting on January 14-15, had endorsed the Politburo resolution of censure on Radek and added a rider of its own to the effect that it was " under an obligation to bring to the notice of IKKI that comrade Radek does not in this question represent the views of the central com-

[1] *Die Lehren der Deutschen Ereignisse* (Hamburg, 1924), pp. 61, 70, 74-75. This accusation was particularly resented by Zinoviev who mentioned it twice in his speech a week later to the thirteenth party conference ; according to him, Radek had already brought this charge against the central committee at a meeting of students in Moscow (*Trinadtsataya Konferentsiya Rossiiskoi Kommunisticheskoi Partii (Bol'shevikov)* (1924), pp. 167, 175).

[2] A brief note on the constitution and proceedings of the commission is in *Die Lehren der Deutschen Ereignisse* (Hamburg, 1924), p. 81, the text of the resolution *ibid.* pp. 95-109.

mittee of the RKP "; and the resolution with this addition was published in *Pravda* on January 16, 1924, the day on which the thirteenth party conference assembled. On January 18 Zinoviev made a long report to the conference on the international situation, the greater part of which was devoted to events in Germany during the past three months. The narrative of events, though marked by Zinoviev's opinions and prejudices, was fairly restrained; Zinoviev himself was vulnerable at too many points of the story. But the report contained a series of indirect and thinly veiled attacks on Trotsky and an outspoken and bitter tirade against Radek who, though he " knew more than anyone about this [i.e. the German] movement and was supposed to be the greatest authority on it ", had none the less " made more mistakes than anyone " and " held back the party by its coat-tails when it ought to have been summoned to battle ". Radek confined his reply to a short and formal statement denying the allegations against him. But his restraint earned him the taunts not only of Zinoviev, but of a delegate from the body of the hall who, recalling the charge against Brandler, shouted that Radek had " retreated without fighting ".[1] A resolution was then carried approving the present attitude of the central committee on the German question, repeating the text of the censure pronounced on Radek on December 27, 1923, by the Politburo, and warning him of his obligation to submit to decisions of the central committee. The resolution was carried unanimously, with one abstention : Radek had presumably not yet been schooled into voting for his own humiliation.[2]

On the day following this debate the presidium of IKKI met to receive the report of its commission. There was no need for further discussion. The presidium rejected two amendments proposed by Pieck, the effect of which would have been to justify the October retreat by the circumstances in which it had occurred, and carried the resolution in the form in which it had left the commission by four votes to two, the noes being once more Zetkin and Radek.[3] What happened behind the scenes after this

[1] *Trinadtsataya Konferentsiya Rossiiskoi Kommunisticheskoi Partii (Bol'-shevikov)* (1924), pp. 169, 178-180.
[2] *VKP(B) v Rezolyutsiyakh* (1941), i, 556.
[3] *Die Lehren der Deutschen Ereignisse* (Hamburg, 1924), pp. 81-82. The number of votes cast for the resolution is omitted from the official record, but

narrow victory is not known. But when the presidium met for its final session on January 21, a few hours before Lenin's death, tension had been somewhat relaxed. Zinoviev, in his concluding speech, handsomely made the admission, which the majority had refused to include in the resolution, of the inevitability of the October retreat :

> Not only as a result of errors and weaknesses in the party, but also as a result of the weakness of the working class the retreat was absolutely necessary. Of course there will be a number of workers who will always say : The moment has been missed.

In response to this concession, Zetkin and Radek, undeterred by Maslow's taunts, declared themselves ready in the name of party unity to vote for the resolution, which was then unanimously adopted by the presidium.[1] A curious declaration by the Polish delegation marked the final stage of the proceedings. Warski, the head of the delegation, had apparently intervened in the debate on behalf of the Right.[2] In his absence the Polish delegation declared in a written statement its acceptance of the terms of the final resolution on the paradoxical ground that " they stick fundamentally to the existing tactics of Comintern, with which the so-called Left in Germany wished to make a radical break ". It denounced the " irresponsible agitation (Hetze) " against the KPD leaders of the Right who, though guilty of errors and omissions, formed " the oldest, most tried and most experienced nucleus of the party ". Having expressed apprehension lest the absence of Lenin and the discrediting of Trotsky by the Russian central committee should weaken " the authority of the direction

---

is given in *Bericht über die Verhandlungen des IX Parteitags der Kommunistischen Partei Deutschlands* (1924), p. 355 ; the four were probably Zinoviev, Kolarov, Kuusinen and an unnamed representative of the Communist Youth International. The Russian text of the resolution appeared in *Pravda*, February 7, 1924.

[1] *Die Lehren der Deutschen Ereignisse* (Hamburg, 1924), pp. 82-89.

[2] According to R. Fischer, *Stalin and German Communism* (Harvard, 1948), p. 373, he defended Trotsky, and " referred to a letter from the Polish central committee to the Russian Politburo in support of Trotsky " (for this letter see p. 235 above); this speech was not included in the official record, which merely mentioned " a few shorter statements by other comrades " as having preceded Zinoviev's main speech (*Die Lehren der Deutschen Ereignisse* (Hamburg, 1924), p. 58)

of the Communist International ", it embarked on a vigorous
defence of Radek :

> We consider the charge of opportunism which has been
> brought against Radek, one of the most meritorious leaders
> of Comintern, as not only unjust but in the highest degree
> damaging to the authority of all leaders of Comintern. . . .
> The differences of opinion between the best known leaders of
> Comintern in the assessment of the German question are of a
> kind which are unavoidable in a living revolutionary party,
> especially in such a difficult situation, and which have in the
> past also occurred in the direction of IKKI without giving rise
> to mutual accusations of opportunism.[1]

These reflexions were clearly prompted as much by the internal
crisis in the Russian party as by the crisis in German affairs
which had become inextricably involved in it. Nor were the
supporters of the official line slow to establish the same equation.
It was stated in unequivocal terms by Guralsky, Zinoviev's
spokesman in Germany :

> The alliance between Brandler-Thalheimer and Radek-
> Trotsky in the German question is no accident. It touches
> fundamental questions : de-Bolshevization of the Russian
> Communist Party and de-Bolshevization of the European
> parties, or maintenance of the Bolshevik tutelage of the Russian
> Communist Party and Bolshevization of the European parties.[2]

The central committee of the KPD met in Halle on February
19, 1924, to consider the results of the Moscow meeting. The
proceedings were little more than formal. Brandler, on behalf
of the old leadership, handed in a statement in which he complained that " our representative was practically excluded in the
debates in Moscow ".[3] The committee unanimously endorsed
the resolution of the presidium of IKKI ; and a further resolution
condemning the former policies of the Right was adopted with

[1] *Die Lehren der Deutschen Ereignisse* (Hamburg, 1924), pp. 92-94 ; the
charge of " opportunism " combated in the Polish statement had not been
made in so many words in the presidium of IKKI, but was the burden of
Zinoviev's bitter attack on Radek at the thirteenth party conference on January
18, 1924 (*Trinadtsataya Konferentsiya Rossiiskoi Kommunisticheskoi Partii (Bol'-
shevikov)* (1924), pp. 172-178).
[2] *Die Internationale*, vii, No. 4 (March 31, 1924), p. 161.
[3] *Ibid.* vii, No. 2-3 (March 28, 1924), pp. 134-139.

only a few dissentients. The new slogan of " the Bolshevization of the party " served both to discredit past policies and to flatter the leaders of Comintern whose powerful influence had transferred the party leadership into the hands of the Centre and Left. A new Zentrale was elected, consisting of five members of the Centre and two of the Left.[1] But the fortunes of the party after the October defeat were at a low ebb. Currency reform and economic revival were on the way in Germany, and the Weimar republic seemed to have taken on a new lease of life. The legal ban on the KPD was removed on March 1, 1924. But its leaders still lived under danger of arrest; and it was not till April that the ninth party congress assembled in Frankfurt. In preparation for the congress, IKKI despatched a letter to the central committee of the party in which " the victory of the Left wing of the KPD " was said to have " immense significance for the destiny of the German revolution ". But the letter was accompanied by an article signed by Zinoviev which, while endorsing the policies of the party Left, contained what was in effect an appeal to the Left not to press its victory too far.[2] The appeal had little effect. At the Frankfurt congress, and once again at the fifth congress of Comintern in Moscow in the following June, the old battles within the German party were fought over with all the old bitterness. But behind them, and under cover of them, new struggles were beginning in a new setting, where issues turned not so much on relations between the KPD and Comintern as between factions in the German party and factions in the Russian party. The ultimate effect of the events of 1923 in Germany, though this did not immediately appear, was to destroy the large measure of independence hitherto enjoyed by the KPD and to turn it into a sparring-ground for Russian factional disputes. This was to be its main significance during the next three years.

[1] *Bericht über die Verhandlungen des IX Parteitags der Kommunistischen Partei Deutschlands* (1924), pp. 64/75.

[2] The letter and the article, both dated March 26, 1924, were printed with the proceedings of the congress (*ibid.* pp. 65-71, 78-85).

CHAPTER 10

RECOGNITION

THE Soviet outlook on the external world in the last half of
1923 had been restricted by the preoccupations of the
domestic crisis. Little attention had been given to events
abroad other than those of the dramatic and abortive Bulgarian
and German revolutions; and it was not till the end of the year
that the Soviet Government became fully aware how much the
European situation had moved in its favour since the anxious days
of the Curzon ultimatum. The causes of the movement were
confused and, in part, fortuitous. As the year 1923 proceeded,
the strength of the reaction against French policy in Germany
became apparent and spread from Europe to the United States.
The appointment in December 1923 of two allied " committees
of experts ", including American experts, to examine every aspect
of the reparations problem, was the sequel to a long diplomatic
argument in which France and Belgium had fought an isolated
rearguard action against the desire of the other European Powers
and of the United States to achieve a pacification of Europe
through a financial settlement with Germany. In Great Britain
the change of sentiment appeared to favour the Left in domestic
politics, since the Liberal and Labour parties had tended ever
since 1919 to mistrust French policy in Europe and support a
more indulgent attitude towards Germany. In 1923, however,
the interests of commerce and finance as well as the interests of
Labour appeared to demand a financial and economic *détente* in
Europe, and British foreign policy took on a marked German
orientation.

From this change of climate Soviet Russia was an unwitting
and unintended beneficiary. Since 1919 the groups in western
Europe which had shown themselves respectively most intransigent
or most conciliatory towards Germany had adopted similar

attitudes towards Soviet Russia; the Rapallo treaty of April 1922 provided a diplomatic form for a community of interests which already existed. The pro-German bias of British opinion and British policy which became increasingly marked throughout 1923 automatically carried with it favourable implications for Soviet Russia. Even in Conservative circles, outside the limited groups which had financial claims against the Soviet Government, the policy of the Curzon ultimatum had enjoyed no great popularity and was felt to have ended in a fiasco. In France, not even the radical Left yet came out openly for conciliation either of Germany or of Soviet Russia; but an undertone of uneasiness was evident about Poincaré's attitude to both these countries, if only because of its dangerous repercussions on Anglo-French relations. In Italy Mussolini had no prejudices, and was clearly prepared for any step in regard either to Germany or to Soviet Russia which promised some immediate advantage to his country or to his régime. In the United States conciliation of Germany did not appear to carry with it the same corollary of conciliation of Soviet Russia. But, even here, the wave of hatred and fear of Bolshevism which had reached its climax in 1919 and 1920 had ebbed; and rational discussion of problems of American-Soviet relations was once more possible.

The second half of 1923 witnessed, therefore, a slow but unmistakable *détente* between the Soviet Government and the western Powers, especially Great Britain. In view of Bolshevik activities in Germany in the autumn of that year, it may seem anomalous to diagnose in Soviet policy a growth of conciliatory attitudes towards the capitalist world. But events in Germany were regarded in the west — and, on the whole, rightly — as an exception attributable to special conditions in Germany rather than to the main tendencies of Soviet policy. It was correctly inferred from the Soviet reaction to the Curzon ultimatum that the Soviet Government was ready to come halfway in search of an accommodation with the western Powers. The development of economic policy since the introduction of NEP seemed full of encouragement. Krasin had worked hard and successfully in London. In a period of slump and unemployment Soviet orders were an important asset and an attractive bait. The resumption of exports of grain suggested further visions of a return to mutually

profitable pre-war commercial relations between Russia and the
west.[1] In August 1923 an important group of British business
men, said to represent no less than eighty British engineering
firms, visited the Soviet Union.[2] They were lavishly entertained,
secured some substantial orders and returned for the most part
convinced advocates of recognition of the Soviet Government.
Above all, the rapid progress made towards the re-establishment
of a stable currency in Soviet Russia — a harbinger of what was
so much required in Germany — and the willingness of Soviet
financiers to follow capitalist prescriptions and to pay their tribute
to the soundness of capitalist practices in international finance
made an excellent impression. As the acting head of the Soviet
trade delegation in London told *Izvestiya*, " the city has long ago
recognized Soviet Russia, and this in England means something ".[3]
At the end of 1923 optimistic " experts " in western Europe
could look forward once again to a prosperous Europe in which
the German and Russian economies, purged of the diseases and
excesses of the nightmare period since 1918, might once more
be incorporated under the aegis of sound finance and orderly
commercial relations.

The year 1923 had also seen the first beginnings of those
extensive American economic activities in Soviet Russia which
continued throughout the 1920s to provide a striking contrast to
the absence of political relations. In January 1923 the Soviet
Government formally endorsed the oil concession in northern
Sakhalin originally granted by the Far Eastern Republic in 1921
to the Sinclair Exploration Company.[4] Thus prompted, the
Sinclair company wrote to the State Department asking for
diplomatic representations to the Japanese Government to permit
the company to develop its concession, but received the chilling
reply that the department could not " take official cognisance of a
contract which purports to have been concluded with a government which has not been recognized by the United States " or

[1] Chicherin in a press interview of January 1924 spoke of the strengthened
international position of the Soviet Union due to the grain exports (*Internationale Presse-Korrespondenz*, No. 5, January 15, 1924, p. 36).
[2] Its arrival in Moscow was prominently reported in *Izvestiya*, August 21,
1923; the same issue reported the arrival of Wirth, the former German
Chancellor. [3] *Izvestiya*, November 11, 1923.
[4] See *The Bolshevik Revolution, 1917–1923*, Vol. 3, pp. 353-354.

take diplomatic action to support it.[1]   Where, however, commercial transactions could proceed without official backing, they were more successful.   Two enterprises set on foot during 1923 assumed important dimensions.   The first was the establishment of a firm under the name of the Allied American Corporation which operated in Moscow as the agent of more than thirty American exporters interested in trade with the Soviet Union. In the summer of 1923 the company concluded a general agreement with Vneshtorg on Soviet-American trade, undertaking to ship to Russia goods to the value of 2,400,000 gold rubles a year, mainly machinery, mining equipment and agricultural implements, and to organize exports from the Soviet Union, mainly of raw materials, to a corresponding value.   A later by-product of this arrangement was a scheme to finance Soviet clothing factories through the American International Garment Workers' Union.[2] The second was the organization of large-scale purchases of raw cotton in the United States by the Soviet Union.   Nogin, the director of the Soviet textile trust, arrived in New York on November 21, 1923, with the announced intention of buying cotton to the value of $1\frac{1}{2}$ million dollars for Soviet factories; and one of the results of his visit was the organization in New York of an All-Russian Textile Syndicate with a loan of 2 million dollars from the Chase National Bank to finance Soviet cotton purchases in the United States.[3]   These and similar transactions revealed the growing strength of economic interest slowly breaking through the barriers of official aloofness.

These developments inspired a revival of hopes of change in the official attitude of the American Government, which had languished since the failure to reopen the issue on Harding's assumption of the presidency in March 1921.[4]   Raymond Robins was once more the driving force behind the campaign for recogni-

[1] *Foreign Relations of the United States, 1923* (1938), ii, 802-804.
[2] Interview with Hammer, the manager of the Allied American Corporation, in *Ekonomicheskaya Zhizn'*, July 29, 1923 (a front-page advertisement had appeared *ibid.* July 22, 1923) ; W. A. Williams, *American-Russian Relations, 1781–1947* (N.Y., 1952), p. 211, and the sources there cited.
[3] *Ekonomicheskaya Zhizn'*, November 24, 1923 ; W. A. Williams, *American-Russian Relations, 1781–1947* (N.Y., 1952), p. 211. Nogin in an interview on his return to Moscow claimed that the " cotton block " of sixty senators and congressmen was now friendly to the Soviet Government (*Trud*, February 14, 1924).
[4] See *The Bolshevik Revolution, 1917–1923*, Vol. 3, pp. 340-341.

tion, in which Borah, the senator from Idaho, now became the public protagonist. In the summer of 1923 Harding, probably in order to stave off persistent pressure rather than with any intention to take action, authorized Robins to make a confidential visit to Moscow and take soundings of the position there. Robins had actually reached Berlin when Harding died on August 2, 1923; he then abandoned the mission as futile and returned to Washington to agitate with Harding's successor, Coolidge.[1] A few days later a group of five American senators and congressmen led by senator King arrived in Moscow : they were enthusiastically welcomed, and toured various parts of the Soviet Union, remaining for several weeks.[2] These proceedings engendered an optimistic mood in Soviet circles. In Washington the Robins-Borah group appear to have entertained great hopes of Coolidge's first address to congress, which was issued on December 6, 1923. The address did little more in substance than repeat the unbending attitude of previous administrations on the conditions of recognition. But it did say that the American Government had no objections to commercial relations between American citizens and Russians, and that the United States was ready to " make very large concessions for the purpose of rescuing the people of Russia " from economic distress; and it added that " we hope the time is near at hand when we can act ".[3] Encouraged by Robins's optimism and by these crumbs of official comfort, *Izvestiya* announced, in a leading article of December 9, that " the movement in favour of agreement with the Soviet republic has spread to America ", and opined that " the struggle for influence in the Pacific, where the United States clashes with Japanese imperialism ", was one of the factors in the change. A week later Chicherin despatched a message to Coolidge welcoming his pronouncement and indicating the willingness of the Soviet Government to discuss " all questions raised in your message, on the understanding that the principle of mutual non-interference in the affairs of the other party will be taken as the basis of the

[1] W. A. Williams, *American-Russian Relations, 1781–1947* (N.Y., 1952), pp. 201-204, based mainly on unpublished material.

[2] *Izvestiya*, August 9, 1923, reported a luncheon in their honour at Narkomindel, and on the following day published a photograph of them with Kamenev; for Trotsky's interview with senator King see p. 216 above.

[3] *Foreign Relations of the United States, 1923* (1938), i, p. viii.

discussions ". But by this time Coolidge had lost interest in the issue and was prepared to leave it in the firmer hands of the State Department. On December 18, 1923, Hughes, the Secretary of State, despatched an unusually prompt reply to Chicherin's misguided overture :

> There would seem to be at this time no reason for negotiations. . . . If the Soviet authorities are ready to repeal their decree repudiating Russia's obligations to this country and appropriately recognize them, they can do so. It requires no conference or negotiations to accomplish these results.[1]

On the following day the State Department released the text of a long letter from Zinoviev to the Workers' Party of America, concluding with the hope that " the party will step by step conquer [embrace] the proletarian forces of America, and in the not distant future raise the red flag over the White House ".[2] A declaration of the Workers' Party of America that the letter was "a forgery from the first word to the last " [3] did not shake the official attitude. Borah secured the appointment of a committee by the Senate to enquire into recognition, and spoke in favour of it in a Senate debate on January 7, 1924.[4] But the Robins-Borah offensive had been beaten off by the skill and pertinacity of the State Department, and the issue remained dormant for several years.

The movement in Europe for recognition of the Soviet Government was less clamorous, but had more solid foundations. France, as hostile to Soviet Russia as to Germany, remained the most stubborn obstacle. Herriot, the Radical leader, had visited Moscow in September 1922. A year later, in August 1923, a Radical senator, De Monzie, came to Moscow, had an equally friendly reception and returned to Paris a firm advocate of recognition. But such individual initiatives by his opponents were unlikely to influence the unbending Poincaré. It was Mussolini who, in a speech of November 30, 1923, made the first dramatic move.

---

[1] *Foreign Relations of the United States, 1923* (1938), ii, 787-788 ; the Russian text of Chicherin's message of December 16, 1923, is in Klyuchnikov i Sabanin, *Mezhdunarodnaya Politika*, iii, i (1928), 294.

[2] *Foreign Relations of the United States, 1923* (1938), ii, 788-790 ; for the Workers' Party of America, at this time the legal cover of the American Communist Party, see *The Bolshevik Revolution, 1917-1923*, Vol. 3, p. 423.

[3] *Internationale Presse-Korrespondenz*, No. 5, January 15, 1924, p. 37.

[4] The debate was reported at some length in *Pravda*, January 9, 1924.

Negotiations for a Soviet-Italian commercial treaty, to replace the abortive agreement of 1921,[1] had begun some weeks earlier. Mussolini now declared himself prepared for *de jure* recognition of the Soviet Government, and indicated that the act of recognition would coincide with the conclusion of the new treaty. This declaration, though it caused a moment of confusion in the ranks of the Italian Communist Party,[2] was triumphantly hailed in Moscow as the first " breach in the old Entente united front against Soviet Russia ".[3] Hitherto, wrote a Soviet commentator, the western countries had hoped to barter political recognition for payment of private debts and restoration of private property : " to Mussolini belongs the merit and the honour of driving the final nail into the coffin of this hope ".[4] But, before effect could be given to Mussolini's initiative, still more important events happened. The general election in Great Britain on December 6, 1923, marked a swing to the Left, for which issues of foreign policy were believed to be partly responsible. The Labour Party was left as the largest single party, but without an absolute majority, so that the prospective Labour government would be dependent on Liberal support. Since, however, both Labour and Liberal parties favoured full recognition of the Soviet Government, this issue, at any rate, appeared to have been settled in principle by popular vote.

Some minor stir was now caused by the question whether Italy or Great Britain would be first in the race to accord *de jure* recognition. When the new Labour government under Ramsay MacDonald took office on January 23, 1924, recognition was assumed to be impending; but many thought that it would be preceded by negotiations between the two governments on outstanding questions. Kamenev, speaking a few days later at the second All-Union Congress of Soviets, admitted that Soviet

[1] See *The Bolshevik Revolution, 1917–1923*, Vol. 3, p. 340.
[2] Bombacci, an Italian communist deputy, in a speech supporting Mussolini's offer of recognition, took up what was later described as " an almost nationalist position ", expressing fears of British and French competition in Soviet trade and failing to condemn the extravagant demands of Italian capitalists and of the Italian Government. His attitude was condemned by the central committee of the Italian party, and subsequently by the presidium of IKKI (*Pravda*, January 8, 1924).
[3] *Izvestiya*, December 4, 1923.
[4] B. Shtein in *Ekonomicheskaya Zhizn'*, December 22, 1923.

R

relations with Great Britain constituted "an enormous and immediate interest in the present stage of world history ". But he professed to have no illusions about the British Labour leaders, and thought that their rise to power would give " the English working class " an opportunity to " verify " their real character.[1] The commercial negotiations in Rome were still held up by difficulties over the status of the future Soviet trade delegation in Italy. On January 31, 1924, Mussolini impatiently intervened with a concession on this point; and it was proposed that the signature of the agreement, carrying with it *de jure* recognition, should take place on February 3. Meanwhile, the British Government had decided on unconditional recognition. On February 1, 1924, Hodgson, the British agent in Moscow, notified the Soviet Government that the British Government " recognize the Union of Socialist Soviet Republics as the *de jure* rulers of those territories of the old Russian Empire which acknowledge their authority ". The note went on to invite the " Russian Government " to send representatives to London to draw up " the preliminary bases of a complete treaty to settle all questions outstanding between the two countries " : the three questions named were the validity of treaties concluded before the revolution, claims and propaganda. Hodgson was given the status of chargé d'affaires. The note made no reference to the appointment of an ambassador; King George V raised personal objections to receiving an ambassador from a Power which he regarded as responsible for the assassination of Tsar Nicholas II, his cousin, and the imperial family.[2]

On the following day Litvinov read Hodgson's note to the second All-Union Congress of Soviets, which passed a resolution welcoming " this historic step ". It noted that the working class of Great Britain had always been " the true ally of the working masses of the Union of Soviet Socialist Republics ", held out a hand of " friendly fraternal greeting to the British people ", and empowered the Soviet Government to enter into negotiations with

[1] *Vtoroi S"ezd Sovetov Soyuza Sovetskikh Sotsialisticheskikh Respublik* (1924), p. 62.

[2] H. Nicolson, *King George the Fifth* (1952), p. 385 ; as late as 1929 the King protested ineffectually against having to receive the first Soviet Ambassador (*ibid.* p. 441). A chargé d'affaires would not need to be personally received by the King.

the British Government on the issues arising out of recognition.[1]
On February 8, 1924, Rakovsky officially notified the satisfaction
of the Soviet Government at the recognition accorded to it, its
acceptance of the invitation to send representatives to London
for negotiations and its appointment of himself as chargé d'affaires
" pending the appointment of an ambassador ".[2] This did not
prevent the despatch on February 6 of a long message on recognition from IKKI to the Communist Party of Great Britain, ending
with the injunction to become " an influential revolutionary mass
party ".[3] Meanwhile, on February 7, Mussolini, deprived by this
precipitate British action of the priority which he had expected,
despatched his note according *de jure* recognition to the Soviet
Government.[4] Having now secured the recognition of two
principal allied Powers, the Soviet Government could indulge
itself in a gesture of triumph. Litvinov gave an interview to
Pravda in which he explained that Great Britain and Italy had
at last abandoned " the illusion that recognition would be of
advantage only to the Soviet republics ", that for other countries
recognition of the Soviet Government was now " of incomparably
greater importance than for the Soviet Government itself ", and
that to future proposals for recognition the Soviet answer would be :
" No negotiations and no preliminary settlement of any questions
whatever ; recognition must be unconditional and unrestricted ".[5]

The formal recognition of the Soviet Government by Great
Britain and Italy strengthened its international prestige without
materially affecting its position. The Soviet-Italian commercial
treaty was signed on February 7, 1924, and ratified a month later.[6]
Austria announced her intention of renewing diplomatic relations ;
and *de jure* recognition came in the next few weeks from Greece,

---

[1] *Vtoroi S"ezd Sovetov Soyuza Sovetskikh Sotsialisticheskikh Respublik*
(1924), pp. 197-198 ; *2ˢ S"ezd Sovetov Soyuza Sovetskikh Sotsialisticheskikh
Respublik: Postanovleniya* (1924), pp. 16-17.

[2] The British note was published in *The Times*, February 2, 1924, Rakovsky's note *ibid.* February 9, 1924 ; Russian texts of both are in Klyuchnikov i
Sabanin, *Mezhdunarodnaya Politika*, iii, i (1928), 295-296.

[3] *Pravda*, February 19, 1924.

[4] For this note and the Soviet reply of February 13 see *SSSR : Sbornik
Deistvuyushchikh Dogovorov, Soglashenii i Konventsii*, i-ii (1928), No. 18, pp.
29-30.

[5] *Pravda*, February 14, 1924.

[6] *SSSR: Sbornik Deistvuyushchikh Dogovorov, Soglashenii i Konventsii*,
i-ii (1928), No. 82, p. 219.

Norway and Sweden.[1] But the large group of European states which were still sensitive to French promptings continued to hold aloof. In particular, France intervened with effect to scotch negotiations between Soviet Russia and Rumania. The ever vexed question of Bessarabia, which had prevented the appearance of Rumanian delegates at the Moscow disarmament conference in December 1922,[2] proved a fatal obstacle a year later to negotiations for a commercial treaty between the two countries which were in progress at Odessa.[3] The question had become almost exclusively one of *amour-propre*. The Soviet Government, though without any immediate ambition to disturb the *status quo*, would make no formal renunciation of claims to Bessarabia; the Rumanian Government would accept nothing less. In these circumstances it was agreed after much difficulty to hold a conference at Vienna in March 1924 to seek for a formula to resolve the issue.[4] But on March 12 the French Government took the significant step, from which it had hitherto refrained, of submitting to the Chamber of Deputies for ratification the treaty of October 28, 1920, which in the name of the allied governments recognized Rumanian sovereignty over Bessarabia; and this act, which evoked an energetic protest from Moscow,[5] was calculated to promote Rumanian intransigence. The conference met at the end of March, with Krestinsky as the chief Soviet delegate, but broke down within a few days on the old question of principle, the final move from the Soviet side being a proposal for a plebiscite which the Rumanian delegation declined.[6] It was clear that

[1] *SSSR : Sbornik Deistvuyushchikh Dogovorov, Soglashenii i Konventsii*, i-ii (1928), Nos. 3, 14, 28, 40, pp. 9, 20, 80, 153.

[2] See *The Bolshevik Revolution, 1917–1923*, Vol. 3, p. 440.

[3] A *communiqué* on the breakdown of these negotiations appeared in *Pravda*, January 8, 1924.

[4] References to these negotiations in the contemporary press are collected in A. J. Toynbee, *Survey of International Affairs, 1924* (1926), p. 263.

[5] Chicherin's two notes to Poincaré of March 16 and 21, 1924, and Poincaré's note of March 20, 1924, appear in abbreviated form in Klyuchnikov i Sabanin, *Mezhdunarodnaya Politika*, iii, i (1928), 305-307 ; the French ratification was finally deposited on April 24, 1924 (*British and Foreign State Papers*, cxix (1924), 515).

[6] L. Fischer, *The Soviets in World Affairs* (1930), ii, 511-512, quoting unpublished records : extracts from Krestinsky's final declaration and the Rumanian reply are in Klyuchnikov i Sabanin, *Mezhdunarodnaya Politika*, iii, i (1928), 307-309. The proceedings were reported with unusual fullness in *Izvestiya*, April 1, 1924, and the following days.

Soviet diplomacy had reached the limit of its achievement in Europe so long as the position of the French Government remained unchanged.   On May 11, 1924, the French general election showed that the French voter had followed the British voter in a move to the Left.   Poincaré gave way to a radical and socialist coalition under Herriot; and this reversal of fortune heralded important changes in French policy towards both Germany and Soviet Russia.   These developments, however, like the Anglo-Soviet negotiations which began in April 1924, belong to the next period.   In the spring of 1924 the British recognition still seemed the decisive factor in the international position of the Soviet Government, and constituted a landmark not less striking than the first Anglo-Soviet trade agreement three years earlier.   It indicated, as Kamenev claimed at the second All-Union Congress of Soviets, " the collapse of all the basic forces which created the Versailles treaty and were trying to impose the standards of the Versailles treaty on the whole of mankind as a guarantee of peace, freedom and national prosperity ".[1]   At a moment when the Soviet Union seemed to have attained a new peak of political, economic and financial stability at home, it had also been readmitted to the circle of European Powers as a full member.

[1] *Vtoroi S"ezd Sovetov Soyuza Sovetskikh Sotsialisticheskikh Respublik* (1924), p. 61.

PART III

THE TRIUMVIRATE IN POWER

CHAPTER II

THE TRIUMVIRATE TAKES OVER

THE crisis which shook the party while Lenin lay dying in the last months of 1923 may be said to date from the second breakdown in his health in December 1922. On November 20, 1922, he had made the last public speech of his life to the Moscow Soviet. Shortly afterwards he had his last conversation with Trotsky — a conversation to which Trotsky in retrospect attached much importance, but for which the earliest authority is an account given by him some five years later. Lenin expressed his horror and fear of the growth of bureaucracy in the Soviet apparatus : it was a favourite theme with him at this time. Trotsky retorted that bureaucracy was to be found not only in state, but in party institutions ; and Lenin half-jestingly proposed " a bloc against bureaucracy in general and against the Orgburo in particular ".[1] On December 12, on medical advice following a renewed deterioration in his condition, Lenin withdrew to his private apartment in the Kremlin, where four days later he had a second stroke which paralysed his right side. Between the date of his withdrawal and that of his second stroke fall several notes attacking the proposal to relax the monopoly of foreign trade.[2] During the next three months, though confined to his apartment, he remained in full possession of his faculties and wrote articles and personal notes on party and governmental affairs. But, so far as can be ascertained, he saw none of the other leaders, and

---

[1] L. Trotsky, *The Real Situation in Russia* (n.d. [1928]), pp. 304 305 ; the account is repeated in L. Trotsky, *Moya Zhizn'* (Berlin, 1930), ii, 215-216.

[2] The first is a note addressed to Stalin as secretary-general for communication to the Politburo and is in Lenin, *Sochineniya*, xxvii, 379-382 ; the others are addressed to Trotsky, Frumkin and Stomonyakov and are in L. Trotsky, *The Real Situation in Russia* (n.d. [1928]), pp. 285-289. On December 21 Lenin wrote again to Trotsky congratulating him on the successful outcome of the proceedings in the party central committee (*ibid.* pp. 289-290). For this episode see *The Bolshevik Revolution, 1917-1923*, Vol. 3, pp. 463-465.

communicated with them solely in writing or by messages through Krupskaya.[1] It was at this time that he first clearly recognized that his days were numbered, and was filled with anxieties for the future. On December 25, 1922, nine days after the second stroke, he dictated the document known in party history as the " testament ", which has been more often quoted to serve particular purposes than studied in its entirety :

> . . . Our party rests upon two classes, and for that reason its instability is possible, and if there cannot exist an agreement between those classes its fall is inevitable. In such an event it would be useless to take any measures or in general to discuss the stability of our central committee. In such an event no measures would prove capable of preventing a split. But I trust that this is too remote a future, and too improbable an event, to talk about.
>
> I have in mind stability as a guarantee against a split in the near future, and I intend to examine here a series of considerations of a purely personal character.
>
> I think that the fundamental factor in the matter of stability — from this point of view — is such members of the central committee as Stalin and Trotsky. The relation between them constitutes, in my opinion, a big half of the danger of that split, which might be avoided, and the avoidance of which might be promoted, in my opinion, by raising the number of members of the central committee to fifty or one hundred.
>
> Comrade Stalin, having become general secretary, has concentrated an enormous power in his hands; and I am not sure that he always knows how to use that power with sufficient caution. On the other hand comrade Trotsky, as was proved by his struggle against the central committee in connection with the question of the People's Commissariat of Communications, is distinguished not only by his exceptional abilities — personally he is, to be sure, the most able man in the present central committee — but also by his too far-reaching self-confidence and a disposition to be too much attracted by the purely administrative side of affairs.
>
> These two qualities of the two most able leaders of the present central committee might, quite innocently, lead to a split; if our party does not take measures to prevent it, a split might arise unexpectedly.
>
> I will not further characterize the other members of the central committee as to their personal qualities. I will only

[1] See p. 342, note 2 below.

remind you that the October episode of Zinoviev and Kamenev was not, of course, accidental, but that it ought as little to be used against them personally as the non-Bolshevism of Trotsky.

Of the younger members of the central committee I want to say a few words about Bukharin and Pyatakov. They are, in my opinion, the most able forces (among the youngest), and in regard to them it is necessary to bear in mind the following : Bukharin is not only the most valuable and biggest theoretician of the party, but also may legitimately be considered the favourite of the whole party ; but his theoretical views can only with the very greatest doubt be regarded as fully Marxist, for there is something scholastic in him (he has never learned, and I think never has fully understood, the dialectic).

And then Pyatakov — a man undoubtedly distinguished in will and ability, but too much given over to administration and the administrative side of things to be relied on in a serious political situation.

Of course, both these remarks are made by me merely with a view to the present time, or supposing that these two able and loyal workers do not find an occasion to supplement their knowledge and correct their one-sidedness.[1]

Except perhaps for the confused and contradictory verdict on Bukharin, and the weakness of the one concrete proposal to increase the numbers of the central committee, the testament shows no signs of failing power. Few of the leading party members would have been perspicacious enough at this time to see in

---

[1] The so-called testament together with its postscript (see p. 263 below) was read to a meeting of leading party members on May 22, 1924 (see pp. 360–361 below) on the eve of the thirteenth party congress, and from that time its contents were widely known in the party ; but the text was first published in 1956. The central committee decided in 1926 to ask " permission " of the next party congress to " print this document " (Stalin, *Sochineniya*, x, 176) ; but it had only restricted circulation. Summaries of it, inaccurate in some details, first appeared in *Sotsialisticheskii Vestnik* (Berlin), No. 15 (85), July 24, 1924, pp. 11-12 A rather clumsy, but correct, English translation obtained by Max Eastman appeared in the *New York Times*, October 18, 1926, and in L. Trotsky, *The Real Situation in Russia* (n.d. [1928]), pp. 320-323 ; this has become the accepted version, and has been used above. The issue is complicated by the fact that in 1925 Trotsky, under pressure from his colleagues in the Politburo to dissociate himself publicly from Eastman's attacks on the party (Stalin, *Sochineniya*, x, 174), published an article, in which he described the charge against the central committee of " concealing " writings of Lenin, including " the so-called ' testament ' ", as " a slander ", and went on : " In the guise of a ' testament ' mention is frequently made in the *émigré* and foreign bourgeois and Menshevik press (in a form distorted to the point of being unrecognizable)

Trotsky and Stalin the two main contestants for power, passing over Zinoviev and Kamenev — not to mention Bukharin. Trotsky's individual ambition and Stalin's reckless exercise of power were lightly touched on; and the diagnosis of a major short-coming common to both Trotsky and Pyatakov — a lack of political, as opposed to administrative, capacity — was extremely acute.[1] But the testament, while it sounded a warning, pointed no way to a solution. In this respect it fell short of what the party had learned to expect from its leader.

Though Lenin in the testament faced the likelihood that the choice of his successor might soon impose itself, his capacity for work seemed at the moment to be recovering after the second stroke. On December 27, he dictated a note to members of the Politburo in part agreeing, and in part disagreeing, with Trotsky's proposals about the functions and powers of Gosplan.[2] Then, under what precise impulse is still not clear, Lenin turned his attention to the Georgian question. Ever since March 1921, when the Georgian SSR had been brought into being and Lenin's proposal for a coalition with the Mensheviks shelved,[3] he had showed signs of uneasiness over this question. Georgia was distinguished as the country where the establishment of a socialist Soviet republic and the incorporation of that republic, through

of one of Vladimir Ilich's letters containing advice of an organizational char-acter " (*Bolshevik*, No. 16, September 1, 1925, p. 68). In spite of this misleading statement, the authenticity of the text is not contested ; passages from it were afterwards quoted by leading Bolsheviks, and the postscript, as well as other passages in it, was quoted by Stalin himself, in a speech in the party central committee on October 23, 1927, reported in *Pravda*, November 21, 1927, and in *Internationale Presse-Korrespondenz*, No. 109, November 8, 1927, p. 2366, and reprinted in J. V. Stalin, *Ob Oppozitsii* (1928), p. 723 (the version of the speech in Stalin, *Sochineniya*, x, 175, omits the direct quotation).

[1] According to a later statement by Molotov, Lenin had already expressed this opinion of Pyatakov at the eleventh party congress in March 1922 : " Com-rade Lenin, who defended comrade Pyatakov and tried in every way to keep him for the work in the Don basin, said at the eleventh party congress : ' Com-rade Pyatakov has over-administered, has distorted the correct party policy, carried it out incorrectly ' " (*Trinadtsataya Konferentsiya Rossiiskoi Kom-munisticheskoi Partii (Bol'shevikov)* (1924), p. 44). In a speech to the All-Russian Congress of Soviets a few months earlier, Lenin spoke of " the Donbass, where comrades such as comrade Pyatakov have worked with extra-ordinary devotion and extraordinary success in the field of heavy industry " (Lenin, *Sochineniya*, xxvii, 133).

[2] See *The Bolshevik Revolution, 1917–1923*, Vol. 2, p. 380.

[3] See *ibid.* Vol. 1, pp. 349-350.

the intermediate stage of a Transcaucasian federation, in the
USSR had proceeded least smoothly, and where Moscow had not
only encountered extensive overt opposition from the local communist party, but had incurred a large measure of international
discredit. When Lenin recovered from his first stroke in the late
summer of 1922, reports of the visit of the Dzerzhinsky commission to Georgia and of the removal of Mdivani and Makharadze [1] renewed his anxieties, though as late as October 1922,
he was still firmly insisting on the submission of the Georgian
party central committee to the decisions of Moscow.[2] It was only
after Georgian opposition had been overruled, and the Transcaucasian Socialist Federal Soviet Republic brought into being

[1] See *ibid.* Vol. 1, p. 396.
[2] See *ibid.* Vol. 1, p. 396. The sequence of events appears to have been
as follows. After the return of the Dzerzhinsky commission to Moscow, accompanied by Mdivani and Makharadze, the Georgian party central committee on September 15, 1922, considered proposals drafted by Stalin for
what was called the " autonomization " of the Soviet republics ; it passed
a resolution with only one dissentient, Eliava (though several non-members
who were present, including Sokolnikov and Enukidze, also opposed it),
rejecting as " premature " the project for " unification in the form of autonomization " and instructing Mdivani to " sound the opinion of comrades
in Moscow " (*Sotsialisticheskii Vestnik* (Berlin), No. 2 (48), January 17, 1923,
p. 19). On September 27, 1922, Lenin, on the eve of his return to work,
circulated to the Politburo a long letter of comments on Stalin's preliminary
draft for the establishment of a union of Soviet republics ; though the
comments did not specifically mention Georgian opposition, a remark in the
letter that he was to see Mdivani tomorrow shows that this was uppermost in
his mind. The comments insisted on the principle of " unification " of formally
equal republics as the basis of the union rather than of their incorporation in
the RSFSR, and made the suggestion of having two central executive committees
(the germ of the eventual division of TsIK into two chambers) : he added the
general comment that " Stalin has a slight aspiration towards haste ". Stalin
in his reply opposed the suggestion for two executive committees, and to the
charge of undue haste made the tart retort that in some of his suggestions
" comrade Lenin himself was a little hasty ", and that " there is hardly a doubt
that this ' hastiness ' will supply fuel to the advocates of independence ".
(Extracts from this correspondence appear in L. Trotsky, *The Real Situation
in Russia* (n.d [1928]), pp. 293-296 : the full text has not been published.) Lenin
stood out for conciliation, writing in a personal note of October 6 : " I declare
life-and-death war on Great Russian chauvinism. . . . It is necessary to insist
that in the TsIK of the Union the Russian, Ukrainian, Georgian, etc., should
hold the presidency in turn " (Lenin, *Sochineniya* (4th ed.), xxxiii, 335). This
time Stalin gave way, and differences were ironed out at a meeting of the party
central committee at which both Lenin and Mdivani were present. The result
seems, however, to have been announced in needlessly uncompromising terms.
On October 15, 1922, Stalin telegraphed to Tiflis the decision of the central
committee to maintain " without any changes whatever " the proposal for a

to sign the act of union, that something occurred to modify and sharpen Lenin's whole attitude. On December 30, 1922, five days after the writing of the testament, and on the very day when the delegates of the RSFSR, of the Ukranian, White Russian republics and of the Transcaucasian federal republic, having listened to an oration by Stalin, voted the formation of the USSR and constituted themselves as its " first congress of Soviets ",[1] Lenin dictated the first instalment of a letter or memorandum on the national question, which was completed in two further instalments on the following day. He began by expressing himself as " seriously to blame before the workers of Russia " for his failure to intervene effectively in this question at an earlier stage. " Evidently this whole scheme of ' autonomization ' was radically wrong and untimely." What advantage could there be in establishing a single state apparatus when the existing Russian apparatus was " still thoroughly alien to us and representative of the bourgeois Tsarist machine " ?

I think [Lenin went on] that a fatal rôle was played here by Stalin's hastiness and administrative impulsiveness, and also by his resentment against the notorious " social-chauvinism " ; resentment altogether plays the worst possible rôle in politics.

Transcaucasian federal republic to be united with the RSFSR and the Ukrainian and White Russian republics in a " union of socialist republics " ; it was added that, in view of this unanimous decision, Mdivani had been " compelled to renounce the proposal of the Georgian committee ". This was followed by an angry meeting of the Georgian party central committee at Tiflis, in the course of which Makharadze described the Transcaucasian federation as " a corpse " and denounced it as being simply " the creation of a bureaucratic apparatus " (quoted in Orjonikidze's article in *Pravda*, April 19, 1923). An indignant telegram of protest was sent to Moscow, addressed not to Stalin or the secretariat but to Bukharin, who was known to favour the views of the Georgian committee (see p. 280 below) ; and on October 21 Lenin despatched in reply a personal telegram evincing extreme irritation at Georgian intransigence : "Astonished at the improper tone of the note by direct wire bearing the signatures of Tsintsadze and others, handed to me for some reason by Bukharin and not by one of the secretaries of the central committee. I was convinced that the difficulties had been eliminated by the decision of the central committee in which I and Mdivani directly participated. Therefore I emphatically condemn the abuse of Orjonikidze, and insist on your dispute being submitted in proper and loyal terms for decision to the secretariat of the central committee." On receipt of this telegram, the Georgian central committee resigned *en bloc* and a new and more pliant committee was formed under the supervision of Orjonikidze (*Sotsialisticheskii Vestnik* (Berlin), No. 2 (48), Jan. 17, 1923, p. 19).

[1] See *The Bolshevik Revolution, 1917–1923*, Vol. 1, pp. 397-398.

Orjonikidze had at one point gone so far as to use physical violence, and Dzerzhinsky had too easily condoned this. Orjonikidze should receive " exemplary punishment ", and Stalin and Dzerzhinsky be held " politically responsible for this truly Great Russian nationalist campaign ". In general the union of socialist republics was necessary and should be maintained for purposes of war and diplomacy (of all the Soviet state apparatus that of Narkomindel was the best, since not a single important person from the old Tsarist bureaucracy had been admitted there) ; but there should be willingness to consider a restoration of the " complete independence " of other commissariats. Lack of coordination here would be a lesser evil than to prejudice the authority of the Soviet power throughout Asia, " even by the smallest harshness or injustice towards our own non-Russians ".[1] Four days later, on January 4, 1923, the sick leader's brooding on these problems provoked another explosion. He dictated a postscript to the " testament " :

> Stalin is too rude, and this fault, entirely supportable in relations among us communists, becomes insupportable in the office of general secretary. Therefore, I propose to the comrades to find a way to remove Stalin from that position and appoint to it another man who in all respects differs from Stalin only in superiority — namely, more patient, more loyal, more polite and more attentive to comrades, less capricious, etc. This circumstance may seem an insignificant trifle, but I think that, from the point of view of preventing a split and from the point of view of the relation between Stalin and Trotsky which I discussed above, it is not a trifle, or it is such a trifle as may acquire a decisive significance.[2]

The testament and its postscript, together with the memorandum on the national question, remained for the moment among Lenin's papers, and were divulged to nobody except his wife and his secretary.

In January 1923 Lenin was still working intermittently. From his jottings of this month there survived two short articles (or perhaps alternative drafts of an article) on the cooperatives dated

[1] *Sotsialisticheskii Vestnik* (Berlin), No. 23-24 (69-70), December 17, 1923, pp. 13-15.
[2] For the sources for the text and the quotation of it by Stalin see p. 259, note 1 above.

January 4 and 6, and notes on Sukhanov's memoirs of the revolution recently published in Berlin : all these were printed some months later in *Pravda* after his final collapse.[1] Next he turned to the People's Commissariat of Workers' and Peasants' Inspection (Rabkrin), over which Stalin had presided from its creation in 1920 down to May 1922,[2] publishing in *Pravda* of January 25, 1923, an article under the title *How to Reorganize Rabkrin: A Proposal to the Twelfth Party Congress.* The article began by referring to the " immense difficulty " of the task and declaring emphatically that it had " not yet been solved ". But, since this was followed by a rejection of the view of " those comrades " who " deny the usefulness or necessity of Rabkrin " and by a sweeping condemnation of the whole of " our state apparatus with the exception of Narkomindel ", any impression that Stalin's former department had been singled out for attack was avoided. The article concluded with the proposal, later adopted by the twelfth congress, for strengthening Rabkrin by amalgamating it with the central control commission of the party.[3] But ten days later, on February 6, 1923, still dwelling on the same subject, Lenin wrote a further article of a very different character, and three times as long as its predecessor, entitled *Better Less but Better*.[4] This was a fierce uninhibited attack on the whole record and organization of Rabkrin.[5] Stalin's name was not mentioned. But the opening sentence, in which Lenin gave the advice " not to run after quantity and not to be too hasty ", echoed the criticism in his memorandum of December 30, 1922, of Stalin's " hastiness and administrative impulsiveness " ; and the emphatic indictment, twice repeated, of " bureaucracy not only in our Soviet institutions, but in our party

[1] Lenin, *Sochineniya*, xxvii, 391-401.

[2] Stalin ceased to be People's Commissar for Workers' and Peasants' Inspection in May 1922 (*Tsentral'nyi Gosudarstvennyi Arkhiv Oktyabr'skoi Revolyutsii i Sotsialisticheskogo Stroitel'stva : Putevoditel'*, ed. V. V. Maksakov (1946), p. 69). This was presumably the result of his appointment as secretary-general of the party, but is not recorded in biographies of Stalin or in the usual works of reference.

[3] Lenin, *Sochineniya*, xxvii, 402-405 ; for the history of Rabkrin and its reorganization in 1923 see *The Bolshevik Revolution, 1917–1923*, Vol. 1, pp. 226-228.

[4] Lenin, *Sochineniya*, xxvii, 406-418 ; the date is recorded in L. A. Fotieva, *Poslednyi Period Zhizni i Deyatel'nosti V. I. Lenina* (1947), p. 21.

[5] The crucial passages are quoted in *The Bolshevik Revolution, 1917–1923*, Vol. 1, p. 228.

institutions " was unequivocally aimed, at the office of the secretary-general.[1]

Even though the development of Lenin's personal animosity against Stalin was still unknown and unsuspected in the party, where Stalin ranked as one of Lenin's most faithful and useful subordinates, the attack on him in this article was unmistakable. Its publication would be an announcement to the party that he no longer enjoyed Lenin's confidence. This explains the extraordinary attempts made to prevent publication. Delaying tactics were at first tried, but impatient messages from Lenin through Krupskaya compelled the Politburo to take a decision. According to Trotsky, all those present at the beginning of the meeting except himself — he names Stalin, Molotov, Kuibyshev, Rykov, Kalinin and Bukharin — were against publication. When the difficulty of Lenin's insistence was raised, Kuibyshev (the third member of the secretariat with Stalin and Molotov) proposed to print a dummy issue of *Pravda* containing the article to be shown to Lenin. The proposal proved embarrassing for some of his less hardened colleagues ; and, when Kamenev, arriving late, took Trotsky's side, the Politburo swung over and resigned itself to publication.[2] The article *Better Less but Better* appeared in *Pravda* on March 4, 1923. The date March 2 appended to it was evidently designed to cover up the delays and hesitations of the Politburo.[3]

By the beginning of March Lenin's health had again deteriorated, and he realized that he would be unable to attend the forthcoming party congress. On March 5 he sent to Trotsky (and, apparently, to no other member of the Politburo) his memorandum of December 30-31, 1922, on the national question, explaining that he could not rely on the " impartiality " of Stalin and Dzerzhinsky, and asking Trotsky to " undertake the defence "

---

[1] Lenin, *Sochineniya*, xxvii, 412-413 ; according to Trotsky he raised the question of the dangers of bureaucracy in the party in his last conversation with Lenin, shortly before Lenin's second stroke (see p. 257, above).

[2] Trotsky's letter of October 24, 1923, in *Sotsialisticheskii Vestnik* (Berlin), No. 11 (81), May 28, 1924, pp. 11-12. Zinoviev and, of course, Lenin were absent ; Tomsky, the remaining member of the Politburo, is not mentioned ; Molotov, Kuibyshev, Rykov and Kalinin were " candidate " members.

[3] The date was removed when the article was reprinted in the first collected edition of Lenin's works edited by Kamenev, who knew that it was a fake (*Sochineniya* (1st ed.), xviii, ii (1925), 129) ; it was restored in later editions.

of his views at the congress ; he also informed him that Kamenev
was leaving for Georgia in two days' time. On the following day
Lenin went much further than he had ever gone before by writing
a letter to Mdivani and Makharadze in which he promised them
his support and denounced the " rudeness " of Orjonikidze and
the " connivance " of Stalin and Dzerzhinsky.[1] This denunciation of colleagues in the party central committee (and, in the case
of Stalin, in the Politburo) to ordinary party members was undoubtedly a breach of normal standards of party behaviour, and
betokens a high degree of nervous exasperation. It is probably
to be connected with an incident which apparently occurred on
the previous evening and led to the writing by Lenin on the
night of March 5-6, 1923, of a letter breaking off " comradely
relations " with Stalin. The immediate occasion of the breach
was, according to all the evidence, personal and not political.
Stalin had had an altercation with Lenin's wife and behaved in a
way which Krupskaya thought insulting. The letter was never
published or seen by any independent person : its existence was,
however, known to Kamenev and through him to Trotsky.[2] The
incident would have been unimportant but for the background
of political suspicion against which it took place. The letter to
Stalin and the letter to the Georgian comrades were, so far as is
known, the last which Lenin wrote. On March 9, 1923, a third
stroke again paralysed his right side, deprived him of the power of
speech, and put an end to his participation in public affairs. The
first bulletin issued on March 12 spoke of " a marked deterioration

[1] L. Trotsky, *The Real Situation in Russia* (n.d. [1928]), pp. 298-299.
Trotsky in his autobiography adds the further details that Lenin in a message
on March 5 warned him against communicating his memorandum to Kamenev
on the ground that " Kamenev will immediately show everything to Stalin, and
Stalin will make a rotten compromise and outwit us " ; that on the following
day Lenin changed his mind, and Trotsky with Lenin's approval showed
Kamenev the documents and enlisted his bewildered support against Stalin ;
and that Kamenev, after reaching Tiflis, received a telegram from Stalin in-
forming him of Lenin's third stroke, whereupon he changed sides again and
settled the Georgian question on lines favourable to Stalin (L. Trotsky, *Moya
Zhizn'* (Berlin, 1930), ii, 222-225). These details, being without either contemporary or documentary confirmation, must be treated with some caution.

[2] L. Trotsky, *The Real Situation in Russia* (n.d. [1928]), p. 308 ; *Moya
Zhizn'* (Berlin, 1930), ii, 223-225. The incident was also referred to by Zinoviev
at the session of the party central committee in July 1926 in a passage quoted
in L. Trotsky, *The Suppressed Testament of Lenin* (N.Y., 1935), pp. 31-32, from
the official record of the session.

in his health " and " a weakening in the movement of the right
arm and the right leg ". On the following day a bulletin published
in an extra edition of *Pravda* reported " in addition to a weakness
in the right arm and the right leg, some disturbance in his speech ".
On that day Rykov, in his capacity as deputy president of Sovnarkom, announced that a consultation had taken place with
" medical authorities who have come from Germany ". The tone
of the statement was grave, but it was stressed that " there is no
danger of a fatal ending " and that " after some time recovery is
possible ".[1] In the next few weeks factual and mildly reassuring
bulletins appeared regularly in the press, daily at first, then at
progressively longer intervals. The assumption at this time,
probably shared with the public by most of Lenin's immediate
colleagues, was that he would make at any rate a partial recovery
from his most recent stroke, as he had done before.

While these events were in progress, the party was preparing
to celebrate the twenty-fifth anniversary of its foundation, which
had taken place at a congress meeting in Minsk on March 1/13,
1898. The theses *For the 25-year Jubilee of the Russian Communist
Party*, issued by the central committee for the occasion, took the
form of an outline history of the party. None of the party leaders
other than Lenin was named except in a single passage towards
the end, which recorded that, during the world war, " the Bolsheviks under the leadership of Lenin and Zinoviev appeared on
an international scale as organizers of the Left elements of international socialism ". The opposition, headed by Zinoviev and
Kamenev, on the eve of the October revolution and immediately
after it was passed over in silence. But mention was made of the
" Left communists " who had resisted Lenin at the time of Brest-
Litovsk and of the opposition groups on the occasion of the tenth
party congress in March 1921.[2] The document was noteworthy,
both for the discreet attention drawn to Zinoviev as co-leader of
the party at a critical period of its fortunes, and for the hint of a
certain discredit attaching to those who had opposed Lenin in
the past.

[1] *Trud*, March 14, 1923 ; *Pravda*, March 22, 1923, gave the names of five
German specialists who had attended Lenin.
[2] The document was published in *Pravda*, February 25, 27, 28, March 1,
1923, and in translation in *Internationale Presse-Korrespondenz*, No. 45, March
12, 1923, pp. 339-347.

The twelfth annual congress of the Russian Communist Party was due to be held in March 1923. Every year since 1918 the party congress had been held in March. The precarious state of Lenin's health and the confusion in the Politburo caused the postponement of the twelfth congress to April 17 : a longer delay in so vital an occasion as the annual party congress could not at this period have been contemplated. But the situation which confronted the party leaders was highly disconcerting. It was now recognized that Lenin's absence from the scene was of indefinite duration. Some may already have suspected that it would be permanent; and even the most optimistic shrank from answering the question whether, and to what extent, Lenin would one day regain his powers. The very existence of the testament and its postscript was still unknown even to the inner circle of leaders. But the incident with the article *Better Less but Better* had been, to say the least, embarrassing; and the memorandum on the national question, which was circulated to the members of the Politburo during March 1923 and soon leaked to other party leaders, showed that Lenin might still strike shrewd and un-expected blows. These uncertainties had not been dissipated as the moment for the congress approached.

An additional problem was created by the prevailing restiveness in the party ranks. The relief and enthusiasm which had followed the introduction of NEP were now spent, and the obvious lack of leadership since Lenin's withdrawal made the clouds on the horizon look all the darker. While the grievances and the demands of the two more or less organized opposition groups — the Workers' Truth and the Workers' Group [1] — were primarily economic, they were both inevitably drawn into criticisms of the constitution and behaviour of the party hierarchy. The Workers' Group in particular combined its economic programme with far-reaching political demands : indeed, contempt was expressed for the " struggle for halfpence ", and " all preaching of strikes in order to improve the material position of the proletariat in leading capitalist countries " was denounced as " a harmful illusion ".[2]

---

[1] See pp. 79–82 above.

[2] V. Sorin, *Rabochaya Gruppa* (1924), pp. 26-27 (for the sources for the Workers' Group manifesto see p. 81 note 3 above).

Much space in the manifesto of the group was devoted to an attack on the united front policy advocated by Comintern in capitalist countries, which was based on belief in the tactical usefulness of limited demands. No compromise with the bourgeoisie could be tolerated : " the party of the proletariat must with all its strength and energy preach civil war in all leading capitalist countries ".[1] The group distrusted the conspicuous rôle of intellectuals in the party, and denounced the party bureaucracy which treated the " grey mass " of the workers as " material out of which our heroes, the communist officials, will build the communist paradise ".[2] Freedom of speech for the workers was vigorously demanded : " let the bourgeois be silent, but who will dare to contest the right of free speech for the proletarian who maintains his power with his blood ? "[3] The manifesto ended with a thorough-going attack on the existing party leadership :

> The stratum which occupies the leading positions is very small, and, although the places are often changed, remains always the same or is replaced by altogether non-proletarian elements. . . . . We are faced with the danger of the transformation of the proletarian power into a firmly entrenched clique, which is animated by the common will to keep political and economic power in its hands — naturally under the guise of the noblest purposes : " in the interests of the proletariat, of world revolution and of other lofty ideas ! "[4]

And in the " appeal " issued after the twelfth party congress in April 1923 as a preface to the manifesto, the complaint was made that the ruling group of the party " will tolerate no criticism, since it considers itself just as infallible as the Pope of Rome ".[5] A further passage of the manifesto enquired whether the proletariat might not be " compelled once again to start anew the struggle — and perhaps a bloody one — for the overthrow of the oligarchy."[6] The Workers' Truth group, although its pronouncements did

---

[1] *Ibid.* pp. 20-21, 32-33 ; *Das Manifest der Arbeitergruppe der Russischen Kommunistischen Partei* (n.d. [1924]), pp. 10-15.

[2] *Ibid.* p. 18 ; V. Sorin, *Rabochaya Gruppa* (1924), p. 94.

[3] *Ibid.* p. 74 ; the full passage from the manifesto has not been available, and it is not clear from the quotations whether freedom was demanded only within the party itself or for all workers' parties.

[4] *Das Manifest der Arbeitergruppe der Russischen Kommunistischen Partei* (n.d. [1924]), p. 21.   [5] *Ibid.* p. 9.

[6] V. Sorin, *Rabochaya Gruppa* (1924), p. 97.

not emulate the uninhibited vigour of the Workers' Group manifesto, voiced the same political discontents. The old " democratic centralism " [1] group did not revive as such ; but Osinsky, the most prominent of its leaders, was still an unrepentant critic of party organization. All these groups, whatever their starting-point, attacked the growing concentration of power in the hands of the party leaders and protested in the name of democracy or of the workers against abuses of that power. At the twelfth congress an anonymous pamphlet was in circulation, though it is uncertain from what source it emanated, which appealed to " all honest proletarian elements ", whether in the party or outside it, associated with the " democratic centralism " group, with the Workers' Truth group, or with the workers' opposition, to unite on the basis of the manifesto of the Workers' Group, and put forward the specific demand for the elimination of Zinoviev, Kamenev and Stalin from the party central committee.[2]

The opposition within the party could be overcome, as it had been overcome at the two preceding congresses, provided the party leadership remained united. This was the major problem which exercised the minds of those engaged on the organization of the congress. The withdrawal of Lenin at once threw into relief the potential rivalry between Trotsky and Zinoviev, the two most obvious candidates for the succession, and isolated Trotsky in the Politburo, where he had owed his outstanding position partly to his own abilities, but partly also to Lenin's protection and support. The personal hostility between Trotsky and Zinoviev was also expressed in political terms. Trotsky had become critical of some of the implications of NEP and was now a strong advocate of planning and support for industry. In these respects he stood near to those opposition groups which claimed to defend the interests of the industrial worker under NEP ; but he was inhibited from appealing to these not only by

---

[1] See *The Bolshevik Revolution, 1917–1923*, Vol. 1, pp. 195-196.

[2] This " anonymous platform " was several times referred to and quoted at the congress (*Dvenadtsatyi S''ezd Rossiiskoi Kommunisticheskoi Partii (Bol'-shevikov)* (1923), pp. 46, 122, 136, 145), but those who spoke for the opposition all disclaimed responsibility for it : in spite of Osinsky's denial, E. Yaroslavsky, *Kratkie Ocherki po Istorii VPK(B)*, ii(1928), 272 (a somewhat dubious source), categorically states that the anonymous platform was the work of Osinsky.

his own party loyalties, but by the animosity he had incurred from these groups (or their predecessors) in the trade union dispute of 1921. Zinoviev, who appealed to the tradition of NEP and the " link " between peasant and worker so ardently preached by Lenin, could count on the collaboration of the other principal members of the Politburo, Kamenev, the leader of the party organization in Moscow, and Stalin, whose key position as manager of the whole party machine was yet scarcely recognized. Talk of a ruling *troika* or triumvirate, consisting of Zinoviev, Kamenev and Stalin, was already current in party circles in the early months of 1923.

The dominant factor in the situation was that both Stalin and Trotsky shrank at this time from bringing the issue to a head. Stalin's position was weakened, or at any rate threatened, by Lenin's personal attacks on him and evident willingness to rely on Trotsky's support against him.   Stalin perceived far more clearly than the vain and obtuse Zinoviev the danger of a breach with Trotsky at the present juncture, and had a strong personal interest in seeing that as little dirty linen as possible should be washed in public at the congress.   The position of Trotsky, conscious of his own isolation and hoping against hope for Lenin's return, was more complex, and the explanation of his failure to strike which he afterwards gave in his autobiography, though undoubtedly offered in good faith, was not free from elements of hindsight and self-justification :

The chief obstacle to this course was Lenin's condition. He was expected to recover again as he had done after his first stroke and to take part in the twelfth congress as he had done in the eleventh.   He himself hoped for this.   The doctors spoke encouragingly though with dwindling assurance.   The idea of a " bloc of Lenin and Trotsky " against the apparatus-men and bureaucrats was at that time fully known only to Lenin and me, though the other members of the Politburo dimly guessed it.   Lenin's letters on the national question and his testament were unknown to anybody.   Action on my part would have been interpreted, or, to speak more accurately, represented, as a personal fight by me for Lenin's place in the party and the state.   The very thought of this made me shudder. I considered that it would have brought a demoralization into our ranks which would have been dearly paid for even in the event of victory. In all plans and calculations, one decisive factor of uncertainty remained : Lenin and his physical condition. Would he be able to speak ? Would he still have time ? Would the party understand that it was a struggle by Lenin and Trotsky for the future of the revolution and not a struggle by Trotsky for the place of the sick Lenin ? [1]

The argument was valid so long as reasonable hope could be entertained of Lenin's return. But the impression is strong that Trotsky's passivity was due in part to the lack of that political sense and acumen which Stalin possessed in a superabundant degree. Trotsky did not act because, with Lenin laid aside, he was conscious of his own helplessness ; and he found more or less plausible reasons to account for his inaction. With both Stalin and Trotsky determined, for their different reasons, to avoid any breach in the party leadership, the preparations for the congress were cautiously taken in hand.

The first step was to decide who was to present the general report of the central committee, made at every congress since 1918 by Lenin. Stalin at once proposed that it should be made on this occasion by Trotsky. Trotsky, declining the invidious honour, proposed that a general report should be dispensed with, and added that there were " differences between us on economic questions ". Stalin, supported by Kalinin, minimized the differences, and continued, without success, to urge that Trotsky should make the report.[2] The dilemma was resolved when Zinoviev, returning from leave of absence and evidently feeling the mantle of Lenin on his shoulders, volunteered to make the report. But the essential which Stalin secured in these preliminary discussions between the leaders was an agreement not to disagree. Zinoviev was satisfied by the mandate to deliver the general report — the major speech of the congress ; Stalin was to make the subsidiary report on party organization. Trotsky took over the special report on industry which would enable him to develop the theme which lay nearest to his heart — industrial planning.

[1] L. Trotsky, *Moya Zhizn'* (Berlin, 1930), ii, 219-220. The statement that Lenin's " letters " on the national question were unknown at this time is in correct.

[2] *Ibid.* ii, 227 ; *id. Stalin* (N.Y., 1946), p.366. According to the later version, Trotsky countered Stalin's offer by proposing that he, Stalin, should make the report as general secretary.

In return, Stalin, as he had done at the tenth congress, was to make the — on this occasion — delicate report on the nationalities question. The principal draft resolutions to be presented with the reports were, in accordance with the usual practice, approved in advance by the party central committee and published in *Pravda* before the congress met.[1] This procedure carried with it a collective responsibility of the leaders for all reports. It was tacitly understood that Trotsky would refrain from attacking the triumvirate, and that the triumvirate would not attack him. This agreement was faithfully observed at the congress except by Zinoviev, who, without mentioning Trotsky's name, indulged in some oblique criticisms of Trotsky's conceptions of planning.[2] Trotsky observed the understanding so literally that he spoke at the congress on no subject other than his industrial report. To secure his silence on the nationalities question, in spite of the appeal made to him in Lenin's letter of March 5-6, was perhaps the most remarkable of Stalin's successes on this occasion.[3]

The twelfth party congress of April 1923, the first since 1917 which was not dominated by the presence of Lenin and the last to be held in his lifetime, produced no sensational results, and was typical of the period of marking time and manœuvring for

[1] Stalin's theses on the national question were published in *Pravda* as early as March 24, 1923, Trotsky's theses on industry on April 11, 1923 : both were described as " approved by the central committee of the party ".

[2] See *The Bolshevik Revolution, 1917–1923*, Vol. 2, pp. 381-382.

[3] Two unpublished letters of Trotsky dating from the eve of the twelfth party congress, one addressed " to the members of the central committee " on April 17, 1923, and the other to Stalin on the following day, appear in English translation in L. Trotsky, *Stalin* (N.Y., 1946), pp. 362-363 ; Trotsky apparently left no commentary on them, and the circumstances giving rise to them have to be inferred from the contents. They relate to a declaration made by Stalin in the central committee on April 16, 1923, in which Stalin apparently accused Trotsky of being improperly in possession of Lenin's memorandum of December 30-31, 1922, on the national question and of divulging its contents without Lenin's authority. Lenin's secretariat confirmed that Lenin had given no directions about any use to be made of the memorandum. In his letter of April 17, Trotsky informed the central committee of the manner in which Lenin had sent the memorandum to him ; he had kept a copy and returned the original to the secretariat, and had not been aware whether Lenin had or had not given any further directions about its use. The letter concluded that, " if anyone thinks that I acted improperly in this matter ", he would demand an enquiry by the conflict commission of the party congress or some other special commission. On the same day Stalin, in personal conversation with Trotsky, withdrew the charge of improper action and promised a written declaration to

position among the party leaders. Its most significant features probably attracted little attention at the time, but foreshadowed much that was to come. The name of Lenin was on the lips of every speaker; and some of those who had the strongest motives to wish his most recent utterances forgotten covered themselves by the most exuberant tributes to his wisdom. Kamenev ingeniously set the tone in opening the congress. " We know ", he exclaimed, " only one antidote against any crisis, against any wrong decision : the teaching of Vladimir Ilich." But he added that Lenin " could not know, and does not know, the agenda for our congress, nor the resolutions prepared by the central committee ", thus contriving to imply that nothing that he had written was relevant to the immediate issues before the congress.[1] Zinoviev began his major speech, as was natural, by recalling how often this speech had been delivered at previous congresses by Lenin :

> When we travelled to these congresses, our purpose first of all was to hear this speech, since we knew in advance that in it we should find not only the considered experience of the time through which we had lived, but firm directions for the future. You remember with what thirst we always listened to this speech — a thirst like the thirst of a man who on a sultry summer day falls upon a deep clear spring to drink his fill.[2]

In this respect, as in others, Stalin distinguished himself from his colleagues in the triumvirate by a studied and pleasing moderation. In the first three months of 1923 his one public utterance had been a long didactic article in *Pravda*, based on lectures delivered to a workers' club and to the Workers' and Peasants' Communist University (the " Sverdlov University "), which he

that effect. On the following morning Trotsky, not having received the declaration, wrote to Stalin saying that, if he did not receive it during the day, he would formally demand an enquiry by the commission. The letter concluded : " You can understand and appreciate better than anyone else that, if I have not done this so far, it was not because it could have hurt my interests in any way ". Since nothing further was heard of the matter, Stalin presumably sent the declaration : this would have accorded with his policy of avoiding any open breach with Trotsky.

[1] *Dvenadtsatyi S"ezd Rossiiskoi Kommunisticheskoi Partii (Bol'shevikov)* (1923), p. 3.
[2] *Ibid.* p. 6.

described as " a compressed and systematic exposition of the fundamental views of comrade Lenin ".[1] In both his reports at the congress — on party organization and on the national question — he plunged straight into his theme, indulged in no rhetorical eulogies of the sick leader, and quoted Lenin only in order to reveal himself in the capacity of a modest disciple and interpreter.[2] It was left for Kamenev, at a ceremonial public session held in the Bol'shoi Theatre to celebrate the twenty-fifth anniversary of the foundation of the party, to follow Zinoviev's lead and strike a note which was to become only too familiar later :

> At this congress Vladimir Ilich could not be present ; but everything that the congress has done shows that, although he was not in the hall where the congress was sitting, he is in thought and deed the leader of the congress. His precepts we have been fulfilling when we took our decisions. His teaching has been our touchstone every time this or that problem, this or that difficult question, confronted us. Inwardly each of us asked himself : And how would Vladimir Ilich have answered this ? [3]

Such phrases heard at the twelfth congress sound like the opening bars of a symphonic movement, pointing the way to what was soon to develop into one of its major themes.[4]

The incipient cult of Lenin was invoked to reinforce the authority of the party leadership in the name of party unity. Zinoviev, conjuring up the nightmare of a fresh foreign intervention timed by the imperialist Powers to coincide with Lenin's absence, demanded loudly that " at this time we must permit on the question of party unity not the slightest ambiguity, no crooked interpretations ", and laid down a maxim whose cutting edge was one day to be felt by the speaker himself :

---

[1] Stalin, *Sochineniya*, v, 160-180 ; a translation of the article appeared in *Internationale Presse-Korrespondenz*, No. 55-56, March 28, 1923, pp. 443-447.

[2] See p. 282 below.

[3] *Dvenadtsatyi S"ezd Rossiiskoi Kommunisticheskoi Partii (Bol'shevikov)* (1923), p. 479.

[4] According to B. Bazhanov, *Stalin* (German transl. from French, 1931), pp. 116-117, Krasin in his speech at the congress told a humorous anecdote dating from 1907 designed to show that Lenin was not infallible, especially when it came to raising loans ; but this clashed so much with the prevailing canons of taste that it was omitted from the record on the orders of the central committee.

Every criticism of the party line, even so-called " Left " criticism, is henceforth objectively Menshevik criticism.[1]

The place left vacant by Lenin could be filled only by " collective will, collective thought, collective energy and collective determination ".[2]   Lenin's denunciation of Rabkrin and far-reaching proposal for its reform had been, as one of the delegates said, " something like a bombshell ".[3]   But Stalin, in his report on party organization, disarmed criticism in advance by repeating and endorsing Lenin's strictures on the bureaucracy.   The time had come, Stalin explained, to train up " a generation of future leaders ", and, for this purpose, to " draw into the work of the central committee new, fresh workers, and in the course of the work to bring them to the top, to bring to the top the most capable and independent ".[4]   The resolution which he submitted to the congress, and which was unanimously adopted by it, carried out Lenin's proposal for the amalgamation of Rabkrin with a much enlarged central control commission of the party.[5]   Since this was Lenin's own prescription for countering the evils of bureaucracy, any plea that it was inadequate or ineffective would have sounded like disloyalty to the sick leader.

These measures did not, however, entirely blunt the edge of criticism.   For the first time the autocratic powers of the party bureaucracy became a major target of attack for all the opposition groups and all the malcontents.   V. Kosior, who led the attack, argued that the organizational policy of the central committee made party unity impossible :

The fundamental question, in my opinion, is that the ruling group of the central committee in its organizational policy

[1] *Dvenadtsatyi S"ezd Rossiiskoi Kommunisticheskoi Partii (Bol'shevikov)* (1923), p. 46 ; Radek, soon to incur Zinoviev's enmity, hastened to express his whole-hearted approval of this formula (*ibid.* pp. 125-126).

[2] *Ibid.* p. 47.

[3] *Ibid.* p. 96.

[4] Stalin, *Sochineniya*, v, 206-208 ; in his later speech Stalin explained a little crudely that by " independent " he meant " independent not of Leninism, . . . free not from our party line, . . . but independent people free from personal influences, from those habits and traditions of struggle within the central committee which have been formed among us " (*Dvenadtsatyi S"ezd Rossiiskoi Kommunisticheskoi Partii (Bol'shevikov)* (1923), p. 182 ; the text in Stalin, *Sochineniya*, v, 226, omits the words " free not from our party line ").

[5] For this resolution see *The Bolshevik Revolution, 1917–1923*, Vol. i, p. 228.

pursues to a large extent a group policy — a policy which in my opinion frequently does not tally with the interests of the party. This policy appears first and foremost in the organizational form in which we manage the recruitment and utilization of responsible workers for party and Soviet work. Dozens of our comrades remain outside this work not because they are poor organizers, not because they are bad communists, but exclusively because at different times and for different reasons they have been members of some group or other, or have taken part in discussions against the official line which was being followed by the central committee.

He instanced wholesale transfers of party members from the Urals and from Petrograd by Uchraspred [1] after the eleventh party congress, and demanded the abrogation of the resolution of the tenth party congress against groups within the party — an emergency measure provoked by the Kronstadt crisis which had been "elevated into a system of party administration".[2] Lutovinov alleged that "not the whole party but the Politburo is the infallible pope", and denounced its claim to "the monopoly right of saving the party without the participation of all the members of the party".[3] Krasin complained that "the leading positions in the party are still arranged in the same way as 20 years ago" and mocked the suggestion that "some group of three or five would replace Lenin and that everything would be left as before".[4] Preobrazhensky urged the dangers of centralization, and, dwelling on a grievance which became one of the key issues in the party controversy, alleged that "30 per cent of all the secretaries of our provincial committees are what are called secretaries 'recommended' by the central committee".[5] At a later stage of the

---

[1] For this institution see *The Bolshevik Revolution, 1917–1923*, Vol. 1, pp. 228–229.

[2] *Dvenadtsatyi S"ezd Rossiiskoi Kommunisticheskoi Partii (Bol'shevikov)* (1923), pp. 92–95.

[3] *Ibid.* pp. 105–106.

[4] *Ibid.* pp. 114–115.

[5] *Ibid.* p. 133. The eleventh party conference in December 1921 had adopted a resolution requiring that secretaries of provincial party committees should have been party members before the October revolution, that secretaries of county committees should be members of at least three years' standing, and that appointments to these posts should be "confirmed by the highest party authority" : this resolution was duly endorsed by the eleventh party congress in April 1922 (*VKP(B) v Rezolyutsiyakh* (1941), i, 412, 436). This apparently innocuous decision was little noticed at the time ; but, coming at a moment

congress, when the national question was under discussion, Rakovsky reverted once more to the attack on the party bureaucracy.[1] The impression which emerged from these attacks was of a widespread, but dispersed and ineffective, opposition, without cohesion, without organization or leadership, and, above all, without policy or tactical plan. Kosior concluded his speech by lamely ruling out any change in the composition of the central committee. Nor was a critical mood characteristic of the congress as a whole. Nogin, a former textile worker and a member of the central committee, who had a reputation for common sense, went out of his way to congratulate the secretariat on the vast improvement in its technical efficiency since the previous congress.[2] Perhaps few delegates paused to reflect how rapidly not only the efficiency, but the authority, of the secretariat had increased since Stalin took office just a year earlier. Rarely had a party congress assembled in an atmosphere of such widespread uncertainty and discontent. Yet every resolution of the congress had been adopted unanimously and with only trivial amendments in the text approved by the Politburo and the central committee ; nor had the congress been accompanied or followed, like its two predecessors, by expulsions, or even threats of expulsion, from the party. Whatever private discontents might still be nourished, the lesson of party discipline appeared to have been learned. Clearly a party manager who could deliver such results with so little outward show of high-handedness was a force to be reckoned with.

The two major debates of the congress were, however, not on organization, but on Trotsky's report on industry and on Stalin's report on the national question. Neither of them produced noteworthy decisions or indeed any concrete results ; but both were significant for the balance of power among the party leaders. The debate on industry showed up Trotsky's isolated position. A prisoner of his own imperious temperament, of his

when the need for strengthening party discipline against opposition groups was widely felt, and on the eve of Stalin's appointment as secretary-general, it proved an important milestone in the bureaucratization of the party apparatus. The right of confirmation by the Orgburo or the secretariat of the appointments to key posts in the party organization became in practice tantamount to a right of " recommendation " or " nomination ".

[1] *Dvenadtsatyi S"ezd Rossiiskoi Kommunisticheskoi Partii (Bol'shevikov)* (1923), p. 532.

[2] *Ibid.* p. 63.

past record, and of his determination not to break the unity of the
Politburo, he could make common cause neither with the so-called
workers' opposition nor with the industrial managers. When
Kosior in his provocative speech declared that Trotsky's services
had not been fully utilized, Trotsky was obliged by loyalty to his
colleagues to denounce the remark as " completely out of place " ;
and it was expunged from the records.[1] Thanks to the bargain
between the leaders, Trotsky was able to present to the congress
without overt dissent a cogent review of the economic situation
and an agreed resolution which embodied the principles of state
planning and state support for industry.[2] But this was a paper
victory so long as Trotsky remained formally committed to the
official policy. His conspicuous refusal to stake out for himself
any claim to leadership now that Lenin was withdrawn from the
scene caused surprise to many — most of all, perhaps, to those
who most feared such a move on his part ; his self-effacement was
still commonly interpreted as a tactical manœuvre.[3] Meanwhile,
the disappointment caused by his failure to take the lead lowered
his prestige among the malcontents of the rank and file who
could most eagerly have rallied to him.

The proceedings of the congress on the national question had
one point in common with the report and debate on industry.
The same formal emphasis was laid on general principles which
nobody contested, while profound differences about the application of these principles were kept as far as possible out of view.
Stalin attempted, as he had done in the report on organization,
to disarm the opposition by unreservedly accepting all Lenin's
criticisms and making them his own. Just as he had expounded
and defended Lenin's proposals for the reorganization of Rabkrin
and so blunted the edge of the attack on himself, so he now
emphatically endorsed the proposal, which he had resisted when

---

[1] *Ibid.* p. 369 : the remark does not figure in the report of Kosior's speech, *ibid.*
pp. 92-95. According to *Sotsialisticheskii Vestnik* (Berlin), No. 15 (61), September 1, 1923, p. 4, Kamenev replied to Kosior by eulogizing Trotsky who,
he declared, had declined " the highest honour " offered him by the Politburo :
nothing of this appears in the record.

[2] For the review and resolution see pp. 20-26 above.

[3] This impression emerges strongly from a belated but well-informed
review of the congress in *Sotsialisticheskii Vestnik* (Berlin), No. 15 (61),
September 1, 1923, pp. 13-15.

Lenin first mooted it in the previous autumn, for a bicameral TsIK and boldly declared that, without a second chamber to represent the nationalities, it would be " impossible to govern in such a state ".[1] The resolution submitted by Stalin to the congress and unanimously adopted by it went further to satisfy the aspirations of the nationalities than any previous party pronouncement on the subject. Makharadze opened his hostile speech with the admission that " in the theoretical sense the national question calls here for absolutely no objections ",[2] and never really effaced the impression sedulously fostered by Stalin that Georgian grievances were the product of a petty local nationalism.

The most significant feature of the debate was, however, the treatment accorded to Lenin's memorandum (generally referred to as a " letter ") of December 30-31, 1922. The presidium of the congress decided not to publish it " in view of the instructions which V. I. himself gave " ; but copies had circulated widely and, as Zinoviev explicitly said, all the delegates had read i⸀.[3] Though the convention was observed that it should not be textually quoted, the remarks of many delegates betrayed a close familiarity with its contents. Mdivani, Makharadze and the Crimean Tatar Said-Galiev all repeated phrases from it, and Makharadze also referred to the earlier Lenin-Stalin correspondence of September 27, 1922.[4] Bukharin, who alone of the party leaders espoused the opposition case, winning for himself the mocking title of an " honorary Georgian ", pertinently asked why Lenin " beat the alarm with such furious energy over the Georgian question ", and why he " said not a word in his letter of the mistakes of the deviators, and used all his words — words five yards long — against the policy which was being conducted against the deviators ".[5] Of the defenders of the official policy only Enukidze dealt

[1] Stalin, *Sochineniya*, v, 258-259 ; see also *The Bolshevik Revolution, 1917–1923*, Vol. 1, p. 400.

[2] *Dvenadtsatyi S"ezd Rossiiskoi Kommunisticheskoi Partii (Bol'shevikov)* (1923), p. 471 ; in an article which appeared in *Pravda* while the congress was sitting, Makharadze expressed his dislike of the Transcaucasian federation, and protested against the methods used by Orjonikidze to secure its adoption (*Pravda*, April 19, 1923).

[3] *Dvenadtsatyi S"ezd Rossiiskoi Kommunisticheskoi Partii (Bol'shevikov)* (1923), pp. 552, 556.

[4] *Ibid.* pp. 455-456, 473-474, 522.   [5] *Ibid.* pp. 563-564.

openly with Lenin's " letter ".   But his attempt to argue that it had not been written " in order to support the deviators and justify their policy *in toto* " was cut short by a curt interruption from Bukharin (" Of course, it was ") ; and he retired to the more tenable ground that Lenin, in the personal parts of the letter, " had been the victim of one-sided and incorrect information ".[1]

But it was Stalin's treatment of the issue which was decisive, and deserves study as an example of his method.   Stalin knew himself vulnerable.   He had felt the barbs of every word directed against him both in the letter of September 27 and in the memorandum of December 30-31, and proceeded in his own manner to disengage himself from them.   He had already resented the charge of " hastiness " in Lenin's earlier letter, and brought the same charge against Lenin in his reply.[2]   Lenin had repeated the same accusation in the memorandum of December 30-31 ; and now, with characteristic tenacity when he had been wounded, Stalin attempted in public a subtler retort.   Quoting Lenin's still earlier proposal for a Transcaucasian federation in November 1921, he recalled that he had written to Lenin on that occasion urging him " not to be in a hurry ", and that Lenin had agreed to a delay of " two or three months " in carrying out the decision.[3]   It was Lenin, not Stalin, who had shown undue hastiness over the proposed federation.   In his major speech on the national question at the congress Stalin returned yet again to the barbed word : " It is no accident that comrade Lenin was in such haste and insisted on the federation being introduced immediately ".[4]   In the same speech he carefully emphasized all the points which Lenin in the September letter and the December memorandum had brought up against him.   Lenin had ended with the warning that " if we fall into imperialist attitudes towards oppressed peoples " the chance of mobilizing Asia against " the international west which defends the capitalist world " would be lost ; Stalin opened his speech with the same argument.   Lenin had demanded a " basis of equality for the union of republics : Stalin declared that " good will and legal equality " were the foundation of the union.   Lenin,

[1] *Ibid.* pp. 540-541.   [2] See p. 261, note 2 above.
[3] Stalin, *Sochineniya*, v, 228-229.   The extract from Lenin's proposal of November 28, 1921, appears in Lenin, *Sochineniya*, xxvii, 94, on the authority of Stalin's quotation ; the document as a whole is presumably not extant.
[4] Stalin, *Sochineniya*, v, 257.

ignoring the danger of local nationalism on which Stalin had hitherto mainly dwelt, had insisted at length on the " Great Russian chauvinism " of the " typical Russian bureaucrat "; Stalin now argued that " in connexion with NEP Great Russian chauvinism is growing among us daily and hourly, trying to sweep away everything non-Russian ", and that this was " our most dangerous enemy which we must overthrow, since if we overthrow it we shall have overthrown nine-tenths of that nationalism which survived and is developing in the individual republics ".[1] So far, he had made no specific reference at all to Lenin's unpublished memorandum. But, when he came to reply to the debate, in the course of which direct or oblique references to it had been made by almost every speaker, he faced the issue with extraordinary astuteness and in a characteristically roundabout manner. He found occasion to quote passages from two of Lenin's articles dating from 1914 and 1916 and introduced both with a cunningly calculated apology :

> Many have referred to notes and articles of Vladimir Ilich. I should have preferred not to quote my teacher, comrade Lenin, since he is not here, and I am afraid that I may perhaps refer to him incorrectly or inopportunely. Nevertheless, I am obliged to quote one axiomatic passage which gives rise to no misunderstanding.

And again :

> Allow me here too to refer to comrade Lenin. I should not have done it, but since there are at our congress many comrades who quote comrade Lenin at random and distort him, permit me to read a few words from one well-known article of comrade Lenin.[2]

Following the main speech in which he had trodden with such meticulous precision in Lenin's footsteps, it was a brilliant stroke. Stalin's claim to call Lenin his teacher seemed as unimpeachable as it was modest. Whatever strictures Lenin from his sick-bed might have passed on the minor mistakes of a persevering and devoted disciple were incidental, and could be charitably explained away. Stalin had extricated himself with tact and honour from an

---

[1] Stalin, *Sochineniya*, v, 237, 242, 245, 262.
[2] *Ibid.* v, 266, 268.

invidious position, and built up a solid reputation for modesty and common sense. Trotsky absented himself altogether from the debates on the national question. He explained that he had been too much occupied with the amendments to his resolution on industry.[1] Once more he had declined to join battle.

The character of the twelfth congress and its place in the history of the party were entirely determined by the absence of Lenin in conditions which made his eventual return uncertain : it was the congress of the interregnum. Its substantive decisions were virtually limited to the reorganization of Rabkrin and an increase in the membership of the central committee to 40, with from 15 to 20 " candidates ".[2] The main resolutions were for the most part platitudinous recitals of agreed principles which concealed, or revealed only in some occasional turn of phrase, the underlying conflicts and rivalries. The function of the congress was to mark time till the question of the succession could be cleared up. In the meanwhile some interim authority was required to fill the vacuum. Zinoviev had clearly offered himself in the rôle of Lenin's deputy when he made the opening report to the congress. But Zinoviev could not and did not aspire to rule alone ; and the need for a defensive alliance against Trotsky's presumed ambitions was never far from the mind of the " old Bolsheviks ". It was Zinoviev who insisted on the need to replace " the authoritative word of Vladimir Ilich " by " collective will, collective thought, collective energy and collective determination ". The threatened dictatorship of Trotsky — the Soviet Bonaparte — must be countered by the dictatorship of the party. In these calculations Zinoviev, backed by his Petrograd organization, could count on the support of Kamenev, the head of the Moscow party organization, always serviceable and not personally ambitious, and of Stalin, still a lesser figure, but important for his efficient management of the party secretariat ; Bukharin, the only other leader of comparable rank and prestige, was too much of a theorist and too little of a politician, and had at the moment ranged himself in opposition to Stalin on the national question. The provisional triumvirate, consisting of Zinoviev, Kamenev and

[1] *Dvenadtsatyi S"ezd Rossiiskoi Kommunisticheskoi Partii (Bol'shevikov)* (1923), p. 577.
[2] *VKP(B) v Rezolyutsiyakh* (1941), i, 501.

Stalin — with the names arranged in that order — had effectively established itself before the congress met. Every opposition at the congress, whatever its political complexion, was directed individually or collectively against the triumvirate. The anonymous platform which proposed the exclusion of Zinoviev, Kamenev and Stalin from the central committee [1] represented the secret ambition of all the opposition groups.

Stalin was the weakest and most vulnerable member of the triumvirate, partly owing to his junior status, partly owing to Lenin's recent attacks on him. It was easy to imagine circumstances in which Zinoviev might be tempted to strengthen his own position by jettisoning an unpopular associate. Hence it was in Stalin's interest above all to build up the authority of the triumvirate and to weld more firmly the link between its members ; at these tasks he worked, inconspicuously but untiringly, before and during the congress. At the congress it was an ill-tempered attack by Osinsky on Zinoviev that gave him his opportunity :

> Comrades, I cannot pass over the outburst which comrade Osinsky permitted himself — an ugly, indecent outburst — which he permitted himself in regard to comrade Zinoviev. He praised comrade Stalin, he praised comrade Kamenev, and he let fly at comrade Zinoviev, having made up his mind that for the moment it was enough to get rid of one and the turn would then come for the others. His line was to break up the core which has been formed within the central committee through years of work, in order gradually, step by step, to break up everything. If he seriously thinks of pursuing that aim, if comrade Osinsky seriously thinks of undertaking such attacks against this or that member of the core of our central committee, I must warn him that he will strike a solid wall, on which, I fear, he will break his own head. Let comrade Osinsky take heed for himself.[2]

How much this passage flattered Zinoviev's vanity is suggested by the fact that he remembered and quoted it two and a half

---

[1] See p. 270 above.

[2] *Dvenadtsatyi S"ezd Rossiiskoi Kommunisticheskoi Partii (Bol'shevikov)* (1923), p. 183. The version in Stalin, *Sochineniya*, v, 227, apart from the routine omission of " comrade " before the names of subsequent offenders (producing in this passage the bizarre effect that Stalin speaks of himself, and of nobody else, as " comrade "), omits the phrase " an ugly, indecent outburst " and the final sentence.

years later, when Stalin had broken with him.[1] He now repaid
the debt, though in far cooler terms, by speaking in support of
Stalin's resolution on the national question. The experience of
the congress sealed the solidarity of the triumvirate, based on fear
of Trotsky and reinforced by the attacks of the opposition ; and
it raised the status of Stalin, who both worked harder and behaved
more sensibly than either of his colleagues, to that of an equal
partner. After the twelfth congress of April 1923 it was no
longer possible to think of Stalin as a secondary figure in the party
hierarchy.

The summer which followed the twelfth party congress was a
period of deceptive tranquillity in party affairs. The period was
in a real sense an interregnum, when the old authority had lapsed
and the nature and character of the authority to come was still
unpredictable. In the meanwhile any claim to sit in a chair not
yet technically vacant was bound to provoke the jealous hostility
of other potential claimants and to seem indecently presumptuous
to the rank and file of the party. The congress had provisionally
invested the triumvirate with the rôle of leadership in Lenin's
prolonged absence. Trotsky, still hoping against hope for Lenin's
recovery, refused to challenge the triumvirate ; and, so long as he
held back, nobody else was strong enough to act. The strife
which Lenin in his testament had foreseen and feared seethed
and festered beneath the surface of party discipline. But its
outward expression was muted by the physical presence of the
stricken leader, and the amenities of controversy between men
professing the same aims and the same ultimate loyalties were
preserved, though with an ever increasing sense of strain. An
anecdote of the period illustrates both the constant irritation that
lay beneath Trotsky's official self-restraint and Stalin's careful
refusal to offer the slightest provocation, or even to return it
when offered. After anxious debate the Politburo approved a
reply to the Curzon ultimatum based on a draft by Trotsky
copiously amended by his colleagues. The two secretaries, subordinates of Stalin, bungled the final text ; and Trotsky seized
the occasion for an attack on the incompetence of Stalin's

[1] *XIV S"ezd Vsesoyuznoi Kommunisticheskoi Partii (B)* (1926), p. 454.

secretariat, which apparently ended in a long discussion between
the members of the Politburo on the handling of secret documents.
Stalin, with all due humility, dismissed the offending secretaries
and appointed in their place one Bazhanov, who a few years later
left Soviet Russia and recounted the incident in his memoirs.[1]

The one conspicuous exhibition of Stalin's growing power in
the summer of 1923 was a blow struck by him in a field which was
particularly his own. A Tatar Bolshevik, Sultan-Galiev by name,
a school-teacher from Kazan, had been in the early days of the
revolution a member of the collegium of Narkomnats and head
of its Muslim commissariat. He was apparently at this time one
of those " russified non-Russians " whose international outlook
made them the strongest supporters of a policy of centralization.[2]
He remained a faithful servant of Moscow throughout the troubles
of 1919-1920 in the eastern borderlands, and the sworn enemy of
Validov and other national leaders who pressed too far the claims
of the Muslim peoples to independence and incurred the charge
of bourgeois nationalism ; and he seems to have been associated
with the movement for a broader toleration of Muslim religious
practices and institutions which was introduced in 1920.[3] It was
only when the new régime in the eastern borderlands and in
Central Asia had begun to consolidate itself, and the evil of Great
Russian chauvinism was rearing its head, that Sultan-Galiev
altered his line, made himself the champion of the oppressed
Muslim peoples and sought to promote common action between
their leaders and spokesmen in the party to secure for them a
larger measure of autonomy. This quickly made him suspect in
Moscow, especially after the trouble with the Georgian Bolsheviks
in the latter part of 1922. In the spring of 1923 the GPU intercepted a letter from Sultan-Galiev to party friends in Ufa complaining that " the policy of the Soviet Government in regard to
the non-Russian peoples differs scarcely at all from the policy
of Great Russian chauvinists " and that " the promises given in
1917 have remained only words ". The writer proposed to hold
conversations with " the Kazakhs and the Turkestanis ", and to
" take common action with them at future congresses of the party

[1] B. Bazhanov, *Stalin* (German transl. from French, 1931), pp. 98-99.
[2] See *The Bolshevik Revolution, 1917-1923*, Vol. i, pp. 278-279.
[3] See *ibid.* Vol. i, pp. 323-327.

and sessions of the executive committee ".[1] Sultan-Galiev was placed under arrest — the first prominent party member to incur this penalty for a political offence. The precedent was significant and fruitful. It is recorded that Stalin sought and obtained the prior assent of Zinoviev and Kamenev to this step.[2]

To announce the downfall of Sultan-Galiev and to extract the appropriate lessons and warnings from it was the main purpose of a conference of the party central committee " with responsible workers of the national republics and regions " which met early in June 1923.[3] Kuibyshev, as president of the central control commission which dealt with questions of discipline, made the main report on the Sultan-Galiev affair. But Stalin also spoke at length on this topic besides delivering a general report on the nationalities question. With a faint touch of irony he pleaded guilty to the charge levelled against him by the " Left " of having in the past protected Sultan-Galiev, just as still earlier he had protected Validov. These concessions to local nationalism, this policy of " patience and precaution ", had been inspired by the hope that nationalists " would develop into Marxists ", and had been necessary in order to keep the local parties together. Sultan-Galiev was, of course, not present to defend himself. But Stalin proceeded to attack by name those delegates who, while condemning Sultan-Galiev's treasonable actions, had not dissociated themselves vigorously enough from his opinions. Stalin ended

[1] What purported to be the text of this letter was published in the Turkish journal *Yana Milli Vol*, No. 10 (1931), pp. 13-15, from the Tatar newspaper *Kzyl Tatarstan*; neither its authenticity nor its accuracy can be regarded as certain. According to Stalin, *Sochineniya*, v, 302-303, Sultan-Galiev wrote two secret letters, of which the first may have been the one quoted above ; the second is said to have contained a proposal to make contacts with the Basmachi and with Validov. But this version is also open to doubt.

[2] Kamenev admitted this in a subsequent conversation with Trotsky (L. Trotsky, *Stalin* (N.Y., 1946), p. 417).

[3] In order to minimize the exceptional character of the occasion it was described as the " fourth " such conference, its predecessors being the two Muslim congresses of November 1918 and November 1919 (see *The Bolshevik Revolution, 1917-1923*, Vol. 1, p. 319) and an otherwise unrecorded conference of Turki-speaking communists in January 1921. The stenographic record of the conference of June 1923 (*Chetvertoe Soveshchanie TsK RKP s Otvetsvennymi Rabotnikami Natsional'nykh Respublik i Oblastei* (1923)) has not been available, and it does not seem to have been reported in the press. But some information can be gleaned from Stalin's two major and two minor speeches (*Sochineniya*, v, 301-341) and the resolutions adopted by it (*VKP(B) v Rezolyutsiyakh* (1941), i, 525-530).

his speech with a long argument built on the theme of the middle way between Right and Left which served him so well at a later stage of his career. The Rights in the national republics and regions were, as the case of Sultan-Galiev showed, in danger of slipping over into a counter-revolutionary position; nationalism was their form of Menshevism. The Lefts objected to necessary and legitimate concessions to bourgeois-democratic elements which were loyal to the Soviet régime.

If the threat from the Rights is that by their subservience to nationalism they may make difficult the growth of our communist cadres in the borderlands, the threat from the " Lefts " is that by their obsession with a simplified and hair-trigger " communism " they may cut off our party from the peasantry and from broad strata of the local population.

Stalin was careful to conform to the current fashion in party leadership by associating his nationalities policy with the conciliation of the peasant and by condemning his antagonists as Mensheviks.[1]

Even more than Stalin's speech, the resolution of the conference on " the affair of Sultan-Galiev " was a significant foretaste of things to come. The charges against Sultan-Galiev were that he had created within the party " an illegal organization for opposing measures taken by the central party organs "; that the work of this organization had been calculated to bring about " a breakdown of the confidence of the formerly oppressed nationalities in the revolutionary proletariat "; that he had attempted to extend this organization beyond the boundaries of the Soviet Union by establishing " contacts with his supporters in certain eastern states (Persia, Turkey) "; and that " the anti-party and objectively counter-revolutionary tasks pursued by Sultan-Galiev and the very logic of his anti-party work led Sultan-Galiev to seek an alliance with openly counter-revolutionary forces " — among which the Basmachi and Validov were specifically named. The resolution concluded that " the criminal activities of Sultan-Galiev in regard to the party and its unity, and also in regard to the Soviet republics, confirmed by his own complete confession, place him outside the ranks of the communist party ". No other penalty was indicated;

[1] Stalin, *Sochineniya*, v, 301-312.

and the remainder of the resolution was devoted to the precautions to be taken in the party to guard against the repetition of such an incident.[1] It may be assumed that disciplinary measures were also taken against Sultan-Galiev's supporters or accomplices. But no suggestion was heard at this time of the pan-Turanian ambitions, and of the desire to create a vast Tatar-Turkish state stretching from the Volga over Central Asia, with which Sultan-Galiev was afterwards credited.[2]

Among the items dealt with in Stalin's general report and in the resolution of the conference were the still unappeased Ukranian grievances about the federal constitution of the USSR.[3] Since clear directives had been given by the party congress to the drafting commission which was engaged in putting the final touches to the constitution, the conference was clearly not competent on this issue. But Rakovsky and Skrypnik both raised it during the debate and drew a sharp concluding retort from Stalin.[4] Rakovsky was president of the Sovnarkom of the Ukrainian SSR and the principal advocate of Ukrainian claims throughout the constitutional discussions; he had also supported Trotsky's opposition in the party central committee to the reintroduction of the vodka monopoly.[5] In July 1923, a month after the nationalities conference, and a few days after the constitution of the USSR had formally come into force, the announcement was made of Rakovsky's appointment to succeed Krasin as Soviet representative in London.[6] It was a reasonable appointment; among leading Bolsheviks few had more obvious qualifications for a diplomatic post in western Europe. Nor is it unusual for governments to select for foreign service prominent individuals whose opinions or personalities are liable to lead to friction at home. Nobody had thought it strange that Krestinsky, after his dismissal from

---

[1] *VKP(B) v Rezolyutsiyakh* (1941), i, 525-526. No other reference to Sultan-Galiev's alleged confession has been found ; but he appears to have been set at liberty after a short period of confinement.

[2] These charges formed the core of the indictment against him in the trial of 1929 when he was condemned to death.

[3] See *The Bolshevik Revolution, 1917–1923*, Vol. i, pp. 399-401.

[4] Stalin, *Sochineniya*, v, 340-341.

[5] M. Eastman, *Since Lenin Died* (1925), p. 110 ; for the vodka monopoly see p. 35, note 2, above.

[6] Rakovsky's impending appointment was first mentioned in *The Times*, July 6, 1923 ; it was formally announced *ibid.* July 14, 1923.

the party secretariat at the tenth congress in March 1921,[1] should be sent on a mission to Germany and should later have become Soviet representative there. But members of the party were just beginning to realize the extent of the power concentrated in Stalin's hands through his responsibility for major appointments, and to guess at the unremitting skill and thoroughness with which that power would be used. The appointment of Rakovsky to London was probably the first to provoke widespread comment from this point of view. It was about the same time that Osinsky, who had made himself conspicuous as a critic of the triumvirate at the twelfth party congress, became Soviet trade representative in Sweden.

The summer of 1923 was marked by an incident which acquired some notoriety in the party and, though it had no immediate consequences, was ominous for the future. Notwithstanding the apparent harmony of the triumvirate, Zinoviev had not been altogether blind to the accretion of power in Stalin's hands resulting from his exclusive control over the party secretariat and his dominant position in the Orgburo. With Lenin laid aside, the secretariat became something altogether different from a secretariat working under Lenin's watchful supervision. Zinoviev, having detected the danger, chose the clumsiest method of attempting to counter it. While most of the leaders were on holiday in the Caucasus in August or September 1923, he invited a few prominent party figures — those known to have been present, besides Zinoviev, were Bukharin, Evdokimov, Lashevich and Voroshilov — to meet in a cave near Kislovodsk. Here he broached a plan to " politicize " the secretariat and bring it under the control of the Politburo : Stalin was to be reinforced by two coadjutors of equal standing with himself, one of them Trotsky, the other either Zinoviev or Kamenev or Bukharin. What Zinoviev's guests thought of the project does not transpire. But, a few days after the meeting, Zinoviev gave to Orjonikidze, who was travelling to Moscow *en route* for a German spa, a letter for Stalin outlining the project.[2] Stalin, more than a match for this

---

[1] See *The Bolshevik Revolution, 1917–1923*, Vol. 1, p. 204.

[2] Our information on this episode is derived from recriminations about it at the fourteenth party congress in December 1925. According to Zinoviev (*XIV S"ezd Vsesoyuznoi Kommunisticheskoi Partii (B)* (1926), pp. 455-456), Frunze and " a number of comrades of completely diverse views " were present

crude diplomacy, replied with a telegram couched in what Zinoviev calls a " coarsely friendly tone " suggesting that there had
been a misunderstanding somewhere ; and shortly afterwards he
arrived in Kislovodsk for talks with Zinoviev and Bukharin. A
compromise was soon reached. Stalin kept his grip on the
secretariat unrelaxed. But Zinoviev, Trotsky and Bukharin were
invited to attend the meetings of the Orgburo. Stalin was an
adept in the organization of business. Zinoviev attended one or
two meetings of the Orgburo without finding anything to object
to or anything in which he could intervene, and came no more.
Trotsky and Bukharin never thought it worth while to attend at
all ; Trotsky, unlike Zinoviev, scarcely even recognized the
gravity of the problem.[1] Zinoviev's naïve plan for curbing
Stalin's power fell to the ground, and nothing more was heard
of it. Stalin's self-confidence and contempt for the qualities of
his fellow-triumvirs can only have been enhanced by the incident.
But for the moment it had no sequel. The three were drawn
more closely together by the common interest in combating the
potentially far more formidable Trotsky.[2]

at the cave meeting ; Voroshilov's more precise and probably more correct
account (ibid. pp. 398-399, 950) limits it to the five named in the text, and states
that Frunze arrived only two days after the meeting ; nor need we take too
seriously Zinoviev's attribution of the project to Bukharin. For Orjonikidze's
rôle see ibid. p. 953.

    [1] Ibid. p. 456. Stalin's only public mention of this incident was an ironi-
cal reference to the " cave men " (ibid. p. 487) ; the bracketed passage in
L. Trotsky, Stalin (N.Y., 1946), pp. 367-368, does not emanate from Trotsky.

    [2] Voroshilov's allegation that Zinoviev made an offer to Trotsky at this
time for a bloc against Stalin and that Trotsky refused is probably an inflated
version of this incident ; as Zinoviev pointed out in his reply, it occurred before
the break with Trotsky (XIV S"ezd Vsesoyuznoi Kommunisticheskoi Partii (B)
(1926), pp. 399, 457).

CHAPTER 12

STRAINS AND STRESSES

THE party crisis of the autumn of 1923 began as a minor outbreak of discontent on the fringes of the party and at its lower levels and culminated in an open division among its highest leaders. Both phases reflected the strains and stresses of an unresolved economic dilemma ; but both also exhibited a widespread uneasiness at the growing strength of the party bureaucracy and of the tendency to stifle differences of opinion in the party or drive them underground. As the crisis deepened, issues arising from the application of " party democracy " outweighed the economic issues out of which it first arose. The discontent in the rank and file of the party was a continuation or recrudescence of that revealed in 1921 and 1922 by the workers' opposition, the Myasnikov group, the Moscow discussion club and " the declaration of the 22 " : [1] indeed many of the old names recurred in the new groupings. Nothing had been done to clear up the ambiguity of the resolution of the tenth party congress on party unity, which, while sternly forbidding all forms of fractionalism, had purported to uphold the principle of democracy in the party.

Of the two secret groups known to be active in party circles at the time of the twelfth party congress in April 1923, the Workers' Group of Myasnikov and Kuznetsov proved the more persistent, and was the first to attract official reprisals. Myasnikov's record of expulsion from the party in the previous year for " fractionalism " made him particularly vulnerable. He was arrested by the GPU at the end of May 1923 ; and Kuznetsov, expelled from the party a few weeks after Myasnikov, became the leader of the group. Moiseev, the third author of the manifesto of the group, who had a clean party record, retired at this point from further participation. Early in June 1923 the group held a conference in Moscow and

[1] See *The Bolshevik Revolution, 1917–1923*, Vol. i, pp. 200-201, 207-210.

elected a " Moscow bureau ". It entered into negotiations with persons who had been associated with former oppositions, notably with Kollontai, Shlyapnikov, Medvedev, Lutovinov and Ryazanov, but with apparently no tangible results ; and it established contacts with groups of discontented industrial workers in provincial centres. Abroad it hoped for support from the Left leader of the KPD, Maslow. Professing loyalty to the party programme,[1] its members are said to have taken an oath — perhaps inspired by the crisis over the Curzon ultimatum — to resist " all attempts to overthrow the Soviet power ". With the wave of strikes and industrial unrest in July and August new perspectives began to open. The opportunity dawned of transforming the economic demands of the workers into political demands, and a proposal was mooted to organize a mass demonstration of workers on the lines of the petition to the Tsar on Bloody Sunday, January 9, 1905.[2] But by this time the GPU had ferreted out the main lines of the " conspiracy "; and in September 1923 Kuznetsov and some 20 members of the group (out of an estimated total in Moscow of 200) were arrested. Of the 28 persons ultimately involved, 5 had already been expelled from the party ; the sentence of expulsion now fell on 9 more ; the remaining 14 escaped with a reprimand.[3] Penalties for breaches of party discipline were still light. Myasnikov, after his arrest in May, had been released and allowed to go to Germany. He was rearrested on his return to Moscow in the autumn. But both he and Kuznetsov appear to have been released after a few months' detention. A little later, similar reprisals were taken against the Workers' Truth group, seven members of its " collective " and six sympathizers being expelled from the party.[4]

No leading member of the party took the Workers' Truth or

---

[1] It defined itself in its manifesto as " a group not organizationally connected with the RKP, but fully recognizing its programme and party statutes " (*Manifest der Arbeitergruppe der Russischen Kommunistischen Partei* (n.d. [1924]), p. 27).

[2] The above particulars came from depositions made by Kuznetsov after his arrest ; but there is no reason at this period to doubt the substantial accuracy of such depositions (V. Sorin, *Rabochaya Gruppa* (1924), pp. 97-100, 109-112).

[3] *Ibid.* pp. 112-114.

[4] *Pravda*, December 30, 1923. According to *Sotsialisticheskii Vestnik* (Berlin), No. 20 (66), November 3, 1923, pp. 13-14, 400 members of the Workers' Truth were arrested at this time. The number is probably exaggerated ; the writer admits that the influence of the group was " for the present evidently not very great ".

the Workers' Goup seriously, or regarded them as anything but a minor recrudescence of the quasi-syndicalist " deviation " which had appeared from time to time in the party since 1917. But it was a symptom which forced attention on the growing industrial unrest, and increased the sense of uneasiness in the party ranks and among the leaders themselves.[1] The central committee took alarm. It was Dzerzhinsky, former president of the GPU and never a member of the opposition, who now argued that " the dying out of our party, the decay of its inner life, the predomin-ance of nomination over election, can become a political danger and paralyse our party in its political leadership of the working class ".[2] The result was the decision, taken by the party central committee at the end of September 1923, to set up three com-mittees on the scissors crisis, on wages and on the internal situation in the party,[3] the last being presided over by Dzerzhinsky. Stalin afterwards made play with the fact that neither Trotsky nor those who were later the most active critics of the policy of the central committee — Preobrazhensky and Sapronov — were in Moscow when this decision was taken, and that the committees were set up on the unprompted initiative of the majority.[4] Trotsky arrived, however, in time to scotch another proposal, which was apparently put before the central committee at the same session, for the reorganization of the Revolutionary Military Council, of which Trotsky had been president since its creation under the title of Supreme War Council in April 1918. This was not the first attempt by Trotsky's rivals to curb his hitherto undisputed authority over the Red Army. A reconstitution of the Revolu-tionary Military Council in July 1919 at the height of the civil war had brought into it Smilga and Gusev, both members of the military faction opposed to Trotsky.[5] It was now proposed to

---

[1] Bukharin afterwards wrote, with explicit reference to the Workers' Group, that the " summer strikes and anti-party groups " of 1923 had " turned the concentrated attention of the party to the necessity of a lowering of prices, to the necessity of a raising of the standard of living and of political activity in our own party organization " (preface to V. Sorin, *Rabochaya Gruppa* (1924), p. 3).

[2] Dzerzhinsky's outburst was narrated by Kamenev in his speech at the Moscow conference of party workers on December 11, 1923 (see p. 312 below), published in *Pravda*, December 13, 1923.

[3] See p. 104 above.   [4] Stalin, *Sochineniya*, vi, 27-28.

[5] A confused account of the change will be found in L. Trotsky, *Stalin* (N.Y., 1946), pp. 276, 313-314.

reinforce and transform the council by adding to it several members
of the party central committee, including Stalin. Trotsky resisted
the new proposal so vigorously that it was dropped. But two
new appointments to the Revolutionary Military Council were, in
fact, made at this time : Lashevich and Voroshilov. Lashevich,
a former non-commissioned officer in the Tsarist army, had won
his spurs in the military preparations for the October *coup*,
Voroshilov in guerrilla warfare in the Ukraine. In the party disputes in the civil war both had incurred Trotsky's enmity, and
repaid it in kind. Lashevich evidently owed his new appointment
to his patron, Zinoviev, Voroshilov to Stalin.[1]

The session of the central committee at which these momentous
events occurred was quickly succeeded by Trotsky's correspondence of October 1923 with the central committee, by the platform
of the 46 of October 15, and finally by the collapse of the German
revolution. The controversy now passed beyond the scope of the
debates on economic policy in which it found its first overt
expression, and developed into a struggle for the control of the
party. Trotsky's letter of October 8, 1923, to the central committee, the economic paragraphs of which have already been
quoted,[2] launched an attack on the party leadership from within
the Politburo itself. It took as its starting-point a recommendation of Dzerzhinsky's committee that members of the party who
had information about groupings in the party should be placed
under a formal obligation to divulge their knowledge to the GPU,
the central committee and the control commission. That it was
thought necessary to enunciate so elementary an obligation seemed
to Trotsky plain evidence of that " incorrect and unhealthy régime
in the party " which was one of the main themes of the letter.
" Very many members of the party, by no means the worst,"
Trotsky went on, " felt the greatest alarm at the methods and
procedures by dint of which the twelfth party congress was constituted " ;[3] and the situation had further deteriorated since the

---

[1] The authority for this episode is Trotsky's letter of October 8, 1923, to
the central committee (*Sotsialisticheskii Vestnik* (Berlin), No. 11 (81), 1924,
p. 10).   [2] See pp. 105-106 above.
[3] According to Yaroslavsky, Trotsky spoke in his letter of the " packing " of
the twelfth party congress (*Trinadtsataya Konferentsiya Rossiiskoi Kommunisticheskoi Partii (Bol'shevikov)* (1924), p. 124) ; whether the letter contained this
phrase, or any further elaboration of this charge, cannot now be established.

twelfth congress. Having next dealt with the shortcomings of economic policy, Trotsky returned to party matters and criticized the method of appointment of party workers, particularly to important posts, by the Orgburo : these were made not on grounds of merit, but " first and foremost from the standpoint how far they may support or hinder the maintenance of the régime in the party which, secretly and unofficially but all the more effectively, is being applied through the Orgburo and the central committee ". In a few pungent phrases Trotsky crystallized the issue of nomination *versus* election to key posts in the party : not even in the hardest days of the civil war had the practice of nomination to party office been carried one-tenth as far as at present.[1] A " secretarial apparatus created from above " had gathered all the threads into its hands, and the participation of the masses of the party in party organizations had become " illusory ". The last year or year and a half had seen the growth of a " secretarial psychology, the principal trait of which is that the secretary is capable of deciding everything ". Discontent in the party with the secretarial apparatus was bound to turn against the old Bolsheviks who were identified with it. Trotsky protested against the recent attempts to interfere in the direction of military affairs, and quoted an alleged cynical comment made to him by Kuibyshev : " We find it necessary to conduct a struggle against you, but cannot declare you an enemy ; that is why we have to resort to such methods ". Finally he demanded that " secretarial bureaucratism " should be replaced by " party democracy — at any rate enough of it to prevent the party being threatened with ossification and degeneracy ". The letter concluded with a threat. For a year and a half, Trotsky explained, he had been struggling against a " false policy ", while refusing to carry the dispute beyond the narrow limits of the party central committee. This restraint had yielded no results, and threatened to produce " *a crisis of exceptional severity* ". He now considered himself free to divulge the facts " to any member of the party whom I consider sufficiently schooled, mature, disciplined and therefore capable of

[1] Trotsky may have remembered that in December 1920 he had defended the practice of " nominating from above " against attacks from the trade unions ; he had then described it as being " in inverse proportion to the enlightenment of the masses, to their cultural standards and political consciousness " (Trotsky, *Sochineniya*, xv, 422).

helping the party to escape from a blind alley without fractional convulsions and upheavals ".[1]

This bombshell in the ranks of the central committee was followed exactly a week later by the circulation of the platform of the 46. No definite evidence exists of collusion between Trotsky and the authors of the platform. The group which had gathered round Trotsky in the trade union controversy of 1920–1921 had dispersed;[2] and he had since been meticulously careful to observe the ban of the tenth party congress on " fractional groupings ". But the signatories of the platform included most of those who, both earlier and later, were Trotsky's closest political associates.[3] It is inconceivable that they should have failed to inform him of their intentions or not invited him to associate himself with the group; had he accepted, he would automatically have become their leader. That Trotsky held aloof was symptomatic of his irresolute attitude and of his unwillingness, so long as Lenin's recovery and return were still possible, openly to challenge the triumvirate. By confining himself to isolated criticism, he avoided the imputation of " fractionalism " and did not finally burn his boats. In the long run his restraint was of little avail. Even if, as may well be the case, Trotsky's letter of October 8, 1923, and the platform of the 46 were composed and issued independently of one another, the similarities between them in general arrangement, in specific content, and even in the choice of language, were sufficient to suggest to nervous party leaders a secretly concerted joint attack. But the fact that the same bitter criticisms should emanate at the same moment from two independent sources was an even more striking symptom of widespread uneasiness in the party. The platform of the 46 denounced " the inadequacy of the leadership of the party, both

[1] For the text of this letter see p. 106, note 1 above.

[2] Of the seven party members who had been finally associated with Trotsky's trade union platform (see *The Bolshevik Revolution, 1917–1923*, Vol. 2, p. 223), Andreev had gone over whole-heartedly to the official line; Bukharin and Dzerzhinsky, though still at this time critical of it, were soon to bow to it; Krestinsky and Rakovsky were in diplomatic posts abroad; Preobrazhensky and Serebryakov signed the platform of the 46 without reservation.

[3] Trotsky in his autobiography names Rakovsky, I. N. Smirnov, Sosnovsky and Preobrazhensky as those to whom he spoke at the time of his conversation with Lenin in November or early December 1922 on the dangers of bureaucracy in the party (L. Trotsky, *Moya Zhizn'* (Berlin, 1930), ii, 215; for the conversation see p. 257 above).

U

in the economic domain and especially in the domain of internal party relations ": and, after three paragraphs devoted to the economic and financial crisis, the signatories turned to their second and principal theme.[1] The document described " the ever increasing and now scarcely concealed division in the party between a secretarial hierarchy and the ' quiet folk ', between professional party officials appointed from above and the general mass of the party which does not participate in the common life ". Ordinary party members who disapproved of something that was being done " are afraid to speak about it at party meetings, and are even afraid to talk about it in conversation, unless the partner in the conversation is thoroughly reliable from the point of view of ' discretion ' ". The " secretarial hierarchy " more and more openly exercised its influence to recruit the membership of conferences and congresses, " which are becoming to an ever greater extent the executive assemblies of this hierarchy ". (This echoed Trotsky's criticism of the preparations for the twelfth congress.) The régime of " dictatorship within the party " dated, it was claimed, from the tenth congress of the party in 1921. Some of the signatories thought that the steps then taken had been necessary as a " temporary measure "; others had regarded them " sceptically or negatively " from the first. But all were now agreed that by the time of the twelfth congress in April 1923 " this régime had outlived itself ". The sting was taken out of the protest by the deprecatory admission that " the present leaders could not in any conditions fail to be appointed by the party to the outstanding posts in the workers' dictatorship " (a confession that no alternative leadership was available), and by the weakness of the one and only concrete recommendation — the immediate summoning of a conference of the central committee and active party workers to consider what should be done. Some of the signatories made reservations as to the description of the existing situation, while accepting the general tenor of the document and its concluding proposal. Radek, who must have been on the eve of his departure for Germany, is said to have written a letter of his own to the

---

[1] For the platform of the 46 see p. 10f above, for the text see pp. 367-373 below : while the economic paragraphs were frequently quoted in subsequent discussions, only a few sentences of the political section seem ever to have found their way into print.

central committee in somewhat similar terms; the text of this has not been disclosed.[1]

About the time it received this second blast, the majority of the Politburo drew up its reply to Trotsky's letter of October 8. The reply was evidently circulated to the central committee, but was not published : only a short extract from the text has ever appeared in print. In this section the Politburo declared itself " unwilling to agree to the dictatorship of Trotsky either in the economic or in the military sphere ". It accused him of failing to exercise the functions already bestowed on him — he never appeared at Sovnarkom or STO, and had refused the offer to become a deputy president of Sovnarkom — and of acting on the formula " all or nothing ". In a passage which has not been preserved, it evidently drew attention to a number of occasions in the past in which Trotsky's views had been opposed to those of Lenin.[2] The reply provoked a stinging retort from Trotsky[3] in which he referred to Lenin's partial conversion to his views on the question of planning, and to the agreement between Lenin and himself, against other members of the Politburo and the central committee, on the maintenance of the monopoly of foreign trade.[4] Then, carrying the war into the enemy's camp, he recalled his correspondence with Lenin on the Georgian question, and Lenin's attack on Rabkrin, and went on : " If we remember who was for the longest period at the head of Rabkrin, it is not difficult to understand at whom this description was aimed, as well as the article on the national question ". He then narrated the embarrassing scene in the Politburo when Kuibyshev had proposed to print a fake number of *Pravda* carrying the article on Rabkrin in order to appease Lenin.[5] The sharpness of the retort, and fear lest publicity might ensue, was probably sufficient to put an end for the time being to this personal controversy.[6]

[1] M. Eastman, *Since Lenin Died* (1925), p. 37.
[2] The extract is in *Sotsialisticheskii Vestnik* (Berlin), No. 11 (81), May 28, 1924, p. 11 ; for the gist of the other passage (which can be inferred from Trotsky's reply of October 24) see *ibid.* p. 8.
[3] *Ibid.* No. 11 (81), May 28, 1924, pp. 11-12.
[4] See *The Bolshevik Revolution, 1917-1923*, Vol. 3, pp. 463-466.
[5] See p. 265 above.
[6] According to *Sotsialisticheskii Vestnik* (Berlin), No. 11 (81), May 28, 1924, p. 8, the Politburo also replied to Trotsky's second letter ; but no text has ever been published.

This was the situation which confronted the party central committee when (in Trotsky's absence, through illness) it met on October 25, 1923, in joint session with the central control commission and delegates of ten leading party organizations. The constitutional laxity which had always allowed the party leaders to arrange joint sessions of the central committee (or of TsIK in the case of the governmental machine) with other bodies, and to treat such gatherings as particularly solemn sessions of the main organ, now for the first time became important when it was desired to arrange demonstrations of party solidarity against the opposition. The central control commission was the custodian of party loyalty and its members could always be relied on for severity against dissentients ; and the ten unnamed party organizations would clearly not have been invited if their fidelity to the party leadership had not been certain. Twelve signatories of the platform of the 46 were also invited to attend and give their views, though only those who were members of the central committee had votes. Preobrazhensky submitted on their behalf a six-point resolution putting forward measures necessary " for the realization in practice of the principles of workers' democracy " as laid down in the resolution of the tenth party congress. The six-point resolution constitutes the most concise statement of what the opposition meant at this time by workers' democracy. Its main points were the discussion of " all the most important questions of internal party, political and economic life " by all ranks of the party ; freedom of expression of opinion, individual and collective, within the party, and the removal of the ban on discussion, especially in party clubs and in the party press ; control over party organs by the " public opinion of the party " ; cessation of the appointment of leading party officials by nomination from the centre, and restoration of the principle of election of party organs and officials ; cessation of the practice of selecting party workers not for their competence but for their submissiveness to orders ; and a review of transfers of party workers effected on the ground of unorthodox opinions.[1] The proceedings lasted three days, but no record of them is extant. The Preobrazhensky draft found no support ; and the only published result of the session was a short resolution

---

[1] *Trinadtsataya Konferentsiya Rossiiskoi Kommunisticheskoi Partii (Bol'-shevikov)* (1924), pp. 106-107.

" On the Internal Party Position ", which was carried by 102 votes to 2 with 10 abstentions.[1] After instructing the Politburo to hasten the work of the three committees set up a month earlier, and to take any action which might be necessary on their reports, it described Trotsky's action " at this most responsible moment through which the international revolution and the party are passing " as " a profound political error " — the more so since it had " served as the signal for a fractional grouping (the declaration of the 46) ". This declaration was " decisively condemned " as " a step of fractional schismatic policy ", thus bringing it under the ban on " fractional activities " pronounced by the tenth party congress in 1921 and justifying the refusal of the central committee to distribute it or publish it.[2] At the same time the resolution reiterated the central committee's acceptance of the principle of workers' democracy. The acute division of party opinion on what were primarily and ostensibly issues of economic policy could no longer be disguised. In an article in *Pravda* on November 7, 1923, entitled *New Tasks of the Party*, Zinoviev proclaimed that it was " indispensable to give practical application to workers' democracy within the party "; and a note appended to the article announced that the columns of the paper would be thrown open for a discussion in which party members, trade unionists and non-party workers were invited to participate. This signalized a major occasion in party history.

Throughout the greater part of November 1923 the debate in the columns of *Pravda* was pursued in comparatively moderate terms, and only secondary figures participated in it.[3] The scissors committee was still sitting behind closed doors, endeavouring to

---

[1] *VKP(B) v Rezolyutsiyakh* (1941), i, 531-532.

[2] According to Rykov's speech of December 29, 1923 (*Pravda*, January 1, 1924), the committee took a formal decision not to distribute it ; after this, any further attempts by its authors to circulate it would have been treated as a contravention of party discipline.

[3] Stalin afterwards wrote of this " first period " that the central committee of the party " did not intervene in the discussion in the pages of *Pravda*, reserving full freedom of criticism to members of the party ", and " did not even think it necessary to reply to inept charges " (Stalin, *Sochineniya*, v, 372) ; the circulation of *Pravda* is said to have doubled during the discussion (*Trinadtsatyi S"ezd Rossiiskoi Kommunisticheskoi Partii (Bol'shevikov)* (1924), p. 62).

reach an agreed solution of the economic issues. But the political issue — the challenge to the principles and methods of the present party leadership — began more and more to dominate the discussion ; and an article in *Pravda* of November 28 from the pen of Preobrazhensky, the first signatory of the platform of the 46 and one of its chief initiators, was fundamental and uncompromising. Since the introduction of NEP, wrote Preobrazhensky, the party had been following " an essentially incorrect line in its internal party policy ". The tenth party congress of March 1921 had proclaimed a " transition from military methods to methods of party democracy " (Preobrazhensky passed over in silence the decisions of the congress on party unity and the prohibition of fractions). What had been needed was " to liquidate military methods within the party, to restore party life somewhat on the lines of the years 1917–1918 ". Instead of this, the line pursued by the central committee had simply " strengthened bureaucracy, officialdom, increased the number of questions decided in advance from above, intensified the division of the party . . . between those who take the decisions and carry the responsibility and the mass of those who execute party decisions but take no part in framing them ". The course had been set " for a good apparatus and a good party official ", but " at the expense of the extinction of internal party life ". The results had been " a dying out of party life " and " the growth of careerism and subservience ". These sweeping attacks on bureaucracy in the party organization were of a kind to evoke a vague but widespread sympathy in the rank and file ; and the party leadership was highly sensitive to the threat to its authority. But the lack of cohesion and unity of purpose among the critics made it possible for the triumvirate to discredit and defeat them in a series of separate engagements. Thus the 46 had kept aloof from the Workers' Group, against which proceedings had, indeed, been taken before the platform of the 46 was elaborated. The rather more delicate task now was to keep Trotsky isolated from the 46, whose affinities to him were much closer and who would eagerly have welcomed his leadership. To avoid an open clash with Trotsky which would drive him into a position of solidarity with the 46 or with other opposition groups, and to heal the incipient breach made by the resolution of October 25, was the overriding tactical aim of the triumvirate at this time; and it could count on the active or tacit support, not only of the other members of the Politburo, but of a majority in the central committee.[1]

An incidental factor of some significance enters the story at this point. In the winter of 1923–1924, for the first recorded time in his career, Trotsky was troubled by persistent ill health. Already in the spring of 1923, in the critical weeks before Lenin's final stroke in March, Trotsky was in bed in the Kremlin with an attack of lumbago.[2] In the latter part of October 1923 he caught a severe chill while on a duck-shooting expedition — an occurrence narrated at some length in his autobiography and accompanied by philosophical reflexions on the rôle of accident in history.[3] The sequel was what he later called " a dogged, mysterious infection the nature of which still remains a mystery to my physicians ".[4] The symptom of intermittent fever persisted well into January 1924, when Trotsky left Moscow for the Caucasus. During this time, he made no appearances in public, though he continued to work, and several articles and letters from his pen were published in December. The historian can scarcely avoid speculating on possible psychological factors in the malady

[1] Trotsky afterwards wrote of a " secret political bureau ", composed of the six full members of the Politburo other than himself and of Kuibyshev, the president of the central control commission, who were " bound by mutual vows " and " undertook not to engage in polemics against one another and at the same time to seek opportunities to attack me " : similar groups were established in local party organizations (L. Trotsky, *Moya Zhizn'* (Berlin, 1930), ii, 240). This is a no doubt exaggerated and over-dramatized picture of the *de facto* situation.

[2] L. Trotsky, *Moya Zhizn'* (Berlin, 1930), ii, 220.

[3] *Ibid.* ii, 234-238.

[4] L. Trotsky, *Stalin* (1946), p. 381. A bulletin signed by Semashko, Foerster, Guétier and three other Kremlin doctors and dated December 31, 1923, described the illness as follows : " L. D. Trotsky fell ill on November 5 of the present year of influenza with symptoms of catarrh in the upper respiratory tubes ; these symptoms rapidly disappeared, but a condition of fever not exceeding 38 degrees has continued up to the present. An external examination revealed loss of weight, loss of colour, reduced capacity for work and lowered appetite ; an examination of the internal organs revealed an enlargement of the bronchial glands due to the above mentioned infection" (*Pravda*, January 8, 1924). Since the purpose of the bulletin was to justify Trotsky's departure from Moscow on sick leave (see p. 331 below), the severity of the symptoms is not likely to have been understated. On the other hand, the date given for the beginning of the illness does not tally with his own statement or with his absence on grounds of illness from the meeting of the party central committee on October 25, 1923.

that condemned Trotsky to inaction, or provided him with a reason for inaction, in this crisis of his fortunes.

It was in these conditions that the triumvirate made its overtures to Trotsky. The task was not easy. Stalin records two " private discussions " between Trotsky and his principal colleagues — Zinoviev explicitly states that all the members of the Politburo were present [1] — in which a basis of agreement on " all questions of an economic or party character " was found ; the drafting of a resolution for the Politburo was then entrusted to a sub-committee consisting of Stalin, Kamenev and Trotsky, which evidently superseded the third of the committees set up by the Politburo at the end of September.[2] Trotsky has left no record of these discussions except a description which he quotes from his wife's unpublished memoirs :

> He was alone and ill and had to fight them all. Owing to his illness the meetings were held in our apartment ; I sat in the adjoining bedroom and heard his speeches. He spoke with his whole being ; it seemed as if with every such speech he lost some of his strength — he spoke with so much " blood ". And in reply I heard only cold, indifferent answers. Everything had, of course, been decided in advance, so what was the need to get excited ? After each of these meetings L. D.'s temperature rose ; he came out of the study soaked through, and undressed and went to bed.[3]

The dilemma was to reconcile the proclaimed need for " party democracy " with the prohibition on fractions and " fractional groupings " : Trotsky was trying to enlarge, and the triumvirate to restrain, the right of the opposition to concert its campaign against the central committee. Stalin afterwards gave a cynical account of the tactics pursued :

> Comrade Kamenev and I decisively raised the question of groupings. Comrade Trotsky protested in the form of an ultimatum, declaring that he could not vote for the resolution in such circumstances. We then confined ourselves to a reference to the resolution of the tenth congress, which comrade Trotsky

---

[1] Speech at IKKI of January 6, 1924, reported in *Internationale Presse-Korrespondenz*, No. 20, Feb. 18, 1924, p. 224.

[2] Stalin, *Sochineniya*, vi, 33, 224 ; for the Politburo committees, see p. 294 above.

[3] L. Trotsky, *Moya Zhizn'* (Berlin, 1930), ii, 240.

had apparently at that time not read, and in which mention is made not only of prohibiting fractions, but of prohibiting groupings.[1]

Broadly speaking, the triumvirate was prepared to go to almost any length to meet Trotsky in the enunciation of general principles, provided that Trotsky could be prevented from placing himself at the head of the opposition and coming out publicly against the central committee. Trotsky, accustomed to see differences within the party fought out and settled through the drafting of party resolutions, attached to a victory on paper a practical value which, in the new conditions of party leadership, it no longer possessed.[2]

The resolution now drafted by Stalin, Kamenev and Trotsky was one of those compromises which are achieved because the aims and calculations of the parties in conflict move on different planes, so that satisfaction can be given to them simultaneously without apparent contradiction. It was a hotchpotch of familiar ideas, whose significance resided only in the distribution of emphasis ; and different interpreters naturally chose to emphasize different points. A brief review of the economic situation offered nothing new, and concluded by drawing attention to " the unique importance of Gosplan, the economic staff of the socialist state ". Broaching the theme of the dangers arising for the party from the contradictions of NEP, the resolution drew up a list of " adverse

---

[1] Stalin, *Sochineniya*, vi, 224. For the resolution of the tenth congress and the definition of " fractionalism " see *The Bolshevik Revolution, 1917–1923*, Vol. i, p. 200 ; the resolution did not prohibit " groups " or " groupings " as such, but only " groups forming themselves on the basis of this or that platform ". The distinction was fine, and quite unreal in practice.

[2] The statement in L. Trotsky, *Stalin* (1946), p. 371 (a passage bracketed to show that it was added to Trotsky's manuscript by the editor), that " Trotsky, who had been ill since the beginning of November and therefore unable to participate in the general discussion, attached his signature to it along with all the other members of the Politburo " conveys a false impression. Trotsky attached the utmost importance to the resolution, which he treated as a vindication of his point of view ; in the heat of the subsequent controversy he described it as initiating a fourth period in party history, the previous periods being " pre-October ", " October " and " post-October " (L. Trotsky, *Novyi Kurs* (1924), p. 9, reprinting an article which first appeared in *Pravda* on December 29, 1923 — see p. 320 below). Six months later he still regarded it as having given him the essentials of what he wanted, and spoke of it in this sense at the thirteenth party congress (*Trinadtsatyi S"ezd Rossiiskoi Kommunisticheskoi Partii (Bol'-shevikov)* (1924), p. 154).

tendencies " which included almost all the points raised by the opposition :

> The sharp differentiation in the material situation of party members in connexion with differences of function, and the so-called " excesses "; the growth of a link with bourgeois elements and the ideological influence of the latter; an official narrowness of outlook, which should be distinguished from necessary specialization, and the consequent weakening of the link between communists engaged in different sectors of work; the danger of the loss of a broad view of socialist construction as a whole and of world revolution; the danger already noted by the congress of a degeneration under NEP of the section of party workers in closest contact, through the nature of their activity, with the bourgeois milieu; the bureaucratization which has been observed in party offices and the threat arising therefrom of a divorce of the party from the masses.

The resolution was, however, less categorical in its prescription of remedies. It did, indeed, demand " a serious change of the party course in the direction of a real and systematic application of the principles of workers' democracy ". But on the crucial issue of the control exercised by the centre over the appointment of local party secretaries it remained equivocal. It recalled that the party statute required the confirmation of such appointments by the highest party authority, but thought that the time had come, " in the light of the experience which we now have, especially of the lower organizations ", to " verify the usefulness " of this and other similar restrictions on the autonomy of local branches. " In any case ", concluded this section of the resolution, " the right to confirm secretaries cannot be allowed to be converted into their virtual nomination." It required much optimism to read into these halting phrases a firm determination to reform established practice. Besides " party democracy ", the other remedy to which the resolution returned in more than one passage was the long-standing panacea of " the influx [into the party] of new cadres of industrial workers "; the existing preponderance of " non-proletarian elements " must be checked by drawing into the party more " industrial workers from the bench ". This was un-impeachable party doctrine, to which lip service had been paid for many years past. Nobody had yet considered to what uses its application might be put.

Apart from these pronouncements on the principles of party organization and structure, the agreed resolution had also to be read as a verdict on the current party controversy. Here, too, it proceeded mainly by implication. Workers' Truth and the Workers' Group were condemned by name. The platform of the 46 was not specifically mentioned. But the resolution cited and endorsed the earlier resolution of the central committee of October 25 approving " the course set by the Politburo for internal party democracy "; and since one of the main purposes of this resolution, adopted in Trotsky's absence, had been to condemn the 46, the implication was clear that they too were included in the renewed censure of " fractional groupings ". Trotsky was induced in this roundabout way to pronounce judgment in the name of party loyalty on his potential supporters. It could even be argued that Trotsky, by agreeing to cite with approval the Politburo resolution which had condemned his own letter of October 8, had accepted the justice of this censure : it was he, not his colleagues on the Politburo, who seemed to have retreated from the position taken up in October. Unity had been restored among the leaders ; and, while Trotsky assumed that it had been restored through the acceptance of his views by his colleagues, others could just as plausibly believe that Trotsky had rallied to the call of party loyalty and accepted in all essentials the majority standpoint. The main fact, however, on either hypothesis was that unity once more reigned in the Politburo. The opposition had been condemned and isolated.

The resolution drafted by Trotsky, Stalin and Kamenev was unanimously approved at a joint session of the Politburo and the presidium of the central control commission on December 5, 1923.[1] The members of the triumvirate could breathe a sigh of relief. The danger of a split in which Trotsky would lead the rank and file of the party against them had once more been averted.

---

[1] The resolution was published in *Pravda*, December 7, 1923 : shorn of the two first paragraphs of the first section relating exclusively to economic questions, it was adopted as the resolution of the thirteenth party conference on party structure (*VKP(B) v Rezolyutsiyakh* (1941), i, 535-540 ; for the two omitted paragraphs see *ibid.* i, 622-623). It appeared once more in its original form in the records of the thirteenth party congress (*Trinadtsatyi S"ezd Rossiiskoi Kommunisticheskoi Partii (Bol'shevikov)* (1924), pp. 733-741).

CHAPTER 13

THE CAMPAIGN AGAINST TROTSKY

THE month of December 1923 proved to be the turning-point in the internal party crisis. It brought all the hidden bitterness to the surface and moulded the party into the new shape in which its destinies were to be cast throughout the coming decade. It opened quietly. Having the agreement with Trotsky now in sight, the triumvirate was slow to make any fresh move. Zinoviev's article in *Pravda* on December 1 on the German revolution [1] contained no hint of any desire to pick a quarrel with Trotsky or Radek on this subject. On the same day Zinoviev made a colourless and unprovocative speech to a conference of the Petrograd provincial party organization. The conference passed a resolution whose key sentence merely repeated the current formula without attempting to bridge the contradiction: " Freedom of discussion in the party on a whole series of questions is essential: freedom of ' groupings ' and ' fractions ' is excluded ".[2] On December 2 the sentences of expulsion or censure on those implicated in the Workers' Group were published in *Pravda* : [3] the decision was an advertisement of the unity of all the responsible party leaders in condemning factious opposition and upholding the discipline of party loyalty. On the same day, which was a Sunday, Stalin addressed a meeting of party members at Krasnaya Presnya, an industrial settlement on the outskirts of Moscow. Disclaiming any right to speak for the central committee, whose committee appointed in September would report shortly on the situation in the party, Stalin cautiously issued a warning against carrying principles too far. The election of secretaries of provincial and other party committees should be

---

[1] See p. 233 above.
[2] The speech and the resolution were printed in *Pravda*, December 7, 1923.
[3] See p. 293 above.

maintained, but it was equally important to uphold the rule confining eligibility to party members of a certain number of years' service. Discussion of differences within the party should be free, but not unlimited; the function of the party was not merely to formulate opinions, but to carry out a programme of action. Here Stalin came to the defence of Trotsky against someone who had attributed to him a description of the party as " a voluntary union of like-minded people ". He did not believe that Trotsky had used such a phrase; for he knew Trotsky as " one of those members of the central committee who emphasize most of all the active side of party work ".[1] The speech was significant only of Stalin's determination to force no issues and not show his hand prematurely. It was full of those clichés which, if they shed no fresh light, are at any rate sure to offend nobody. Whatever ironical undertones may be detected in his defence of Trotsky, it was noteworthy as the last occasion on which he spoke of Trotsky in public without open animosity. On December 5 *Pravda* published a bewildered little note, apparently from a provincial correspondent, complaining that " the discussion of internal party questions has taken the provinces unawares ", and that most party members did not know what to think, fearing " a conspiracy of silence ". Next day's *Pravda* carried an article by Trotsky bearing the title *About the Link* (*More Accurately: About the Link and about False Reports*). It was an exposition of Lenin's views of the " link " between the proletariat and peasantry, and a refutation of current reports (conveniently attributed to the nepman) of divergences between Lenin and Trotsky on this question; and it repeated, like everything else written by Trotsky at this time, his conviction of the need for " a consciously calculated, planned approach to the market and, in general, to economic tasks ".[2] The article provoked no retort and no public comment in party circles. On the following day, December 7, the agreed Politburo resolution of December 5 appeared in *Pravda*.

The resolution of December 5, 1923, while it was accepted by all concerned as a means to avert or postpone the threatened

---

[1] Stalin, *Sochineniya*, v, 354-370 ; the speech was originally published in *Pravda*, December 6, 1923.

[2] The article was reprinted in L. Trotsky, *Novyi Kurs* (1924), pp. 93-99.

split in the leadership, had precisely the opposite effect. It proved
to be the last document on which the triumvirate and Trotsky
registered, with whatever secret reservations, their common
agreement. What exactly precipitated the rupture is even now
not certain. When a stroke has been long meditated and prepared,
the moment of its delivery is often determined by a sudden fear
of the consequences if it is delayed any longer; this is perhaps
the most plausible explanation of what followed. The occasion
of the rupture was a letter written by Trotsky on December 8
to a party meeting apologizing for his failure to attend, which was
published in *Pravda* with a postscript on December 11. The
letter took the form of a commentary on the resolution of December
5 : it was an exposition of what Trotsky assumed the resolution
to mean and a rebuttal of any other potential interpretations. It
was not, as was afterwards pretended, a deliberate attack on the
agreed text or on other members of the Politburo and of the
central committee. The views stated were those which Trotsky,
as he naïvely believed, had persuaded or compelled his colleagues
to share. All that the letter did was, in Trotsky's intention, to
dot the i's and cross the t's of the resolution and to register his
victory. The resolution would, Trotsky suggested, be criticized
only by those " conservatively minded comrades who are inclined
to overrate the rôle of the machine and to underrate the independence of the party ". The result of the resolution was that " the
centre of gravity incorrectly shifted under the old course to the
side of the machine must now, with the new course, be shifted to
the side of the activity, of the critical independence, of the self-
administration of the party ". This led Trotsky to the reflexion
which was afterwards most resented. The bureaucracy, he
remarked, which was naturally manned by " comrades of most
experience and longest service ", weighed most heavily on the
rising generation; and it was for this reason that " youth, the
surest barometer of the party, reacts most sharply against party
bureaucracy ". History had often witnessed " the transformation
of an ' old guard ' ", i.e. its lapse into " opportunism " : the
German social-democratic leaders in the period before 1914 were
a conspicuous example.[1] Some " bureaucratized representatives

[1] The example was familiar in party literature, and Trotsky himself had
used it to point the same moral before the present crisis arose. The preface

of the machine " might even now be preparing " formally to ' take note of ' the resolution, i.e. *bureaucratically to annihilate it* ". Having issued this warning, Trotsky wound up with a reference to " the dangers of fractionalism ". But this was qualified by the italicized remark that " *the bureaucracy of the machine is one of the chief sources of fractionalism* ", and carried a good deal less conviction than his attack on the " machine ". A postscript, published with the letter, but written after the letter had been read and discussed at several party gatherings, attempted to rebut the charge of having set the younger generation against the " old guard ". The reference to the social-democrats before 1914, it was now explained, had not been intended to suggest a precise parallel between the two periods. But it was right to " draw attention to the dangers of NEP, which were closely connected with the *protracted* character of the international revolution ".[1] The postscript was unlikely to reassure those who had been made uneasy by the original letter.

Simultaneously with the circulation of Trotsky's letter the opposition redoubled its exertions in party meetings. Though no identification of Trotsky's views with those of the opposition was yet admitted, the remedies demanded by the opposition were clearly relevant to the ills which Trotsky diagnosed. The most active protagonists of the opposition were at this time Preobrazhensky and Sapronov (Pyatakov apparently did not return

---

to a recent German edition of some of his articles and speeches, dated May 4, 1923, referred to the rapid degeneration of the German social-democrats when immediate revolutionary prospects were no longer in sight, and went on : " This danger arises to a certain extent even for our own party, in the land of the proletarian dictatorship. Our work necessarily becomes specialized and is lost in details. . . . The present protracted period conceals within itself the possibility of sharp breaks in tempo and profound disturbances. Our sober, cautious, calculating policy must preserve the capacity to make sharp turns. Otherwise a new revolutionary wave might take the communist party by surprise and throw it off its balance. That would almost certainly mean a new defeat of the revolution " (L. Trotsky, *Grundfragen der Revolution* (Hamburg, 1923), preface).

[1] The letter and postscript were reprinted in L. Trotsky, *Novyi Kurs* (1924), pp. 77-86. It was apparently sent by Trotsky to several party meetings, where it was read out ; the translation which appeared in *Internationale Presse-Korrespondenz*, No. 8, January 21, 1924, pp. 69-71, wrongly described it as a letter addressed to " the enlarged plenum of the central committee ". It was later often referred to as an article under the title *The New Course* which Trotsky gave to the collection in which it was published.

from Germany till the middle of December); and a resolution proposed by Preobrazhensky at a party meeting in an industrial district of Moscow on December 8 or 9 was typical of the opposition programme. It demanded " the abolition of nomination as a system "; " the introduction of election (as a rule) of party organs and of responsible workers in the apparatus "; " *de facto* responsibility of party organs to the mass of the party "; " a precise formulation of the question of fractions "; " the reservation to party cells in the first instance of decisions to apply disciplinary measures to members of the party "; and " the carrying out of elections to all party organs hitherto recruited by nomination ".[1] These demands, vague as some of them were, were clearly calculated to appeal to the rank and file. Yet the total impression was confused, and the call for democracy in the party carried little weight. Apart from measures of discrimination and repression applied by the party authorities, two defects continued to militate against the success of the opposition : lack of leadership, and reliance on discontent with the existing policy rather than on a positive programme of reform.

The members of the triumvirate, who learned of the contents of Trotsky's letter on December 8 or 9,[2] showed no great haste to react to it, and did not at once decide to treat it as a declaration of war on the resolution of December 5. A large meeting of the Moscow city party organization held in the columned hall of the House of the Trade Unions (the former House of the Nobility) on December 11, the day on which Trotsky's letter had appeared in *Pravda*, found the triumvirate without any clear or concerted plan of campaign. Kamenev opened the proceedings with a long and moderately worded defence of the central committee and of the " apparatus ", in which he referred to the attacks of Preobrazhensky, Sapronov and Smirnov, but did not mention Trotsky at all. Sapronov, who led for the opposition, did not show the

---

[1] *Pravda*, December 12, 1923 ; the same issue records two other similar meetings at which the official line was defended by Sokolnikov and Kamenev respectively. These were probably among the meetings at which Trotsky's letter of December 8 was read.

[2] According to a statement at the thirteenth party conference, Stalin was present at a meeting on December 8, and Zinoviev and Kamenev at meetings on December 9, at which the letter was read (*Trinadtsataya Konferentsiya Rossiiskoi Kommunisticheskoi Partii (Bol'shevikov)* (1924), pp. 131-132).

same restraint and interlarded his speech with quotations from Trotsky's letter. A general debate followed, with speakers for the central committee and for the opposition fairly well balanced. Radek, freshly returned from Germany, tried to take up a middle position; but the tone of his speech was hostile to the leadership. " The proletariat," he caustically observed, " which went through the civil war and has now spent three years studying Marxism, wants itself to discuss the affairs of the party." He regretted Trotsky's comparison of the old Bolsheviks with the German revisionists, but noted that Preobrazhensky and Smirnov were in agreement with Trotsky about Gosplan. He thought that both sides were " inflaming the question ". Zinoviev carried the debate on to a more sensational plane. Drawing attention to the fact that most of the present opposition leaders (Preobrazhensky, Osinsky, Radek, Pyatakov and V. Smirnov among them) had been Left communists in 1918, he recalled a recent (and apparently unreported) speech of Bukharin, who had described how in the Brest-Litovsk crisis Left SRs had approached the Left communists with a project to arrest the whole Sovnarkom " with Lenin at its head ", and the Left communists had seriously canvassed the names of a new Sovnarkom " with Pyatakov at its head ".[1] His handling of Trotsky, who in 1918 had stood with Lenin against the Left communists, was far more restrained. But he thought that Trotsky's letter " bodes no good ", and " we shall see how the matter proceeds ". He added ominously : " whoever violates the agreement which we reached will answer for it to the whole party ". Preobrazhensky did not mention Trotsky, but made a direct attack on the " leading triumvirate " in the Politburo, to which Stalin had referred at the twelfth party congress.[2] The triumvirate had, of course, no basis in the party constitution. But Preobrazhensky's attempt to depict it as an illegal " fraction " was a somewhat hollow debating point. Yaroslavsky, who was secretary of the central control commission and was beginning to be recognized as a Stalin man, made the only direct attack on Trotsky, whom he accused in bitter terms of attempting to destroy the party "apparatus". But the record shows that the passage was ill received and the speaker almost shouted down by a hostile audience. To attack Trotsky

[1] See *The Bolshevik Revolution, 1917–1923*, Vol. 1, p. 188.
[2] For Stalin's words see p. 284 above.

X

openly at a party meeting was still a hazardous and unpopular proceeding.

Kamenev wound up the debate in a speech which revealed a cunning consciousness of the need to walk delicately. He took Sapronov's quotations from Trotsky as his text. It was natural that Sapronov should declare his solidarity with Trotsky.

> It sounds well to say : " I am in agreement with Trotsky ". . . . That Sapronov agrees to accept Trotsky's formula in order to beat the central committee, I do not doubt ; but whether Trotsky is in agreement with Sapronov, I do not know.

Encouraged by the applause which greeted this passage, Kamenev went on to share Radek's regret that Trotsky should have " introduced the comparison of the ' heads of our party ' with the degeneration of Bernstein, etc." He suggested that Trotsky's article had dangerous implications, and concluded :

> Evidently Trotsky's article needs supplementing and explaining in order that, in the lower ranks of the party workers, doubts may not arise that Trotsky is demanding the removal of the " apparatus-men ".

The meeting then passed an anodyne declaration of confidence in the resolution of December 5 and in the unity of the party. Preobrazhensky pursued on this occasion the tactics of submitting a resolution which differed so little from the official line that it seemed difficult to quarrel with it. It hailed the resolution of December 5 as "a first step on the way to carrying out measures for which the party had long been ripe " and referred to it as " the new course of party policy ". It was none the less rejected by an overwhelming majority.[1] At the party conference a month later Stalin expressed hypocritical surprise that this innocuous

---

[1] A verbatim, though no doubt abbreviated, record of the meeting of December 11 appeared in *Pravda*, December 13, 14, 15, 16 and 18, 1923. Kamenev's opening speech and the text of the two resolutions appeared on December 13, Sapronov's speech and Kamenev's concluding speech on December 14 ; then followed the other speeches, probably in the order in which they were delivered. Stalin did not speak, though a reference to the meeting in *Sochineniya*, vi, 12, implies that he was present. Translations of Kamenev's and Zinoviev's speeches appeared in *Internationale Presse-Korrespondenz*, No. 7, January 18, 1924, pp. 52-59, 63-68.

resolution of Preobrazhensky should " for some reason " have been rejected.[1]

The Moscow meeting of December 11, 1923, deserves perhaps to be remembered as the last occasion of frank and fully reported public debate capable of swaying opinion within the party. A turning-point was at hand. The next two or three days were evidently occupied in anxious deliberation by the triumvirs. On December 13 Radek's reference to Trotsky's prestige and popularity in foreign communist parties, soon to be followed by the letter of the Polish central committee in support of Trotsky,[2] injected into the situation a fresh irritant and a fresh source of apprehension. On December 14 came another cautious leading article in *Pravda*, which deprecated any attempt to drive a wedge between older and younger generations in the party, but did not mention Trotsky's name.[3] Then, on December 15, a concerted offensive was opened. On that day *Pravda* carried an article by Stalin, who had not broken silence since his speech of December 2. He now suggested that the discussion was on the point of ending in the complete defeat of the opposition, which he described as " a bloc of a part of the ' Left ' communists (Preobrazhensky, Stukov, Pyatakov, etc.) with the so-called democratic centralists (Rafail, Sapronov, etc.) " ; and he went on to criticize in detail a speech by Rafail, who had compared the discipline imposed on the party with the discipline of an army, and articles by Preobrazhensky and Sapronov. Then, in a concluding section, which may well have been added as an after-thought, he abruptly turned to a sharp attack on Trotsky, who had not hitherto been mentioned in the article. Trotsky's letter could only be regarded as " an attempt to weaken the party's will for unity in support of the central committee and of its attitude ". Stalin quoted Trotsky's reflexions on the " transformation " of the Bolshevik " old guard ", and drove home with heavy irony what was to become henceforth one of his favourite themes — the hollowness of Trotsky's claim to be numbered among the old Bolsheviks :

First of all, I must clear up one possible misunderstanding. Comrade Trotsky, as his letter shows, counts himself one of the

---

[1] Stalin, *Sochineniya*, vi, 12.   [2] See pp. 234-235 above.

[3] This article is attributed, no doubt rightly, to Bukharin, then editor of *Pravda*, in *Diskussiya 1923 Goda*, ed. K. A. Popov (1927), p. 97.

Bolshevik old guard, thereby showing readiness to take on himself all possible charges which may fall on the head of the guard, if it really undergoes a transformation. It must be admitted that this readiness to sacrifice oneself is beyond doubt an honourable trait. But I must defend comrade Trotsky from comrade Trotsky, since he cannot and should not, for understandable reasons, bear responsibility for a possible transformation of the basic cadres of the Bolshevik old guard. The sacrifice is, of course, a fine thing, but do the old Bolsheviks need it ? I think they do not.

Stalin gently defended the old Bolsheviks against the charge of degeneracy : the danger of a transformation came surely not from them, but from " a part of the Mensheviks, who entered our party *unwillingly* and have not yet outlived their old opportunist habits ". Once again the hit at Trotsky was sly, but palpable. Stalin described " the unity of the ' old ' and ' young ' ", which Trotsky had tried to undermine, as " the fundamental strength of our revolution ". Finally, having hinted that Trotsky's letter was " diplomatic " and " two-faced ", he delivered the verdict in a single curt sentence :

> Comrade Trotsky is in a bloc with the democratic centralists and a part of the " Left " communists : that is the political meaning of comrade Trotsky's action.[1]

Nearly everything that Stalin was to say or write about Trotsky in the next four years was contained in embryo in these few paragraphs.

The same issue of *Pravda* which carried Stalin's article also printed a note signed by Stalin in his capacity as secretary of the central committee inviting party members outside Moscow " in every nook and corner of the U.S.S.R." to organize discussions of the party situation, " not, however, going so far as to form groupings, which were forbidden by the tenth congress of the party ". It also contained a report of an opposition resolution at a local meeting which, according to a brief editorial note appended to the report, was " made up of quotations from comrade Trotsky's letter " and was " an example of the fractional utilization of that letter ". On the evening of the same day Zinoviev, no doubt encouraged by Stalin's willingness at long last to come out into

---

[1] Stalin, *Sochineniya*, v, 383-387.

the open against Trotsky, opened his campaign at a large meeting of party workers in Petrograd. He began quietly by taking issue with Preobrazhensky on the admissibility of " fractional groupings " in the party. He pointed out that 55 members or candidate members of the central committee supported the majority, only 3 the case of the opposition. Then he unmasked his guns : " It is particularly disagreeable to me to dispute against comrade Trotsky in his absence, but unfortunately comrade Trotsky was unable to come ". He attacked the " democratic centralism " group with the familiar quotations from Lenin. On this subject Trotsky had at first " not spoken out clearly " ; but, when he saw that the central committee was determined to take action against " his present allies of the democratic centre ", he " abandoned his reserve " and wrote his letter on the " new course ". Having gone so far, Zinoviev receded a little and summed up this charge in more tenable terms :

> The attitude of comrade Trotsky is extremely unclear ; but we, the majority of the central committee, see plainly in it not a support, but a contradiction, of the attitude of the central committee and of its unanimous resolution.

Zinoviev then plunged into the past. " It is known to you that ' Trotskyism ' " — the first appearance of the word in the current controversy — " represents a definite tendency in the Russian workers' movement ". He passed lightly over Trotsky's neglect of the peasant — this theme had not yet been thoroughly worked up — in order to deal at length with Trotsky's long-standing conception of the party as " a conglomerate of individual fractions and tendencies ". Trotsky's attacks on the party apparatus and on the " old guard " of the party were inspired by the same conception, which was the antithesis of Bolshevism. In his peroration Zinoviev, as if frightened by what he had done, retreated once more to solid ground : " Come what may, the collaboration of comrade Trotsky in the Politburo and in other organs is indispensable ". But a cautious and shamefaced beginning had been made with the work of building up, side by side with the new and sacrosanct canon of " Leninism ", a new and satanic credo of " Trotskyism ".

Zinoviev's oratory, when not exposed to the ordeal of cold

print, proved as effective as ever. A long document, taking the form of a " letter to all members of the party" from the Petrograd party organization, was approved with only 5 noes and 7 abstentions in a gathering of 3000 persons. It accused Trotsky of violating the unanimity of the Politburo to which he had hypocritically subscribed only a few days before.[1] Similar meetings were now organized throughout the country ; and, from December 16 onwards, *Pravda* began to publish reports of meetings from many centres, almost all of which expressed confidence in the central committee and defeated motions of support for Trotsky and the opposition by overwhelming majorities — the technique already employed by Stalin in the trade union controversy three years earlier.[2] On the next day the Politburo, in Trotsky's absence, passed a resolution whose guarded terms betrayed the diffidence still prevailing among the leaders. It declared that Trotsky's letter (here referred to as an article) had been "utilized by the opposition to make the internal struggle more acute ", and had necessarily raised objections " on the part both of the central organ of the party (*Pravda*) and of individual members of the central committee (article of comrade Stalin) ". But it was a " malicious invention " to suggest that there was a single member of the central committee or of the Politburo " who could imagine the work of the Politburo, of the central committee or of the organs of state power without the active participation of comrade Trotsky ". The Politburo considered " friendly and joint work with comrade Trotsky " absolutely essential. By a coincidence the issue of *Pravda* which published this resolution [3] also carried a letter of one sentence from Trotsky in which he declined to answer in print the accusations which were being made against him.

The phase of the struggle in which the columns of *Pravda* provided a main battle-ground for the disputants was, however,

---

[1] The resolution was published in *Pravda*, December 18, 1923, Zinoviev's speech in *Pravda*, December 20, 21 ; none of the other speeches delivered at this meeting was printed in *Pravda* — a significant variation from the treatment accorded to the Moscow meeting of December 11. Translations of Trotsky's letter of December 8 with its postscript, of Stalin's article of December 15 and of Zinoviev's speech of the same day appeared in *Internationale Presse-Korrespondenz*, No. 8, January 21, 1924, pp. 69-82.

[2] See *The Bolshevik Revolution, 1917–1923*, Vol. 2, p. 223, note 1.

[3] *Pravda*, December 18, 1923 ; the resolution was reprinted in *Diskussiya 1923 Goda*, ed. K. A. Popov (1927), pp. 25-26.

now coming to an end. The new phase which began with the opening of the direct campaign against Trotsky on December 15, 1923, was accompanied by a significant change in the policy and management of the party newspaper. The announcement of November 7, 1923, throwing open the columns of *Pravda* to party discussion, had been followed by the publication in the section of the paper headed " Party Life " of many articles critical of the central committee. This section was in charge of a young man of twenty-three named Konstantinov, a party member of six years' standing. Early in December Zinoviev, alarmed at the large number of such attacks,[1] demanded to see the portfolio of unpublished articles, and from it selected four, whose publication he requested. The mild Bukharin, the responsible editor of *Pravda*, had no objection. But Konstantinov declared that this request was an act of " pressure " contrary to the resolution of December 5 on party democracy, and resigned when one of the articles was published. He was replaced by his assistant Vigilyansky, aged twenty.[2] When, however, the editorial board decided that Vigilyansky was too young for so delicate an appointment and placed a reliable party member over him, he also went on leave and did not return. These events, coinciding with the opening of the grand campaign against Trotsky and the opposition, were hailed on the one side as proof that Konstantinov and Vigilyansky had been engaged in making *Pravda* a tool of the opposition, and on the other as evidence that *Pravda* had now shed all pretence of impartiality.[3]

From this moment, therefore, the exceptional licence accorded by the announcement of November 7 tacitly lapsed. After the middle of December *Pravda* resumed its normal status as the organ of the central committee ; and, as the campaign grew

[1] It was afterwards stated that 44 per cent of the articles published in *Pravda* emanated from the opposition (resolution of the presidium of the central control commission of January 7, 1924, quoted in *Diskussiya 1923 Goda*, ed. K. A. Popov (1927), p. 44) — for what period is not clear.

[2] He was presumably the author of an article supporting freedom of discussion which appeared in *Pravda*, November 27, 1923, over the signature " N. Vigilyansky ".

[3] The report of the central control commission from which these particulars are taken is quoted in *Diskussiya 1923 Goda*, ed. K. A. Popov (1927), pp. 45-46 ; it may be assumed to put the case in the least favourable light for the two young men.

progressively more bitter, only a few further articles of the opposition — and then only with special precautions — were admitted to its columns. Rafail's rejoinder to Stalin's article of December 15, and a brief note by Sapronov, were printed in the issues of December 22 and 23, but were in each case both preceded and followed by articles supporting the central committee. Trotsky elaborated his views in two articles, *On Groupings and Fractional Formations* and *The Question of the Party Generations*, which appeared on December 28 and 29. The second article, which was written first,[1] did not repeat the panegyric of the younger generation which had given so much offence in the letter of December 8, but shifted the veiled attack on the old guard to a somewhat different, though related, ground : the power exercised by the party apparatus. The recent crisis had revealed "to what an extent the party is living on two different levels : on the upper level, they decide ; on the lower level, they learn about the decisions taken ". The older generation had become " accustomed to think and decide for the party " ; and " some comrades " had " sincerely not noticed the bureaucratic danger, being themselves the carriers of it ". The article *On Groupings and Fractional Formations* admitted that " some adherents of the old course " had voted for the resolution of December 5 " in the conviction that everything could remain as before ". But this was to evade the problem : " to declare groupings and fractions an evil is not in the least an adequate way to render their formation automatically impossible ". The article failed to resolve the inherent contradiction between the assertion of freedom of discussion in the party and the prohibition of fractional groupings ; nor did a reference to "the danger of *bureaucratic-conservative fractionalism*" really clarify the issue.

By way of counteracting any effect which Trotsky's articles might be expected to produce on the readers of *Pravda*, they were accompanied by the first two instalments of a long unsigned article from Bukharin's pen under the title *Down with Fractionalism*, which was described as "the reply of the central organ" to the

---

[1] In a note appended to the second article Trotsky explained it had been intended to precede the other and to appear on December 25 ; when its publication was delayed, he had reversed the order. They were reprinted in L. Trotsky, *Novyi Kurs* (1924), pp. 7-14, 22-31.

critics, and ran through five successive issues of *Pravda*.[1] It was the first systematic essay in that unashamed exploitation of Trotsky's past differences with Lenin which afterwards became a major feature of the campaign against him. Trotsky in his last article had appealed to his colleagues " to attempt to understand one another " first and " get heated " afterwards. It was Trotsky, retorted Bukharin, who had been guilty of " fractional heat " Three years ago Lenin had written of Trotsky, in the trade union controversy of the day, as "one member of the central committee out of 19, who collects a group outside the central committee, appears with the 'collective' 'work' of this group in the shape of a ' platform ', and invites the congress to ' choose between *two* tendencies ' ".[2] History was now repeating itself. " In questions of *internal party* policy the fraction of Trotsky, Sapronov and Preobrazhensky willy-nilly *departs from Leninism* " It was Bolshevism which had always stood for strict party discipline, while Menshevism was content with "freedom of opinions ", " freedom of groupings"," freedom of tendencies ". The hint of Trotsky's former Menshevik affiliations was not further developed. But no such restraint was shown in dealing with party history since 1917. In this period, wrote Bukharin, the party had passed through three major crises : the Brest-Litovsk crisis, the trade union crisis of 1920–1921 and the present crisis. In all of them Trotsky had endeavoured to fasten on the party a solution not in accord with reality. In the Brest-Litovsk controversy, he was associated with the Left communists, who preached either " revolutionary war " or " the

[1] *Pravda*, December 28, 29, 30, 1923, January 1, 4, 1924. The authorship appears to have been an open secret ; Stalin referred to it in his speech at the thirteenth party conference a month later (Stalin, *Sochineniya*, vi, 38). A translation appeared in *Internationale Presse-Korrespondenz*, No. 13, January 28, 1924, pp. 128-138. This article may be said to mark the definitive adhesion of Bukharin to the policy of the triumvirate. Alone of the members of the Politburo he had taken an independent line on the Georgian question (see p. 280 above) ; at the beginning of the discussion on democracy in the party he made a speech complaining that voting in local party meetings in Moscow had become a farce and that " elections to party organizations are being turned into elections in inverted commas " : this speech does not appear to have been published, but was quoted with effect by Trotsky at the thirteenth party congress in May 1924 (*Trinadtsatyi S"ezd Rossiiskoi Kommunisticheskoi Partii (Bol'-shevikov)* (1924), pp. 155-156).

[2] The passage is quoted from Lenin, *Sochineniya*, xxvi, 114 ; a few lines later Bukharin himself was denounced as "an accomplice in the worst and most noxious fractionalism ".

worthless formula: no peace, no war ". In the trade union controversy he had failed to understand the "mass psychology" of the peasants who demanded " the removal of the fetters of war communism".[1] Now he was exhibiting the same one-sided and utopian predilection for planning and for "the dictatorship of industry ". These considerations were offered in proof of Trotsky's "deviation from Leninism".

Trotsky's appeal to the younger generation against the potential degeneracy of the "old guard " was more effectively countered by quoting a speech of Trotsky himself at the eleventh party congress, in which he had said that youth lacked "the experience of the class struggle which created and hardened the party " and that " the young worker has not within him the foundation of class experience, of struggle ". But the element of prejudice was more conspicuous in Bukharin's article than the element of reasoned argument.

At the turn of the year the change of attitude in *Pravda* was the subject of a strong challenge from Trotsky, Radek and Pyatakov.[2] In a memorandum, which referred to "the régime of fabrications prevailing in the party section of *Pravda* ", they demanded the suspension of two workers on the paper, Nazaretyan and Sapronov, and the appointment by the Politburo of a committee to investigate their allegations and report within twenty-four hours.[3] The committee appears to have been appointed. The nature of its report can be judged from a resolution of the presidium of the central control commission of January 7, 1924, which, having censured the behaviour of Konstantinov and Vigilyansky, went on to explain that " the organ of the central committee is obliged to carry out the perfectly definite line of the central committee ". This sentiment was endorsed by the full meeting of the control commission a few days later;[4] and the

[1] Piquancy is added to these misrepresentations of Trotsky's position by the recollection of Bukharin's own attitude on both these occasions (see *The Bolshevik Revolution, 1917–1923*, Vol. 2, pp. 221-226, Vol. 3, pp. 36-40).

[2] Their collaboration in this matter probably preceded their joint theses for IKKI on the future of the KPD (see p. 237 above) ; but the precise chronology is uncertain.

[3] Quotations from the memorandum are in *Sotsialisticheskii Vestnik* (Berlin), No. 11 (81), May 28, 1924, p. 8 ; no complete text has been published.

[4] Both resolutions are quoted in *Diskussiya 1923 Goda*, ed. K. A. Popov (1927), p. 44 ; the latter is also in *Trinadtsataya Konferentsiya Rossiiskoi Kommunisticheskoi Partii (Bol'shevikov)* (1924), p. 191.

thirteenth party conference, with three dissentients, congratulated *Pravda* on having " taken up a fighting Bolshevik position and consistently defended the fundamental ideas of Leninism through the whole course of the discussion ".[1]   The party crisis of November–December 1923 was the last occasion on which *Pravda* provided a forum for the controversial pronouncements of conflicting groups within the party.   Thereafter it spoke exclusively with the official voice of the central committee or of the Politburo.

The history of the severe party crisis which came to a head in the last weeks of Lenin's life still contains many obscure elements.   The public events are well documented.   But evidence on which to base a reliable estimate of the forces in play is less plentiful.   In the autumn of 1923, at the acute stage of an economic crisis and with the party still disorganized by the confusion and uncertainty of Lenin's prolonged illness, the opposition could rally round itself a mass of potent, though vaguely formulated, discontent against a fumbling leadership.   Whatever else the rank and file of the party wanted, it could be won for the general proposition that a change of direction was needed at the top.   It was, no doubt, in the long run a source of weakness that the opposition relied mainly on a negative programme.   But for the moment the symptoms were sufficiently alarming to leaders jealous for their own supremacy.   " It was a struggle ", exclaimed Stalin in retrospect, " for the life and death of the party." [2] Rykov more realistically said that the struggle " brought the Moscow organization to the very verge of a split ".[3]   Since the party press tended to give prominence only to results favourable to the official line, it is difficult to gauge the amount of sympathy enjoyed by the opposition.   But there is a record of a large party meeting in a region of Moscow at which Kamenev, appearing as spokesman of the central committee, could muster only six votes against an overwhelming majority of opposition supporters ; and Rykov admitted that both Pyatakov and other opposition speakers

[1] *Trinadtsataya Konferentsiya Rossiiskoi Kommunisticheskoi Partii (Bol'-shevikov)* (1924), p. 218.

[2] Stalin, *Sochineniya*, vi, 253.

[3] *Trinadtsataya Konferentsiya Rossiiskoi Kommunisticheskoi Partii (Bol'-shevikov)* (1924), p. 91.

" frequently " obtained majorities at party meetings.[1] Nor could
support for the opposition always be measured by the voting
figures, since fear of reprisals, whether justified or not, certainly
operated as a restraining factor, particularly in the later phases
of the discussion. In a situation so delicately poised it is not
surprising that the attitude of the triumvirate towards Trotsky
should have been dominated by the determination to prevent this
formidable leader from taking the field against them.

The resolution of the thirteenth party conference afterwards
noted that the opposition campaign had been especially active in
the party cells in the army and in higher educational institutions ; [2]
and there is evidence to show that the apprehensions of the
triumvirate were particularly acute in these two quarters. The
prestige of Trotsky as People's Commissar for War stood high in
the Red Army and in the military administration. It was not
suggested, even by his bitterest adversaries, that he himself
attempted to exploit this in the party struggle. But two signatories
of the platform of the 46 — Antonov-Ovseenko, head of the
political administration of the Red Army,[3] and I. N. Smirnov,
an important member of the administration — were less cautious.
The charges brought against Antonov-Ovseenko were that he
organized meetings of party members in military training institutions for political discussions without the knowledge or approval
of the central committee ; that on December 24, 1923, he sent
out to party cells in military units a circular on internal party
democracy, disregarding a request from the party secretariat to
submit any such documents in advance to the central committee ;
and that, when called to order for this act of insubordination, he
wrote an insulting answer in which he accused the central committee of "shameless and unprincipled attacks on one who in the

---

[1] *Trinadtsataya Konferentsiya Rossiiskoi Kommunisticheskoi Partii (Bol'-
shevikov)* (1924), p. 108.   [2] *VKP(B) v Rezolyutsiyakh* (1941), i, 541.

[3] Antonov-Ovseenko was a former Tsarist officer who deserted after 1905
to join the Russian Social-Democratic Party, adhering to its Menshevik wing.
In 1915 he was the main promoter of the anti-war journal in Paris, *Nashe Slovo*,
in which Trotsky and Martov collaborated. In 1917, having joined the Bolshevik party with Trotsky, he was a member of the revolutionary committee
of the Petrograd Soviet and played a prominent part in the October revolution,
being himself in command of the detachment which seized the Winter Palace.
In October 1923 he signed the platform of the 46, and for the next two years
was probably, next to Rakovsky, Trotsky's closest collaborator.

eyes of the broad masses is the leader, the organizer and the in-spirer of the victory of the revolution ".   Antonov-Ovseenko was not surprisingly recalled from his post by the Orgburo.   It appears to have been the first case of overt disciplinary action against one of the 46.   Of Smirnov nothing more specific was recorded than that he encouraged hostility to the central committee in party cells in the Red Army, and then boasted that one-third of the cells supported the opposition.   For the moment he was left untouched.[1]

The other main danger spot was the mass of students in technical institutions and universities, whose youth and en-thusiasm easily ranged them on the side of the opposition.   *Pravda* of December 10, 1923, reported a recent series of meetings of 400 young party members from the training school of the People's Commissariat of Communications, at which such statements had been made, apparently with general approval, as that Gosplan was pursuing a policy of capitulation to the nepman ; that the party consisted of 40,000 members with hammers and 400,000 with portfolios ; that the central committee had driven the party underground ; and that the leadership was worthless since " there was a split in the Politburo even on such a question as the German revolution ".   If such sentiments were typical of the student body of the capital,[2] the alarm generated by Trotsky's sudden appeal to the younger generation as " the surest barometer of the party ", the safeguard against the abuses of bureaucracy and the degeneracy of the " old guard ", needs no explanation.

It is wholly inadequate [Trotsky had written] for youth to repeat our formulae.   Youth must adopt its revolutionary formulae fighting, convert them into flesh and blood, work out its own opinions, its own front, and be capable of struggling for its own opinions with the courage born of sincere conviction and independence of character   Passive obedience, mechanical

---

[1] The sources for these charges are a resolution of the central control com-mission of January 12-13, 1924 (*Trinadtsataya Konferentsiya Rossiiskoi Kom-munisticheskoi Partii (Bol'shevikov)* (1924), p. 190), and speeches by Yaroslavsky and Stalin at the thirteenth party conference (*ibid.* pp. 123-124 ; Stalin, *Sochineniya*, vi, 42-43).

[2] Yaroslavsky admitted at the thirteenth party conference that a majority of the party cells in higher educational institutions had voted for the opposition (*Trinadtsataya Konferentsiya Rossiiskoi Kommunisticheskoi Partii (Bol'shevikov)* (1924), p. 126) ; Zinoviev made the same admission in an article reprinted in *Partiya i Vospitanie Smeny* (1924), pp. 10-11.

uniformity under orders, lack of individuality, subservience careerism — out of the party with them.[1]

In the current atmosphere the words could hardly be read otherwise than as an incitement to the young to defy the edicts of the central committee. Weapons of defence were not easy to find. *Pravda* on January 1, 1924, published an article by nine members of the central committees of the Komsomol and Communist Youth International, in which Trotsky was accused of " dragging in the question of youth by the hair ", and Lenin quoted to the effect that "we must not flatter the young" and that "theoretical clearness and firmness " could not be expected from the young. Two days later Krupskaya, in an article stressing the need to recruit more workers into the party, added that this had been forgotten by Trotsky " when he appeals to the party to turn in the direction of the youth ". But this did not amount to much; and the article of the nine was answered by a group of eight members of the Komsomol (including two members of its executive committee) in a statement sent to Trotsky and published by him, defending Trotsky against the charge of flattering the young and of attacking the old guard.[2] Order was not restored till a majority of the members of the central committee of the Komsomol — 15 in all — had been dismissed and sent to the provinces; and discontent long continued to disturb the organization, and especially its Petrograd branch.[3]

The section of the rank and file of the party whom the opposition at this time was least successful in rallying to its side were the industrial workers. The material appeal of the opposition was to the interests of industry, but to the managers and technicians rather than to the industrial proletariat. Its ideological appeal for party democracy was to a western tradition which was powerful only in a diminishing minority of party intellectuals. Nothing either in its economic or in its political platform was likely to catch the imagination of the worker or to touch his immediate material interests; nothing was done to relate the platform to his current grievances. The principal members of the opposition were singularly free from the gifts of demagogy. The party

[1] L. Trotsky, *Novyi Kurs* (1924), pp. 81-82.   [2] *Ibid.* pp. 100-104.
[3] *XIV S"ezd Vsesoyuznoi Kommunisticheskoi Partii (B)* (1926), pp. 459-460, 526.

leadership had little difficulty in creating the impression that they were factious politicians, without a practical programme, anxious only to pick a quarrel with authority and to raise the banner of democracy in the interest of their own discontents and ambitions. " The workers will ask me ", cried a railway worker at the Moscow meeting of December 11, 1923, " what your fundamental differences are ; to speak frankly, I do not know how to answer." [1] In Moscow, at a time when a majority of the students in the party were voting for the opposition, the opposition could win only 67 out of 346 cells of industrial workers.[2]   While the reply that workers were afraid to come out on the side of the opposition for fear of losing their jobs had probably some foundation, there is ample evidence to support Larin's assertion that the opposition relied chiefly on the non-proletarian elements in the party.[3]   A dissident trade union delegate at the thirteenth party congress, a transport worker, who denounced the official wages policy, none the less joined with bitterness and vigour in the attack on Trotsky.[4] While the defeat of the opposition is rightly attributed to Stalin's infinitely superior skill in organization, it is also and more profoundly true that the opposition was doomed to fail because it lacked any broad social and economic basis of support within the party, and, specifically, because it dared not, and could not, identify itself with the cause of the industrial proletariat.   Some of the blame for the failure may be placed on Trotsky, who, by his policy of the militarization of labour and of the " statization " of the trade unions, had done more than anyone to justify the charge that the dictatorship of the proletariat had been transformed into a dictatorship over the proletariat, and had made it impossible to rally the forces of the proletariat behind him in the party crisis.   It was this paradox which made Trotsky in his new rôle as the champion of party democracy so vulnerable to the charge of inconsistency.[5]   But the real causes of the failure lay deeper. The small, vigorous and highly class-conscious section of the proletariat which had acted as the spear-head of the revolution in

---

[1] *Pravda*, December 18, 1923.

[2] *Trinadtsataya Konferentsiya Rossiiskoi Kommunisticheskoi Partii (Bol'-shevikov)* (1924), p. 134.

[3] *Ibid.* p. 67.

[4] *Trinadtsatyi S"ezd Rossiiskoi Kommunisticheskoi Partii (Bol'shevikov)* (1924), pp. 172, 174-175.   [5] See pp. 336-337 below.

Petrograd and Moscow had, in the hour of enthusiasm, carried on its shoulders the mass of semi-illiterate, semi-proletarianized peasants who still provided the majority of factory workers. In the aftermath of disillusionment, hunger and disorganization, the proletariat itself had begun to disintegrate. The flight from the factories and cities and the stagnation of industry brought with it more than economic disaster : it altered the balance of the social and political forces which made the revolution. The coming of NEP had arrested and reversed the process of economic decline, but had not yet affected the political consequences flowing from it. The failure of the opposition to base itself on the proletariat was a symptom of the weakness, not merely of the opposition, but of the proletariat itself. It was one more tragic illustration of the practical dilemma of the attempt to build socialism in a country which still lacked both the economic and the political presuppositions of democracy.

From the middle of December 1923 preparations went forward for the general party conference which was to meet in the middle of January. It was preceded by a number of other important gatherings in Moscow, all of them dominated by the struggle against the opposition. On January 6, 1924, the presidium of IKKI opened its session, and listened to a long statement by Zinoviev on the dissensions in the Russian party. Much of Zinoviev's speech was devoted to a heavy-handed effort to destroy the prestige and popularity enjoyed by Trotsky in foreign communist parties, which had become a matter of serious concern to the Russian leaders. Zinoviev began by defending the ban on fractions as an essential element of the Bolshevik tradition, and praised the party apparatus, unjustly assailed by the champions of party democracy, as the "iron instrument" for ensuring party unity. He refuted Trotsky's attempt to set the young generation against the old and to convict the Bolshevik old guard of degeneracy. Then he turned to Trotsky's economic criticism and hinted at his neglect of the peasant :

> He has no feeling for real economic relations in Russia : he never had it. That is a psychological factor which cannot be left out of account.

Even Trotsky's predilection for planning was a sign of bourgeois affiliations ; for Gosplan " consists of 300 professors and specialists, who were formerly active in economic affairs, whose experience and knowledge are very useful to us, but who nevertheless represent by and large ordinary bourgeois elements ". Trotsky's career was passed in searching and hostile review. His opposition to Lenin before 1914, at Brest-Litovsk and in the trade union controversy of 1920–1921 was recalled. He " overlooked the needs of agriculture ". He was " an outspoken individualist " ; for this reason he was " never able to create a solid fraction ". Zinoviev assured his audience that the supporters of the central committee in the rank and file of the party outnumbered the opposition in the proportion of nine to one; even in Moscow, where the opposition was strongest, it did not muster more than 20 to 25 per cent of the party membership. The speech ended with a bitter attack on Radek, and on the central committee of the Polish party for its " intervention in favour of the Trotsky faction ".[1]   Subsequent proceedings showed that Zinoviev had failed to dissipate the indignation aroused in many quarters in Comintern by the treatment meted out to Trotsky.[2]

The next occasion was a Moscow provincial party conference, which sat on January 10-11, 1924, under the presidency of Kamenev. It showed its unwillingness to proceed to extremes by electing Lenin, Zinoviev, Stalin and Trotsky (in that order) as honorary presidents and by sending greetings to Lenin and Trotsky, both absent through illness. Kamenev contrived to accuse Trotsky of opportunism and Menshevism and, at the same time, to describe him as essential to the party — an inconsistency with which Preobrazhensky taunted him in the leading speech for the opposition. Nevertheless, Kamenev obtained 325 votes for a resolution of confidence in the central committee ; only 61 delegates supported the opposition motion of Preobrazhensky, and nine a freak resolution of Ryazanov.[3] This easy margin of success in the stronghold of the opposition must have been reassuring to the party leaders. On January 12-13 the central

---

[1] *Internationale Presse-Korrespondenz*, No. 20, February 15, 1924, pp 215-226 ; for the Polish intervention see pp. 234-235 above. The Russian record of this session of the presidium of IKKI does not appear to have been published see p. 237, note 1, above).

[2] See pp. 240-241 above.   [3] *Pravda*, January 12, 13 and 15, 1924.

Y

control commission of the party met and passed a long resolution. It dealt with the behaviour of Antonov-Ovseenko and with the irregularities in *Pravda*,[1] and gave a strong hint to the party to show no tenderness to the rebels :

> The plenum of the central control commission draws the attention of the whole party to the necessity of eradicating and overcoming as quickly as possible those mutually embittered fractional relations which arose among some of our party comrades at the time of the discussion. . . . The best method of achieving this is, however, in the opinion of the plenum of the central control commission, not to relegate to silence and obscurity the differences which have arisen or may arise, but on the one hand to promote a comprehensive and full explanation of these differences, and on the other hand to carry decisively and actively into effect the resolutions adopted by the party.

Several paragraphs of the resolution formed the basis of the eventual resolution of the party conference on the results of the discussion. But the commission made one recommendation which was not endorsed or discussed by the party conference, and not carried into effect :

> The plenum of the central control commission thinks it indispensable to cancel the decision of the October plenum of the central committee and the central control commission forbidding the circulation of the correspondence of the central committee with comrade Trotsky and of all the documents leading up to the discussion — the appeal of the 46, etc. The limits of the circulation of these documents should be fixed by the presidium of the central control commission together with the Politburo of the central committee.[2]

These documents were never published or circulated to the party, and full texts are not even now available. The meeting of the central control commission was immediately followed, on January 14-15, by a meeting of the party central committee, which made the final preparations for the conference. According to the brief note of its proceedings which was published in *Pravda*, it heard reports from a number of members who had been working

---

[1] See pp. 319, 324-325 above.
[2] *Trinadtsataya Konferentsiya Rossiiskoi Kommunisticheskoi Partii (Bol'-shevikov)* (1924), pp. 190-192.

in the provinces, and who " sharply and categorically condemned
the line of the opposition (Trotsky, Radek, Pyatakov, etc.) ",
approved the resolution of the Politburo condemning Radek [1] and
fixed the agenda for the coming conference. [2]

Among the anxieties weighing on the party leaders as they
prepared for the conference, the question whether Trotsky would
or would not take the field against them in person must have
bulked large. The answer to the question was provided by a
bulletin signed by six Kremlin doctors, including Semashko, the
People's Commissar for Health, on December 31, 1923, and
published a week later. The doctors, having diagnosed Trotsky's
condition, ended with a recommendation :

> In view of the prolongation of the illness, which may take a
> more acute form in local climatic conditions, we consider it
> indispensable to give the patient immediate leave with release
> from all duties for a climatic cure for a period of not less than
> two months. [3]

Trotsky bowed to the recommendation, and left Moscow for the
Caucasus in the middle of January 1924 at the moment when the
thirteenth party conference was about to assemble. On the eve
of his departure a pamphlet was published under the title *The
New Course* containing his letter of December 8, 1923, his articles
which had appeared in *Pravda* during the same month, and four
hitherto unpublished articles on the theme of the party discussion.
In one of these, entitled *Tradition and Revolutionary Policy*, he
attempted a personal reply to attacks on his party record :

> I came to Lenin fighting, but I came to him fully and
> wholly. Apart from my activities in the service of the party, I
> can offer no one any supplementary guarantees. And if the
> question is to be put on the plane of biographical investigations,
> then it must be done properly. In that case it would be necessary
> to answer some pointed questions : Was everyone who was
> faithful to the teacher in little things faithful to him also in
> great things ? Does everyone who showed obedience in the
> presence of the teacher thereby guarantee his own consistency
> in the absence of the teacher ? Is Leninism confined to
> obedience ? . . .

---

[1] See p. 236 above.   [2] *VKP(B) v Rezolyutsiyakh* (1941), i, 533-534.
[3] *Pravda*, January 8, 1924 ; the earlier part of the bulletin has been quoted
p. 303, note 4, above.

The traditions of Bolshevism in their full amplitude are not less dear to us than to anyone. But let nobody dare to identify bureaucracy with Bolshevism or tradition with officialdom.[1]

The publication of the pamphlet was hailed as an admission that he had placed himself at the head of the opposition, though he was not present to sustain the rôle; and this made it doubly easy to treat him as the principal target for attack at the conference, even though he was not there to defend himself.

The thirteenth party conference opened on January 16, 1924, and lasted for three days. Conferences were smaller and less broadly representative, as well as less authoritative, than congresses; the conference of January 1924 mustered only 128 voting delegates. But the membership was recruited on the same basis. Delegates were selected by provincial party conferences, which were in turn composed of delegates from district or county conferences. The constitution of these conferences was a matter which, under Stalin's expert management, constantly preoccupied party headquarters. The platform of the 46 had already alleged that party conferences and congresses were gerrymandered by the " secretarial hierarchy ";[2] and the one point on which the triumvirate had withstood the inroads of workers' democracy in the resolution of December 5 was in insisting on the right of the central committee to nominate the secretaries of provincial and local party committees, who played an important part in making the elections. Not much is known of what happened outside Moscow in the election of delegates in December 1923 and January 1924. The opposition is said to have captured the party organizations in Ryazan, Penza, Kaluga, Simbirsk and Chelyabinsk — a result which an opposition spokesman plausibly attributed to the predominance in these provincial capitals of party officials transferred from the centre as a reprisal for their heterodox opinions.[3] But the core of the opposition was in Moscow; and it was here that the battle was fought and lost. Of all delegates to the conferences of district party organizations in the Moscow province which were held in December 1923, 36 per cent were supporters of the opposition. At the Moscow provincial party conference on

---

[1] L. Trotsky, *Novyi Kurs* (1924), pp. 48-49.   [2] See p. 298 above.
[3] *Trinadtsataya Konferentsiya Rossiiskoi Kommunisticheskoi Partii (Bol'-shevikov)* (1924), pp. 124, 133.

January 10-11, 1924, the immediate prelude to the all-Union conference, 18 per cent of the delegates belonged to the opposition. But both the elections themselves, and the calculations made as the result of them, were the subject of endless recriminations. Hitherto, where differences of opinion had occurred at local party conferences, it had apparently been the practice to elect delegates to the higher conference proportionally to the votes cast. Now, feelings ran so high that the majorities at the district conferences — whether for the central committee or for the opposition — attempted to appoint delegations representing exclusively the majority view; and this attempt sometimes succeeded and some times failed. Allegations of " pressure from the party apparatus " on the choice of delegates were freely made. The dwindling support accorded to the opposition was attributed by official spokesmen to growing realization of the dangers of a split in the party, and by the opposition to fear that anyone who came out openly against the central committee would lose his job; party officials known to favour the opposition had every reason to expect transfer to remote and less congenial posts. Direct and open reprisals were apparently not taken against critics of the party line, other than those formally condemned for " fractional " activities, before the thirteenth party conference. But indirect discrimination was certainly employed; and fear of these and more drastic measures to come was already a powerful factor in moulding party opinion and, still more, in determining the selection of delegates.[1]

Plans for the conference had been carefully laid. It had been decided that Rykov should introduce the resolution on economic policy, Stalin the resolution on party questions and Zinoviev the resolution on the international situation. Kamenev

[1] Evidence of these proceedings can be found in the speeches of Yaroslavsky, for the central committee, and Sapronov, for the opposition, at the thirteenth party conference (*Trinadtsataya Konferentsiya Rossiiskoi Kommunisticheskoi Partii (Bol'shevikov)* (1924), pp. 123-127, 130-131); the official records, though evidently censored to some extent, are still revealing. Two years later Krupskaya put the point bluntly at the fourteenth party congress : " If we go on writing resolutions about internal party democracy and at the same time create such conditions for every individual member that he can be transferred to another post for the open expression of his opinion, all one's good intentions about internal party democracy will remain on paper " (*XIV S"ezd Vsesoyuznoi Kommunisticheskoi Partii (B)* (1926), p. 572).

presided. His rôle was limited to formal opening and closing speeches and to a subsidiary speech in the economic debate; and it was noteworthy that his name now followed those of Lenin, Zinoviev and Stalin in the list of the presidium approved at the opening session.[1] When the conference began Stalin had already ceased to rank as junior member of the triumvirate. The debate on economic policy was the most prolonged, probably because it came first on the agenda rather than because it was regarded as the most important; it ended in the rout of the opposition in the person of Pyatakov.[2] Stalin then rose to deliver the most delicate and important speech of the conference.[3] He set the tone at the outset with a little mild banter on the sensitiveness of the opposition to attacks on Trotsky, who had never been slow to attack others. Then, taking his stand on the resolution of December 5, and adopting a schematic arrangement which became characteristic of all his major speeches, he enumerated two conditions of the realization of internal party democracy — the growth of industry and the industrial proletariat, and freedom from external menace — and three present obstacles to its realization — the psychological consequences of war communism, the pressure of the state bureaucracy on the party and the low cultural level of many party workers. All this was on the theoretical plane, and relatively uncontroversial. It was followed by a very brief retrospect on the recent stages of the party crisis, concluding with a reference to Trotsky's letter of December 8; and this led up to what was evidently the *clou* of the speech — a list of " six serious errors " involved in Trotsky's action.

The six errors were all related in one way or another to Trotsky's letter, which Stalin now for the first time unequivocally denounced as " a new platform opposed to the unanimously adopted resolution of the central committee ". The first was that Trotsky, by his action, had set himself apart from the other members of the central committee and against them, thereby violating fundamental party discipline; he had " elevated himself into a superman standing above the central committee, above its laws, above its decisions ". The popular charge against Trotsky

[1] *Trinadtsataya Konferentsiya Rossiiskoi Kommunisticheskoi Partii (Bol'-shevikov)* (1924), p. 4.
[2] See pp. 125-130 above.   [3] Stalin, *Sochineniya*, vi, 5-26.

of personal ambition was thus faintly hinted at. The second error was that Trotsky had failed to state clearly whether he was for or against the central committee, for or against the opposition ; the discussion had not been intended to encourage " evasions ". This was a shrewd thrust at Trotsky's major weakness — his undeclared and intermediate position in the party struggle. But it was Stalin who, by the compromise resolution of December 5, had helped to ensnare him in the trap. The third error was that Trotsky had opposed the apparatus to the party, as if party work could be carried on without the apparatus. Stalin did not, he suavely explained, dream of placing Trotsky on the same footing as the Mensheviks : but, all the same, this was an " anarcho-Menshevik view ". The fourth error was that he had opposed youth to the old guard : Stalin recognized the demagogic qualities of the appeal, and countered with some rather false pathos about the comparison of the Bolshevik old guard with the German social-democrats. The fifth error was the emphasis placed by Trotsky on the rôle of intellectuals and students in the party ; fortifying himself with quotations from Lenin, Stalin argued that Trotsky, by exalting the intellectuals, was depreciating the claims of the workers and proposing " to break with the organizational line of Bolshevism ". Finally, the sixth error was Trotsky's attempt to draw a distinction between groupings and fractions and to assert the admissibility of groupings : in the dangerous conditions of NEP the central committee would never tolerate groupings. Stalin kept his bombshell for the end. He read to the conference the secret " point 7 " of the resolution of the tenth congress on the conditions in which disciplinary action might be taken against members of the central committee,[1] and proposed that it should be included in the resolution of the conference and made public. The warning to highly placed members of the opposition was unmistakable.

Preobrazhensky replied to Stalin on behalf of the opposition. He devoted much time to the history of the dispute, and depicted a conservative and somnolent central committee driven to take action in October, and once again driven to accept the resolution of December 5, by opposition pressure. Alone among the opposition spokesmen, he had the courage to attack the central committee

[1] For the text see *The Bolshevik Revolution, 1917–1923*, Vol. 1, p. 201.

for its treatment of Trotsky as " an outsider in our Bolshevik family ", and protested against the revival of old quarrels for the purpose of branding the opposition as " Menshevik ", and the use of the term " Leninism " to justify bureaucracy. But his speech was coldly received by a well-drilled audience. After this the debate rapidly degenerated. Lominadze and Yaroslavsky, both eager to earn their spurs as Stalin men, saw no reason to imitate their master's studied restraint, indulged in much cruder abuse of the opposition and called for drastic measures. Yaroslavsky read alleged letters addressed to Trotsky by members of the Workers' Truth group and intercepted by the central control commission, thus attempting to involve Trotsky in complicity not only with the 46, but with an earlier and much less reputable opposition group. It was noteworthy that Lashevich, hitherto counted as an adherent of Zinoviev, in casually mentioning the members of the triumvirate by name, put Stalin first — perhaps the first time he appeared in this position. Two or three members of the opposition, including Radek, raised their ineffectual voices, and were subjected to mild heckling. " Perhaps we have only a few hours left of full democracy," cried one of the opposition speakers, Vrachev, to his interrupters; " allow us to use these hours ". And at the end of Vrachev's speech, when he was speculating what the secretary-general would report at the next party congress, Lominadze called out rudely from his seat: " You won't be there to hear ". Preobrazhensky and Stalin wound up the debate. Preobrazhensky tried, not altogether successfully, to refute the charge that the opposition had no positive policy.[1] Stalin's concluding speech, almost as long as his first and far more loosely constructed, ranged far.[2] Professing to be absolved from his former restraint by Preobrazhensky's excursion into party history, he plunged headlong into the campaign to discredit members of the opposition by digging up their past records. He spoke openly of " the opposition headed by Trotsky ", and pointed a finger of scorn at Trotsky as " the patriarch of bureaucrats " who now declared that " he cannot live without democracy " — the same Trotsky who had formerly

[1] The debate is in *Trinadtsataya Konferentsiya Rossiiskoi Kommunisticheskoi Partii (Bol'shevikov)* (1924), pp. 104-148.
[2] Stalin, *Sochineniya*, vi, 27-45.

demanded " a shake-up " of the trade unions from above.[1] Preobrazhensky had been against Lenin in the Brest-Litovsk debate, Sapronov at the tenth party congress; yet both now claimed Lenin as their master. Radek was one of those people who " are servants of their tongue and are governed by it ". The opposition, he concluded, " represents the tendencies and the strivings of non-proletarian elements in the party and outside the party ".

At the end of the debate on the party crisis it was announced that the conference would be invited at once to confirm the Politburo resolution of December 5, 1923, and that a further resolution would be submitted later on the results of the discussion. A minor contretemps occurred on the first point. A delegate from Kazakhstan handed in an amendment to the resolution of December 5, emphasizing the importance of " workers' democracy " in the party and especially in local organizations, and drawing attention to " the indispensable necessity of further bringing comrade Trotsky into participation in the work of leading the party and the country ". The president announced that an amendment had been received but, without disclosing its content, declared it unacceptable. The resolution was then put to the vote and carried unanimously. No protest against this procedure appears in the records. But the fact that the text of the rejected amendment was read from the chair at the evening session, though nobody spoke in support of it, suggests that influential objections had been raised to its suppression.[2] Party conferences and congresses were the last stronghold of the tradition of free speech in the party.

The third item on the agenda was the international situation. This was relegated to the last evening of the conference, and the proceedings were confined to two speeches by Zinoviev and a short statement by Radek.[3] Zinoviev began by retailing amid general hilarity the rumours about the Russian party crisis current in the foreign press — that Trotsky had been arrested, that Trotsky had taken refuge in an armoured train, that Krestinsky the Soviet Ambassador in Berlin was one of the leaders of the opposition

---

[1] See *The Bolshevik Revolution, 1917–1923*, Vol. 2, p. 221; for Trotsky's defence of bureaucracy at the time of the trade union controversy see p. 83 above.

[2] *Trinadtsataya Konferentsiya Rossiiskoi Kommunisticheskoi Partii (Bol'shevikov)* (1924), pp. 156, 180.

[3] *Ibid.* pp. 158-180.

and that the Soviet Union was on the eve of a " political NEP ". He spoke of the early prospect of recognition of the Soviet Government by Great Britain, France and Italy. He taunted the opposition with being unable to decide whether it wanted, like Krasin, to intensify NEP by further concessions to foreign capital, or to return to war communism. But the major part of his speech was devoted to the recent events in Germany; and here he too took his modest share in the work of discrediting Trotsky, and, more particularly, Radek. The appropriate resolution was then adopted.[1] But both the debate and the resolution were the shortest of the conference. The decisions relating to the KPD were being taken in IKKI. The contribution which international issues could make to the discomfiture of the opposition was still small and incidental.

When the international debate was over, it remained for the conference formally to adopt the resolutions on economic policy and on the discussion of the party crisis. The economic resolution was accepted with minor amendments. The party resolution gave more trouble. The central committee draft was confronted with an alternative draft submitted by Preobrazhensky, deploring the fact that criticism, whether of bureaucracy in the party or of an unsystematic economic policy, had been denounced as an attempt to destroy the authority of the central committee, and that the defence of bureaucracy was identified with defence of the principles of Bolshevism. But the conclusion was the vague recommendation of " a régime of activity on the part of the party masses ".[2] Preobrazhensky secured only three votes, the remainder going to the draft resolution of the central committee. This was a long and detailed history of the controversy designed to associate Trotsky unequivocally with the opposition, and to establish his baleful rôle as its leader and as the source of whatever authority it possessed. Trotsky was now openly held responsible, not only for the platform of the 46, but for the whole subsequent campaign against the leaders. The acute stage of the struggle had been initiated by his " fractional manifesto " of December 8. The

---

[1] For this part of Zinoviev's speech, as well as for Radek's statement and the resolution, see p. 239 above.

[2] *Trinadtsataya Konferentsiya Rossiiskoi Kommunisticheskoi Partii (Bol'-shevikov)* (1924), pp. 180-184.

opposition was described as " not only an attempt to revise Bolshevism, not only a direct departure from Leninism, but a plainly declared petty bourgeois deviation "; the label of " Menshevism " was avoided. The conclusions were set forth in fifteen points. These were, in brief : (1) to admit not less than 100,000 " workers from the bench " as new members of the party, barring entry meanwhile to all non-proletarian elements; (2) to admit non-party workers to all Soviets and Soviet organs; (3) to undertake " most careful explanatory work " in cells whose loyalty to the party line had been dubious; (4) to cut down the number of students in the party, but to improve their material position and " strengthen the quality of the work in higher educational institutions "; (5) to improve the study of party history, " especially of the basic facts of the struggle of Bolshevism with Menshevism, of the rôle of different fractions and tendencies at the time of this struggle, and in particular of those eclectic fractions which tried to ' reconcile ' Bolshevism with Menshevism " (these were the only mentions of Menshevism in the resolution); (6) to introduce in all party organizations " circles for the study of Leninism "; (7) to strengthen *Pravda* in order to enable it " systematically to explain the foundations of Bolshevism and to conduct a campaign against all deviations from it "; (8) to remove the present discussion from the columns of *Pravda* to a separate " discussion sheet " (this was perhaps a tactful way of ending the publication of dissentient views, since no further " discussion sheets " seem to have been issued); (9) to keep freedom of discussion within the limits of party discipline; (10) to impose severe penalties " down to exclusion from the party " for the dissemination of " unverified rumours " or prohibited documents; (11) to improve the circulation of party literature; (12) to " punish with particular severity " attempts to introduce fractional activities into the Red Army; (13) to confirm the prohibition of the tenth party congress on fractional groupings; (14) to publish the secret " point 7 " of the resolution of the tenth congress; and (15) to take the most decisive measures, " down to exclusion from the party ", against those who had organized a " fractional grouping " in Moscow. The resolution ended with a declaration that the discussion was now closed and with an appeal for unity.[1]

[1] *VKP(B) v Rezolyutsiyakh* (1941), i, 540-545.

The draft of the central committee having been approved by the conference, a few minor amendments were either accepted or rejected by show of hands. Two of these had some interest. On the proposal of Orjonikidze a phrase in the original text noting the adherence to the opposition of " a number of comrades who had entered the party from the ranks of the Mensheviks and SRs " was omitted; the intention was presumably to give an assurance that former Mensheviks or SRs who now remained loyal to the party line would not have their past brought up against them. The second amendment would have included among the 100,000 to be admitted to the party not only workers from the bench, but " poor peasants and agricultural labourers ". Stalin resisted this amendment on the ground that, though unexceptionable in principle, it would delay the urgent task of " drawing the industrial proletariat into the party "; and it was accordingly rejected.[1] Stalin at this time shared none of Zinoviev's enthusiasm for the peasant. The charge of under-estimating the peasant was one of the few elements in the later amalgam of " Trotskyism " which did not appear in Stalin's indictment of Trotsky at the conference.

Notwithstanding its formally subordinate status, the thirteenth party conference of January 1924 was a more decisive occasion in party history than either the twelfth congress which had preceded it in April 1923 or the thirteenth congress which followed it in May 1924. It put an end to the acrimonious discussion which had been shaking the party for more than three months, and reasserted the authority of the triumvirate against the challenge of the opposition. It had, however, a novel and disquieting character. It was the first representative party assembly at which it could be clearly seen that personalities rather than principles were at stake. To discredit the opposition, not to secure the adoption or rejection of a policy, was the primary preoccupation of the party leaders. The struggle for power had assumed a naked form. But the conference also marked a new and decisive stage in this struggle. Down to the middle of December 1923 the leaders had been anxiously concerned to drive a wedge between Trotsky and the opposition and to minimize the extent of the common ground between them; and a certain caution had been

[1] *Trinadtsataya Konferentsiya Rossiiskoi Kommunisticheskoi Partii (Bol'-shevikov)* (1924), pp. 184-185.

observed on this point even after the opening of the direct campaign of attack against Trotsky.   At the thirteenth conference this caution was thrown to the winds as no longer requisite.   The former tactics were reversed, and every effort made to identify Trotsky with the opposition in every particular.   This was the symptom of a new confidence felt by the leaders, and especially by Stalin, in the strength of their position.   No longer was it necessary for them to manœuvre to divide their enemies.   Both Trotsky and the whole opposition had been so far weakened and disarmed that the position could be carried by direct assault.

CHAPTER 14

THE DEATH OF LENIN

AFTER the stroke of March 9, 1923, Lenin was never able to utter more than a few incoherent monosyllables. His right side was for a time totally paralysed and his left side partially affected. When he was removed to the country villa at Gorki on May 15 the medical prognostications were " very gloomy ".[1] The change of scene produced some alleviation of the symptoms. A minor crisis in June was followed by a marked and progressive improvement during the next three or four months, which brought a partial recovery once more within the range of hope. Throughout this time Lenin communicated intelligibly, though painfully, by signs. The devoted Krupskaya read newspapers to him and attempted, apparently without success, to teach him to write with the left hand. It is probable that he never again saw any of his political colleagues after the stroke of December 1922. During the next three months, he communicated with them only in writing or through Krupskaya. After the stroke of March 9, 1923, it is specifically recorded that " he decisively refused all meetings with impatient political leaders ".[2]

[1] The most detailed and apparently reliable account of Lenin's last months was given three years later by Osipov, one of the physicians in constant attendance on him from May 1923 till the moment of his death (*Krasnaya Letopis'*, No. 2 (23), 1927, pp. 237-246). Medical accounts published immediately after his death (*Pravda*, January 24 and 31, 1924 ; *Izvestiya*, January 29, 1924 ; *Proletarskaya Revolyutsiya*, No. 3 (26), March 1924, pp. 16-23) are more conventional in tone, and, so far as can be judged, less accurate in detail.

[2] *Krasnaya Letopis'*, No. 2 (23), 1927, p. 243. Trotsky, *The Real Situation in Russia* (n.d. [1928]), pp. 304-305, and Chicherin in *Izvestiya*, January 30, 1924, specifically mention that they saw Lenin for the last time before the stroke of December 1922 ; no other political leader has claimed a later meeting. Zinoviev recorded an occasion when he, Kamenev and Bukharin were at the villa in Gorki, and watched from a window while Lenin was taken out for a drive (*Izvestiya*, January 30, 1924) ; but it is clear that they were not brought face to face with him. Zinoviev's statement reported in *Izvestiya*, August 30, 1923, that he had " seen " Lenin two days earlier evidently refers to this or a similar occasion.

On the other hand he received from time to time delegations of peasants and workers, presumably from the surrounding districts, and replied to their greetings with " friendly gestures ". He was regularly driven out in a car, and presently recovered the use of the paralysed right leg sufficiently to move about unaided. Once, on October 21, 1923,[1] he manifested a strong desire to be driven into Moscow and overcame the reluctance of those attending him. He was able to climb the stairs to his old office in the Kremlin and spent some minutes there, looking about him and idly fingering some books from the shelves. Then he was driven back to Gorki, which he never again left. In the late autumn a " new and final deterioration " set in. The last occasion on which he was able to receive a workers' delegation was on November 2.[2] But no specific symptoms of collapse were visible till January 19, 1924, when he appeared extremely exhausted and showed signs that his sight was affected. On Monday, January 21, at six o'clock in the evening, he had another severe stroke and died fifty minutes later.

During the whole of this time little information about Lenin's condition had been given to the world.[3] Towards the end of April 1923 the bulletins in the press ceased ; and those who had access to the confidential medical reports in May and June must have had ground to suspect that Lenin would never return. It may have sounded ominous in some ears when the central committee of the party decided, at the instance of a party conference in Moscow, to set up a Lenin Institute where Lenin's manuscripts and documents relating to him would be collected, and issued a notice signed by Stalin and Kamenev asking that any such material should be sent to the latter,[4] or when a " Lenin corner " commemorating Lenin's life and the history of the party was set up in the " central peasant's house " at the agricultural exhibition.[5] On August 30, 1923, which was noted as the anniversary of the attempt to assassinate Lenin five years earlier, *Izvestiya* reported speeches by Zinoviev and Kamenev describing a recent

[1] L. A. Fotieva, *Poslednyi God Zhizni i Deyatel'nosti V. I. Lenina* (1947), p. 23, gives the date as October 19.
[2] *Ibid.* pp. 23-24.
[3] For the first medical bulletins of March–April 1923 see pp. 266-267 above.
[4] *Ekonomicheskaya Zhizn'*, July 8, 1923.
[5] *Izvestiya*, August 28, 30, 1923.

improvement in his condition.   On October 9 the press published a detailed statement made two days earlier by Molotov at a training course for party secretaries.   Molotov reported that during the summer Lenin's condition had been very grave and had given rise to keen anxiety ;   in the last two months, however, his health had shown a great improvement, and the chief difficulty was now the restoration of his speech.   The statement ended by expressing hopes for his speedy and complete recovery.   A few days later Semashko, the People's Commissar for Health, made a similar statement at a festive gathering at the agricultural exhibition :

> Since the beginning of August such marked improvement has occurred in the health of V. I. Lenin as to surprise the doctors attending him.
> Vladimir Ilich in general feels well, reads the papers and is interested in various questions, including the exhibition.   But, of course, he must undergo a cure and a rest before he can again begin to work.[1]

Zinoviev spoke about the same time at a Komsomol meeting of a " continuous improvement " in Lenin's health during the past two months, adding the characteristically fulsome comment that " it is not the doctors who are directing the cure of the great leader, but he himself who directs the course of his cure " ; [2] and Tomsky followed suit by declaring that " the doctors are surprised at the change that has occurred, and assure us that now matters will improve rapidly ".[3]   Before the end of October this flow of reassuring statements came to a stop.   Thereafter the silence was unbroken by any official report.   But the mood of anxious optimism continued to prevail.   At a meeting of railwaymen in Bryansk addressed by Lezhava in the middle of December 1923 a voice called out :   " We want to know about Ilich's health " ; and Lezhava replied that Lenin's health was improving, and that " the time is not distant when, if he does not fully take over the rudder of administration, he will be able to give us directions and counsels ".[4]

The end came on the evening of January 21, 1924, before any news of Lenin's immediately critical condition had reached Moscow.   The second All-Union Congress of Soviets and the

[1] *Trud*, October 14, 1923.
[2] *Ibid*. October 18, 1923.
[3] *Ibid*. October 23, 1923.
[4] *Pravda*, December 16, 1923.

eleventh All-Russian Congress of Soviets were in session; earlier
in the day Zinoviev had just wound up the protracted session
of the presidium of IKKI.[1] The issues of the newspapers for
January 22 had already gone to press; but special sheets were
issued announcing Lenin's death. Late on the same evening the
leading Bolsheviks drove out to Gorki in sleighs. The party consisted of Zinoviev, Bukharin, Tomsky, Kalinin, Stalin and
Kamenev; Rykov was prevented from joining it by illness.[2]
Zinoviev has described the scene at Gorki. It was a frosty moonlit
night. Lenin's body had been placed on a table surrounded with
flowers and fir branches in a room opening on to the terrace where,
Zinoviev remembered, the leaders had met in the summer of 1920
to discuss the advance on Warsaw. Having paid homage to the
dead leader, they returned to Moscow to attend a ceremonial
meeting of the party central committee which had been summoned
for 2 A.M., and for which they arrived an hour late. Next morning
an autopsy took place, and it was announced that the cause of
death had been " disseminated arterio-sclerosis of the vessels of
the brain ".[3]

On the same day, January 22, the central committee published
its valedictory tribute. It was addressed " To the party, to all
toilers ". Before passing on to Lenin's achievements as the leader
of the October revolution, it described him (not quite truly, but
Trotsky was not there to protest, even had he been so inclined)
as " the man under whose leadership the invincible ranks of the
Bolsheviks fought in the year 1905 ". It noted Lenin's main
contributions to Marxist theory : " his elaboration of the doctrine
of the proletarian dictatorship, of the alliance of the workers and
peasants, of the whole significance for the struggling proletariat
of the national and colonial questions, and finally his teaching on
the role and nature of the party ". It spoke of " our whole
communist family " as " the collective embodiment of Lenin ",
and ended with a proud claim to pre-eminence :

[1] See p. 240 above.
[2] A long account of this journey was given by Zinoviev in *Pravda*, January
30, 1924. In the translation of the article which appeared in *Internationale
Presse-Korrespondenz*, No. 17, February 7, 1924, pp. 179-181, Stalin's name
was omitted from the list ; the omission can hardly have been other than accidental.
[3] *Proletarskaya Revolyutsiya*, No. 3 (26), March 1924, p. 17 ; the medical
communiqué appeared in *Pravda*, January 24, 1924.

z

In the European ruins we are the only country which is being reborn under the power of the workers and looks forward boldly to its future.[1]

The newspapers did not appear on January 23. The issue of *Pravda* of January 24 was entirely devoted to tributes and commemorative articles.

The succeeding ceremonial was the expression of a sincere and widely felt popular emotion as well as the first experience of the revolutionary régime in the organization of official pomp and circumstance. On Wednesday, January 23, the members of the party central committee proceeded to Gorki and escorted the coffin on the short railway journey to Moscow. On arrival there the funeral procession was joined by delegates of the second All-Union Congress of Soviets and the eleventh All-Russian Congress of Soviets, and walked to the House of the Trade Unions, where the body lay in state till the funeral, flanked by guards of honour drawn from the ranks of leading Bolsheviks. The conspicuous absentee was Trotsky, who, having left Moscow some days earlier on a trip to the Caucasus, received the news of Lenin's death in Tiflis on the evening of January 21. Next day, according to his own story, he telegraphed to Moscow to enquire about the funeral and was informed by Stalin that it had been fixed for Saturday, January 26, which would not have allowed time for the four days' railway journey from Tiflis to Moscow. (In fact, the funeral took place on Sunday, January 27.) Trotsky proceeded on his journey to Sukhum.[2] After the verdict passed by the thirteenth party conference three days before Lenin's death, Trotsky's absence from the ceremonies can hardly have been other than a relief to his colleagues. Stalin, for his part, had learned during the past year the importance of appearing in the rôle of Lenin's modest and most faithful disciple. The opportunity now occurred to put the lesson into practice, and he was unlikely to miss it. But not until the eve of the funeral did he strike a distinctive note. On that day, January 26, the second Union

---

[1] *VKP(B) v Rezolyutsiyakh* (1941), i, 557-558.
[2] The story is in L. Trotsky, *Moya Zhizn'* (Berlin, 1930), ii, 250, and is repeated in almost the same words in L. Trotsky, *Stalin* (N.Y., 1946), pp. 381-382. Whether the deception about the date was deliberate is doubtful; the change in date from January 26 to 27 was first announced in *Petrogradskaya Pravda*, January 24, 1924.

Congress of Soviets held a solemn session at which prominent Bolsheviks spoke in praise of their dead leader. Stalin spoke fourth, after Kalinin, Krupskaya and Zinoviev. While the other orators couched their eulogies in the traditional vocabulary of Bolshevism, Stalin's contribution was singular both in content and in form. In content, the relation of the party to Lenin was depicted as that of humble disciples honouring and obeying their founder, their law-giver, their leader, the hope of the dispossessed and despised throughout the world. The hard-headed analysis of Marx had given place to a devotional appeal. In form and in language, the speech, as carefully studied as anything that ever came from Stalin's pen, evidently owed its liturgical inspiration to Stalin's early ecclesiastical training. Its phraseology was biblical. Its structure was antiphonal, the enunciation of each successive " commandment " of Lenin being followed by a uniform response on behalf of the worshippers. The flavour of the document emerges from its opening paragraph and from the series of " responses " :

Comrades ! We communists are people of a special mould. We are fashioned out of special stuff. We are they who form the army of the great proletarian general, the army of comrade Lenin. There is nothing higher than the honour of belonging to this army. There is nothing higher than the calling of a member of the party whose founder and leader is comrade Lenin. Not to every man is it given to be a member of such a party. Not to every man is it given to endure the tribulations and tempests which go with membership of such a party. Sons of the working class, sons of need and strife, sons of unexampled privations and heroic strivings — such are the men who, first and foremost, are fitted to be members of such a party. That is why the party of Leninists, the party of communists, is also called the party of the working class.

Leaving us, comrade Lenin enjoined on us to hold high and keep pure the great calling of member of the party. We vow to thee, comrade Lenin, that we will with honour fulfil this thy commandment.

.   .   .   .   .

Leaving us, comrade Lenin enjoined on us to keep the unity of our party as the apple of our eye. We vow to thee, comrade Lenin, that we will with honour fulfil this thy commandment.

.   .   .   .   .

Leaving us, comrade Lenin enjoined on us to keep and strengthen the dictatorship of the proletariat. We vow to thee, comrade Lenin, that we will not spare our strength to fulfil with honour this thy commandment.

.   .   .   .   .   .

Leaving us, comrade Lenin enjoined on us to strengthen with all our might the union of workers and peasants. We vow to thee, comrade Lenin, that we will with honour fulfil this thy commandment.

.   .   .   .   .   .

Leaving us, comrade Lenin enjoined on us to strengthen and extend the union of republics. We vow to thee, comrade Lenin, that we will fulfil with honour this thy commandment.

.   .   .   .   .   .

Leaving us, comrade Lenin enjoined on us loyalty to the principles of the Communist International. We vow to thee, comrade Lenin, that we will not spare our lives to strengthen and extend the union of the toilers of the whole world — the Communist International.[1]

To many Bolsheviks reared in the western tradition such ritual exaltation of the leader must have sounded as alien as it would have seemed to Lenin himself. But for those who had grown up in a Russian environment without knowledge of the west it may well have struck some familiar half-forgotten chord of emotion, and lent to their mourning a sense of warmth and colour which were lacking in the austere intellectual climate of Marxism.

The same session of the congress which listened to these speeches also approved a number of proposals for the honouring of Lenin's memory. The first was to change the name of Petrograd, the city of the revolution, to Leningrad.[2] The proposal was presented by Kalinin in a formal speech on behalf of VTsIK and adopted without discussion. The hour was now late, and the

---

[1] Stalin, *Sochineniya*, vi, 46-51. The liturgical impression is enhanced in the collected edition of Stalin's works by printing the " responses " in capital letters throughout ; but this has no authority in *Pravda*, January 30, 1924, where the speech was originally printed, or in the official records of the congress.

[2] This was the first city to be renamed for honorific reasons after the revolution. The next was Ekaterinburg which became Sverdlovsk on November 7, 1924 (*Bol'shaya Sovetskaya Entsiklopediya*, 1 (1944), 407) ; shortly afterwards (the date is not recorded, *ibid.* xxvii (1933), 51) Elizavetgrad became Zinovievsk — the first city named after a living Bolshevik leader ; Tsaritsyn became Stalingrad on April 10, 1925 (*ibid.* lii (1947), 625).

remaining motions were adopted *en bloc* without further formality. It was decided to make January 21, the anniversary of Lenin's death, a day of national mourning, to set up monuments to Lenin in the principal cities of the USSR and to publish a collected edition of his works. The final decision was :

(1) to preserve the body of Vladimir Ilich Lenin in a mauso-leum, making it accessible to visitors ;
(2) to construct the mausoleum under the Kremlin wall among the fraternal graves of the warriors of the October revolution.[1]

Nothing is known of the original authorship of these different proposals or of the discussion of them which presumably took place in the Politburo or among the leaders. In the atmosphere of the moment any project to honour the memory of Lenin, once put forward, was almost automatically carried by acclamation.[2]

The funeral on Sunday, January 27, was conducted with traditional ceremony. At nine o'clock the coffin was carried from the House of the Trade Unions by Stalin, Zinoviev and six workers ; it was then taken over by Kalinin, Kamenev, Kursky, four workers and a peasant, and borne in procession across the Red Square. Here the multitudes stood hour by hour throughout the day in the intense cold, while innumerable delegates and representative persons laid wreaths and made speeches in honour of the dead. It was not till four o'clock that Stalin, Zinoviev, Kamenev, Molotov, Bukharin, Rudzutak, Tomsky and Dzerzhin-sky once more raised the coffin and lowered it into the hastily

---

[1] Only the decision to change the name of Petrograd was included in the official proceedings of the congress (*Vtoroi S"ezd Sovetov Soyuza Sovetskikh Sotsialisticheskikh Respublik* (1924), pp. 54-55) ; the others, not having been actually discussed at the congress, were published in *2ᵗ S"ezd Sovetov Soyuza Sovetskikh Sotsialisticheskikh Respublik: Postanovleniya* (1924), pp. 7-9.

[2] The party tradition that Krupskaya was opposed to much of this com-memorative ceremonial, including the embalming of Lenin's body, lacks documentary evidence, but derives some confirmation from Krupskaya's letter of thanks for messages of condolence published in *Pravda*, January 30, 1924 : " I have a great request to you : do not allow your mourning for Ilich to take the form of external reverence for his person. Do not raise memorials to him, palaces named after him, solemn festivals in commemoration of him, etc. : to all this he attached so little importance in his life, all this was so burdensome to him. Remember how much poverty and neglect there still is in our country. If you wish to honour the name of Vladimir Ilich, build crèches, kindergartens, houses, schools, libraries, medical centres, hospitals, homes for the disabled, etc., and, most of all, let us put his precepts into practice."

constructed vault in front of the Kremlin wall — soon to be replaced by the more permanent mausoleum.[1] Through the next days and weeks Soviet newspapers and periodicals carried articles praising Lenin and relating the experiences and impressions of their authors in meetings with him. Of all these commemorative writers Zinoviev was the most copious and eloquent. His association with Lenin in Switzerland throughout the war gave him a unique place in party history. He had returned to Petrograd in April 1917 in the sealed train as the leader's recognized and indispensable first lieutenant; and when, in the "July days", the party decided that its leader must at all costs not expose himself to arrest, it was Zinoviev who accompanied Lenin into hiding. His opposition to the seizure of power, and Lenin's castigation of him at the time, were scarcely known except to the few party stalwarts in the central committee. When Lenin died it was easy for Zinoviev to build up for himself an almost uncontested position as Lenin's most intimate follower and the high priest of the new creed of Leninism.

Lenin is dead [ran the peroration of his long commemorative article in *Pravda* on January 30], Leninism lives. It lives in our great party, in Comintern, in the revolutionary movement of the whole world. When the proletarian revolution conquers throughout the world, that will be first and foremost the victory of Leninism.

Stalin, who had not much to boast of in the way of personal association with the dead leader, behaved with self-effacing modesty. But his speech at the Union Congress of Soviets was followed on the day after the funeral by an address to students of the party military school in the Kremlin. Here, before reaching the customary eulogies of the revolutionary leader and genius, he briefly told the story of his own early meetings with Lenin — at Tammerfors, in Stockholm, in London — prefacing it with a

---

[1] The arrangement of names in the report of the funeral in *Pravda*, January 30, 1924, cannot be fortuitous, and it is significant that Stalin is mentioned first in the party newspaper at the opening and concluding stages of the ceremony; there is, however, no other indication of any special importance attached to him or to his office. *Trud*, January 30, 1924, named "Zinoviev, Tomsky, Kamenev, Stalin and others" as those who carried the coffin to the vault. Subsequent accounts (e.g. the chronology in Stalin, *Sochineniya*, vi, 418-419) which make Stalin the most prominent figure throughout the proceedings are not confirmed by contemporary records.

new episode for which there is no other authority beyond this single mention by himself. He related how, on reading the first numbers of *Iskra* and other early party writings, he had been impressed to find that Lenin stood out head and shoulders above all the other Bolsheviks like " a mountain eagle ". He wrote of this impression to an unnamed friend, who showed the letter to Lenin ; and at the end of 1903 Stalin, then in exile in Siberia, received from Lenin " a simple but deeply significant letter ", which " through the habits of an old underground worker " he had immediately burned.[1] Austere critics have relegated this story to the category of historical fiction. Whether true or false, its function in its present context was clear. It strengthened Stalin's credentials as an old Bolshevik who thus early in the history of the party had attracted the attention of the future leader. Trotsky had first come to Lenin in London in 1902.

The formal succession to Lenin's public offices gave no trouble and was a matter of no great moment. Rykov became president of the Sovnarkom of the USSR, combining this post with that of president of the Sovnarkom of the RSFSR : he was succeeded as president of Vesenkha by Dzerzhinsky. Kamenev took Lenin's place as president of STO, and Tsyurupa succeeded Krzhizhanovsky as president of Gosplan : these two also became deputy presidents of Sovnarkom. Lenin had been both leader of the party and head of the state executive. These appointments, which were confirmed by TsIK on February 2, 1924,[2] showed that there was henceforth to be a division of function, and that the centre of gravity resided in the party. A few days after Lenin's funeral the central committee of the party met to confirm the resolutions of the thirteenth party conference ; since this had been only a conference, its findings lacked formal authority till they were endorsed by the central committee in the name of the sovereign congress. The moral of the conference resolution " On the Results of the Discussion ' was driven home by pointing to the ever greater need for party unity " now that comrade Lenin has fallen out of the

[1] Stalin, *Sochineniya*, vi, 52-54 ; the address was originally published in *Pravda*, February 12, 1924.
[2] *Pervaya Sessiya Tsentral'nogo Ispolnitel'nogo Komiteta Soyuza Sovetskikh Sotsialisticheskikh Respublik* (1924), pp. 5-6, 8.

ranks ".[1] But the main business was to make arrangements for the recruitment of "workers from the bench" into the party, which had been decided on at the conference. The central committee now declared that the death of Lenin had intensified the pressure among the workers for admission to the party, and decreed a three months' recruiting campaign. The rules governing admission were relaxed to the extent that workers applying for it were to be brought into touch with existing members, if possible workers from the same factory, who could attest their reliability. General meetings of workers would be summoned for this purpose; but admission presupposed "the preliminary scrutiny of every individual candidature", and special precautions must be taken with former members of other parties. Finally, the teaching in party schools for members and candidates for membership must be reviewed in order to ensure "that the chief attention in these schools of *politgramota* will be concentrated on the history of the party in connexion with the exclusive rôle played in it by the leading ideas of comrade Lenin ".[2]

The decision to swell the party ranks by a large recruitment of "workers from the bench" had attracted no great attention at the January conference, and seemed more like a conventional gesture to the doctrine of party democracy than an innovation in practice. It proved highly significant in regard both to the numbers and to the composition of the party. From small beginnings the party had expanded steadily after the February revolution of 1917, and still more after the seizure of power in October. Before the first great purge of 1921 the membership had stood at rather more than 650,000. The purge dramatically reversed this process of growth. Not only did it reduce the membership to less than 500,000 at a single stroke,[3] but it set a precedent of stringent periodical reviews of membership, which had further reduced the total to 350,000, together with 120,000 candidates, by the beginning of 1924.[4] These decisions reflected

---

[1] *VKP(B) v Rezolyutsiyakh* (1941), i, 559.   [2] *Ibid.* i, 561-562.
[3] See *The Bolshevik Revolution, 1917–1923*, Vol. i, pp. 205-207.
[4] A. Bubnov, *VKP(B)* (1931), p. 613. The system of "candidates" was first laid down in the revised statute approved by the party conference of December 1919 : candidates for admission to the party remained on probation for not less than two months in the case of workers and peasants, not less than six months in the case of others (*VKP(B) v Rezolyutsiyakh* (1941), i, 318).

Lenin's emphatically expressed views. In 1919 he had boasted that " the party of the revolutionary working class " was " the only party in power which concerns itself not with increasing its membership, but with improving its quality " ; [1] and on the eve of the eleventh party congress of 1922, the last which he attended, he was still pressing for stricter limitation of party membership :

> If we have in the party 300,000 to 400,000 members, even such a number is excessive, since decidedly these facts point to an insufficient level of preparation among members of the party.[2]

The decision of the thirteenth party conference of January 1924, taken while Lenin was on his death-bed, reversed this process of contraction, and provided for an accretion to party ranks which would automatically provide an answer to the demand for more " party democracy ". From this moment onwards the party was launched on a process of expansion, which continued without interruption throughout all its later vicissitudes.

The decision to confine the new recruitment to " workers from the bench " proved equally significant, but represented no novelty in party doctrine. The weakness of the proletarian element in the party had been a standing complaint from the earliest years of its existence : Lenin at the third party congress in 1905 had demanded that party committees should contain eight workers to every two intellectuals.[3] The rapid increase in the size of the party after the October revolution presented new problems by bringing into it large numbers of recruits who " join the ruling party simply because it is the ruling party ". Among those who joined it for careerist reasons, non-proletarians were, if not the most numerous, at any rate the most conspicuous ; and it was reasonable to assume that the evil could be countered by limiting the proportion of non-proletarian members. Lenin concluded his diagnosis of the problem at the end of 1919 by recommending the party " to admit, apart from the working class, only those products of other classes

The periods of probation were later substantially increased (*ibid*. i, 432, 454). Before 1922 candidates were not included in the statistics of party membership (A. Bubnov, *VKP(B)* (1931), p. 612).
    [1] Lenin, *Sochineniya*, xxiv, 484.   [2] *Ibid*. xxvii, 209.
    [3] *Ibid*. vii, 282 ; cf. Krupskaya, *Memories of Lenin* [i] (Eng. transl., 1930), p. 140.

whom it is able to test with the utmost experience ".[1] The most
recent specific party pronouncement on the subject was a decision
of the ninth party conference in September 1920 to regulate
admissions to the party in such a way as " to reduce all formalities
for workers and for proletarian elements of the peasantry, and to
increase to the maximum the obstacles to the entry of non-
proletarian elements into the party ".[2] In this respect the decision
of the January conference fully corresponded to the views of
Lenin and every other responsible party leader.

Throughout February, March and April 1924 what came to
be known in party history as " the Lenin enrolment " went on.
The rules of admission had been laid down with such vagueness
as to leave an almost unlimited discretion to local party officials ;
and the efficient party machine created by Stalin's secretariat had
an opportunity of proving itself. When the central committee met
at the end of March to make preparations for the thirteenth party
congress, it decided that candidates for membership of the party
(meaning, presumably, those registered as such by the local
party organs) should be entitled to vote on the same footing as
members in the election of delegates to the party congress.[3] This
ensured that the new enrolment would carry its full weight at the
congress even if there had not been time enough to complete the
procedures of admission. When the congress met at the end of
May 1924 it was announced that 128,000 new members had been
admitted before May 1, bringing the total membership of the
party up to 600,000, and that by the end of May it was hoped to
have raised the number of new admissions to 200,000.[4] In the
event, even this limit was exceeded ; the " Lenin enrolment "
reached 240,000, increasing the total membership of the party,
including candidates, by more than 50 per cent. Since the new
members were almost all " workers from the bench ", the proportion of industrial workers in the party rose for the first time
to well over a half. The already heavy preponderance of the

[1] Lenin, *Sochineniya*, xxiv, 571-572.
[2] *VKP(B) v Rezolyutsiyakh* (1941), i, 350-351.
[3] *Ibid.* i, 563 ; this decision, which was a contravention of the party statute,
required and obtained the subsequent endorsement of the congress itself
(*Trinadtsatyi S"ezd Rossiiskoi Kommunisticheskoi Partii (Bol'shevikov)* (1924),
pp. 12-13).
[4] *Ibid.* p. 122.

Great Russian element was also increased, since Great Russians still supplied an overwhelming majority of industrial workers.[1]

The most important change brought about by the Lenin enrolment was, however, in the political implications of party membership. With the achievement of power the party itself had changed its character. Not all Lenin's efforts could keep alive the conception of the party as a homogeneous group of devoted revolutionaries in conditions where this conception was, in fact, no longer applicable. After 1917, and still more clearly after 1921, the party was no longer an association of bold adventurers banded together to win freedom by overthrowing the rule of injustice and oppression; it was imperceptibly transformed into a political machine geared to manage and supervise the affairs of a great state. The older members of the party were enthusiastic intellectuals or thoroughly class-conscious workers who had joined it in order to achieve the revolution. But by 1923 only 10,000 of these " old Bolsheviks " remained ; and not all of these were still active.[2] Of those who had entered the party since 1917, many — especially, perhaps, the young — had been fired by sincere revolutionary ardour, had sacrificed themselves in the precarious battles of the civil war and had laboured unsparingly for the building of a new socialist society. But, as time went on, an increasing number of the new recruits were men who, having remained outside the party in the period of storm and stress, now entered it not to overthrow an old order or to demand new rights, but to conserve an established organization and to enjoy the privileges of participation in it. Down to the time of Lenin's death the self-seekers in the party had perhaps been found mainly among members recruited from the former bourgeoisie — its intellectuals and its managers ; and what these had sought in the party ticket was an avenue to influence and authority quite as much as to material advancement. Indeed the restrictions still in

---

[1] According to Molotov, a Ukrainian party conference had named 65-70 per cent as its target for the proportion of workers in the party at a time when it already contained more than 70 per cent of workers (*Trinadtsatyi S"ezd Rossiiskoi Kommunisticheskoi Partii (Bol'shevikov)* (1924), p. 535) ; the high proportion of workers in the Ukrainian party was doubtless connected with Great Russian predominance in it (see *The Bolshevik Revolution, 1917–1923*, Vol. 1, p. 290).

[2] *Dvenadtsatyi S"ezd Rossiiskoi Kommunisticheskoi Partii (Bol'shevikov)* (1923), p. 134.

force on the earnings of party members often meant that a party member employed in economic administration received less in terms of financial reward than his non-party colleague. The Lenin enrolment opened fresh inducements of self-interest to a wider class. It was the first large-scale recruitment to the party planned and organized for a conscious and specific purpose. Members of the party had always thought of themselves as possessing special privileges and special duties. But the privileges now for the first time began to assume a predominantly material form — in times of unemployment party members were the first to be chosen and the last to be discharged; and among the duties whose punctual performance guaranteed the enjoyment of the privileges the duty of loyalty to the party authorities ranked higher than ever before. The Lenin enrolment was undertaken under the pervading influence of the struggle with the opposition. It seemed both a celebration of the victory just achieved and a guarantee against any renewal of the struggle. The unity of the party and fidelity to its leaders were proclaimed more clearly than ever as the supreme ideal. " The development of the party in the future ", declared Molotov, " will undoubtedly be based on this Lenin enrolment." [1]

The progress of the Lenin enrolment was accompanied by a corresponding purge. No formal party decision to set the purge machinery in motion was recorded, and what was done probably did not differ from the periodical reviews of membership which had been carried out from time to time since the original purge of 1921. It was not the first time that abuses had occurred in the conduct of the purges; Lenin, shortly before his last stroke, had emphatically complained of the prevalence of " a squaring of personal or local accounts " in the practice of the local party commissions in charge of the purge.[2] Now the process was bound to fall most heavily on supporters of the opposition. The accusations of discrimination against them made by Preobrazhensky, both privately and at the thirteenth party congress, may have been exaggerated, but are not likely to have been unfounded. It would have been better, complained Preobrazhensky, if members had been openly expelled for their support of the opposition

---

[1] *Trinadtsatyi S"ezd Rossiiskoi Kommunisticheskoi Partii (Bol'shevikov)* (1924), p. 515.

[2] Lenin, *Sochineniya*, xxvii, 300.

instead of on pretexts which left them "politically and morally dishonoured ". According to official spokesmen, the purge was confined in the first instance to the four cities of Moscow, Leningrad, Odessa and Penza, was directed against " non-proletarian elements " which had "attached themselves to the party " and included " unprincipled people who had .ven voted in favour of the central committee ". It was admitted that " mistakes " had been made.[1] Coming at this moment, the purge could not fail to be felt as a fresh weapon in the hands of a party leadership determined to enforce disciplined obedience to its decisions — a weapon less discreet, but more promptly and ruthlessly effective, than the control of admissions to the party. But an incident of the period which received publicity in *Pravda* — no doubt as a warning to others — was a better index of the promptness of the party authorities to take disciplinary action. Two young party members were convicted of " distributing secret documents, knowing that they were secret and that the party did not permit their publication ". The offence was admitted, and seriously aggravated by the refusal of the accused to divulge to the central control commission of the party the names of those from whom they had obtained the documents. This was described in the report of the commission as " a question of principle " : Lenin in one of his last articles had described it as the duty of the central control commission to ensure that " no authority should prevent it from conducting an examination, verifying documents and obtaining unconditional information ". The two offenders were expelled from the party with permission to apply for re-instatement in six months' time — presumably on condition of disclosing the required names.[2]

While the Lenin enrolment was in progress, Stalin repeated on a larger scale his gesture of the previous spring when, in advance of the twelfth party congress, he had given two lectures to a workers' club and to the Sverdlov university, which revealed him as an earnest student and disciple of Lenin the revolutionary theorist.[3] Now, a year later, on the eve of the thirteenth congress, he once more entered the field of party doctrine with a series of

[1] *Trinadtsatyi S"ezd Rossiiskoi Kommunisticheskoi Partii (Bol'shevikov* (1924), pp. 202-203, 208, 234-235, 283-285.
[2] *Pravda*, February 22, 1924.   [3] See pp. 274-275 above.

lectures at the Sverdlov university, which appeared in *Pravda* in April and May 1924 entitled *On the Foundations of Leninism*. His exposition of Leninism, which he defined as " Marxism of the epoch of imperialism and of the proletarian revolution ", was bald, orderly and highly schematic. It wisely made no claim to originality or profundity, but once more showed its author in the rôle of a patient and faithful disciple. A few points only seemed significant. In the section on theory, without mentioning Trotsky by name, he attacked the champions of " permanent revolution ", and endeavoured to explain how the teaching of Lenin (who, like Marx, had also used the phrase) differed from theirs :

> Lenin proposed to " exhaust " the revolutionary capacities of the peasantry, to drain the revolutionary energy of the peasantry to the bottom in order completely to liquidate Tsarism and to bring about the transition to the proletarian revolution, whereas the advocates of " permanent revolution " did not understand the weighty rôle of the peasantry in the Russian revolution, under-estimated the strength of the revolutionary energy of the peasantry, under-estimated the strength and capacity of the Russian proletariat to draw the peasantry after it, and thus made difficult the liberation of the peasantry from the influence of the bourgeoisie, the grouping of the peasantry around the proletariat. . . . Lenin proposed to crown the work of revolution by the transfer of power to the proletariat, whereas the advocates of " permanent " revolution thought to *begin* the work directly from the power of the proletariat.[1]

Having thus attempted to disqualify Trotsky's claim to be a follower of Lenin by convicting him of support of a non-Leninist doctrine, of neglect of the peasantry and (more subtly) of a failure to understand peculiarly Russian conditions, Stalin none the less proceeded, in a passage which underwent omissions and modifications in later editions, to re-state the conventional position that socialism could be realized only on an international basis :

> But to overthrow the power of the bourgeoisie and establish the power of the proletariat in one country does not yet mean the complete victory of socialism. The principal task of socialism — the organization of socialist production — has still

[1] Stalin, *Sochineniya*, vi, 103 ; for Lenin's and Trotsky's views on permanent revolution before 1917 see *The Bolshevik Revolution, 1917–1923*, Vol. 1, pp. 56–60.

to be fulfilled. Can this task be fulfilled, can the final victory
of socialism be achieved, in one country, without the joint
efforts of the proletarians in several advanced countries ? No,
it cannot. To overthrow the bourgeoisie the efforts of one
country are sufficient ; this is proved by the history of our
revolution. For the final victory of socialism, for the organization of socialist production, the efforts of one country, particularly of a peasant country like Russia, are insufficient ; for that,
the efforts of the proletarians of several advanced countries are
required.[1]

In a later section on the peasantry, Stalin guarded himself
against the opposite extreme of enthusiasm for the peasant professed in some party circles. It was, he declared, " completely
untrue " to treat the peasant question as " the fundamental in
Leninism ". The fundamental question was the dictatorship of
the proletariat : Leninism was a doctrine " which regards the
toiling masses of the peasantry as a reserve of the proletariat ".
Stalin was, even at this date, cautiously steering a middle course.
But there was nothing in his pedestrian pronouncements to attract
the attention, favourable or unfavourable, of the other party
leaders ; nor does anyone seem to have attached any particular
importance to his appearance in a field where he had hitherto
shown little ambition to shine.

On the eve of the thirteenth party congress in May 1924 an
embarrassing scene was enacted. Lenin's " testament " seemed
by its highly personal character designed for his immediate
party colleagues rather than for the party as a whole ; on the
other hand, Krupskaya, who must have known Lenin's wishes
and intentions, desired that it should be read at the forthcoming
congress, which could then pass judgment and take action on it.
There is no evidence to show at what moment the party leaders
became cognizant of the contents and text of the testament. But
the consternation with which it was received by them can be
easily imagined. Zinoviev and Kamenev were pointedly reminded
that their failure at the crucial moment of the revolution was " not

---

[1] This passage appeared in *Pravda*, April 30, 1924, and in *Ob Osnovakh
Leninizma* (1924), p. 60, and was quoted by Stalin himself in a pamphlet, *K
Voprosam Leninizma*, of January 1926, where he explained that it represented
an " incomplete and therefore incorrect " formulation, and had been modified
in editions of the pamphlet subsequent to December 1924 (Stalin, *Sochineniya*,
viii, 61-62).

accidental "; Trotsky, though criticized for his shortcomings, was described as " the most able man in the present central committee "; Stalin, treated in the testament itself with carefully balanced commendation and criticism, was the target of a direct attack in the postscript, which recommended his removal from the post of general secretary of the party.[1] Both the question of the action to be taken on the testament and the question of the publicity to be given to it were acutely delicate. None of the leaders, except perhaps Trotsky, had anything to gain from its publication; Stalin had merely rather more to lose than the others. The triumvirate was once more united by a common interest in resisting Trotsky.

A party meeting to consider the matter was held on May 22, 1924.[2] The testament was read by Kamenev, who presided at the proceedings. Then Zinoviev spoke in terms which have been recorded from memory by one of those present :

> Comrades, the last wish of Ilich, every word of Ilich is without doubt law in our eyes. More than once we have vowed to fulfil everything which the dying Ilich recommended us to do. You know well that we shall keep that promise. . . . But we are happy to say that on one point Lenin's fears have not proved well founded. I mean the point about our general secretary. You have all been witnesses of our work together in the last few months ; and, like myself, you have been happy to confirm that Ilich's fears have not been realized.

Kamenev followed in support of the plea not to carry out the injunction to depose Stalin. Nobody seems to have taken up the indictment against him. Many of those present may have shared Lenin's doubts, but were no more able than Lenin to suggest a concrete alternative. Trotsky remained silent throughout the proceedings. If, however, Stalin (and with him the present leadership) was to remain, nothing but harm could be done by divulging Lenin's reflexions and apprehensions to the world. By

---

[1] For the text see pp. 258-259, 263 above.

[2] All accounts agree in treating this as a meeting of the party central committee except L. Trotsky, *The Suppressed Testament of Lenin* (N.Y., 1935), pp. 11-12, which describes it as " a council of seniors ", to whom the question had been remitted owing to disagreement in the central committee. Trotsky's account was not written till 1932, but he is unlikely to have been mistaken on this formal point, which other writers may well have forgotten or treated as irrelevant : the distinction had, in fact, no significance.

a majority of some 30 votes to 10, and against the opposition of
Krupskaya, it was decided not to read the testament to the
congress, but to communicate it confidentially to the heads of the
delegations attending the congress.[1] The vote averted a blow
which might have ended Stalin's party career. But it did not in
itself increase his stature. Even Lenin's penetrating diagnosis of
his qualities and capacities had not taught the party as yet to
think of him as its future leader.

   The thirteenth party congress met on May 23, 1924. Its
opening day was marked by a ceremony indicative of the rapid
growth of the cult of Lenin's memory. A parade of young
" pioneers " organized by the Communist League of Youth was
held at Lenin's tomb on the Red Square, at which the name of
" Leninist " was solemnly bestowed on them, and a revised form
of the pioneers' oath was adopted under which they promised
" unswervingly to observe the laws and customs of the young
pioneers and the commandments of Ilich ". Kamenev, Bukharin,
Trotsky and Klara Zetkin were among those who addressed them
on the occasion.[2] The congress itself, while it inaugurated no
fresh move in any direction, served to drive home the discomfiture
and defeat of the opposition. At first some pretence was made of
avoiding controversy and allowing wounds to heal. Zinoviev, who,
as at the twelfth congress, made the principal report, reserved his
polemics for a short section at the end of his speech. He drew
attention to the dangers of " the growth of a new bourgeoisie "
under NEP and, with it, of a " new Menshevism " — what he
called " the Indian summer of Menshevism " ; but he refrained
from overtly connecting this danger with the party opposition,

---

[1] The fullest report of this meeting is in B. Bazhanov, *Stalin* (German transl.
from French, 1931), pp. 32-34. It is written in Bazhanov's highly coloured
style, and the remarks attributed to Zinoviev cannot claim textual accuracy ; but the account is probably correct in substance. Other details are in
M. Eastman, *Since Lenin Died* (1925), p. 28, and in L. Trotsky, *The Suppressed
Testament of Lenin* (N.Y., 1935), p. 13 ; the reference in L. Trotsky, *Stalin*
(N.Y., 1946), p. 376, gives the false impression that the meeting took place
while Lenin was still alive.
[2] The proceedings were reported in the press on the following day and the
speeches are in *Trinadtsatyi S"ezd Rossiiskoi Kommunisticheskoi Partii (Bol'-
shevikov)* (1924), pp. 629-633.

   2 A

and did not name Trotsky throughout his speech. The concluding passage referred to the disputes in the party during the past year, and ended with a rhetorical appeal :

> The most sensible step, and most worthy of a Bolshevik, which the opposition could take is what a Bolshevik does when he happens to make some mistake or other — to come before the party on the tribune of the party congress and say : " I made a mistake, and the party was right " . . .
> There is one way really to liquidate the controversy and end it once for all — to come forward on this tribune and say : " The party was right, and those were wrong who said that we were on the brink of ruin".

The orator seemed to be sounding a note of appeasement, which was greeted with " stormy and prolonged applause ". In fact, he was setting for the first time in party history the fateful precedent of demanding from an opposition not loyal submission to the will of the majority, but a recantation of its opinions. But few delegates at the congress were impressed by the innovation or guessed its significance for the future — least of all, Zinoviev himself. Stalin, who followed with the report on party organization, contented himself with a factual review of the year's work, and did not mention the opposition at all. His reputation for studied moderation in controversy, and for not making himself conspicuous, still stood him in good stead.

Trotsky found himself in a cleft stick. It was unthinkable that he should be present at a party congress without speaking, or that he should speak and ignore Zinoviev's much applauded peroration. He could not fight against the party decision : faced with genuine " old Bolsheviks " like Zinoviev and Stalin, Trotsky was always in the weak position of the newcomer to the faith who has to compensate for his tardy conversion by doubly fervent protestations of his fidelity. The " far-reaching self-confidence " which Lenin had noted as the hall-mark of his character did not permit him to believe himself in error ; and he was incapable of tactical dissimulation. In a speech much shorter than those which party congresses had been used to hear from him, he re-emphasized the dangers of bureaucracy in the party, supporting himself with a quotation from Bukharin, reiterated the ambiguous phraseology of the resolution of December 5, 1923, on the question

of fractions and groupings in the party, and put in his customary
plea for more and better planning. But the full pathos of his
situation was visible in the contorted sentences of the concluding
passage in which he attempted a direct reply to Zinoviev's appeal :

> Comrades, an invitation was given here to all who have
> erred to declare that they have erred. Nothing is simpler,
> morally and politically easier, than to confess to this or that
> mistake before one's own party. For that, I think, no great
> moral heroism is required.

But the resolution of December 5 constituted an admission by the
central committee that it had made mistakes and that a new course
should be set. Those whose warnings had prompted that resolution could not now declare themselves to have been wrong.

> Comrades [Trotsky went on], none of us wishes to be right,
> or can be right, against his party. The party is in the last resort
> always right, because the party is the unique historical instru-
> ment given to the proletariat for the fulfilment of its funda-
> mental tasks. I have already said that nothing is easier than to
> say before the party : " All this criticism, all these declarations,
> warnings and protests, were simply a sheer mistake ". But,
> comrades, I cannot say this, because I do not think so. I know
> that one cannot be right against the party. One can be right
> only with the party and through the party, since history has
> created no other paths to the realization of what is right. The
> English have a historical proverb : " My country, right or
> wrong ". With far greater historical right can we say : " Right
> or not right in individual particular concrete questions, but it
> is my party ".

But he could not vote for the resolution of the thirteenth party
conference which had condemned him :

> Not only the individual member of the party, but the party
> itself may make particular mistakes, such as the particular
> resolutions of the last conference which I consider in certain
> parts incorrect and unjust. But the party cannot take any de-
> cisions, however incorrect and unjust, which could shake by
> one jot our boundless devotion to the cause of the party, the
> readiness of each one of us to bear on his shoulders the discipline
> of the party in all conditions. And if the party carries out a
> decision which one or other of us thinks an unjust decision, he

will say : " Just or unjust, but this is my party, and I bear the consequences of its decision to the end ".[1]

More than one of those who heard these words was later to make a similar declaration to his own conscience in a predicament far more fearful than that which now confronted Trotsky.

In the ensuing debate minor figures in the party — Uglanov,[2] Zakharov and Rudzutak — attacked Trotsky ; and Preobrazhensky confined himself to a defence of the economic policies of the opposition. Uglanov attempted to discredit the opposition on the ground, already adumbrated at the January conference, that it relied for its support on intellectuals and former bourgeois elements. He related that at the Sormovo works, where he had been when Trotsky's " letters " were published, the workers, both party and non-party, had supported the central committee and the engineers had come out for Trotsky. " There ", exclaimed Uglanov triumphantly, " you have the class essence of the attitude of different strata to comrade Trotsky's pronouncements." [3] Kamenev replied to both Trotsky and Preobrazhensky, insisting on the verdict of the January conference that the opposition constituted a " petty bourgeois deviation ". Krupskaya desperately attempted to prevent a further widening of the rift. Life, she declared, always showed in the end whether the party was right or not ; Stalin and Zinoviev had been right to rest their argument on the fact that life had justified the line of the central committee. But the important thing now was to face the new tasks ahead and not to " duplicate the discussion of the past ". Zinoviev had been wrong to call on the opposition to confess its errors from the tribune : " psychologically that is impossible ". It was sufficient that the opposition should be willing to work with the party. Trotsky had accepted this when he declared in his speech against

[1] *Trinadtsatyi S"ezd Rossiiskoi Kommunisticheskoi Partii (Bol'shevikov)* (1924), pp. 153-168.

[2] Soon after this Uglanov was appointed to clean up the Moscow organization after the inroads made by the opposition in November and December 1923 ; according to B. Bazhanov, *Stalin* (German transl. from French, 1931), pp. 37-38, he was a nominee of Zinoviev and Kamenev, but was quickly won over by Stalin.

[3] *Trinadtsatyi S"ezd Rossiiskoi Kommunisticheskoi Partii (Bol'shevikov)* (1924), p. 169 ; at a later stage of the congress Molotov alleged that the authors of the platform of the 46 " reflected the negative influence of strata alien to the proletariat " (*ibid.* p. 523).

fractions and groupings. What was necessary now was " to put an end to further discussion and concentrate chiefly on those questions which life is setting before the party ".[1] For the last time a party congress heard, on the lips of Lenin's widow, Lenin's appeal to warring factions in the party to work together for the common cause.

But it was too late for counsels of appeasement to be heard — as the apprehensions expressed by Lenin himself in the testament clearly revealed. Stalin, speaking in the congress on the day after Krupskaya's appeal, retorted that he also was against " duplicating debates about differences ", and for that reason had ignored these differences in his first speech. But now that Trotsky and Preobrazhensky had given their version of the story, it would be " unthinkable " and " criminal " to be silent ; and Stalin plunged into another bitter attack on Trotsky's defiance of the resolution of December 5 in his letter and articles on the " new course ", and on his refusal to recognize the verdict of the thirteenth party conference in January on these proceedings. Zinoviev followed more ponderously and more garrulously in the same strain.[2] The main resolution of the congress confirmed the verdict of the January conference on the " petty bourgeois deviation " of the opposition, and praised the central committee for its " firmness and Bolshevik uncompromisingness . . . in defending the foundations of Leninism against petty bourgeois deviations ".[3] Trotsky was among those elected by the congress to the central committee of the party. The number of votes obtained by each candidate was no longer publicly announced. But, according to current rumour, Trotsky was fifty-first on the list of 52 successful candidates.[4]

The thirteenth party congress of May 1924, four months after

[1] *Ibid.* pp. 220-221, 235-237.

[2] Stalin, *Sochineniya*, vi, 220-223 ; *Trinadtsatyi S"ezd Rossiiskoi Kommunisticheskoi Partii (Bol'shevikov)* (1924), pp. 259-267.

[3] *VKP(B) v Rezolyutsiyakh* (1941), i, 566.

[4] *Sotsialisticheskii Vestnik* (Berlin), No. 15 (85), July 24, 1924, p. 13. According to M. Eastman, *Since Lenin Died* (1925), p. 128, Zinoviev supported by Kamenev " demanded Trotsky's exclusion from the Politburo ", but the demand was opposed by Stalin " for his own reasons " : Eastman was in Moscow during the thirteenth party congress, and was in a position to know much that went on behind the scenes. Stalin's opposition was consistent with his general caution at this time.

Lenin's death, marked the culmination and the end of the period of hesitation and confusion in party affairs dating from Lenin's final removal from active work in December 1922. During this time the members of the triumvirate had held closely together, linked by the firm determination to exclude Trotsky from the leadership, conscious of their dependence on one another, resolved to pursue a waiting policy and to make all such compromises, with one another or with other elements in the party, as might be needful to maintain their authority. Thanks to the good harvest, it had been possible to hold the economic situation with a minimum of modifications in the ramshackle structure of NEP and to score a conspicuous success in the achievement of the currency reform. The opposition had been skilfully divided against itself and its attacks beaten off. Trotsky, isolated and without stomach for the fight, had been routed in his absence at the party conference in January; his presence at the thirteenth party congress, far from redressing the balance, only confirmed the bankruptcy of his platform and the eclipse of his authority in the party. But Trotsky's decline quickly loosened the cement that held together the triumvirate. At the thirteenth congress Zinoviev — the typical figure of the interregnum — appeared for the second and last time in the rôle of provisional party leader which he had usurped at the twelfth congress in April 1923. Kamenev had clearly accepted relegation to a secondary rôle. Stalin continued to exhibit the qualities of self-effacement, cunning and infinite patience. Having emerged from the ordeal of Lenin's testament, and having, unperceived, immensely fortified his control over the rank and file of the party through the Lenin enrolment, he now only awaited the moment to show his hand and reveal the full scope of his power and his ambitions. The uneasy balance, marked by the pursuit of policies of compromise and marking time, would not outlive the summer of 1924. The period of the interregnum was over.

NOTE A

THE PLATFORM OF THE 46

To the Politburo of the Central Committee of the
Russian Communist Party

Secret

THE extreme seriousness of the position compels us (in the interests of our party, in the interests of the working class) to state openly that a continuation of the policy of the majority of the Politburo threatens grievous disasters for the whole party. The economic and financial crisis beginning at the end of July of the present year, with all the political, including internal party, consequences resulting from it, has inexorably revealed the inadequacy of the leadership of the party, both in the economic domain, and especially in the domain of internal party relations.

The casual, unconsidered and unsystematic character of the decisions of the central committee, which has failed to make ends meet in the economic domain, has led to a position where, for all the undoubted great successes in the domain of industry, agriculture, finance and transport — successes achieved by the economy of the country spontaneously and not thanks to, but in spite of the inadequacy of, the leadership or, rather, the absence of all leadership — we not only face the prospect of a cessation of these successes, but also a grave economic crisis.

We face the approaching breakdown of the chervonets currency, which has spontaneously been transformed into a basic currency before the liquidation of the budget deficit ; a credit crisis in which Gosbank can no longer without risk of a serious collapse finance either industry or trade in industrial goods or even the purchase of grain for export ; a cessation of the sale of industrial goods as a result of high prices, which are explained on the one hand by the absence of planned organizational leadership in industry, and on the other hand by an incorrect credit policy ; the impossibility of carrying out the programme of grain exports as a result of inability to purchase grain ; extremely low prices for food products, which are damaging to the peasantry and threaten a mass contraction of agricultural production ; inequalities in wage payments which provoke natural dissatisfaction among the workers with the budgetary chaos, which indirectly produces chaos in the state apparatus. " Revolutionary " methods of making reductions in drawing up the budget, and new and obvious reductions in carrying it out, have ceased to be transitional measures and become a regular phenomenon which constantly disturbs the state apparatus and, as a result of the absence of plan in the reductions effected, disturbs it in a casual and spontaneous manner.

These are some of the elements of the economic, credit and financial crisis which has already begun. If extensive, well-considered, planned and energetic measures are not taken forthwith, if the present absence of leadership continues, we face the possibility of an extremely acute economic breakdown, which will inevitably involve internal political complications and a complete paralysis of our external effectiveness and capacity for action. And this last, as everyone will understand, is more necessary to us now than ever ; on it depends the fate of the world revolution and of the working class of all countries.

Similarly in the domain of internal party relations we see the same incorrect leadership paralysing and breaking up the party ; this appears particularly clearly in the period of crisis through which we are passing.

We explain this not by the political incapacity of the present leaders of the party ; on the contrary, however much we differ from them in our estimate of the position and in the choice of means to alter it, we assume that the present leaders could not in any conditions fail to be appointed by the party to the outstanding posts in the workers' dictatorship. We explain it by the fact that beneath the external form of official unity we have in practice a one-sided recruitment of individuals, and a direction of affairs which is one-sided and adapted to the views and sympathies of a narrow circle. As the result of a party leadership distorted by such narrow considerations, the party is to a considerable extent ceasing to be that living independent collectivity which sensitively seizes living reality because it is bound to this reality with a thousand threads. Instead of this we observe the ever increasing, and now scarcely concealed, division of the party between a secretarial hierarchy and " quiet folk ", between professional party officials recruited from above and the general mass of the party which does not participate in the common life.

This is a fact which is known to every member of the party. Members of the party who are dissatisfied with this or that decision of the central committee or even of a provincial committee, who have this or that doubt on their minds, who privately note this or that error, irregularity or disorder, are afraid to speak about it at party meetings, and are even afraid to talk about it in conversation, unless the partner in the conversation is thoroughly reliable from the point of view of " discretion " ; free discussion within the party has practically vanished, the public opinion of the party is stifled. Nowadays it is not the party, not its broad masses, who promote and choose members of the provincial committees and of the central committee of the RKP. On the contrary the secretarial hierarchy of the party to an ever greater extent recruits the membership of conferences and congresses, which are becoming to an ever greater extent the executive assemblies of this hierarchy.

The régime established within the party is completely intolerable ; it destroys the independence of the party, replacing the party by a recruited bureaucratic apparatus which acts without objection in normal times, but which inevitably fails in moments of crisis, and which threatens to become completely ineffective in the face of the serious events now impending.

The position which has been created is explained by the fact that the régime of the dictatorship of a fraction within the party, which was in fact created after the tenth congress, has outlived itself. Many of us consciously accepted submission to such a régime. The turn of policy in the year 1921, and after that the illness of comrade Lenin, demanded in the opinion of some of us a dictatorship within the party as a temporary measure. Other comrades from the very beginning adopted a sceptical or negative attitude towards it. However that may have been, by the time of the twelfth congress of the party this régime had outlived itself. It had begun to display its reverse side. Links within the party began to weaken. The party began to die away. Extreme and obviously morbid movements of opposition within the party began to acquire an anti-party character, since there was no comradely discussion of inflamed questions. Such discussion would without difficulty have revealed the morbid character of these movements both to the mass of the party and to the majority of those participating in them. The results have been illegal movements which draw members of the party outside the limits of the party, and a divorce of the party from the working masses.

Should the position thus created not be radically changed in the immediate future, the economic crisis in Soviet Russia and the crisis of the fractional dictatorship in the party will deal heavy blows at the workers' dictatorship in Russia and the Russian Communist Party With such a load on its shoulders, the dictatorship of the proletariat in Russia and its leader the RKP cannot enter the phase of impending new world-wide disturbances except with the prospect of defeats on the whole front of the proletarian struggle. Of course it would be at first sight most simple to settle the question by deciding that at this moment, in view of all the circumstances, there is not and cannot be any room to raise the question of a change in the party course, to put on the agenda new and complicated tasks etc. etc. But it is perfectly apparent that such a point of view would amount to an attitude of officially shutting one's eyes to the real position, since the whole danger resides in the fact that there is no real unity in thought or in action in face of an extremely complicated internal and foreign situation. The struggle that is being waged in the party is all the more bitter the more silently and secretly it proceeds. If we put this question to the central committee, it is precisely in order to bring about the most rapid and least painful issue from the contradictions which are tearing the party asunder and to set the party without delay on a healthy foundation. Real unity in opinions and in actions is indispensable. The impending difficulties demand united fraternal, fully conscious, extremely vigorous, extremely concentrated action by all members of our party. The fractional régime must be abolished, and this must be done in the first instance by those who have created it ; it must be replaced by a régime of comradely unity and internal party democracy.

In order to realize what has been set forth above and to take the measures indispensable for an issue from the economic, political and party crisis, we propose to the central committee as a first and urgent step to call a conference of members of the central committee with the most prominent and active party workers, providing that the list of those invited should include a number of comrades holding views on the situation different from the views of the majority of the central committee.

Signatures to the Declaration to the Politburo
of the Central Committee of the RKP
on the Internal Party Situation of
October 15, 1923 [1]

E. Preobrazhensky
B. Breslav
L. Serebryakov

Not being in agreement with some of the points of this letter explaining the causes of the situation which has been created, but considering that the party is immediately confronted with questions which cannot be wholly resolved by the methods hitherto practised, I fully associate myself with the final conclusion of the present letter.   A. Beloborodov

With the proposals I am in full agreement,

[1] The signatures are so arranged in the copy from which this translation has been made that it is impossible to be certain that the original order has been preserved.

though I differ from certain points in the motiva-
tion.

A. Rozengolts
M. Alsky

In essentials I share the views of this appeal.
The demand for a direct and sincere approach
to all our ills has become so urgent that I entirely
support the proposal to call the conference suggested in order to lay down practical ways of
escape from the accumulation of difficulties.

Antonov-Ovseenko
A. Benediktov
I. N. Smirnov
Yu. Pyatakov
V. Obolensky
        (Osinsky)
N. Muralov
T. Sapronov

The position in the party and the international position is such that it demands, more
than ever before, an unusual exertion and concentration of party forces.   I associate myself
with the declaration and regard it *exclusively* as
an attempt to restore unity in the party and to
prepare it for impending events.   It is natural
that at the present moment there can be no question of a struggle within the party in any form
whatever.   It is essential that the central committee should assess the position soberly and
take urgent measures to remove the dissatisfaction within the party and also in the non-party
masses.

A. Goltsmar
V. Maksimovsky
D. Sosnovsky
Danishevsky
O. Shmidel
N. Vaganyan
I. Stukov
A. Lobanov
Rafail
S. Vasilchenko
Mikh. Zhakov
A. M. Puzakov
N. Nikolaev

Since I have recently been somewhat aloof from the work of the party centres I abstain from any judgment on the first two paragraphs in the introductory section ; for the rest I am in agreement.

Averin

I am in agreement with the exposition in the first part of the economic and political situation of the country. I consider that in the part describing the internal party situation a certain exaggeration has crept in. It is completely indispensable to take measures *immediately* to preserve the unity of the party.

I. Bogoslavsky
P. Mesyatsev
T. Khorechko

I am not in agreement with a number of opinions in the first part of the declaration ; I am not in agreement with a number of the characterizations of the internal party situation. At the same time I am profoundly convinced that the condition of the party demands the taking of radical measures since the condition in the party at the present time is not healthy. I entirely share the practical proposal.

A. Bubnov
A. Voronsky
V. Smirnov
E. Bosh
I. Byk
V. Kosior
F. Lokatskov

With the assessment of the economic position I am in complete agreement. I consider a weakening of the political dictatorship at the present moment dangerous, but an elucidation is indispensable. I find a conference completely indispensable.

Kaganovich
Drobnis
P. Kovalenko
A. E. Minkin
V. Yakovleva

With the practical proposal I am in full agreement.

       B. Eltsin

I sign with the same reservation as comrade Bubnov.

       L. Levitin

I sign with the same reserves as Bubnov, though I do not endorse either the form or the tone, the character of which persuades me all the more to agree with the practical part of the declaration.

       I. Palyudov

I am not in full agreement with the first part which speaks of the economic condition of the country ; this is really very serious and demands extremely attentive consideration, but the party has not hitherto produced men who would lead it better than those who are hitherto leading it. On the question of the internal party situation I consider that there is a substantial element of truth in all that is said, and consider it essential to take urgent measures.

       F. Sudnik

LIST OF ABBREVIATIONS

Comintern	= Kommunisticheskii Internatsional (Communist International).
CPGB	= Communist Party of Great Britain.
Glavkomtrud	= Glavnyi Komitet Truda (Chief Labour Committee).
Gosbank	= Gosudarstvennyi Bank (State Bank).
Gosplan	= Gosudarstvennaya Obshcheplanovaya Komissiya (State General Planning Commission).
GPU	= Gosudarstvennoe Politicheskoe Upravlenie (State Political Administration).
GUM	= Gosudarstvennyi Universal'nyi Magazin (State Universal Store).
IFTU	= International Federation of Trade Unions.
IKKI	= Ispolnitel'nyi Komitet Kommunisticheskogo Internatsionala (Executive Committee of the Communist International).
Inprekorr	= *Internationale Presse-Korrespondenz.*
Komvnutorg	= Komissiya Vnutrennei Torgovli (Commission of Internal Trade).
KPD	= Kommunistische Partei Deutschlands (German Communist Party).
Narkomfin	= Narodnyi Komissariat Finansov (People's Commissariat of Finance).
Narkomindel (NKID)	= Narodnyi Komissariat Inostrannykh Del(People's Commissariat of Foreign Affairs).
Narkomprod	= Narodnyi Komissariat Prodovol'stiya (People's Commissariat of Supply).
Narkomput'	= Narodnyi Komissariat Putei Soobshcheniya (People's Commissariat of Communications).
Narkomsoben	= Narodnyi Komissariat Sotsial'nogo Obespecheniya (People's Commissariat of Social Security).
Narkomtrud	= Narodnyi Komissariat Truda (People's Commissariat of Labour).
Profintern	= Krasnyi Internatsional Professional'nykh Soyuzov (Red International of Trade Unions).
Prombank	= Torgovo-Promyshlennyi Bank (Bank of Trade and Industry).

Rabkrin	= Narodnyi Komissariat Rabochei i Krest'yanskoi Inspektsii (People's Commissariat of Workers' and Peasants' Inspection).
RKK	= Rastsenochno-Konfliktnye Komissii (Assessment and Conflict Commissions).
RKP(B)	= Rossiiskaya Kommunisticheskaya Partiya (Bol'-shevikov) (Russian Communist Party (Bolsheviks)).
Sovnarkom	= Sovet Narodnykh Komissarov (Council of People's Commissars).
SPD	= Sozial-Demokratische Partei Deutschlands (German Social-Democratic Party).
Tsentrosoyuz	= Vserossiiskii Tsentral'nyi Soyuz Potrebitel'skikh Obshchestv (All-Russian Central Union of Consumers' Societies).
TsIK	= Tsentral'nyi Ispolnitel'nyi Komitet (Central Executive Committee).
Uchraspred	= Uchet i Raspredelenie (Account and Distribution Section).
USPD	= Unabhängige Sozial - Demokratische Partei Deutschlands (German Independent Social-Democratic Party).
Vesenkha	= Vysshii Sovet Narodnogo Khozyaistva (Supreme Council of National Economy).
Vneshtorg	= Narodnyi Komissariat Vneshnei Torgovli (People's Commissariat of Foreign Trade).

INDEX

Account and Distribution Section (Uchraspred), 277

Agrarian Institute, Moscow, 199-200

Agrarian policy: legislation relating to, under NEP, 5-7 ; and effect of NEP, 7-8, 149, and grain exports, 13-14, 17-18, 22, 26, 31, 88, 114, 118, 149 ; and industry, 13-15, 21-22, 24, 85-89, 114-115, 145 ; and twelfth party congress, 16-19, 24, 26-27 ; and " decree on land ", 18 ; and scissors crisis, 21-22, 26, 89, 113-114 ; and emancipation of serfs, 88 ; and thirteenth party congress, 146-149 ; and agricultural communes, 147 ; and Soviet farms, 147 ; and peasant committees of mutual aid, 148-149 ; and " committees of poor peasants ", 148 ; and cooperation, 149. *See also* Industrial policy ; Peasantry ; Prices ; Scissors crisis

Allied American Corporation, 246

All-Russian Congress of Soviets : tenth : and exports, 7 ; eleventh : and wages, 136-137

All-Russian Textile Syndicate, 246

All-Union Communist Party (Bolsheviks) [*formerly* Russian Communist Party (Bolsheviks)] : and NEP, 4, 14-15 ; and industrial policy, 14-16, 18-20, 118, 273, 278-279 ; twelfth congress (1923), 16-26, 46, 50, 110, 268-285 ; and economic policy, 16-26, 46, 50, 110, 334, 338, 366 ; and scissors crisis, 21, 87 n., 90-91, 95, 104-107, 113-117, 125-130, 294, 301-302 ; opposition within, 79-84, 268-270, 276-278, 284-285, 292-302, 304, 307-308, 311-341, 356-357, 361-362, 364-366 ; and Workers' Truth, 79-80, 268-270, 293-294, 307, 336 ; and Workers' Group, 80-84, 268-270, 292-294, 302, 307-308 ; and " industrial " opposition, 83, 120-121, 124-130 ; and " platform of the 46 ", 106, 108, 120, 228, 295, 297-298, 300 302, 307, 324-325, 367-373 ; and succession to leadership, 270-274, 283-285, 290-291, 295, 340-341 ; and emergence of triumvirate, 271, 273, 283-285, 290-291, 302-305, 307-308, 310, 312-313, 315, 323, 332, 334, 336, 340, 360, 366 ; and party unity, 275-276, 292, 307, 314, 351, 356 ; and party organization, 276-278, 283, 292, 295-298, 300, 302, 306-307, 310-313, 320 ; central committee of, 283, 335, 339 ; interregnum in, 285, 366 ; and arrest of Sultan-Galiev, 287-289 ; thirteenth congress (1924), 144-146, 354, 359, 361-365 ; and economic recovery, 144-146, 366 ; and agrarian policy, 146-149 ; and Ruhr crisis, 163, 215 ; and revolution in Germany (1923), 201-206, 212-215, 218-219, 227-229, 233, 238-239 ; and European revolution, 214-215 ; crisis in, 228, 233-236, 238-239, 241, 257, 292, 295, 308, 315, 323-328, 338-341, 367-373 ; and foreign communist parties, 234-235, 241 ; and German Communist Party, 234-236, 241-242 ; and Polish Communist Party, 234-235 ; and national question, 265-266, 273, 275, 278-283, 287-289 ; twenty-fifth anniversary of, 267, 275 ; and " democratic centralism ", 270, 315-317 ; and Ukraine, 289 ; and party democracy, 292, 294, 300-302, 304, 306-307, 312, 319, 324, 326-327, 332, 333 n., 334, 336, 352-353 ; and " fractionalism ", 292, 297, 301, 304-305, 307-308, 310-312, 316-317, 320-321, 328-330, 339 ; committee on internal situation in, 294-295, 304 ; and Revolutionary Military Council, 294-295 ; central control commission of, 300, 319 n., 322, 329-330, 357 ; and " old Bolsheviks ", 310, 315-317, 320, 325 ;

THE END